John Timbs

Knowledge for the Time

A manual of reading, reference, and conversation on subjects of living interest,

useful curiosity, and amusing research

John Timbs

Knowledge for the Time
A manual of reading, reference, and conversation on subjects of living interest, useful curiosity, and amusing research

ISBN/EAN: 9783337219420

Printed in Europe, USA, Canada, Australia, Japan

Cover: Foto ©Thomas Meinert / pixelio.de

More available books at **www.hansebooks.com**

KNOWLEDGE
FOR THE TIME:

A Manual

OF

READING, REFERENCE, AND CONVERSATION ON SUBJECTS OF LIVING
INTEREST, USEFUL CURIOSITY, AND AMUSING RESEARCH:

HISTORICO-POLITICAL INFORMATION.
PROGRESS OF CIVILIZATION.
DIGNITIES AND DISTINCTIONS.
CHANGES IN LAWS.
MEASURE AND VALUE.
PROGRESS OF SCIENCE.
LIFE AND HEALTH.
RELIGIOUS THOUGHT.

Illustrated from the best and latest Authorities.

By JOHN TIMBS, F.S.A.

AUTHOR OF CURIOSITIES OF LONDON, THINGS NOT GENERALLY KNOWN,
ETC.

LONDON:
Lockwood and Co., 7 Stationers'-hall Court.
—o—
M D CCC LXIV.

TO THE READER.

THE great value of contemporary History—that is, history written by actual witnesses of the events which they narrate, —is now beginning to be appreciated by general readers. The improved character of the journalism of the present day is the best evidence of this advancement, which has been a work of no ordinary labour. Truth is not of such easy acquisition as is generally supposed ; and the chances of obtaining unprejudiced accounts of events are rarely improved by distance from the time at which they happen. In proportion as freedom of thought is enlarged, and liberty of conscience, and liberty of will, are increased, will be the amount of trustworthiness in the written records of contemporaries. It is the rarity of these high privileges in chroniclers of past events which has led to so many obscurities in the world's history, and warpings in the judgment of its writers; to trust some of whom has been compared to reading with "coloured spectacles." And, one of the features of our times is to be ever taking stock of the amount of truth in past history; to set readers on the tenters of doubt, and to make them suspicious of perversions; and to encourage a whitewashing of black reputations which sometimes strays into an extreme equally as unserviceable to truth as that from which the writer started.

It is, however, with the view of correcting the Past by *the light of the Present*, and directing attention to many salient points of Knowledge for the Time, that the present volume is offered to the public. Its aim may be considered great in proportion to the limited means employed ; but, to extend what is, in homely phrase, termed a right understanding, the contents of the volume are of a mixed character, the Author having due respect for the

b

emphatic words of Dr. Arnold: "Preserve proportion in your reading, keep your views of Men and Things extensive, and *depend upon it a mixed knowledge is not a superficial one:* as far as it goes, the views that it gives are true; but he who reads deeply in one class of writers only, gets views which are almost sure to be perverted, and which are not only narrow but false."

Throughout the Work, the Author has endeavoured to avail himself of the most reliable views of leading writers on Events of the Day; and by seizing new points of Knowledge and sources of Information, to present, in a classified form, such an assemblage of Facts and Opinions as may be impressed with warmth and quickness upon the memory, and assist in the formation of a good general judgment, or direct still further a-field.

In this Manual of abstracts, abridgments, and summaries—considerably over Three Hundred in number—illustrations by way of Anecdote occur in every page. Wordiness has been avoided as unfitted for a book which has for its object not the waste but the economy of time and thought, and the diffusion of concise notions upon subjects of living Interest, useful Curiosity, and amusing Research.

The accompanying Table of Contents will, at a single glance, show the variety as well as the practical character of the subjects illustrated; the aim being to render the work alike serviceable to the reader of a journal of the day, as well as to the student who reads to "reject what is no longer essential." The Author has endeavoured to keep pace with the progress of Information; and in the selection of new accessions, some have been inserted more to stimulate curiosity and promote investigation than as things to be taken for granted. The best and latest Authorities have been consulted, and the improved journalism of our time has been made available; for, "when a river of gold is running by your door, why not put out your hat, and take a dip?"*

The Author has already published several volumes of "Things not generally Known," which he is anxious to *supplement* with the present Manual of Knowledge for the Time.

---

* Douglas Jerrold.

THE FRONTISPIECE.

CAPTAIN COLES'S IRON TURRET-SHIP-OF-WAR.

THE precise and best mode of constructing Iron Ships-of-War, so as to carry heavy guns, is an interesting problem, which Captain Coles believes he has already satisfactorily solved in his Turret ship, wherein he proposes to protect the guns by turrets. Captain Coles offered to the Admiralty so long ago as 1855 to construct a vessel on this principle, having a double bottom; light draught of water, with the power of giving an increased immersion when under fire; sharp at both ends; a formidable prow; her rudder and screw protected by a projection of iron; the turret being hemispherical, and not a turn-table, which was unnecessary, as this vessel was designed for attacking stationary forts in the Black Sea.

Captain Coles contributed to the International Exhibition models of his ship; admitting (he states) from 7 to 8 degrees depression. In two this is obtained by the deck on each side of the turret sloping at the necessary angle, to admit of the required depression; in the other two it is obtained by the centre of the deck on which the turret is surmounted being raised sufficiently to enable the shot, when the gun is depressed, to pass clear of the outer edge of the deck. A drawing published in 1860, of the midship section from which these models were made, also gives a section of the *Warrior*, by which it will be seen that supposing the guns of each to be 10 feet out of water, and to have the usual depressions of guns in the Navy (7 degrees), the *Warrior's* guns on the broadside will throw the shot 19 feet further from the side than the shield ship with her guns placed in the centre, that being the distance of the latter from the edge of the ship: thus, with the same depression, the shield ship will have a greater advantage, this being an important merit of the invention, which Captain Coles has already applied to the *Royal Sovereign*. The construction of these turrets, the guns, and the turn-tables on which they are placed, with the machinery to work 'them, is very interesting ; but its details would occupy more space than is at our command. (See *Times*, Sept.'8, 1863.)

Captain Coles, in a communication to the *Times*, dated November, 4, 1863, thus urges the application of the turret to sea-going vessels, and quotes the opinion of the present Contractor of the Navy on the advantages his (Captain Coles) system must have over the old one, in strength, height out of water, and stability, and consequent adaptation for sea-going ships. The Captain states :

" I believe I have already shown that on my system of a revolving turret, a heavier broadside can be thrown than from ships armed on the broadside ; but it possesses this further advantage, that my turrets *can be adapted to the heaviest description of ordnance* ; indeed, no other plan has yet been put in practice, while it is impossible to adapt the broadside ships to them, without the enlargement of the ports, which would destructively weaken the ships, and leave the guns' crew exposed to rifles, grape-shot or shells." Captain Coles then quotes the armaments of the *Prince Albert* (now constructing at Millwall,) and the *Warrior*, and shows that although the broadside of the *Prince Albert* is nominally reduced to 1120 lbs. (still in excess of the *Warrior's* if compared with tonnage) ; it still gives this great advantage, that whereas late experiments have demonstrated that $4\frac{1}{2}$-inch plates can be made to resist 68-pounder and 110-pounder shot, they have also shown that the 300-pounder smashes them when formed into a " Warrior target" with the greatest ease. The *Prince Albert*, therefore, can smash the *Warrior*, though the *Warrior* carries no gun that can injure her ; nor can she, as a broadside ship, be altered to carry heavier guns.

The Engraving represents Captain Coles's Ship cleared for action, and the bulwarks down.

CONTENTS.

KNOWLEDGE FOR THE TIME.

Historico-Political Information.

Politics not yet a Science.

Mr. Buckle, in his thoughtful *History of Civilization*, remarks: " In the present state of knowledge, Politics, so far from being a science, is one of the most backward of all the arts; and the only safe course for the legislator is to look upon his craft as consisting in the adaptation of temporary contrivances to temporary emergencies. His business is to follow the age, and not at all to attempt to lead it. He should be satisfied with studying what is passing around him, and should modify his schemes, not according to the notions he has inherited from his fathers, but according to the actual exigencies of his own time. For he may rely upon it that the movements of society have now become so rapid that the wants of one generation are no measure of the wants of another; and that men, urged by a sense of their own progress, are growing weary of idle talk about the wisdom of their ancestors, and are fast discarding those trite and sleepy maxims which have hitherto imposed upon them, but by which they will not consent to be much longer troubled."

The Philosopher and the Historian.

" I have read somewhere or other," says Lord Bolingbroke, " in Dionysius Halicarnassus, I think, that History is Philosophy teaching by Example."

Walter Savage Landor has thus distinguished the respective labours of the Philosopher and the Historian. " There are," Mr. Landor writes, " quiet hours and places in which a taper may be carried steadily, and show the way along the ground; but you must stand a tip-toe and raise a blazing torch above your head, if

B

you would bring to our vision the obscure and time-worn figures depicted on the lofty vaults of antiquity.   The philosopher shows everything in one clear light; the historian loves strong reflections and deep shadows, but, above all, prominent and moving characters."

In writing of the Past, it behoves us to bear in mind, that while actions are always to be judged by the immutable standard of right and wrong, the judgment which we pass upon men must be qualified by considerations of age, country, situation, and other incidental circumstances; and it will then be found, that he who is most charitable in his judgment, is generally the least unjust.

It is curious to find one of the silken barons of civilization and refinement, writing as follows.   The polite Earl of Chesterfield says: " I am provoked at the contempt which most historians show for humanity in general: one would think by them that the whole human species consisted but of about a hundred and fifty people, called and dignified (commonly very undeservedly too) by the titles of emperors, kings, popes, generals, and ministers."

Sir Humphry Davy has written thus plainly in the same vein: " In the common history of the world, as compiled by authors in general, almost all the great changes of nations are confounded with changes in their dynasties; and events are usually referred either to sovereigns, chiefs, heroes, or their armies, which do, in fact, originate entirely from different causes, either of an intellectual or moral nature.   Governments depend far more than is generally supposed upon the opinion of the people and the spirit of the age and nation.   It sometimes happens that a gigantic mind possesses supreme power, and rises superior to the age in which he is born: such was Alfred in England, and Peter in Russia.   Such instances are, however, very rare; and in general it is neither amongst sovereigns nor the higher classes of society that the great improvers and benefactors of mankind are to be found."—*Consolations in Travel,* pp. 34, 35.

Whig and Tory Ministries.

The domestic history of England during the reign of Anne, is that of the great struggles between Whig and Tory; and Earl Stanhope, in his *History of England,* thus points out a number of precisely parallel lines of policy, and instances of unscrupulous resort to the same censurable set of weapons of party warfare, in the Tories of the reign of Queen Anne and the Whigs of the reign of William IV.

" At that period the two great contending parties were distinguished, as at present, by the nicknames of Whig and Tory. But it is very remarkable that in Queen Anne's reign the relative meaning of these terms was not only different but opposite to that which they bore at the accession of William IV. In theory, indeed, the main principle of each continues the same. The leading principle of the Tories is the dread of popular licentiousness. The leading principle of the Whigs is the dread of royal encroachment. It may thence, perhaps, be deduced that good and wise men would attach themselves either to the Whig or to the Tory party, according as there seemed to be the greater danger at that particular period from despotism or from democracy. The same person who would have been a Whig in 1712 would have been a Tory in 1830. For, on examination, it will be found that, in nearly all particulars, a modern Tory resembles a Whig of Queen Anne's reign, and a Tory of Queen Anne's reign a modern Whig.

" First, as to the Tories. The Tories of Queen Anne's reign pursued a most unceasing opposition to a just and glorious war against France. They treated the great General of the age as their peculiar adversary. To our recent enemies, the French, their policy was supple and crouching. They had an indifference, or even an aversion, to our old allies the Dutch. They had a political leaning towards the Roman Catholics at home. They were supported by the Roman Catholics in their elections. They had a love of triennial parliaments in preference to septennial. They attempted to abolish the protecting duties and restrictions of commerce. They wished to favour our trade with France at the expense of our trade with Portugal. They were supported by a faction whose war-cry was ' Repeal of the Union,' in a sister kingdom. To serve a temporary purpose in the House of Lords, they had recourse (for the first time in our annals) to a large and overwhelming creation of peers. Like the Whigs in May, 1831, they chose the moment of the highest popular passion and excitement to dissolve the House of Commons, hoping to avail themselves of a short-lived cry for the purpose of permanent delusion. The Whigs of Queen Anne's time, on the other hand, supported that splendid war which led to such victories as Ramillies and Blenheim. They had for a leader the great man who gained those victories. They advocated the old principles of trade. They prolonged the duration of parliaments. They took their stand on the principles of the Revolution of 1688. They raised the cry of ' No Popery.' They loudly inveighed against the subserviency to France, the desertion of our old allies, the outrage wrought upon the peers, the deceptions practised upon the sovereign, and the other measures of the Tory administration.

" Such were the Tories and such were the Whigs of Queen Anne. Can it be doubted that, at the accession of William IV., Harley and St. John would have been called Whigs; Somers and Stanhope, Tories? Would not the October Club have loudly cheered the measures of Lord Grey, and the Kit-Cat find itself renewed in the Carlton ?"

The defence of the Whigs against these imputations seems to be founded upon the famous Jesuitical principle, that the end justifies the means. They do not deny the facts, but they assert, that while the Tories of 1713 resorted to such modes of further-ing the interests of arbitrary power, they have employed them in advancing the progress and securing the ascendancy of the demo-cracy.

Protectionists.

This name was given to that section of the Conservative party which opposed the repeal of the Corn-laws, and which separated from Sir Robert Peel in 1846. A " Society for the *Protection* of Agriculture," and to counteract the efforts of the Anti-Corn Law League, gave the name to the party. Lord George Bentinck was their leader from 1846 till his death on September 21, 1848. The administration under Lord Derby not proposing the restoration of the corn-laws, this society was dissolved February 7, 1853.

Rats, and Ratting.

James, in his *Military Dictionary*, 1816, states:—

" Rats are sometimes used in military operations, particularly for set-ting fire to magazines of gunpowder. On these occasions, a lighted match is tied to the tail of the animal. Marshal Vauban recommends, therefore, that the walls of powder-magazines should be made very thick, and the passages for light and wind so narrow as not to admit them (the rats)."

The expression *to rat* is a figurative term applied to those who at the moment of a division desert or abandon any parti-cular party or side of a question. The term itself comes from the well-known circumstance of rats running away from decayed or falling buildings.—*Notes and Queries*, 2 S., No. 68.

The Heir to the British Throne always in Opposition.

Horace Walpole somewhere remarks, as a peculiarity in the history of the *Hanover family*, that the heir-apparent has always been in opposition to the reigning monarch. The fact is true enough ; but it is not a peculiarity in the House of Hanover. It is an infirmity of human nature, to be found, more or less, in every analogous case of private life ; but our political system de-velopes it with peculiar force and more remarkable effects in the

Royal Family. Those who cannot obtain the favours of the father will endeavour to conciliate the good wishes of the son; and all arts are employed, and few are necessary, to seduce the heir-apparent into the exciting and amusing *game* of political opposition. He is naturally apt enough to dislike what he considers a present thraldom, and to anticipate, by his influence over a faction, the plenitude of his future power. This was the mainspring of the most serious part of the political troubles of the last century: let us, however, hope that it will never be revived; and this we are encouraged to hope from our improved Constitution, as well as from the improved education of our Royal Family.

Legitimacy and Government.

It is an unguarded idea of some public writers that "the Sovereign holds her crown not by hereditary descent but by the will of the nation." This doctrine is too frequently stated in and out of Parliament; and without qualification or explanation it would be apt to breed mischief in the minds of an ignorant and excited multitude, if the instinctive feelings of common sense did not invariably correct the popular errors of theorists.

" They who have studied the Constitution attentively hold that her Majesty reigns by hereditary right, though her predecessor in 1688 received the Crown at the hands of a free nation. To refer to the right of election, which can be exercised only during a revolution, and to be silent on hereditary right, is to lower the Regal dignity to the precarious office of the judges when they held their patents *durante bene placito*. Suppose a nation so divided that one casting vote would carry a plebiscite, changing the form of government, or the dynasty, and there would be a practical illustration of a principle—if principle at all—which, when taken as a broad palpable fact, is undeniable in the founder of a dynasty, but when erected into a legal theory it becomes neither more nor less than a permanent code of revolution. Hence the successor of that founder, if his power be not supported by military despotism, is invariably a staunch advocate of his indefeasible hereditary right, though originally derived from the consent of the nation."— *Saturday Review.*

" The Fourth Estate."

The Press has been described as the Fourth Estate of the realm; but it is not so. If we remember rightly, it was Lord Stanley who characterized it as a second representation of the Third Estate.

This is nearer the mark, though it is not exactly true, seeing that the press represents, or professes to represent, all the three estates. Its influence on the State is a fact either not acknowledged at all or acknowledged as an evil to be held in check by stringent laws and safeguards. Its place of power is not defined by any written Constitution, and its acts are in our day controlled, for the most part, by no written statute, but only by its own good sense. In its modes of expression, the newspaper press of our country usually keeps far within the bounds which the law prescribes; it voluntarily prescribes for itself a law which has no authority save that of taste. There is not a greater power under the Constitution than this press, which is indeed the source of power to much besides itself. What would public meetings be without the press? Within the present century the method of influencing public opinion by means of great gatherings of the people under the direction of leagues and associations has been perfected. It is a method which derives its momentum from the multiplication of reports. It is a matter of indifference to an orator what or where is his audience, provided through the reporters he can address all England. The Press has thus neutralized one of the evils of democracy as it was known in the olden time. A democratic Assembly meant a rabble, a packed multitude of noisy citizens into which the more quiet and thoughtful class of people did not care to venture. In the democratic Assemblies now every man in England virtually sits. We have good seats, for we are at our own firesides with the newspapers in our hands. In the quiet of our chosen retreats we listen to the "cheers," and the "hear, hear," and the laughter which the speech of the orator evokes, and we can calmly measure the words of the demagogue. Upon the very manner of public speaking, too, we imagine that the system of newspaper reporting has had some effect. If we may judge by the very imperfect reports which we have of speeches delivered in the last century, orators were then more inflated and inflammatory in their style than they are now, the momentary impression which they created was beyond anything we can now conceive, and if eloquence is to be judged from its immediate effect they were greater masters of the art than any we can now boast of. If this appears a hard thing to say, when we have such orators among us as Lord Derby, Mr. Gladstone, Mr. Bright, and Mr. Disraeli, let us remember the other side of the question—let us take into account that our contemporary first-class orators speak with the full knowledge that in cool blood their speeches will be read word for word on the morrow. They know right well that much of the bombast which might safely be addressed to an admiring and heated audience will expose them only to ridicule when it is reduced to print. Insensibly a more sober standard of oratory is thus established, to the great gain of our deliberative assemblies, and acting as some check upon rhetorical demagogues.—*Times.*

Writing for the Press.

The organization of a great Newspaper establishment is a remarkable result of practical ability profiting by accumulated experience; but an account of the progress and development of the system is as tedious as a history of the iron manufacture or of the cotton trade. A readable narrative must include matters of more human interest than tables of figures which represent the successive numbers of copies and of advertisements; and although newspapers, like power-looms, may not have sprung into existence of themselves, the names of their obscure founders and managers are deservedly forgotten. Mr. Perry's name is still known in consequence of his connexion with the old Whig party; Mr. Stuart enjoys a parasitic fame as the employer of Coleridge and of Mackintosh; and the late Mr. Walter exhibited an effective sagacity in the conduct of his business which places him on a level with the Arkwrights and Boltons of manufacturing history. It would not be worth while to extend the list of able editors and spirited proprietors. Successful men of business must be contented to make their own fortunes and to benefit the world at large, without desiring the supererogatory reward of posthumous fame. When the gods, in Schiller's apologue, had given away the earth and the sea, they reserved the barren sky for the portionless poet; and ever since, the lightest touch of genius, the smallest act which indicated inherent greatness, has been found to retain its place in the memory of men long after capitalists and mechanical inventors have joined the multitude of the dead; *abierunt ad plures.* The clever lecturer who employs himself in diffusing information on the mechanism of watches probably finds the attention of his audience flag when he attempts to delineate the qualities and virtues of deceased generations of watchmakers.— *Saturday Review.*

Shorthand Writers.

Stenography, or the art of short writing, is generally stated to have been invented by Xenophon, the historian; first practised by Pythagoras; and reduced to a system by the poet, Ennius. To this art we owe full reports of the proceedings in Parliament. The system of Gurney was employed for this purpose; shorthand notes upon which were found among the Egerton MSS.

The shorthand-writer of the House of Commons states in his Evidence before the Select Committee on Private Bill Legislation that he receives two guineas a-day for attendance before committees to take notes of the evidence, and 9*d*. per folio of 72 words for making a copy from his notes. In 1862, he received for business thus done for the committees on private Bills 6667*l.*, consisting of 1682*l.* for attendance fees and 4985*l.* for the transcripts; this does not include the charges in respect of committees on public matters. He is appointed for the House of Lords also. So much of the business as he cannot execute by his own establishment he transfers to other shorthand writers on rather lower terms, but he himself keeps a staff of ten shorthand writers. Each of these has at least one clerk who can read his shorthand; but the most efficient course is found to be that he have two such clerks, each of whom (and himself also), taking in hand a portion of the notes, dictates to quick writers, so that the mode of transcribing is by writing from dictation, and not by copying. There is a great strain and pressure in order to get the transcript to the law-stationers in time for the requisite number of copies to be ready when the committee meet next morning. In the height of the session, the witness mentions, he provides refreshments for about fifty persons employed at his office during the evening, many of them until midnight, and often later.

The Worth of Popular Opinion.

Popular Opinion is generally founded on the most prominent and the most striking, but for that reason, often the most superficial feature in the interesting object of which a knowledge is pretended. That Cromwell had a wart on his nose; that Byron had a club-foot, which gave him more anxiety than the critiques on his poems; that the head of Pericles was too long, for which reason the sculptors always made his bust helmeted, while that of Julius Cæsar was bald, which made it doubly grateful to that great commander to have his brow encompassed with an oaken wreath, or the coveted kingly diadem; such prominent and superficial accessories of personal appearance, in the case of well-known characters, will often be familiar to thousands who know nothing more of the persons so curiously characterized. But these, so far as they go, are true; they are accurate knowledge, not mere opinion.   Even vulgar opinion is not so often altogether false as it is partial and inadequate, and therefore unjust.   Of Mahomet, for instance, everybody knows that he was the prophet of an intolerant religion, which its most sincere professors have always most zealously propagated with the sword.   This is quite true; but it is far from embracing the whole truth with regard to the religion of the Koran; and he who with the inconsiderate haste of popular logic, uses this accurate knowledge about a fraction of a thing, as if it were the just appreciation of the whole, falls not the less certainly into the region of mere delusion; for though the thing that he believes is true, it is not true as he gives it currency.   He is in fact doing a thing in the region of ideas which is equivalent to passing a farthing for a guinea; an act whereby he swindles the public and himself very nearly as much as if he were to pass off a piece of painted pasteboard for the same value.— *Professor Blackie; Edinburgh Essays*, 1856.

Machiavelism.

It has been well said of Machiavelli, that he has the credit or discredit of having been the first to erect into a science, and reduce it to theory, the art of obtaining absolute power by deception and cruelty; and of maintaining it afterwards by the simulation of leniency and virtue.   In political history, he was the first who gave at once a general and a luminous development of great events in their causes and connexion.

Sir Walter Raleigh, in his *History of the World,* says:—" The doctrine which Machiavel taught unto Cæsar Borgia, to employ men in mischievous actions, and afterwards to destroy them when they have performed the mischief, was not of his own invention. All ages have given us examples of this goodly policy; the latter having been apt scholars in this lesson to the more ancient, as the reign of Henry VIII. here in England can bear witness; and therein especially the Lord Cromwell, who perished by the same unjust law that himself had devised for the taking away of another man's life."

Free-speaking.

Archbishop Whately, in his very able Lecture on Egypt, referring to the writers on Public Affairs at home, reprehends the practice of exaggerating, with keen delight, every evil that they can find, inventing such as do not exist, and keeping out of sight what is good. An Eastern despot, reading the productions of one of these writers, would say that, with all our precautions, we are the worst governed people on earth; and that our law-courts and public offices are merely a complicated machinery for oppressing the mass of the people; that our Houses of Lords and Commons are utterly mismanaged, our public men striving to repress merit, and that our best plan would be to sweep away all those, as, with less trouble, matters might go on better, and could not go on worse. Charges of this nature cannot be brought publicly forward in the Turkish Empire. In Cairo, a man was beheaded because he made too free a use of his tongue. He was told not to be speaking of the insurrection in Syria, and had dared to be chatting of the news; and there are other countries, also, where because such charges are true, it would not be safe to circulate them. But these writers do not mean half what they set forth. They heighten their descriptions to display their eloquence; but the tendency of such publications is always towards revolution, and the practical effect on the minds of the people is to render them incredulous. They understand that these overwrought representations are for effect, and they go about their business with an impression that the whole is unreal. If one of these writers were visited himself with a horrible dream that he was a peasant under an Oriental despot, that he was taxed at the will of the Sovereign, and had to pay the assessment in produce, valued at half the market-price, that he was compelled to work and receive four-fifths of his low wages in food consisting of hard, sour biscuit — let him then dream that he had spoken against the Ministry, and that he finds himself bastinadoed till he confesses that he brought false charges; that his grown-up son had been dragged off for a soldier, and himself deprived of his only support, and he would be inclined to doubt whether ours is the worst system of Government.

Speakers of the Houses of Parliament.

The late Sir George Cornewall Lewis, in a communication which appeared in *Notes and Queries*, in the week of the author's lamented death, states the following:

" In modern legislative chambers it has been customary for the Chamber to appoint one of its own members as president. In the English House of Lords the Lord Chancellor is President by virtue of his office. Although a member of the executive Government, and holding his office at the pleasure of the Crown, he is nevertheless a high judicial officer, and is deemed to carry his judicial impartiality into the performance of his presidential functions. In general, however, the president of a legislative chamber is not, according to modern practice, a member of the executive Government. He is an independent member of the legislature, who is appointed by the chamber, and holds his office at its pleasure, such as the Speaker of the English House of Commons.

"The principal functions of the Speaker of the House of Commons were not originally (as the title of his office indicates) what they are at present. The House of Commons were at first a set of delegates summoned by the Crown to negotiate with it concerning the payment of taxes. They might take advantage of the position of superiority which they temporarily occupied to remonstrate with the Crown about certain grievances, upon which they were generally agreed. In this state of things it was important that they should have an organ and spokesman with sufficient ability and knowledge to state their views, and with sufficient courage to contend against the displeasure of the Crown. The helpless condition of a large body which is called upon to conduct a negotiation without any appointed organ is well described by Livy. When the Roman plebeians seceded to the Mount Aventine, after the Decemvirate, the Senate sent three ambassadors to confer with them, and to propose three questions. 'Non defuit,' says Livy, 'quid responderetur; deerat qui daret responsum, nullodum certo duce, nec satis audentibus singulis invidiæ se offerre' (iii. 50). Since the Revolution of 1688, and the increased power of the House of Commons, the functions of the Speaker have undergone a change. His chief function has been no longer to speak on behalf of the House; that which was previously his accessary has become his principal duty. He has been simply chairman of the House, with the function of regulating its proceedings, of putting the question, and of maintaining order. The Speaker of the House of Commons is now virtually disqualified by his office from speaking; but as their debates have become more important, his office of moderator of these debates has acquired additional importance.

"The position of the Speaker of the Irish House of Commons was similar to that of the Speaker of the English House (see Lord Mountmorres's *History of the Irish Parliament*, vol. i. p. 71—79); but in Scotland the three estates sat as one House; there was no separate House of Commons, and the Lord Chancellor presided over the entire assembly." (See Robertson's *History of Scotland*, b. 1, vol. i. p. 276, ed. 1821.)

The National Conscience.

When we come to the proofs from fact and historical experience, we might appeal to a singular case in the records of our Exchequer, viz., that for much more than a century back, our *Gazette* and other public advertisers have acknowledged a series of anonymous remittances from those who, at some time or other, had appropriated public money. We understand that no corresponding fact can be cited from foreign records. Now, this is a direct instance of that compunction which our travelled friend insisted on. But we choose rather to throw ourselves upon the general history of Great Britain: upon the spirit of her policy, domestic or foreign; and upon the universal principles of her public morality. Take the case of public debts, and the fulfilment of contracts to those who could not have compelled the fulfilment; we first set this precedent. All nations have now learned that honesty in such cases is eventually the best policy; but this they learned from our experience, and not till nearly all of them had tried the other policy. We it was who, under the most trying circumstances of war, maintained the sanctity from taxation of all foreign investments in our funds. Our conduct with regard to slaves, whether in the case of slavery or of the Slave Trade—how prudent it may always have been we need not inquire—as to its moral principles they went so far ahead of European standards that we were neither comprehended nor believed. The perfection of romance was ascribed to us by all who did not reproach us with the perfection of Jesuitical knavery; by many our motto was supposed to be no longer the old one of *divide et impera*, but *annihila et appropria*. Finally, looking back to our dreadful conflicts with the three conquering despots of modern history, Philip II. of Spain, Louis XIV., and Napoleon; we may incontestably boast of having been single in maintaining the general equities of Europe by war upon a colossal scale, and by our counsels in the general congresses of Christendom.—*De Quincey*.

" *The Nation of Shopkeepers*."

In the Præludia to the *Chronicon Albeldense*, attributed to Bulcidius, Bishop of Salamanca, a Spanish writer at the end of the ninth century, we find the following singular refutation of an ungraceful compliment hitherto paid to us by our Gallic neighbours. In a paragraph headed *De Proprietatibus Gentium*, we see the tables turned in our favour:—" 1. Sapientia Græcorum; 2. Fortia Gothorum; 3. Consilia Chaldæorum; 4. Superbia Romanorum; 5. Ferocitas Francorum; 6. Ira Britannorum; 7. Libido Scotorum; 8. Duritia Saxonum; 9. Cupiditas Persarum; 10. Invidia Judæorum; 11. Pax Æthiopum; 12. Commercia Gallorum!" This discovery seems to be invested with an additional interest at a time when our Allies very handsomely acknowledge that they have hitherto laboured under a mistake in their estimate of our national peculiarities.

Results of Revolutions.

Sir George Cornewall Lewis, in his last work, *On the Best Form of Government*, has this summary: " There are some rare cases in which a nation has profited by a revolution. Such was the English Revolution of 1688, in which the form of the Government underwent no alteration, and the person of the King was alone changed. It was the very *minimum* of a revolution; it was remarkable for the absence of those accompaniments which make a revolution perilous, and which subsequently draw upon it a vindictive reactionary movement. The late Italian revolution has likewise been successful; by it the Italian people have gained a better government and have improved their political condition. It was brought about by foreign intervention; but its success has been mainly owing to the moderation of the leaders in whom the people had the wisdom to confide, and who have steadily refrained from all revolutionary excesses. The history of forcible attempts to improve governments is not, however, cheering. Looking back upon the course of revolutionary movements, and upon the character of their consequences, the practical conclusion which I draw is that it is the part of wisdom and prudence to acquiesce in any form of government which is tolerably well administered, and affords tolerable security to person and property. I would not, indeed, yield to apathetic despair, or acquiesce in the persuasion that a merely tolerable government is incapable of improvement. I would form an individual model, suited to the character, disposition, wants, and circumstances of the country, and I would make all exertions, whether by action or by writing, within the limits of the existing law, for ameliorating its existing condition and bringing it nearer to the model selected for imitation; but I should consider the problem of the best form of government as purely ideal, and as unconnected with practice, and should abstain from taking a ticket in the lottery of revolution, unless there was a well-founded expectation that it would come out a prize."

Sir William Hamilton has well observed that " No revolution in public opinion is the work of an individual, of a single cause, or of a day. When the crisis has arrived, the catastrophe must ensue; but the agents through whom it is apparently accomplished, though they may accelerate, cannot originate its occurrence. Who believes that but for Luther or Zwingli the Reformation would not have been? Their individual, their personal energy and zeal, perhaps, hastened by a year or two the event but had the public mind not been already ripe for their revolt, the fate of Luther and Zwingli, in the sixteenth century, would have been that of Huss and Jerome of Prague in the fifteenth. Woe to the revolutionist who is not himself a creature of the revolution! If he anticipate, he is lost; for it requires, what no individual can supply, a long and powerful counter-sympathy in a nation to untwine the ties of custom which bind a people to the established and the old."

Worth of a Republic.

Mr. Baron Alderson is described as having a temper too calm for the stormy floor of the House of Commons; but he studied politics as a science, from a safe distance; and his letters contain his opinions on some points expressed with a very deliberate care. To Mrs. Opie, who had been writing against Republics and Republican Government, he says: " I entirely agree with your view of a Republic. As long as men are so wicked, it is an impossibility for it to be a lasting government, for it does not govern, but obey. America is no exception to this rule. In the first place, at its commencement, I believe it was a remarkably moral population; and so the evils would not at first appear And, since that time, the immensity of its territory has enabled its most active and least self-restrained population to expand itself with less inconvenience. But will the thing last? When the wilderness is peopled, will not the wickedness, which is now expended on the Indians and the weak without observation, become intolerable, and a government strong enough to protect, be the result? Such a one, I think, will hardly be a republic, but, I fear, a despotism, for men always run into extremes. Lynch law is, in fact, an ill-regulated despotism."

"Safe Men."

Dean Hook, in his *Lives of the Archbishops of Canterbury*, has the following judicious observations upon appointments of this practically useful class :

" Among the archbishops," says the Dean, "there are a few eminent rulers distinguished as much for their transcendent abilities as for their exalted station in society; but as a general rule they have not been men of the highest class of mind. In all ages the tendency has very properly been, whether by election or nomination, to appoint 'safe men;' and as genius is generally innovating and often eccentric, the safe men are those who, with certain high qualifications, do not rise much above the intellectual average of their contemporaries. They are practical men rather than philosophers and theorists, and their impulse is not to perfection but *quieta non movere*. From this very circumstance their history is the more instructive ; and, if few among the archbishops have left the impress of their mind upon the age in which they lived, we may in their biography read the character of the times which they fairly represent. In a missionary age we find them zealous but not enthusiastic ; on the revival of learning, whether in Anglo-Saxon times or in the fifteenth century, they were men of learning, although only a few have been distinguished as authors. When the mind of the laity was devoted to the camp or the chase, and prelates were called to the administration of public affairs, they displayed the ordinary tact and diplomatic skill of professional statesmen, and the necessary acumen of judges ; at the Reformation, instead of being leaders, they were the cautious followers of bolder spirits ; at the epoch of the Revolution they were anti-Jacobites rather than Whigs; in a latitudinarian age they have been, if feeble as governors, bright examples of Christian moderation and charity."

Church Preferment.

Lord Chancellor Thurlow, on reading Horsley's Letters to Dr. Priestley, at once obtained for the author a Stall at Gloucester, saying that " those who supported the Church should be supported by it."

Peace Statesmanship.

There is nothing more wholesome for both the people and their rulers, than to dwell upon the excellence of those statesmen whose lives have been spent in the useful, the sacred, work of Peace. The thoughtless vulgar are ever prone to magnify the brilliant exploits of arms, which dazzle ordinary understandings, and prevent any account being taken of the cost and the crime that are so often hid in the guise of success. All merit of that shining kind is sure of passing current for more than it is really worth; and the eye is turned indifferently upon, or even scornfully from, the unpretending virtue of the true friend to his species, the minister who devotes all his cares to stay the worst of crimes that can be committed, the last of calamities that can be endured by man.

The Burial of Sir John Moore.

It had been generally supposed that the interment of General Sir John Moore, who fell at the Battle of Corunna, in 1809, took place *during the night ;* a mistake which, doubtless, arose from the justly-admired lines by Wolfe becoming more widely known and remembered than the official account of this solemn event in the Narrative of the Campaign, by the brother of Sir John Moore. In Wolfe's monody, the hero is represented to have been buried

> By the struggling *moonbeam's misty light*,
> And the lanterns dimly burning,—

an error of description which has, doubtless, been extended by many pictorial illustrations of the sad scene, "darkly at dead of night." The Rev. J. H. Symons, who was chaplain to the brigade of Guards attached to the army under Moore's command, and who attended the hero in his last moments, relates that during the battle Moore was conveyed from the field into the quarters on the quay at Corunna, where he was laid on a mattress upon the floor, and the chaplain remained with him till his death. During the night, the body was removed to the quarters of Colonel Graham, in the citadel, by the officers of his staff; whence it was borne by them, assisted by Mr. Symons, the chaplain, to the grave which had been prepared for it on one of the bastions of the citadel. It being now daylight, the enemy had discovered that the troops had been withdrawing and embarking during the night; a fire was soon opened by them, upon the ships which were still in the harbour; the funeral service was, therefore, performed without delay, under the fire of the enemy's guns; and, there being no means to provide a coffin, the body of the general,

> With his martial cloak around him,

was deposited in the earth, the Rev. Mr. Symons reading the funeral service.

The Ancestors of Washington.

While America feels a just pride in having given birth to George Washington, it is something for England to know that his ancestors lived for generations upon her soil. His great-grandfather emigrated about 1657, having previously lived in Northamptonshire. The Washingtons were a Northern family, who lived some time in Durham, and also in Lancashire, whence they came to Northamptonshire. The uncle of the first Lawrence Washington was Sir Thomas Kitson, one of the great merchants, who, in the reigns of Henry VII. and VIII., developed the wool-trade of the country, which depended mainly on the growth of wool, and the creation of sheep-farms in the midland counties. That he might superintend his uncle's transactions with the sheep proprietors, Lawrence Washington settled in Northamptonshire, leaving his own profession of a barrister. He soon became Mayor of Northampton, and at the dissolution of the monasteries, being identified with the cause of civil and religious liberty, he gained a grant of some monastic land, including Sulgrave. In the parish of Brington is situated Althorp, the seat of the Spencers: the Lady Spencer of that day was herself a Kitson, daughter of Washington's uncle, and the Spencers were great promoters of the sheep-farming movement. Thus, then, there was a very plain connexion between the Washingtons and the Spencers.

For three generations the Washingtons remained at Sulgrave, taking rank among the nobility and gentry of the county. Then their fortunes failed: they were obliged to part with Sulgrave, and retired to Brington, under, as it were, the wing of the Spencer family. From this depression the Washingtons recovered by a singular marriage. The eldest son of the family had married the half-sister of George Villiers, Duke of Buckingham, which at this time was not an alliance above the pretensions of the Washingtons: they rose into great prosperity. The emigrant, above all others of the family, continued to be on intimate terms with the Spencers, down to the very eve of the Civil War; he was knighted by James I. in 1623, and in the Civil War took the side of the king. The emigrant who left England in 1657, we leave to be traced by historians on the other side of the Atlantic.

" George Washington, without the genius of Julius Cæsar or Napoleon Bonaparte, has a far purer fame, as his ambition was of a higher and a holier nature. Instead of seeking to raise his own name, or seize supreme power, he devoted his whole talents, military and civil, to the establishment of the independence and the perpetuity of the liberties of his own country. In modern history no man has done such great things without the soil of selfishness or the stain of a grovelling ambition. Cæsar, Cromwell, Napoleon, attained a higher elevation, but the love of dominion was the spur that drove them on. John Hampden, William Russell, Algernon Sidney, may have had motives as pure, and an ambition as sustained, but they fell. To George Washington alone, in modern times, has it been given to accomplish a wonderful revolution, and yet to remain to all future times the theme of a people's gratitude, and an example of virtuous and beneficent power."—*Earl Russell's Life and Times of Charles James Fox.*

The " Star-spangled Banner" of the United States.

The people of the United States understand little of the proper form, proportion of size, number of stripes even, of their own national flag, the " Star-spangled Banner."

The standard for the army is fixed at six feet and six inches, by four feet and four inches ; the number of stripes is thirteen—viz., seven red and six white. It will be perceived that the flag is just one-half longer than it is broad, and that its proportions are perfect when properly carried out. The first stripe at the top is red, the next white, and so down alternately, which makes the last stripe red. The blue field for the stars is the width and square of the first seven stripes—viz., four red and three white. These seven stripes extend from the *side* of the field to the extremity of the flag ; the next stripe is *white*, extending the entire length of it, and directly *under* the field ; then follow the remaining stripes alternately. The number of stars on the field is now thirty-one, and the Army and Navy add another star on the admission of a new State into our glorious union. In some respects, the " Banner" resembles the flag of the Sandwich Islands.—*American Journal.*

Ancestry of President Adams.

John Adams, second President of the United States of America, is commonly but erroneously represented to have been the son of a cobbler. Now, he was the son of a clergyman. His descent would have graced any Court in Europe. He was descended from one of the oldest families in Devonshire and Gloucestershire, one of whom sat as an English Baron in the Parliaments of Edward the First. His father, Adam Fitzherbert, was lineally descended from the ancient Counts de Vermandois. Lord ap-Adam's wife (the ancestress of this second President of America) was the daughter and sole heiress of John Lord de Gournay, of Beverston Castle, Gloucestershire, the representative of the ancient House of Harpitré de Gournai, a branch of the great house of " Yvery," which was connected with every Sovereign house in Europe. It would be difficult to find a higher descent. The late Mr. Edward Adams, M.P., of Middleton Hall, Carmarthenshire, was a descendant of the elder branch of this family; and Mr. Anthony Davis, of Misbourne House, Chalfont Saint Giles, Bucks, is its representative.

The Irish Union.

It was after the exhaustion caused by the Rebellion in Ireland, that Pitt brought forward his project of the Union, and Lord Cornwallis successfully accomplished it. Mr. Massey describes at great length the means by which, in Castlereagh's phrase, " the fee simple of Irish corruption was bought;" and the Irish Parliament, like Tarpeia, perished beneath the weight of stipulated bribery. No person acquainted in the least with history, or having any regard for Ireland, will fail to rejoice at the success of a measure which relieved her instantly from a worthless Legislature, and by incorporating her with Great Britain assured her the prospect of just government. But the delay in the grant of Catholic Emancipation, which Pitt had intended to accompany the Union, retarded for many years its benefits; and another part of the Minister's scheme, a State provision for the Catholic priesthood, remains to this day unaccomplished. Pitt incurred a heavy responsibility on this account. It appears certain from the Castlereagh correspondence that the Irish Catholics supported the Union on something like an implied pledge that they should obtain their political rights; and on this ground, and on that, besides, of the State necessity for emancipation, Pitt can hardly escape the censure of history for not having insisted more strongly in carrying out his policy as a whole, and especially for having, in 1805, consented not to press the subject on the King when he formed his second brief Administration. It is doubtful, however, Mr. Massey observes, whether Pitt could at any period have extorted compliance from George III., or, indeed, from the people of England; and, though his conduct in this matter was not chivalrous as an individual, he may have conceived, as a public man, that he had satisfied honour by his resigning in 1801, and that afterwards he would have not been justified in depriving the country of his services for the sake of a policy impracticable at the moment.— *Times review of Massey's Hist. England.*

The published Correspondence of Lord Cornwallis gives, with painful minuteness, the details of management and bribery by which the Union between Great Britain and Ireland was carried to a conclusion; but most readers of the history of the period are satisfied with knowing that the Union was a political necessity, that the parties to be dealt with in effecting it—the Irish Parliament and its patrons—were utterly corrupt, and that *persuasion* was the only method which it was possible to employ. The result was inevitable. The Government bid high, and as it bid the vendors raised their prices, and still the Government bid higher. At last the owners of seats were gorged with the sum of 15,000*l.* for each disfranchised borough, and the whole amount of compensation thus extorted reached the magnificent figure of 1,260,000*l.* We can hardly be thankful enough that Lord Grey's Government had the firmness to resist the application of so inconvenient a precedent in the Reform Bill of 1832.

The House of Bonaparte.

The *Moniteur* in 1862 contained five columns on the pedigree of Bonaparte, from Anno Domini 1170, when the first of that name headed an Italian league at Treviso against the German invaders under Frederic Barbarossa. John Bonaparte signs a treaty at Constance on behalf of Italy, and writes himself *consul*, being in fact *le premier consul* of his race, in 1182. Two centuries after the Bonaparte escutcheon on their house in St. Andrew's-square, at Treviso, is ordered to be broken by Venice; and 440 years afterwards that republic is suppressed by a Bonaparte at the treaty of Campo Formio. Details are given of the family's removal to Florence, San Miniato, and Corsica; of the sack of Rome, at which Jacopo Bonaparte assisted in 1520, and of a comedy, *La Vedova*, from the pen of another about the same period. Muratori's *Antiquitates Italicæ*, vols. 8, 9, and 12, folio, contain numerous diplomatic documents signed by members of this stirring house, ever active in all the revolutions of mediæval Italy. The *Moniteur* becomes quite an enthusiast about the land that produced this chosen race. The oddest revelation is the fact, that *Mala-parte* was the original name before 1170, just as it was of the Bolognese family *Malatesta*, the change having been voted by popular acclaim in public assembly at Treviso. So far the *Moniteur*. But it might be added that the Beauharnais family, through which the present Emperor comes, had undergone a precisely similar change of name at the request of Marie Antoinette. That house had been known for ages in Poitou as Seigneurs de Bellescouilles, an appellation not quite fitting the Court at Versailles, and altered accordingly. It is rather remarkable that Napoleon I., in the *Moniteur* of 22nd Messidor, an XIII., 1805, had scouted all idea of ancestry, and ordered a formal declaration to be inserted that his house dated from Marengo, quoting the lines of La Fontaine—"*Rien n'est dangereux qu'un sot ami,*" meaning the person who had drawn out his pedigree.

The Register of the Imperial family is a large folio volume, bound in red velvet, and having at the corners ornaments of silver-gilt, with the family cipher ' N ' in the centre. It was commenced in 1806, and the first entry made was the adoption of Prince Eugène by the Emperor. The second, made the same year, relates to the adoption of the Princess Stephanie de Beauharnais, who died Grand Duchess of Baden, and who was cousin of the Empress Joséphine. Next comes the marriage of the Emperor Napoleon I.; then several certificates of the birth of Princes of the family, and lastly of the King of Rome, which closes the series of the certificates inscribed under the reign of the First Emperor. This register was confided to the care of Count Regnault de Saint-Jean-d'Angely, Minister and Councillor of State, and Secretary of the Imperial family. It was to him, under the First Empire, as it is now to the Minister of State under the Second, that was reserved the duty of drawing up the *procès verbaux* of the great acts relative to Napoleon. At the fall of the First Empire, Count Regnault de Saint-Jean-d'Angely carefully preserved the book, which at his death passed into the hands of the Countess, his widow. That lady handed it over to the President of the Republic when Louis Napoleon was called by universal suffrage to the Imperial throne.

A Correspondent of the *Literary Gazette* writes: " I have been afforded an opportunity of examining many of the letters of Napoleon which figure in the Imperial collection; and I assure you that the commission charged with the duty of saying what should and what should not be published, had a most arduous task to perform. For of all the ' cramped pieces of penmanship' that were ever seen his are the most cramped and unintelligible. The manner in which the letters are formed would frighten a writing-master into fits, and the lines never run straight, whilst not unfrequently they come into collision. And what is singular is that a great many of the words are grossly misspelt, and that others are only half-written. O vanity of human genius! O triumph for dull little schoolboys! The man who conquered more kingdoms than Alexander knew not orthography !"

Invasion of England projected by Napoleon I.

The 9th volume of the *Correspondance de Napoléon I.*, published at Paris, in 1862, brings to light, for the first time, the whole of his schemes for invading England, which he planned in 1803, when he led a mighty host to Boulogne, in the hope of repeating the scene of the Conquest. The following passage in this volume shows how Napoleon struggled to remove his inferiority in fleets:

"Collect 3000 workmen at Antwerp. Wood, iron, and materials can be brought there from the North. War is no impediment to shipbuilding

at Antwerp.   If we are three years at war, we must build there not less
than 25 ships of the line.   Anywhere else this would be impossible.   We
must have a powerful fleet ; and we should not have less than 100 ships
of the line.   We must also commence building frigates and smaller vessels.
St. Domingo cost us 2,000,000f. a month ; the English having captured it,
this sum must be appropriated to the increase of our navy."

Such were the conditions of this attack ; and such the forces
with which Napoleon expected " to conquer the world in London ;" and his letters to Soult, to Bruix, to Déeres must convince
the reader that he was in earnest in his scheme of " planting the
tricolour on the Tower."   The problem for Napoleon to solve
was how to transport across the Channel an army of 150,000
men, with horses, cannon, baggage, and equipments, in spite of
the naval superiority of England.   In these first preparations we
must allow he succeeded beyond our worst expectations.   Within
fourteen months from the commencement of the war he had
gathered within ten leagues of our coast, and had placed beyond
the power of attack, a flotilla mounting 2000 guns, and able to
transport his superb army, which, though numbering 150,000
men, could embark in less than a single tide, and were fully
trained for a naval encounter.

So far, at least, as regards the Government, it must be confessed
that our preparations to meet this attack were unequal to the
danger.   In the Channel especially—the point menaced—the naval
arrangements made by the Admiralty were very faulty and even
ridiculous.   Such a Power as England should never have allowed
the flotilla to assemble at Boulogne at all ;   and when it had
assembled it should have been assailed by a mass of gunboats and
light vessels, which we might have sent out in enormous numbers.
Yet the Admiralty persisted in encountering the flotilla with 18
and 12-pounder frigates, which drew too much water to close
the shore, and, at long range, were no match for their powerfully
armed, though small antagonists ; the result was that on no
occasion were we able to damage the enemy seriously, and that
on some we suffered severely.

In England as well as in France it was thought that the flotilla
was to risk the passage unaided, its heavy armament suggesting
the notion that Napoleon believed it a match for our fleet in the
narrow strait between Dover and Calais.   We now know, however, that this was an error, and that Napoleon never intended to
embark unless supported by a covering squadron, which, having
for a time the command of the Channel, would completely protect
the flotilla and the army.   In order to have the mastery of the

Channel for the forty-eight hours required for the transit, the problem was so to manœuvre his fleets as to bring a superior force off Boulogne, in spite of the numerous English squadrons which watched or blockaded them in all their harbours.   He devised a twofold scheme for this end, adapted to the circumstances of the seaboard, and which experience proved to be feasible.

This volume, however, proves sufficiently that, brilliant as were Napoleon's designs, he could not inspire Villeneuve and Ganteaume with the daring energy of Nelson and Cochrane, or make British seamen of his sailors.   The want of discipline, the timidity, and the inexperience, of which there are proofs, explain how Napoleon's deep-laid designs were brought to an end on the day of Trafalgar.

However, in 1805, Napoleon renewed his invasion scheme, the details of which he thus narrates in the 11th volume of his *Correspondance*, 1863 :

" I wished to bring together forty or fifty sail of the line by operating their junction from Toulon, Cadiz, Ferrol, and Brest; to move them all together to Boulogne; to be there for a fortnight master of the Channel; to have 150,000 men and 10,000 horses encamped on the coast, with a flotilla of nearly 4000 vessels, and then, upon the arrival of my fleet, to embark for England and seize London. . . . . To secure a prospect of success it was necessary to collect 150,000 men at Boulogne, with the flotilla, and an immense materiel, to embark the whole, yet to conceal my plan. I accomplished this though it appeared impossible, and I did so by reversing what seemed probable."

Thus, in the spring of 1805 Napoleon collected within ten leagues of our shores a flotilla of nearly 4000 vessels, which, moored under the batteries of Boulogne, and armed with very heavy cannon, had long repelled our attempts to destroy them. Encamped around lay the veteran legions which had been selected for the descent, and had been trained with such care to embark and expedite the passage, that Napoleon writes, " 150,000 men with a due proportion of guns and horses could within four tides effect a landing."

His plan was marked with much ingenuity.   The aspect of an armed flotilla induced our Admiralty to think that Napoleon relied on it alone to cross; and they felt assured that when at sea, three or four ships would suffice to destroy it.   Accordingly, our Channel fleet was reduced to a force of not more than six sail ; and the mass of the British Navy was employed either in blockading the enemy's squadrons or in distant expeditions on the ocean. Could, therefore, one of the blockaded fleets effect its junction with another, and penetrate into the unguarded Channel, a temporary ascendancy at sea might be gained, under cover of which the flotilla could cross and ferry over the French army.

It is only in this volume that we see how nearly Napoleon's design succeeded so far as regards the descent, and also what were the causes of its failure. Whatever we may think of his project as a whole, it must be allowed that in August, 1805, when Villeneuve put to sea from Ferrol, the Emperor had good reason to expect that his Admirals would fulfil their mission:—

"The squadrons of Nelson and Calder have joined the fleet off Brest, *and Cornwallis has been foolish enough to send twenty sail to blockade the French fleet off Ferrol. On the 17th of August—that is, three days after our squadron left Ferrol, Calder left Brest for Ferrol with a northerly wind.* What a chance was there for Villeneuve! *He could either, by keeping a wide offing, avoid Calder, reach Brest, and fall upon Cornwallis, or with his thirty sail-of-the-line beat Calder's twenty, and acquire a decided preponderance.* So much for the English, whose combinations are so talked of."

In England the Whigs laughed at the idea of the invasion as a ministerial bugbear. "Can anything equal," says Lord Grenville in 1804, "the ridicule of Pitt riding about from Downing-street to Wimbledon, and from Wimbledon to Cox-heath, to inspect military carriages, impregnable batteries, and Lord Chatham's reviews? Can he possibly be serious in expecting Bonaparte now?" So also wrote Fox a year afterwards—"The alarm of invasion here was most certainly a groundless one, and raised for some political purpose by the Ministers." Whatever the Whigs might then think, there is no doubt now as to Bonaparte's intentions. "Let us be masters of the Channel for six hours, and we are masters of the world," are his famous words. His design to invade this country was never relinquished, was cherished as the darling scheme of his life, until within a month or two before Pitt's death, when the battle of Trafalgar destroyed his hopes for ever.—*Selected and abridged from reviews in the Times.*

Fate of the Duc d'Enghien.

While the First Consul was meditating the descent upon England, in 1804, his life and government were imperilled by the conspiracy of Georges, Moreau, and Pichegru. The Duc d'Enghien, as is well known, was the innocent victim of this affair, having been arrested on neutral territory, and shot in a ditch, without a trial, in order to strike the Bourbons with terror. While the printed account shows that the plot was a formidable one, that the death of Napoleon and a counter-revolution were really not remote contingencies, and that there were some slight grounds to suspect an intrigue between Dumouriez and the Duke, it also impliedly acquits that Prince of any share in the main conspiracy, and throws the guilt of his cruel fate exclusively on the First Consul. From the list of charges against the Duke, entirely in Napoleon's writing, it is plain that he did not possess any proofs, sufficient even for the tribunal of Vincennes to convict the prisoner of a design against his life.

These monstrous charges speak for themselves, and accord well with the midnight dungeon, the irresponsible conclave, the undefended prisoner, and the grave dug before the trial for the victim! Moreover, the volume of Napoleon's *Correspondance* in which these details are given, has not a trace of the alleged over-rapidity of Savary, of the suppression of the Prince's letter by Talleyrand, of the order said to have been given to Real to suspend the execution after the sentence, and to await the result of a regular examination—of the hundred and one excuses, in short, which have been urged for Napoleon by his apologists. On the contrary, from the following letter we infer that he wished to avoid discussion about a purpose already determined, and that he feared lest public opinion should condemn his design on the Duc d'Enghien. It is addressed to the Commandant of Vincennes:—

"A person, whose name is to remain unknown, will be brought to the fortress confided to your care; you are to put him in a vacant cell, and to take every precaution for his safe keeping. The intention of the Government is to *keep all proceedings concerning him most secret.* No question is to be put to him as to who he is, or why he is detained. Even you are not to know who the prisoner is. No one is to communicate with him but yourself; no one else is to see him until fresh orders. He will probably arrive this night."

Napoleon's Government, though very despotic, was not, however, usually cruel; and this great crime which, perhaps, was caused by the haunting dread of an assassin's arm, was an exception to its general tenor.—*Times review.*

Last Moments of Mr. Pitt.

The news of Austerlitz was the last blow which killed Pitt. The gout, which had hitherto confined its attacks to his extremities, assailed some vital organ. He was not without hopes of getting better. Lord Wellesley found him in high spirits, though before the interview was over Pitt fainted in his presence. His last moments are described by the Hon. James Stanhope, who was present in the room when he died; so that at last we seem to have authentic information of a scene which has hitherto been very imperfectly described. "I remained the whole of Wednesday night with Mr. Pitt," says Mr. Stanhope in a paper drawn up by him, and of which Earl Stanhope has availed himself in his *Life of Pitt.* "His mind seemed fixed on the affairs of the country, and he expressed his thoughts aloud, though sometimes incoherently. He spoke a good deal concerning a private letter from Lord Harrowby, and frequently inquired the direction of the wind; then said, answering himself, 'East; ah! that will do; that will bring him quick.' At other times he seemed to be in conversation with a messenger, and sometimes cried out 'Hear, hear,' as if in the House of Commons. During the time he did not speak he moaned considerably, crying, 'Oh, dear! Oh, Lord!' Towards twelve the rattles came in his throat, and proclaimed approaching dissolution. . . . . . At about half-past two he ceased moaning. . . . . . . I feared he was dying; but shortly afterwards, with a much clearer voice than he spoke in before, and in a tone I never shall forget, 'Oh, my country! how I leave my country!' [referring, as it was natural for him to do, to the disastrous state of the continental war produced by the battle of Austerlitz.] From that time he never spoke or moved, and at half-past four expired without a groan or struggle," 23rd January, 1806. He received the Sacrament from the Bishop of Lincoln. Mr. Pitt gave his watch to his servant, who handed it over to Mr. Dundas, M.P., more than twenty years after Mr. Pitt's death. That watch, a mourning-ring, and box containing the hair, were bequeathed to the Rt. Hon. R. N. Hamilton; and the watch is now preserved in the Fitzwilliam Museum, at Cambridge.

"Pitt is the most forgiving and easy-tempered of men," says Lord Malmesbury. "He is the most upright political character I ever knew or heard of," says Wilberforce. "I never once saw him out of temper," says George Rose. One day, when the conversation turned upon the quality most needed in a Prime Minister, and one said "Eloquence," another "Knowledge," and a third "Toil," Pitt said, "No; Patience." It was an answer worthy of the great statesman, and recalls that of Newton, who said that he owed his splendid discoveries to the power of fixed attention. Pitt was wonderfully patient, and this which is commonly regarded as a slow virtue he combined with uncommon readiness and rapidity of thought. "What an extraordinary man Pitt is!" said Adam Smith; "he makes me understand my own ideas better than before." The Marquis Wellesley has left this character of Pitt—a man of princely hospitality and amiable nature :

"In all places, and at all times, his constant delight was society. There he shone with a degree of calm and steady lustre which often astonished me more than his most splendid efforts in Parliament. His manners were perfectly plain, without any affectation ; not only was he without presumption or arrogance, or any air of authority, but he seemed utterly unconscious of his own superiority, and much more disposed to listen than to talk. He never betrayed any symptom of anxiety to usurp the lead or to display his own powers, but rather inclined to draw forth others, and to take merely an equal share in the general conversation : then he plunged heedlessly into the mirth of the hour, with no other care than to promote the general good humour and happiness of the company. His wit was quick and ready, but it was rather lively than sharp, and never envenomed with the least taint of malignity ; so that, instead of exciting admiration or terror, it was an additional ingredient in the common enjoyment. He was endowed, beyond any man of his time whom I knew, with a gay and social heart. With these qualities, he was the life and soul of his own society ; his appearance dispelled all care; his brow was never clouded, even in the severest public trials; and joy, and hope, and confidence, beamed from his countenance in every crisis of difficulty and danger."—*Communicated to the Quarterly Review.*

This was "the Heaven-born Minister." This was "the pilot to weather the storm." This is he who stands forth as the greatest of our statesmen, and the story of whose life, as fitly told by Lord Stanhope, will have undying interest throughout the world.

Who would have supposed forty years ago that a day was coming when a Frenchman would unhesitatingly write the apology —we had almost said the panegyric—of William Pitt—*ce Pitt,* as the members of the Jacobin Club used to call him ? And yet such is the case. By way of preface to a translation of Lord Stanhope's last work, M. Guizot has given a very good estimate both of the political relation in which England stands to France, and also of the character of the great British statesman. He conclusively shows that Pitt was positively opposed to a war with France, and did all he could to prevent the inevitable catastrophe.

What drove George the Third mad.

How strange is it to find, upon a close examination of the biography of Mr. Pitt, that early in the present century, the *mention* of the measure which twenty-eight years later became the law of the land, had the effect of disturbing the reason of the Sovereign: yet so it was. " Pitt had become in a manner pledged on the union of the Irish with the British Legislature to provide for what has since been called the Emancipation of the Catholics. The probability is, that from the first he had underrated the King's repugnance to the measure; but it has been suggested that had there been no treachery in the camp, and had he been the first to broach the subject to George III., he might have had his own way, and carried the acquiescence of the King. As it was, Lord Loughborough had, contrary to all rule, made the King aware of Pitt's intentions, and had, for his own selfish purposes, sought to strengthen His Majesty in a most absurd view of his duty. So it happened that instead of Pitt breaking the subject to the King, the King, in a fit of impatience, breaks out upon Dundas. Referring to Lord Castlereagh, who had recently come from Dublin, he said, " What is it that this young lord has brought over which they are going to throw at my head ? . . . The most Jacobinical thing I ever heard of! I shall reckon any man my personal enemy who proposes any such measure." " Your Majesty," replied Dundas, " will find among those who are friendly to that measure some whom you never supposed to be your enemies." The time for action had evidently come: it was necessary for Pitt to break the silence; he wrote to the King explaining his views, and pointing out that if they were not ac- ceptable it would be necessary for him to resign. Pitt did resign; his successor was appointed, but before the formal transfer of office could take place, the King went mad, and it was this Catholic question that drove him mad. He recovered in a fort- night and told his physician to write to Pitt, " Tell him I am now quite well—quite recovered from my illness; but what has *he* not to answer for who is the cause of my having been ill at all?" Pitt was deeply touched, and at once conveyed an assurance to the King through the same physician that never again during the King's reign would he bring forward the Catholic question. Pre- vious to that illness, Pitt had two clear alternatives before him —" Either I shall relieve the Catholics, or I shall resign,"—and he resigned accordingly. But after the illness all was changed. Any one attempting to relieve the Catholics would incur the risk of the King's derangement. There was but a choice of evils, and it was natural that Pitt should regard it as the lesser evil to postpone indefinitely the settlement of the Catholic claims, which, nevertheless, he regarded as of the utmost importance."—*Times review.*

The Rt. Hon. George Rose, when Secretary of the Treasury, had frequent conversations with George III., whom he occasionally received at his house at Cuffnells. Evidently the King took the lion's share in every dialogue. His remarks and his gossip must have been often amusing, and not always uninstructive. He invariably turned the conversation to personal subjects, and he commented freely on the numerous politicians whom he had in his time employed and baffled. He had a peculiar dislike to Lord Melville, he resented Lord Grenville's pride, and he accurately described Lord Auckland as an inveterate intriguer. Of himself he said that he seldom forgot and never forgave, but that he always tried to believe the best of every man until he had proved his demerit. Many, he added, improved when they found that they had received more than justice; but it never occurred to him that his own opinion might not form an accurate and sufficient standard of merit.

During the latter part of the time, George III., notwithstanding the continuance of some delusions, was perfectly competent to understand the state of affairs, and there was every reason to suppose that he would become convalescent before his son could take his seat as Regent. For the remainder of his reign, his Ministers and his subjects regarded his occasional insanity as one of the ordinary contingencies of the Constitution. Mr. Pitt, during his second •Administration, sometimes obtained from the physicians a written certificate of the King's competence before he entered his presence for the transaction of business.

Predictions of the Downfal of Napoleon I.

Brialmont and Gleig, in their *Memoirs of Wellington*, relate —Mr. Pitt received, during dinner, when Sir Arthur Wellesley and other eminent persons were present, intelligence of the capitulation of Mack, at Ulm, and the march of the Emperor upon Vienna. One of the friends of the Prime Minister, on hearing of the reverse, exclaimed, " All is lost! there are no other means of opposing Napoleon." " You are mistaken," said Pitt, " there is yet hope, if I can succeed in stirring up a national war in Europe—a war which ought to begin in Spain. Yes, gentlemen, Spain will be the first nation in which that war of patriotism shall be lighted up which can alone deliver Europe."

At a moment when the prestige of the Empire was accepted everywhere, Wellington not only expressed doubts as to the stability of that edifice, which seemed as if it must endure for ages, but pointed out distinctly the causes which must operate to throw it down, and the means by which its fall might be hastened. From that hour, whilst prosecuting the war in Spain, he took care as much as possible, to regulate his own proceedings according to the general state of Europe. Something told him that the little army on the Mondego had a mighty part to play in the sanguinary drama which agitated the world; and that not the fate of the Peninsula alone was at stake, nor yet the question of England's supremacy, but the independence and liberty of all nations, menaced by the ambition of one man.

In December, 1811, Wellington wrote to Lord William Bentinck: " I have long considered it probable that we shall see a general resistance throughout Europe to the horrible and base tyranny of Bonaparte, and that we shall be called upon to play a leading part in the drama, as counsellors as well as actors."

In a letter to Lord Liverpool, in 1811, Wellington wrote: " I am convinced, that if we can only hold out a little longer, we shall see the world emancipated." And to Dumouriez, July, 1811: " It is impossible that Europe can much longer submit to the debasing tyranny which oppresses it."

Brialmont and Gleig summarily observe: " It may truly be said that the Duke foretold in succession, the final success of the war in Spain—the influence which that war would exercise over public opinion in other nations — *the general rising of Europe against Bonaparte*—the fall of the Empire—the disastrous campaign in Russia — and the awakening of the public spirit in Germany."

When, in 1807, Haydon dined with Sir George and Lady Beaumont, he met there Humphry Davy, who was very entertaining, and made a remark which turned out a singularly successful prophecy; he said, " Napoleon will certainly come in contact with Russia, by pressing forward in Poland, and *there*, probably, will begin his destruction." This was said five years before it happened.

Lord Mulgrave, afterwards Marquis of Normanby, first raised Haydon's enthusiasm for Wellington by saying, one day, at table, " If you live to see it, he will be a second Marlborough."

Wellington predicts the Peninsular Campaign.

The following is illustrative of the prophetic perception of Wellington at the outset of the contest :—" He dined in Harley-street one day in June, 1808, just before he set out in command of the expedition which was assembling in Cork harbour. The ladies had withdrawn, and he sat *tête-à-tête* with his host, and was silent. On being asked what he was thinking of, he replied, ' To tell you the truth, I was thinking of the French whom I am going to fight. I have never seen them since the campaign in Flanders, when they were already capital soldiers; and a dozen years of successes must have made them still better. *They have beaten all the world, and are supposed to be invincible. They have besides, it seems, a new system, which has out-manœuvred and over-whelmed all the armies of Europe. But no matter, my die is cast. They may overwhelm, but I do not think they will out-manœuvre me. In the first place, I am not afraid of them, as everybody else seems to be; and secondly, if what I hear of their system of manœuvres be true, I think it a false one against troops steady enough—as I hope mine are—to receive them with the bayonet.* I suspect that all the continental armies were more than half beaten before the battle began. I, at least, will not be frightened beforehand.' "

The Battle of Waterloo.

M. Thiers, in the 20th volume of his *Histoire du Consulat et de l'Empire*, presents to his reader a tissue of intellectual illu-sions in his extraordinary account of the last struggle of Napoleon in Belgium. Common sense and history agree that that effort bears many traces of his hero's genius, though marked by one characteristic mistake, and that it was baffled by the ability of his antagonists, who crushed him at last by superior numbers. This volume, however, has been written to prove that in every move in this famous contest Napoleon was an infallible com-mander; that victory must have crowned his standards had his inspiration been only understood; and that his final overthrow was due, not to Wellington's skill or Blucher's daring—not to British heroism or Prussian valour, but to the errors and fears of his subordinates. Deserting the region of fact and circum-stance, M. Thiers leads us into a dream-land, where the Emperor, like a strategic Providence, holds his puny foes in the hollow of his hand, and predestinates his legions to conquest—where the French army performs prodigies beyond the energies of mortal men—where but for Ney, D'Erlon, and Grouchy, the downfal of its adversaries was certain—and where the inability of these satellites to launch the bolts of military fate was the only cause of the final issue. The above and the following remarks are from *The Times* review,—

Why the issue of this campaign was so different from that of many of its splendid forerunners may be accounted for with perfect certainty. The Duke and Blucher were different men, of greater ability, and better united than the Generals of any previous coalition, and the large majority of their troops were capable of heroic exertions. The Duke was not the man to allow an accident of time to ruin an ally, and at the crisis of the campaign, on the 16th, he baffled the Emperor by his tactical skill and the intrepidity of his British infantry. Of the subsequent moves by which he won the greatest battle of modern times, it is enough to say that they defy criticism, while the heroism of two-thirds of his army has not been surpassed in military annals. As for the Prussian troops, their stand at Ligny and their subsequent rally and advance to Waterloo, are worthy of the highest commendation; and Blucher's celebrated march from Wavre is said to have wrung from Napoleon himself the admission that " it was a flash of genius." It was this combination of talent and valour, unlike anything he had encountered before, that brought the superior numbers of the allies to bear upon Napoleon at last, and involved him and his army in ruin.

As for the armies that met in this bloody strife, we Englishmen think it enough to say that, except the Belgian and Nassau levies, they all did their duty like soldiers. The weak falsetto of M. Thiers detracts from the manhood of that dauntless cavalry " who rode round our squares like their own," and from the renown of that veteran infantry " who bore nine rounds before they staggered." Nor will the heroism of Ligny be forgotten, nor the glory of England at Waterloo fade, because an historian chooses to write that the Prussian army " was well beaten," and that the " English, excellent in defence, are very mediocre on the offensive." At this time, surely, a French historian might describe the campaign of 1815 with a candid regard to truth alone, and without pandering to the ignoble worship of military despotism.

Wellington's Defence of the Waterloo Campaign.

Wellington would never have fought at Waterloo unless certain of the aid of Blucher; it is idle, therefore, to speculate on the chance of what the event of the day might have been had this support been unexpectedly wanting. French writers assert that he must have been crushed; but the Duke held a different opinion. The Rev. Mr. Gleig tells us that—

" After dinner the conversation turned on the Waterloo campaign, when Croker alluded to the criticisms of the French military writers, some of whom contended that the Duke had fought the battle in a position full of difficulty, because he had no practicable retreat. The Duke said: ' At all events, they failed in putting it to the test. The road to Brussels was practicable every yard for such a purpose. I knew every foot of the ground beyond the forest and through it. The forest on each s.de of the chaussée was open enough for infantry, cavalry, and even for artillery, and very defensible. Had I retreated through it, could they have followed me? The Prussians were on their flank, and would have been on their rear. *The co-operation of the Prussians in the operations I undertook was part of my plan, and I was not deceived. But I never contemplated a retreat on Brussels. Had I been forced from my position, I should have retreated to my right, towards the coast, the shipping, and my resources. I had placed Hill where he could have lent me important assistance in many contingencies, and that might have been one.* And, again, I ask, if I had retreated on my right, would Napoleon have ventured to have followed me? The Prussians, already on his flank, would have been on his rear. *But my plan was to keep my ground till the Prussians appeared, and then to attack the French position; and I executed my plan.*' "

It matters little whether it be a pleasing tradition or an historical fact, but it was commonly said that after the Peace, which crowned the immortal services of the Duke of Wellington, that great general, on seeing the playing-fields at Eton, said, there had been won the crowning victory of Waterloo.

Lord Castlereagh at the Congress of Vienna.

By the publication of the *Supplementary Despatches of the Duke of Wellington*, vol. ix., the reputation of Lord Castlereagh will profit by such of his letters as had not appeared before. A writer in the *Saturday Review* remarks:—

" Contemporaries saw that many small States were crushed by the arrangements of Vienna, and that one or two of the larger monarchies, especially that of Russia, were sensibly strengthened. Therefore they concluded that the aim and end of the Congress of Vienna was to aggrandise the greater monarchies, and that the English Minister, biassed by political prejudices or dazzled by royal condescension, had unworthily lent himself to the accomplishment of that object. As the confidential correspondence of that period makes its appearance bit by bit, we are learning to form a juster estimate of what Lord Castlereagh effected at the Congress.   It is hard to set limits to the evils which would have been the result of greater facility or less caution on the part of the English plenipotentiary.   That Alexander would, but for Lord Castlereagh's obstinate resistance, have absorbed the whole of Poland into the Russian empire, and that Prussia would have indemnified herself by the annexation of the whole of Saxony, appears certain ; and that France and Austria would have plunged Europe back into war, in their efforts to resist, seems not improbable.   The greediness of the Powers who had met to divide the spoil threatened incessantly to bring them into collision ; and it was on Lord Castlereagh that the ungracious task of moderating their extravagant pretensions fell.   If he had failed, and the Congress had come to the abrupt and angry close which seemed more than once inevitable, Napoleon's return would have been safe and easy.   It was hard, but it was unavoidable, that those who only saw the result in a considerable accession to Alexander's frontier, should have accused Lord Castlereagh of being his tool, when he had been, in reality, resisting Alexander's pretensions up to the very brink of war."

This late justice to the eminent diplomatic services of Lord Castlereagh, reaches us some forty years after his death; thus giving the lie to the coarse and unfeeling ribaldry of the so-called " Liberal," upon the awful termination of the statesman's life.

The Cato-street Conspiracy.

Early in the year 1820—a period of popular discontent—a set of desperate men banded themselves together with a view to effect a revolution by sanguinary means, almost as complete in its plan of extermination as the Gunpowder Plot.   The leader was one Arthur Thistlewood, who had been a soldier, had been involved in a trial for sedition, but acquitted, and had afterwards suffered a year's imprisonment for sending a challenge to the minister, Lord Sidmouth.   Thistlewood was joined by several other Radicals, and their meetings in Gray's-Inn-lane were known to the spies Oliver and Edwards, employed by the Government. Their first design was to assassinate the Ministers, each in his own house ; but their plot was changed, and Thistlewood and his fellow conspirators arranged to meet at Cato-street, Edge-ware-road, and to proceed from thence to butcher the Ministers assembled at a Cabinet dinner, on Feb. 23rd, at Lord Harrowby's,

39, Grosvenor-square, where Thistlewood proposed, as "a rare haul, to murder them all together." Some of the conspirators were to watch Lord Harrowby's house; one was to call and deliver a despatch-box at the door, the others were then to rush in and murder the Ministers as they sat at dinner; and, as special trophies, to bring away with them the heads of Lords Sidmouth and Castlereagh, in two bags provided for the purpose! They were then to fire the cavalry-barracks; and the Bank and Tower were to be taken by the people, who, it was hoped, would rise upon the spread of the news.

This plot was, however, revealed to the Ministers by Edwards, who had joined the conspirators as a spy. Still no notice was apparently taken. The preparations for dinner went on at Lord Harrowby's till eight o'clock in the evening, but the guests did not arrive. The Archbishop of York, who lived next door, happened to give a dinner-party at the same hour, and the arrival of the carriages deceived those of the conspirators who were on the watch in the street, till it was too late to give warning to their comrades who had assembled at Cato-street, in a loft over a stable, accessible only by a ladder. Here, while the traitors were arming themselves by the light of one or two candles, a party of Bow-street officers entered the stable, when Smithers, the first of them who mounted the ladder, and attempted to seize Thistlewood, was run by him through the body, and instantly fell; whilst, the lights being extinguished, a few shots were exchanged in the darkness and confusion, and Thistlewood and several of his companions escaped through a window at the back of the premises; nine were taken that evening with their arms and ammunition, and the intelligence conveyed to the Ministers, who, having dined at home, met at Lord Liverpool's to await the result of what the Bow-street officers had done. A reward of 1000l. was immediately offered for the apprehension of Thistlewood, and he was captured before eight o'clock next morning while in bed at a friend's house, No. 8, White-street, Little Moorfields. The conspirators were sent to the Tower, and were the last persons imprisoned in that fortress. On April 20th, Thistlewood was condemned to death after three days' trial; and on May 1st, he and his four principal accomplices, Ings, Brunt, Tidd, and Davidson, who had been severally tried and convicted, were hanged at the Old Bailey, and their heads cut off. The remaining six pleaded guilty; one was pardoned, and five were transported for life.

D 2

Southey relates this touching anecdote of Thistlewood's last hours:—

"When the desperate and atrocious traitor Thistlewood was on the scaffold, his demeanour was that of a man who was resolved boldly to meet the fate he had deserved; in the few words which were exchanged between him and his fellow-criminals, he observed, that the grand question whether or not the soul was immortal would soon be solved for them. No expression of hope escaped him; no breathing of repentance, no spark of grace, appeared. Yet (it is a fact which, whether it be more consolatory or awful, ought to be known), on the night after the sentence, and preceding his execution, while he supposed that the person who was appointed to watch him in his cell was asleep, this miserable man was seen by that person repeatedly to rise upon his knees, and heard repeatedly calling upon Christ his Saviour to have mercy upon him, and to forgive him his sins."—*The Doctor*, chap. lxxi.

The selection of *Cato*-street for the conspirators' meeting was accidental; and the street itself is associated but indirectly in name with the Roman patriot and philosopher. To efface recollection of the conspiracy of the low and desperate politicians of 1820, Cato-street has been changed to Homer-street.

Money Panic of 1832.

When, in May, 1832, the Duke of Wellington was very unpopular as a minister, and *it was believed* that he had formed a Cabinet which, *it was thought*, would add to his unpopularity, a few agitators got up " a *run* upon the Bank of England," by means of placarding the streets of London with the emphatic words:—

> TO STOP
> THE DUKE,
> GO FOR GOLD.

advice which was followed to a prodigious extent. On Monday, May 14, (the bills having been profusely posted on Sunday!) the run upon the Bank for coin was so incessant, that in a few hours upwards of half a million was carried off: we remember a tradesman in the Strand bringing home, in a hackney-coach, 2000 sovereigns. Mr. Doubleday, in his *Life of Sir Robert Peel*, states the placards to have been " the device of four gentlemen, two of whom were elected members of the Reformed Parliament. Each put down 20*l*.; and the sum was expended in printing housands of these terrible missives, which were eagerly circuated, and were speedily seen upon every wall in London. The effect is hardly to be described. It was electric." The agent was a tradesman of kindred politics, in business towards the east end of Oxford-street; and it must be admitted that he executed the order completely.

A Great Sufferer by Revolutions.

King Louis of Bavaria, who abdicated after an insurrection in 1848, has seen his family extensively affected by the dynastic changes which have taken place since 1859. His second son is Otho, the ex-King of Greece, born on the 1st of June, 1815; his third, Luitpold, is married to the daughter of the Grand Duke of Tuscany; one of his daughters to the Duke of Modena; and one of his grandsons, or his youngest son Adalbert, was to have succeeded Otho on the throne of Greece. Lastly, the Queen of Naples and her sister, the Countess de Trani, belong to a collateral branch of the Royal family, that of Maximilian, Duke of Bavaria. The House of Wittelsbach has therefore suffered most materially from the revolutions of Germany, Italy, and Greece, and its members might give a second representation of the famous dinner at Venice mentioned in Voltaire's *Candide.—Le Temps*.

Origin of the Anti-Corn-Law League.

The first hint of this great political Association is to be found in the writings of the very individual whose labours tended so much to crown its efforts with success. In the well-known pamphlet, entitled *England, Ireland, and America, by a Manchester Manufacturer*, Mr. Cobden says:

" Whilst agriculture can boast almost as many associations as there are British counties, whilst every city in the kingdom contains its botanical, phrenological, or mechanical institutions, and these again possess their periodical journals (and not merely these, for even *war* sends forth its *United Service Magazine*)—we possess no association of traders, united together, for the common object of enlightening the world upon a question so little understood, and so loaded with obloquy, as free-trade.

" We have our Banksian, our Linnæan, our Hunterian Societies, and why should not at least our greatest commercial and manufacturing towns possess their Smithian Societies, devoted to the purpose of promulgating the beneficent truths of the ' Wealth of Nations'? Such institutions, by promoting a correspondence with similar societies that would probably be organized abroad (for it is our example in questions affecting commerce that strangers follow), might contribute to the spread of liberal and just views of political science, and thus tend to ameliorate the restrictive policy of foreign governments through the legitimate influence of the opinions of its people.

" Nor would such societies be fruitless at home. *Prizes might be offered for the best essay on the corn question, or lecturers might be sent to enlighten the agriculturists, and to invite discussion upon a subject so difficult and of such paramount interest to all.*"

The pamphlet from which the preceding extract is taken, was published in the early part of the year 1835, about four years before the formation of the Anti-Corn-Law League, and at a time when, owing to the very low price of grain, and the prosperity of the manufacturing districts, the question of the Corn-laws scarcely attracted the slightest attention, either in Manchester or in any other part of the country.

Wellington's Military Administration.

Much misconception exists with respect to the military administration of the Duke of Wellington, who was, at the close of his life, commander-in-chief of the army. He is said to have been wedded to " Brown Bess," but he is known to have encouraged the introduction of the Minié ; and several of the reforms executed by Lord Herbert had been discussed by the Duke with approval. The celebrated letter of 1847 shows what were the thoughts of this great man in reference to our national defences, and they are not perhaps the least valuable legacy which Wellington has bequeathed to England. The following scheme of defence by the Duke, which Mr. Gleig for the first time published, is not perhaps the less interesting because it has been in part accomplished :—

" He considered the Channel Islands—Jersey, Guernsey, and Alderney— to be the key of our outer line of defence. In each of these he required that a harbour of refuge should be constructed of sufficient capacity and depth of water to receive a stout squadron ; and then, with Portsmouth well guarded on one flank and Plymouth on the other, he held that England would be perfectly safe from invasion on a large scale. . . . If Government gave him the *Channel Islands, Seaford, Portsmouth, and Plymouth, all completely fortified, and ready to receive respectively their squadrons,* then he was satisfied that, though it might be impossible to prevent marauding parties from landing here or there, England would be placed beyond the risk of invasion on such a scale as to endanger her existence, or even to put the capital in jeopardy. . . . . Establishing then an outer line of defence, he asked for men and material wherewith to meet an enemy if he succeeded in breaking through that line. He would be satisfied with an addition of 20,000 men to the regular army, *provided such a force of Militia were raised as would enable him to dispose of* 70,000 *men among the principal fortresses and arsenals of the kingdom;* keeping at the same time two corps of 50,000 men in hand, one in the neighbourhood of London, the other near Dublin. He should thus have open to him all the great lines of railway, which would enable him to meet with rapidity any danger, from whatever side of the capital it might threaten."

If we read Volunteers for Militia, we shall see that Wellington's plan of defence is nearly that contemplated in 1863.

Gustavus III. of Sweden.

In a paper contributed to the Royal Society of Literature, Dr. Hermann has traced the eventful history of the Swedish monarch with great skill, from the period when he ascended the throne, in 1771, to his assassination by Ankerström at the masked ball in 1792. Dr. Hermann shows that Gustavus united in his own person and character most of those qualities, intellectual and moral, which distinguished the latter half of the eighteenth century. Thus, like Catherine of Russia and Frederick the Great, though not to the same extent, he was a believer in those doctrines whose chief expositors were Voltaire and the Encyclopædists; while, in the government of his country, he was ever striving after a system of optimism, which, however beautiful in theory, is wholly impracticable. The reign of Gustavus is chiefly remarkable for the spirit with which he broke down a tyranny of certain noble families, which had long usurped nearly the whole of the royal prerogative, and had thrown the monarch into the background; for the zeal with which he carried out many reforms of the greatest benefit to the more indigent classes of his people; for the remarkable rashness with which, unsupported by a single other European power, he rushed madly into a war with the Russian Empress; and for the extraordinary victory in which, at the close of his second campaign, in July, 1791, he destroyed the entire Russian fleet, in the Bay of Swöborg, and captured no less than 1412 Russian cannon.

The assassin, Ankerström, was discovered and executed: in his character and in his last moments, a striking similarity may be traced to Bellingham, who assassinated Mr. Perceval in 1812: both expressed the same fanatical satisfaction at the perpetration of the crime, and the same presumptuous confidence of pardon from the Almighty.

Gustavus, in his parting moments, strictly forbad, for *fifty years*, the opening of the chests at Upsal, in which his papers were deposited; and the injunction was strictly obeyed. On March 30, 1842, the chests were opened, in the presence of many spectators; but in neither was found, as was expected, any clue to the conspiracy of which Ankerström was the agent; but the king's autograph instructions do not refer to any papers later than 1788, when the bequest was made. The Swedish instructions, in Gustavus's handwriting, prove that the king enjoyed the reputation of being a great author without even knowing how to spell.—See *Curiosities of History*, p. 107.

Fall of Louis-Philippe.

Sir John Herschel, in a paper on Humboldt's *Kosmos*, in the *Edinburgh Review*, January, 1848, has the following sentence, which reads strangely now, for it was given to the public just before the catastrophe which overthrew the throne of Louis-Philippe, and led in a few months to the Italian and Hungarian wars. Herschel's words are: "A great and wondrous attempt is making in civilized Europe at the present time—neither more nor less than to stave off, *ad infinitum*, the tremendous visitation of war." The retrospect has been thus sketched:

Seventeen years Louis-Philippe sat on his elective throne: great increase of wealth and physical progress were the results of his reign at home, peace preserved abroad, and foreign policy alike successful; yet *the King was not popular at home*. He was hated alike by the Legitimist party, in whose eyes he was but a usurper, and by the revolutionists, who sighed for entire emancipation from kingly rule. Besides, there are deep and dark stains upon the reign of the "Napoleon of Peace," as Louis Philippe liked to be called. His reign was a period of corruption in high places, of jealousy and illiberal restriction towards his own subjects, of a fraudulent and heartless policy towards the allies of his country, whose good will he more especially forfeited by his over-reaching conduct in regard to the marriage of the Duc de Montpensier to a Spanish princess. His downfal was long predicted by the leading journalists of England, where public opinion is unfettered by arbitrary laws. In France, too, it was understood that Louis-Philippe was, in great measure, restrained in his views by his sister, Madame Adelaide, who died Dec. 30, 1847. "Then it came to pass that the heart of the nation became alienated from their king ; and when a trifling disturbance in February, 1848, was aggravated into a popular riot through the audacity of a few ultra-republicans, Louis-Philippe felt that he stood alone and unsupported as a constitutional king, both at home and abroad, and that the soldiery were his only means of defence.   He shrank from employing their bayonets against his people : he fell in consequence, and his house fell with him.   The King fled in disguise from Paris to the coast of Normandy, and taking ship again found a safe refuge on the shores of England, to which his family had already made their escape.   He landed at Newhaven, March 3rd, 1848.   The Queen of England—who, in 1843, had enjoyed the hospitality of Louis Philippe at the Château d'Eu, his royal residence near Dieppe, and who had enter-· tained him in the following year at Windsor, and conferred on him the order of the Garter—immediately assigned Claremont, near Esher, as a residence for himself and his exiled family.   From the time of his arrival in England, his health began visibly to decline: he died on the 26th of August, 1850, in the presence of Queen Amelie and his family, having dictated to them the conclusion of his memoirs, and having received the last rites and sacraments of the church at the hands of his chaplain.   He was buried on the following 2nd of September at the Roman Catholic chapel at Weybridge, Surrey, and an inscription was placed upon his coffin, stating that his ashes remain there, Donec Deo adjuvante in patriam avitos inter cineres transferantur" (*Saturday Review*). They have not been removed !

The Chartists in 1848.

The Tenth of April, 1848, is a noted day in our political calendar, from its presenting a remarkable instance of nipping in the bud apparent danger to the peace of the country by means at once constitutional and reassuring public safety.   It was on this day that the Chartists, as they were called, from developing their proposed alterations in the representative system, through "the People's Charter," made in the metropolis a great demonstration of their numbers: thus hinting at the physical force which they possessed, but probably without any serious design against the public peace.   On this day the Chartists met, about 25,000 in number, on Kennington Common, whence it had been intended to march in procession to the House of Commons with the Charter petition; but the authorities having intimated that the

procession would be prevented by force if attempted, it was
abandoned. Nevertheless, the assembling of the *quasi* politicians
from the north, by marching through the streets to the place
of meeting, had an imposing effect. Great preparations were
made to guard against any mischief; the shops were shut in the
principal thoroughfares; bodies of horse and foot police, assisted
by masses of special constables, were posted at the approaches
to the Thames bridges; a large force of the regular troops was
stationed out of sight in convenient spots; two regiments of
the line were kept ready at Millbank Penitentiary; 1200 infantry
at Deptford, and 30 pieces of heavy field ordnance were ready at
the Tower, to be transported by hired steamers to any required
point. The Meeting was held, but was brought to "a ridiculous issue, by the unity and resolution of the Metropolis, backed
by the judicious measures of the Government, and the masterly
military precautions of the Duke of Wellington."

"On our famous 10th of April, his peculiar genius was exerted to the
unspeakable advantage of peace and order. So effective were his preparations that the most serious insurrection could have been successfully encountered, and yet every source of provocation and alarm was removed by the
dispositions adopted. No military display was anywhere to be seen. The
troops and the cannon were all at their posts, but neither shako nor bayonet
was visible; and for all that met the eye, it might have been concluded
that the peace of the metropolis was still entrusted to the keeping of its
own citizens. As an instance, however, of his forecast against the worst,
on this memorable occasion, it may be observed that orders were given to
the commissioned officers of artillery to take the discharge of their pieces
on themselves. The Duke knew that a cannon-shot too much or too
little might change the aspect of the day; and he provided by these remarkable instructions, both for imperturbable forbearance as long as forbearance was best, and for unshrinking action when the moment for action
came."—*Memoir; Times*, Sept. 15-16, 1852.

The Chartists' Petition was presented to the Commons, on the
above day, signed, it was stated, by 5,706,000 persons. The
principal points of the Charter were universal suffrage, vote by
ballot, annual parliaments, the division of the country into equal
electoral districts, the abolition of property qualification in members, and paying them for their services. Chartism and the
People's Charter grew out of the shortcomings of the Reform
Act. The Chartists then divided into the Physical Force and
the Moral Force Chartists; and then arose the Complete Suf-
fragists; the latter principally from the Middle Classes, the
former from the working-classes; though their objects were very
similar.

Revival of the French Emperorship.

Soon after the breaking-out of the French Revolution, in 1848, the Count d'Orsay called at the office of the *Lady's Newspaper*, in the Strand, and besought the proprietor, Mr. Landells, to engrave in that journal a portrait which he (the Count) had sketched of Louis Napoleon. The proprietor hesitated, when the Count told him it was the Prince's intention to go over to France; and he added, emphatically, "the English people do not understand him; but, take my word for it, if he once goes over to France, *the French people will never get rid of him.*" This prediction has been strictly verified: the assertion was equally correct, that the English people did not understand the Emperor.

Mr. B. Ferrey, in a communication to *Notes and Queries*, 3rd S., remarks:—"For a considerable time, Napoleon was held up to ridicule by the Press of England; yet there were some who then foretold his coming greatness, while the multitude charged him with folly and rashness. Mr. William Brockedon, author of *Passes of the Alps*, who was well acquainted with the Prince's habits, used to say, at the period when the Prince, amidst much derision, was aspiring to become the President of the French Republic,—'Mark my words, that man is not the fool people take him for: he only waits an opportunity to show himself one of the most able men in Europe;' justifying this prediction by relating a discussion he had heard at a public meeting, between the Prince and some civil engineers, respecting a projected railway across the Isthmus of Panama, in which the former displayed great ability, showing an amount of scientific knowledge which amazed everybody present; not only stating his case with clearness, but combating all objections in a most masterly way."

The newspapers of London, with one "base exception," condemned the French choice; and after Louis Napoleon had taken the first step towards the establishment of his rule, the journalists foretold his speedy failure: the "base exception," the *Morning Post*, predicted the reverse, and maintained Louis Napoleon to be the only man capable of rescuing France from the throes of revolution. We happen to know that for another journal of very extensive circulation, chiefly among the influential classes, a leading article of similar tone and confidence to that of the *Morning Post*, was written by the Editor, but omitted by desire of the Proprietor, and an article of opposite tone substituted: the advocacy would have been too bold a step for the time.

The career of Louis Napoleon has been well described as a

great revival in the fortunes of France, the accomplishment of which has been the result of a far-seeing estimate of the French character; thus sketched by a master hand:

"Louis Bonaparte seems to have had the key of the mystery. It may be that, as in the human subject, one part of the system acts upon another, so that a disorder of the brain may affect other seemingly unconnected organs, so political discontent, even though without any just cause, may deaden the enterprise of a people. How else could it be that France, with a citizen King, a philosophical Minister, and the alliance of a nation of shopkeepers, could not be made to feel that her greatness must henceforth be dependent on her mercantile enterprise? While she saw not only England and America, but the German States, making long strides to the attainment of wealth, she lagged behind, and encouraged among the rising generation the delusion that business was unworthy of a warlike and gifted people. That this generation has thoroughly unlearnt the doctrines which were fashionable in its youth, is certainly among the achievements of Napoleon III. If we look back to the days of Louis Philippe, when, though even Germany had its railways and its electric telegraph, we jolted out of Paris in the diligence and saw the old semaphores at work, we shall be able to appreciate the change which ten years of Imperialism have made." —*Times*, Jan. 29, 1862.

French Coup d'Etat Predictions.

The late Baron Alderson, in a letter to Mrs. Opie, written just after the intelligence of the *Coup d'Etat* had arrived, hazards rather a curious speculation with regard to the probable issue of this unexpected crisis. He was just on the point of starting for Paris when the news reached him, and put an end to the expedition:

"I was going there [he writes to Mrs. Opie], but of course do not dream of it now. They seem in a bad way. A nation so unfit for freedom—if that be freedom which requires those who love it to be *first* wise and good—does not exist. The Celts seem to me to be 'a bad lot.' I suppose it will end in Louis Napoleon's becoming dictator, and then (not unlikely), being shot by an assassin, and the game will begin over again then. The fear is, that the Prætorian guards will make him go to war for their own profit. It is a fearful crisis, I think: and the best that can happen will be for him to be made. King or Emperor, and hold his ground in spite of conscience, oaths, and faith which he pledged to the Republic."

Statesmanship of Lord Melbourne.

Sir Bulwer Lytton, in an eloquent lecture upon the historical and intellectual associations of Hertfordshire, pays this willing tribute to the character of Viscount Melbourne; referring to "the fair park of Brocket, which our posterity will find historical as the favourite residence of one who, if not among the greatest Ministers who have swayed this country, was one of the most accomplished and honourable men who ever attained to the summit of constitutional ambition. And it is a striking anecdote of Lord Melbourne, that he once said in my own hearing—' He rejoiced to have been Prime Minister, for he had thus learnt that men were much better, much more swayed by conscience and honour, than he had before supposed;' a saying honourable to the Minister, and honourable still more to the public virtue of Englishmen."

Lord Melbourne was proverbially a good-natured man; but in his preferences he acted with a sense of duty more stringent than might have been expected. It appears that Lord John Russell had applied to Lord Melbourne for some provision for one of the sons of the poet Moore; and here is the Premier's very judicious reply:—

"MY DEAR JOHN,—I return you Moore's letter. I shall be ready to do what you like about it when we have the means. I think whatever is done should be done for Moore himself. This is more distinct, direct, and intelligible. Making a small provision for young men is hardly justifiable; and it is of all things the most prejudicial to themselves. They think what they have much larger than it really is; and they make no exertion. The young should never hear any language but this : ' You have your own way to make, and it depends upon your own exertions whether you starve or not.'—Believe me, &c.

"MELBOURNE."

Ungraceful Observance.

Mr. Torrens M'Cullagh, in his *Life of Sir James Graham*, relates the following instance of want of graciousness in this unpopular statesman. In 1837, on the death of King William, Lord John Russell came to the bar of the House of Commons charged with a Message from the Queen. Hats were immediately ordered off, and even the Speaker announced from the chair that members must be uncovered. Every one present complied with the injunction except Sir James Graham, who continued to wear his hat until the first words of the Message were pronounced. His doing so was the subject of some unpleasant remarks in the newspapers; and at the meeting of the House next day he rose to explain that in not taking off his hat until the word *Regina* was uttered he but followed the old and established custom—a custom which he deemed better than that observed by everybody else in the House. The Speaker then said that Sir James Graham was quite right, that he was strictly within rule in not uncovering until the initiatory word of the Message was delivered. If Sir James Graham had the letter of the law on his side, still there was a stiffness in his conduct which, considering that the message came from a young Queen, and was her first message to her faithful Commons, was not over attractive.

The Partition of Poland.

Some twenty years before the dismemberment of Poland, this disgraceful act was foretold by Lord Chesterfield, in Letter CCCIV., dated Dec. 25, 1753, commencing with " The first squabble in Europe that I foresee, will be about the crown of Poland." The leading data of the fall of Poland will show how far this prediction was realized. Poland was dismembered by the Emperor of Germany, the Empress of Russia, and the King of Prussia, who seized the most valuable territories in 1772.

At the bottom of the Convention signed on the 17th Feb., 1772, we read this declaration of the Empress Queen Maria-Theresa of Austria, dated the 4th March, 1772: " Placet, since so many learned personages will that it should be so; but long after my death it will be seen what will be the result of having thus trampled under foot all that has been hitherto held to be just and sacred."

The royal and imperial spoliators, on various pretexts, poured their armies into the country in 1792. The brave Poles, under Poniatowski and Kosciusko, several times contended against superior armies, but in the end were defeated. Then followed the battle of Warsaw, Oct. 13, 1794; and Suwarrow's butchery of 30,000 Poles, of all ages and conditions, in cold blood. We can scarcely believe such wholesale atrocities to have been perpetrated upon European soil within seventy years of the time we are writing. Poland was finally partitioned and its political exist-ence annihilated in 1795. The transaction, in its earlier stage, is detailed in the *Annual Register* for 1771, 1772, and 1773, sup-posed to have been written by Edmund Burke. Professor Smythe says, diffidently:—" After all, the situation of Poland was such as almost to afford an exception (perhaps a single ex-ception) in the history of mankind to those general rules of justice that are so essential to the great community of nations. I speak with great hesitation, and you must consider the point yourselves;

I do not profess to have thoroughly considered it myself."— (*Lectures on Modern History.*) Sir James Mackintosh contributed to the *Edinburgh Review* a valuable paper on Poland.

The ' Invasion of England.*

In contemplating the possibility of an Invasion, we have some right to count upon the changes which modern civilization has introduced into the methods of warfare. It is not improbable that, if it entered into the French Emperor's plans to invade England, he would make the attempt upon several points at once. The campaign which he sketched out for the use of the allied generals in the Crimea, and which they rejected as impracticable, was based upon this principle. His forces were to be distributed at various points on the circumference of a circle, of which the enemy was to occupy the centre. The enemy was to have all the advantage of concentration; he and his allies were to have all the weakness of division. It is a mode of fighting which is rather at variance with the old Napoleonic ideas, and which would require an overwhelming force to give it effect. As in military numeration the rule of addition is somewhat at fault,— two and two do not always make four, and 200,000 men cannot be computed as ten times stronger than 20,000—we may rest assured that for the successful invasion of England, whether the attack be made by a single armament or by several, a tremendous force must be necessary; and preparations, which will prevent us from being taken altogether by surprise, must be some time in progress.

We shall have a little time to prepare. There is no necessity for our arming to the teeth, and standing to our guns, as if the Philistines were upon us; for there is no need to play the fire-engines before the fire breaks out; but, on the other hand, if we delay our defences on the plea of saving our money till the danger actually comes, when we shall be able to spend it without stint, " it is as if, for a security against fire, you laid by your money at interest, to be expended in making engines and organizing a proper fire brigade as soon as the conflagration commences." Sir John Burgoyne adds, by way of practical illustration, that 10,000 additional British infantry would have taken Sebastopol before the month of December, 1854, and saved all the sufferings of the winter campaign; " but not all the boasted wealth of England could supply the British infantry required."—(*Military Opinions.*)

* This paper relates to the Invasion Tactics, as illustrated by Sir John Burgoyne : the Paper at page 21-24 refers to the project of Napoleon I.

Suppose the descent to have taken place where it was least expected. Sir John Burgoyne attributes to the invading force the power of landing with marvellous rapidity. People imagine that because, after long training on a particular beach, Napoleon could embark 100,000 soldiers in a space of time measured by minutes, the process of debarkation on an unknown shore must be proportionately rapid. Perhaps no nation can do these things more quickly than our French friends, but they sometimes exaggerate. On landing in the Crimea, where there was no resistance, they indeed succeeded in throwing 6000 men on shore in about twenty-two minutes; and at the end of nearly seven hours (namely a little before two o'clock) Marshal St. Arnaud sent word to Lord Raglan that the disembarkation was complete. But observe that here were seven hours required to land 23,600 men without opposition, and the fact was that the whole of these French troops had really not landed in the time specified. The Special Correspondent of the *Times* stated that the French were not more advanced than ourselves in the disembarkation, which was carried on long after sunset. More than this, Sir John Burgoyne asks us to consider what would have been the effect of following St. Arnaud's proposal to land at the mouth of the Katcha. He raises before us a vision of boats closely packed, and rowing on shore in the proper order at the rate of about two miles an hour. From the first they are exposed to the fire of artillery, and for the last 600 yards to a fire of musketry which they are unable to return. Even a small force could, in such circumstances, have punished the allies severely, although ultimately they might have been unable to prevent a landing. If so, it really seems to us that the invasion of our island, though perfectly possible, is not likely to be the simple stepping on shore which some of our military men seem to regard as within the bounds of possibility.—*Times review of Sir John Burgoyne's " Military Opinions."*

What a Militia can do.

Lord Macaulay, in his epitome of the arguments that were used in the year 1697, against the maintenance of a standing army in England, says, illustratively:—

" Some people, indeed, talked as if a militia could achieve nothing great. But that base doctrine was refuted by all ancient and modern history. What was the Lacedæmonian phalanx in the best days of Lacedæmon? What was the Roman Legion in the best days of Rome? What were the armies that conquered at Cressy, at Poictiers, at Agincourt, at Halidon, or at Flodden? What was that mighty array which Elizabeth reviewed at Tilbury?* In the 14th, 15th, and 16th centuries Englishmen who did not live by the trade of war had made war with success and glory. Were the English of the 17th century so degenerate that they could not be trusted to play the men for their own homesteads and parish churches?"

Gibbon, the historian, who at one part of his life was a captain in the Hampshire regiment of militia, remained ever after sensible of a benefit from it, which he testifies as follows:

"It made me an Englishman, and a soldier. In this powerful service I imbibed the rudiments of the language and science of tactics, which opened a new field of study and observation. The discipline and evolutions of a modern battalion gave me a clearer notion of the phalanx and the legion; and the captain of the Hampshire grenadiers, (the reader may smile,) has not been useless to the historian of the Roman Empire."— *Miscellaneous Works*, vol. i. p. 136.

White-Boys.

These ferocious rioters in the south of Ireland, early in the reign of George III., were known by the above name, because, as a mark among themselves in their attacks, they frequently wore a shirt over their clothes. Lord Chesterfield writes in 1765, to the Bishop of Waterford:—"I see that you are in fear again from your White-Boys, and have destroyed a good many of them; but I believe that if the military force had killed half as many landlords it would have contributed more effectually to restore quiet,

---

* We have now learned from Mr. Motley's researches to estimate more correctly the worth of the army at Tilbury. "There were," he says (*History of the United Netherlands*, vol. ii. p. 515 et seq.), "patriotism, loyalty, courage, and enthusiasm in abundance;" but "there were no fortresses, no regular army, no population trained to any weapon." "On the 5th of August no army had been assembled—not even the body-guard of the Queen—and Leicester, with 4000 men, unprovided with a barrel of beer or a loaf of bread, was about commencing his entrenched camp at Tilbury. On the 6th of August the Armada was in Calais Roads, expecting Alexander Farnese to lead his troops upon London." Good fortune and gallant sailors saved us from this calamity; but the undisciplined mob which was assembled under an incompetent commander on shore would have done little to avert it; and we have in this case a sufficient proof of the difficulty of improvising an army in an interval of "diplomatic correspondence."—*Quarterly Review*, No. 223.

The poor people in Ireland are used worse than negroes by their lords and masters, and their deputies of deputies of deputies."

Naval Heroes.

The register of the church of Burnham Thorpe contains the entry of Lord Nelson's birth; with a note by his father recording the investiture of Nelson with the order of the Bath, his rear-admiralship, and creation as Lord Nelson of the Nile, and of Burnham Thorpe. It is somewhat remarkable that three great contemporaneous admirals were all born in one small village of Norfolk—the village of Cockthorpe, which hardly contains more than six houses. The admirals are Sir Cloudesley Shovel, Sir Christopher Minors, and Sir James Narborough; it is also remarkable that this small village and the village of Burnham Thorpe should have produced four such great men.—*Proc. Norfolk and Norwich Archæological Society.*

How Russia is bound to Germany.

In his last Will, Peter the Great said that Russia must endeavour to increase her influence in Germany "by means of marriages, dowries, and annuities;" and that the value of the advice has been properly appreciated by his successors, the *Morgen Post*, in 1863, thus shows:—

"Prussia was bound to Russia by means of the marriage of Nicholas I. with Alexandra, the daughter of Frederic William III., and it may with truth be said that for a quarter of a century the King of Prussia obeyed the behests of his imperious son-in-law. Würtemberg is bound to Russia by three ties. The first wife of William I. was Catherine of Russia; the Crown Princess of Würtemberg is Olga Nicolajevna; and one of the King's nieces is the Grand Duchess Helen, widow of the Grand Duke Michael. The Grand Duke of Oldenburg is a member of the Russian dynasty. The Grand Duchess Helen Paulovna (one of the sisters of the Emperor Nicholas) was married to the hereditary Grand Duke of Mecklenburg-Schwerin. Prince George of Mecklenburg-Strelitz married the Grand Duchess Catherine Michaelovna in 1851. The mother of the present Grand Duke of Saxe-Weimar was Maria Paulovna, another sister of the Emperor Nicholas. The Grand Duke Constantine, at present Stattholder in Poland, is married to a Princess of the House of Saxe-Altenburg. The late Grand Duke Constantine, the uncle of the last-mentioned Prince, was married to Anna Theodorovna, a Princess of Saxe-Coburg. The wife of the Emperor Alexander II. is a scion of the Grand Ducal House of Hesse-Darmstadt. Prince Frederick, the heir-presumptive to the throne of Hesse-Cassel, was married to

Alexandra, the daughter of the late Emperor Nicholas. The wife of the Grand Duke Michael, who is now Stattholder in the Caucasus, is Olga Theodorovna of Baden-Baden. The first wife of Duke Adolphus of Nassau was the Grand Duchess Elizabeth Michaelovna. The Dowager-Queen of the Netherlands, the mother of King William III., is a Princess of the House of Russia. The Russian dynasty is connected with Bavaria by means of the Leuchtenbergs, and with Hanover by means of Queen Maria Alexandrine, who is the sister of the above-mentioned Grand Duchess Constantine."

Count Cavour's Estimate of Napoleon III.

Of the character and policy of Louis Napoleon, Cavour was accustomed to speak with much freedom. No one had better opportunities than Cavour of sounding their depths. He was the only living man who had ventured to grapple with him face to face, and who had used him for his purpose. The estimate he had formed of his capacity was not a high one ; but he fully admitted his fertility of resource, his physical and moral courage, and his knowledge of the people he governs. " He has no definite policy," he remarked to an English friend. " He has a number of political ideas floating in his mind, none of them matured. They would seem to be convictions founded upon instinct. He will not steadily pursue any single idea if a serious object presents itself, but will give way and take up another. This is the *mot d'énigme* to his policy. It is by steadily keeping this in view that I have succeeded in thwarting his designs, or in inducing him to adopt a measure. The only principle—if principle it can be called —which connects together these various ideas is the establish- ment of his dynasty, and the conviction that the best way to se- cure it is by feeding the national vanity of the French people. He found France, after the fall of the Orleanist and Republican Governments, holding but a second place among the great Powers ; he has raised her to the very first. Look at his wars, look at his foreign policy ; he has never gone one step beyond what was absolutely necessary to obtain this one object. The principle ostentatiously put forward in the first instance has been forgotten or discarded as soon as his immediate end has been ac- complished. It was so in the war with Russia ; it has been so in the war with Austria. In the Crimea he was satisfied with the success of his army in the capture of Sebastopol, which took from the English troops the glory they had earned by their devo- tion and courage, and to which they would have added had the war continued. In the struggle with Austria, he was astounded by the greatness of the victories of Magenta and Solferino. The military glory of France had been satiated, and he thought no more of the liberty of Italy, of that free and united nation which he was to have called into existence from the Alps to the Adriatic.

"It is this uncertain policy guided by dynastic and selfish considerations, which makes him so dangerous to you, and which renders it necessary that you should ever be on your guard. Not that he is hostile to England, or that he has any definite design against her. On the contrary, he has much affection for your country. He is a man of generous impulses, and has strong feelings of gratitude towards those who have served and befriended him. At the bottom of his heart he is greatly attached to Italy. His earliest recollections are bound up with her. He is to this day a *carbonaro* in his desire for Italian freedom and hatred of Austria. He has not forgotten the kindness and hospitality shown to him when an exile in England. He admires your institutions and the character of the English people. But all this is as nothing when compared with the maintenance of his dynasty, the establishment of which he looks upon almost in the light of a religious obligation. If the moment came when he thought a sacrifice necessary to sustain it, however great that sacrifice might be, however painful or repugnant to his feelings, he would make it. No one has had better opportunities of knowing him than I have. He has talked to me with the greatest openness of his future plans. But he has invariably assured me at the same time that his first object was to maintain peace and good understanding with England. I believe," he solemnly added, "that, from policy, as well as from affection, such are his views; and that only in a moment of the utmost emergency, when he was convinced that his influence in France depended upon it, would he depart from them. But that moment may come, and you would be madmen if you were not prepared for it."—*Quarterly Review*, No. 222.

The Mutiny at the Nore.

In 1797, when Capt. William Linder had the *Thetis*, and was returning to England, having on board the "Prussian subsidy," amounting to nearly half a million sterling, he was taken prisoner by the mutineer William Parker, and detained, with his vessel and valuable cargo, for a week at the Nore. The rebel, little suspecting the prize he had within his grasp, credited the assertion of Capt. Linder that the aid would shortly arrive, and that he was to be the medium of its transmission to this country. By this *ruse*, and a promise of assistance by which Parker decided that he would take the grand fleet into Brest, he obtained a pass (it is believed the only one given) from William Parker, and arrived safely with his immense treasure at the Tower, where he immediately landed his golden cargo, and forthwith proceeded to the Admiralty,—also giving information to the minister, Mr. Pitt, of his fortunate escape, which, had it been otherwise, would certainly have turned the tide of success of Old England at that time. Mr. Pitt generously offered him a commission; but Capt. Linder having a fine vessel of his own, and a noble and independent spirit, which he retained to the last, respectfully declined; nor could he be induced in after years to solicit for any recompense or popularity. He died in 1862, May 21, at the age of eighty-seven.—*Athenæum.*

Catholic Emancipation and Sir Robert Peel.

It having been stated, in a leading article of a journal, April 14, 1862, that the Liberal party forced upon the Duke of Wellington and Sir Robert Peel that concession to the cause of Catholic emancipation " which Sir Robert Peel declares he entirely disapproved to the latest day of his life," drew from the present Sir Robert Peel the following corrective reply:

" I do not know upon what authority that statement is made, but, so far from disapproving the measure, Sir Robert Peel has distinctly stated that in passing Catholic Emancipation he acted on a deep conviction that the measure was not only conducive to the general welfare, but imperatively necessary to avert from the Church, and from the interest of institutions connected with the Church, an imminent and increasing danger."

The House of Coburg.

Some fifty years ago, a young prince of a then obscure German House was serving under the Emperor Alexander in the great war against Napoleon. He was brave, handsome, clever, and, as events have proved, possessed of prudence beyond the ordinary lot of princes or private men. In 1814 he accompanied the Allied Sovereigns to England, and there his accomplishments attracted the attention and engaged the affection of the heiress to the English throne, the Princess Charlotte of Wales. They were married, and though an untimely death was destined soon to sever the union, yet from that time the star of the successful young officer

and of the House of Coburg has been in the ascendant. From
the vantage-ground of a near connexion with the British Royal
Family they have been able to advance to a position in Europe
almost beyond the dreams of German ambition. The Coburgs
have spread far and wide, and filled the lands with their race.

They have created a new Royal House in England. The
Queen is a daughter of Leopold's sister; her children are the
children of Leopold's nephew. The Coburgs reign in Portugal;
they are connected with the royal though fallen House of Orleans,
and more or less closely related to the principal families of their
own country. Prince Leopold himself has for thirty years
governed one of the most important of the minor States of Europe,
and his eldest son is wedded to an Archduchess of the Imperial
House of Austria. Jealousy and detraction have followed these
remarkable successes, but the Coburgs can afford to smile when
their rivals sneer, for they have the solid rewards of skill, prudence, and that adaptability to all countries and positions which
has distinguished the more able members of their family. It
may be added, as the last memorable events in their annals, that
two of them have successively had the refusal of the Crown of
Greece.

The talents of the Coburgs have been conspicuous. King
Leopold, the late Prince Consort, and the present Duke of Saxe-
Coburg-Gotha, have been men much above the ordinary standard.
They have had great opportunities, and they have known how to
use them. Neither the Prince Consort nor the King of Portugal
could, without offence, have taken a share in the politics of England and Portugal unless they had been gifted with much prudence
and circumspection. No one who studies their history will believe
that they and their kinsmen have merely had greatness thrust upon
them. But, on the other hand, it cannot be doubted that they owe
all to the excellent start which Prince Leopold's good fortune gave
their House. Had it not been for the elevation of the young
soldier to the highest station in England, the Coburgs, instead
of planting dynasties everywhere, might have been no more than
any other of the five-and-thirty German reigning families, or the
multitude of Princely and Serene, but mediatized personages who
are scattered through the land. But when Leopold became an
English prince, and his sister was the mother of the heiress pre-
sumptive to the British throne, the path to greatness was open to
the enterprise of the family. How much one success leads to
another in princely life has been shown in their history, and we
have adverted to it because, if report speak true, another family,

which, a few years since, was of hardly more account in Europe, is at this moment entering on a similar career.—*Times*.

A Few Years of the World's Changes.

Little more than a dozen years have elapsed since there were witnessed in Europe events so stirring that they constitute one of the most remarkable epochs in the history of the world. Since then France has undergone three revolutions—the fall of the constitutional monarchy, the stormy interlude of a democratic republic, and the restoration of a military empire. The old rulers of Lombardy, of Tuscany, and of Naples have disappeared, and the map of the world has been altered in order to admit of the introduction of the kingdom of Italy. Austria, long the haughtiest representative of the principle of absolute monarchy, has commenced the experiment of constitutional government, and Russia has laid the foundation of a new political and social existence in recognising the value of free labour, and abolishing the institution of serfdom. China has opened her ports to our merchants and her capital to our ambassadors. We ourselves have twice gone through the calamities of war in the siege of Sebastopol and the suppression of the Indian revolt, and we have been twice reminded this evening that the great republic which boasted a superb exemption from the perils and the evils which beset ancient states and monarchical forms of government, has been violently rent in twain, and whatever may be the issue of that struggle in which we see at present only a lavish expenditure of blood and treasure, still there is no dispassionate bystander who can believe that the union can ever be restored, and no far-sighted politician who can suppose that the curse of slavery can long survive that separation of which it is the most ostensible, though not the only, nor perhaps the most powerful cause. Such important events, all leading to effects so vast and so permanent in their relation to the advancement of the human race, have probably never before occurred within so short a space of time.—*Speech of Sir E. Bulwer Lytton*.

We may supplement the above by the following strange passage in the career of Louis Napoleon, three-and-twenty years since:

A correspondent of *The Reader* writes:—" It was at Vimereux, the site of the old camp of Boulogne, that Charles Louis Bonaparte, now Emperor of the French, landed on his famous adventure of the 5th of August, 1840. I was in Boulogne when he reached that town, at about 5.30 a.m., with about sixty followers. In proceeding to the beach to bathe, I was startled by the appearance of a rabble, some of whom were clothed as English footmen and grooms, and some as French soldiers. In the midst of this somewhat boozy battalion the then pretender, now the Emperor of the French, marched, closely encircled by adherents. I followed him and them to the barracks; and never did I see a more careworn or crestfallen set of conspirators. In all fifty-six persons, eight horses, and two carriages had embarked at Margate aboard the steamer, which was now cruising in the offing of Boulogne after landing its human freight. When the enterprise at the barracks failed, the present Emperor of the French, with eleven of his adherents, got into a boat with a view to escape; but they allowed the oars to be taken from them by one Guillaume Tutelet, a bather. The boat subsequently capsized, and the present Emperor of the French swam for the steamer, the City of Edinburgh, which was at some distance. In this attempt he failed, and was forced to cling to a buoy till he was picked up and placed in safety by the English captain. But he did not long remain thus, for the Lieutenant du Port collected his force, and boarded the steamer, bringing her, with his prisoner, close to the Quai la Douane."

Noteworthy Pensions.

The finance accounts for 1862 give, as usual, a rather serious list of Pensions charged upon the Consolidated Fund, and therefore not otherwise stated than in these accounts.

" Among the larger entries are five ex-Chancellors of England receiving 5000*l.* a year each, two ex-Chancellors of Ireland with 3692*l.*, four retired English judges with 3500*l.*, two Irish with 2400*l.*, and five County Court judges dividing 4600*l.* between them. But these are pensions earned by personal service; perhaps not so much can be said of some others. The Earl of Ellenborough has a compensation annuity of 7700*l.* as chief clerk of the Court of Queen's Bench; the Rev. T. Thurlow, 4028*l.* as clerk of the hanaper, in addition to 7352*l.* as patentee of bankrupts. Viscount Avonmore receives 4199*l.* as late registrar of the Irish Court of Chancery; the Earl of Roden 2698*l.* as late auditor-general of the Irish Exchequer. But these pensions will come to an end; even that cannot be said of some others. There is above 23,000*l.* a year paid in perpetual pensions, payable as long at least as there shall be an Earl Amherst or Nelson, a Lord Rodney, a Viscount Exmouth, an heir of William Penn, or of the Duke of Schomberg, and so forth. Of the limited number of first-class pensions of 2000*l.* a year to statesmen who have been in high office, and who claim the pensions, only two are now payable—viz., to Lord Glenelg and Mr. Disraeli; Sir G. Grey's is suspended, he being again in office. Several pensions ceased in the course of the year; among them that to the family of George Canning, and that to the door-keeper of the Irish House of Lords; but the housekeeper still lives to receive her annual compensation for loss of emoluments by the Union."

𝔓rogress of 𝔊ivilization.

How the Earth was peopled.

THE record of the actual *origines* of the human race, as communicated by God Himself, tells us that one spot was selected, for the purpose in question, by Creative Power; and that to one aboriginal pair was consigned the office and destiny of replenishing the earth. The same record, moreover, informs us, that, when the *earth was corrupt before God,* through the wickedness of their posterity, the whole race was destroyed, save the family of one man; and that, of the three sons of that one man *was the whole earth overspread.* And, lastly, we have this account confirmed to us by the testimony of an inspired servant of God, who has declared, that *He hath made, of one blood, all nations of men, for to dwell on the face of the earth.*

Now, according to this account, Noah may be considered, for the purposes of ethnological inquiry, as the sole forefather of the existing race of man. Of antediluvian men, all, except Noah, are entirely out of the question. Of the remarkable physical varieties of complexion, stature, or temperament, among the races before the Flood (if any such varieties existed), we are profoundly ignorant. We do read, it is true, that there were *giants* in those days; but the meaning of this term seems very doubtful. It is most generally understood to indicate a gigantic scale of iniquity, licentiousness, and violence, rather than of corporeal bulk and might. At all events, Noah himself, and his three sons, were the only males spared from the general destruction: and the mother of these three sons, together with their three respective wives, the only females; eight persons in all. And, so far as race or family are concerned, the sons are clearly identified with their father. It is, indeed, just possible that all these four females may have been of so many different tribes or races. But this surmise is wholly gratuitous, and very far from probable. And, even were it admitted, it could not affect any argument respecting the origin of the present inhabitants of the earth, without assuming the falsehood of that part of the sacred narrative which traces them all, Noah and his *whole* family included, to one and the same common parentage.

Since the days of the patriarch upwards of 4000 years have
elapsed, and we now find the earth inhabited by at least eight
hundred millions of souls. And, so it is, that these vast multitudes exhibit, *within certain limits,* almost every imaginable variety
of form, of constitution, and of stature.—*English Review,* No. 2.

Nevertheless, the Unity of the Human Race is a much-vexed
question among ethnologists. Mr. Dunn is convinced of the
original unity of the human species, and, after adducing the best
ethnological evidence attainable, he earnestly appeals to the philolo-
gists to help him. Admiral Fitzroy reduces mankind to one, or,
at least, to three types; and these three varieties he reverently
ascribes to the three sons of Noah, with the help of the hypothesis
that they may have been the sons of different mothers. On the
other hand, Mr. Craufurd, President of the Ethnological Society,
admits of no compromise with orthodoxy, maintaining that the
hypothesis of the unity of our race is without foundation. There
are, he says, some forty races of men, which to pack into the five
pigeon-holes of Cuvier and Blumenbach, or the seven of Prichard,
would produce confusion instead of order. The supposition of
a single race peopling all countries by migration he holds to be
"monstrous," and contradictory to the fact that some of them
to this day do not know how to use or construct a canoe.
Migration, he contends, is the achievement of races possessed
of resources in food and means of transport. It is to little purpose that Admiral Fitzroy dwells on the capacities of rafts,
double canoes, and ocean currents. Mr. Craufurd is incredulous
as ever, and fights for his forty Adams with unchecked vivacity,
kicking a tremendous hole in the "frail canoe," and leaving
the ocean currents to deal with it *more oceanico.*

Revelations of Geology.

Geology attests that man was the last of created beings in this
planet. If her *data* be consistent and true, and worthy of scientific consideration, she affords conclusive evidence that, as we
are told in Scripture, he cannot have occupied the earth longer
than 6000 years. (*Hitchcock, Religion of Geology.*)

Sir Isaac Newton's sagacious intellect had arrived at a similar
conclusion from different premises, and long before the geologist
had made his researches and discoveries. " He appeared," said
one who conversed with him, not long before his death, and
has carefully recorded what he justly styles " a remarkable and
curious conversation," " to be very clearly of opinion, that the in-

habitants of this world were of short date; and alleged as one reason for that opinion, that all arts—as letters, ships, printing, the needle, &c.—were discovered within the memory of history, which could not have happened if the world had been eternal; and that there were visible marks of ruin upon it, which could not have been effected by a flood only."—*Brewster's Life of Newton.*

The Stone Age.

Admiral Fitzroy adduces the following striking facts strongly bearing on the great geological inquiry of "Flint Tools," and "Implements in the Drift."

Tierra del Fuego, with its innumerable islands and rocky islets, like mountain ranges half sunk in ocean, combines every variety of aspect—storm-beaten rocky summits, several thousand feet above the sea—glaciers so extensive that the eye cannot trace their limits—densely wooded hillsides—grand cascades and sheltered sandy coves,—altogether such a combination of Swiss, Norwegian, and Greenland scenery as can hardly be realized or believed to exist near Cape Horn. Yet, even there—by lake-like waters, though so near the wildest of oceans—thousands of savages exist, and migrate in bark canoes!

In 1830 four of those aborigines were brought to England. In 1833 three of them were restored to their native places (one having died). They had then acquired enough of our language to talk about common things. From their information and our own sight are the following facts:—The natives of Tierra del Fuego use stone tools, flint knives, arrow and spear heads of flint or volcanic glass, for cutting bark for canoes, flesh, blubber, sinews, and spears, knocking shell-fish off rocks, breaking large shells, killing guanacoes (in time of deep snow), and for weapons. In every sheltered cove where wigwams are placed, heaps of refuse—shells and stones, offal and bones—are invariably found. Often they appear very old, being covered deeply with wind-driven sand, or water-washed soil, on which there is a growth of vegetation. These are like the "kitchen middens" of the so-called "stone age" in Scandinavia.

No human bones would be found in them (unless dogs had dragged some there), because the dead bodies are sunk in deep water with large stones, or burnt. These heaps are from six to ten feet high, and from ten or twenty to more than fifty yards in length. All savages in the present day use stone tools, not only in Tierra del Fuego, but in Australia, Polynesia, Northernmost

America, and Arctic Asia. In any former ages of the world, wherever savages spread, as radiating from some centre, similar habits and means of existence must have been prevalent; therefore asual discovery of such traces of human migration, buried in or under masses of water-moved detritus, may seem scarcely sufficient to define a so-called "stone age."

What are Celtes?

Celtes are certain ancient instruments, of a wedge-like form, of which several have been discovered in different parts of Great Britain. Antiquaries have generally attributed them to the Celtæ, but, not agreeing as to their use, distinguish them by the above unmeaning appellation. Mr. Whitaker, however, is of opinion that they were British battle-axes, and in this he has been generally followed. Such is the statement in the eighth or last edition of the *Encyclopædia Britannica*.

The Welsh etymologists, Owen and Spurrell, furnish an ancient Cambro-British word *celt*, a flint-stone. M. Worsae (*Primeval Antiq.*, p. 26) confines the term to those instruments of bronze which have a hollow socket to receive a wooden handle; the other forms being called paalstabs on the Continent In the "Latin Vulgate," our translators have rendered "an iron pen" in the book of Job, chap. xix. v. 24, there translated *celte*.

But the origin and application are variously explained among antiquarian writers. The Abbé Cochet states, in a letter to the French journals, 1863, that hatchets are found almost all over Europe. They are common in France, and are generally found in groups. Some of them have been analysed, and found to be composed of fourteen parts of tin and eighty-six of copper. The bronze is the same as that of an antique poniard brought from Egypt and analysed by Vauquelin, from which it would appear that the composition of ancient Gallic bronze came from Egypt. Archæologists generally attribute hatchets of this kind to the Celts and Gauls, and give them the general name of Celtic.

In opposition to this statement, it is, however, maintained that "the word is not derived from its use by the Celts or Kelts, but from the Latin word 'celtis,' which means chisel, or hatchet." Dr. Smith (*Dictionary of Greek and Roman Antiquities*) obtains the term from "celtes, an old Latin word for a chisel, probably derived from cælo, to engrave." Mr. Wright (in *The Celt, Roman, and Saxon*) says that Hearne first applied the word to such implements in *bronze*, believing them to be

" Roman *celtes*, or chisels;" and that "subsequent writers, as-
cribing these instruments to the Britons, have retained the name,
forgetting its origin, and have applied it indiscriminately not only
to other implements of bronze but even to the analogous instruments of stone." Mr. Wright objects to the term, "as too
generally implying that things to which it is applied are Celtic;"
and it is now generally allowed that there is no connexion between this word and the name of the nation (Celtæ).—(Abridged
from *Notes and Queries*, No. 203). Fosbroke (*Encyclopædia of
Antiquities*, p. 286) has an excellent column of authorities upon
the subject, which is still hotly contested. An admirable paper
was read to the Archæological Institute, in 1849, by Mr. James
Yates, illustrating "The Use of Bronze Celts in Military Operations," with several woodcuts.—See the *Archæological Journal*,
December, 1849, pages 363-392. See also "Notes on Bronze
Weapons," by A. W. Franks, F.S.A., *Archæologia*, vol. xxxvi.,
pp. 326-331 : and Papers by Mr. John Evans, F.S.A.; *Archæologia*, vol. xxxviii. p. 280; also, vol. xxxix. p. 57. The subject is
of immediate interest in illustration of "The Antiquity of Man."

Roman Civilization of Britain.

If the commencement of the Roman rule in England was,
say, fifty years before the birth of Christ (or 1910 years ago)
and each generation lasted on the average thirty years—rather a
high rate of vitality probably in the Early and Middle Ages—
we find that about sixty-four generations have gone to dust since
then. The archæological information obtained of late years
shows that at the time of the Roman invasion there was a larger
amount of civilization in Ancient Britain than has been generally
supposed : that in addition to the knowledge of the old inhabitants in agriculture, in the training and rearing of horses, cows,
and other domestic animals, they were able to work in mines, had
skill in the construction of war-chariots and other carriages, and
in the manufacture of metals; and there is evidence that cheese
and other British manufactures and materials were exported to
certain parts of the Continent, probably in British vessels. The
ancient coinage of this period is well worthy of attention. To
what country may the style of art be traced? To what people
do we owe the mysterious circle of Stonehenge? Mr. Fergusson
and others say to the Buddhists rather than to the Druids.

In connexion with the Ancient British period, it would seem
that probably 2000 years before the Roman times there had been

in Great Britain a certain degree of civilization, which from various causes declined in extent. If Stonehenge may be considered as of the same antiquity as similar remains in various parts of the East—which are reckoned by good authorities to be 4000 years old—we had in this country a degree of civilization which was contemporary with the prosperous period of the Egyptian empire; and, in times more immediately preceding the Roman occupation, we know that Britain was the grand source of Druidical illumination (whatever relation that may have had to a true civilization) to the whole of Continental Europe.

That the Ancient Britons, even after they were conquered by the Romans, had still a strength considered dangerous, is shown by the fact that upwards of forty barbarian legions which had followed the Roman standards were settled chiefly upon the northern and eastern coasts; and it is supposed that a force of about 19,200 Roman foot and 1700 horse was required to secure peace, and the carrying out of certain laws in the island. It is calculated by some writers that a revenue of not less than 2,000,000l. a year was raised by the conquerors of Britain from the land-tax, pasture-tax, and customs, besides legacy duties, and those levied on the sale of slaves, auctions of goods, &c.; and it may be remarked that these customs were levied by the Roman governors in lieu of direct tribute, to which, it seems, the spirit of the Britons would not submit. —*The Builder*, 1860.

Roman Roads and British Railways.

We have no means of estimating the cost of a mile of Roman road by any audited account of expenses, and it is not easy to make a comparison of labour. Its cost is vaguely calculated as insignificant by the side of that of our leviathan railways. The following is stated to be the average cost of a mile of railway:

Land	6000l.
Earthwork	5000l.
Tunnelling	3000l.
Masonry	3000l.
Viaduct and large Bridges	3000l.
Permanent Iron Road , ...	5000l.
Stations	4000l.
Law expenses, Engineering, Surveying, &c. . .	3000l.
	32,000l.

If this be multiplied by 5000, which was the aggregate length of

British railways in 1851 (now it is nearly 12,000), and we have the almost fabulous amount of 160 millions, a sum fully equal to ten times the revenue of all the Roman provinces in the time of Augustus.

In estimating the value of a Roman road, we have to deduct 7800*l.* a mile for land and law: every mile of railway cost 6000*l.* for land, whereas the Roman road-makers cut through the country without asking the price, and dispensed with all juries for assessing damages. Next, we must deduct 4000*l.* for stations; the Roman *mutationes* were but hovels where horses were changed; and lastly, is to be deducted 5000*l.* for iron, before we come to the materials the Romans were enabled to use; in other words, the materials of the Roman road and labour would not be more than half the cost of our railways, from the mere fact of certain expenses being absent, which they could not understand; but, although inferior to the Britons of the nineteenth century in the art of spending money, if judged by the present state of the science, they could not be despicable engineers—their levels were chosen on different principles, but their lines of roads passed through the same countries, and generally in the same direction, as our railways. A diagram taken from an article of the *Quarterly Review*, exhibiting a general view of the direction of the principal Roman roads in England, shows that on comparing one or two of our principal lines, we shall find that the Great Western, *e.g.*, supplies the place, with a little deviation near Reading, of the Roman iter from London to Bath and Bristol; the Liverpool and Manchester, and on to Leeds and York, replace the northern Watling-street; the Eastern Counties follows a Roman way, and so of the rest.

In boasting of the gigantic steps which the art of road-making has taken in our time, we cannot afford to depreciate either the genius or the magnificence of the ancient Romans in this matter. If we have our railway under the cliffs of Dover, Trajan had his road under 2000 feet of perpendicular cliff along the Ister; if we have our 12,000 miles of rails, the Romans had their 4000 miles of chosen road, reaching from one extremity of the empire to the other; if we have our leviathan bridges and viaducts, the Romans had theirs over greater rivers and wider vales than we have to deal with; and, finally, if we had our glass bazaar, one-third of a mile long, in Hyde Park, they had a golden palace, which reached a whole mile on the Esquiline Hill. If we rise superior and look down upon the works of the Romans, it is not so much that we have gained in unskilful labour, as in science. Without the iron and the science, their works would be as great as ours; it is in mental rather than in any physical energies, that we have the pre-eminence.

We may acquire some idea of this branch of Roman economy from the following details : —From the wall of Antonius to Rome, and from thence to Jerusalem, that is, from the north-west to the south-east point of the empire, was measured a distance of 3740 English miles; of this distance 85 miles only were sea-passages, the rest was the *road of polished silex*. Posts were esta-blished along these lines of high road, so that a hundred miles a day might be with ease accomplished. A fact related by Pliny affords an example of the quickest travelling in a carriage in an-cient times. Tiberius Nero, with three carriages, accomplished a journey of 200 miles in twenty-four hours, when he went to see his brother Drusus, who was sick in Germany.—*Rev. R. Burgess, B.D.*

Domestic Life of the Saxons.

Were it possible for an archæologist to report the gossip of the Saxon hinds over their ale or mead, we should have learnt more of their daily life from such a specimen of their conversation than from all the cautious inferences from manuscripts and records. Let us conceive the presence of a modern reporter in the mead-hall of Hrothgar, and we may be certain that his literal transcript of a single hour's talk there would be worth all that we can now learn from the Romance of Beowulf. "Then," says the poem, " there was for the sons of the Geats (Beowulf and his followers altogether), a bench cleared in the beer-hall ; there the bold spirit, free from quarrel, went to sit; the thane observed his office, he that in his hand bare the twisted ale-cup ; he poured the bright sweet liquor ; meanwhile the poet sang serene in Heorot (the name of Hrothgar's palace) ; there was joy of heroes." Al-though our conceptions of the scene are faint and vague, the antiquary is enabled to represent certain items as "the twisted ale-cup," a favourite fashion of our forefathers, many of whose ale-cups, as discovered in their barrows or graves, are incapable of standing upright, implying that their proprietors were thirsty souls, and that it was not, as we supposed, the Prince Regent who first invented *tumblers*. From the mead-hall and the other Saxon houses of the period, we also get the type of the modern English mansion, with its *enceinte* and its lodge-gate, as distin-guished from its hall-door. The early Saxon house was the whole enclosure, at the gate of which—the *ostium domus*—beggars assembled for alms, and the porter received the arms of strangers. The whole mass enclosed within this wall constituted the burgh, or tun, and the hall, with its duru, or door *par excellence*, was the chief of its edifices. Around it were grouped the sleeping chambers, or *bowers*, as they were designated till a late age, with the subordinate offices. Mr. Wright (in his able work on the *Domestic Life of the Middle Ages*) draws many of his inferences from the description of the mead-hall of Hrothgar, and adds that he believes Bulwer's description of the Saxonized Roman house inhabited by Hilda is substantially correct. Still, though we can identify to this day the Saxon derivatives of many of our houses and much of our crockery-ware, this helps us little as regards the sentiments of the originators of these familiar types. They have left us some memorials of their manners ; but, substantially speaking, their sentiments on a great variety of subjects are lost to us, and there is little trace of them, even in their barrows and sepulchral surroundings.—*Times review.*

Love of Freedom.

There is something absolutely touching in the simplicity of the following incident, derived from Aelfric's *Colloquium*, composed in the eleventh century. A teacher examines a ploughman on the subject of his occupation. " What sayest thou, ploughman ; how dost thou perform thy work ?" " O, my lord," he answers, " I labour excessively : I go out at dawn of day, driving my oxen to the field, and yoke them to the plough : there is no weather so severe that I dare rest at home, for fear of my lord ; but having yoked my oxen, and fastened the share and coulter to the plough, every day I must plough a whole field (acre ?) or more." The teacher again asks, " Hast thou any companion ?" " I have a boy who urges the oxen with a goad, and who is now hoarse with cold and shouting." " What more doest thou in the day ?" "Truly, I do more yet. I must fill the oxen's mangers with hay, and water them, and carry away their dung." " O, it is a sore vexation !" " Yea, it is great vexation ; because *I am not free.*"

The Anglo-Saxon clergy went so far as to make the giving of Freedom an Atonement for all Sins, by encouraging the manumission of theows gratuitously, as an action of merit in the eyes of the church. Among the early benefactors of the abbey of Ramsey, it is recorded that Athelstan Mannesone manumitted thirteen men in every thirty, " for the salvation of his soul," taking

F

them as the lot fell upon them, and "placing them in the open road, so that they were at liberty to go where they would." Many, indeed, were freed, from feelings of piety. Thus it appears from the celebrated "Exeter book" in the cathedral, that, at Exeter, on the day when they removed the bodies of bishops Osbern and Leofric from the old minster to the new one, William, bishop of Exeter, "proclaimed Wulfree Pig free and sackless of the land at Teigtune," and "freed him for the love of God and of St. Marie, and of all Christ's saints, and for the redemption of the bishops' souls and his own." Sometimes a man who had no theow of his own, bought one of another person, in order to emancipate him, "for the love of God and the redemption of his soul." Such were the fruits that ripened from Roman teaching in the olden time !—*Archæologia,* vol. xxx.

The Despot deceived.

Nothing can be more erroneous than the notion that the despot, though he may himself oppress his people, can prevent others from doing the same. He is cheated by his subordinates, and they cheat the people.—*Archbishop Whately.*

True Source of Civilization.

The killing of animals for food is, after all, merely the resource of the savage, and domesticated animals and cultivated plants are indispensable to the earliest advances of civilization. It may be safely averred, says Mr. Craufurd, that no people ever attained any great civilization without, for example, the possession of some cereal, and without having domesticated the horse, or the ox, or the buffalo. No evidence exists of a people emerging from barbarism whose food consisted of the cocoa-nut, the banana, the date, the bread-fruit, sago, the potato, the yam, or the batata. Such articles are too easily produced, require too little skill and ingenuity to raise ; and when they fail, there is nothing to fall back upon—nothing between the people cultivating them and starvation. The higher, too, the cereal the better, wheat standing at the top of the list in temperate regions, and rice in warm ones. Thus, the cereals of Egypt, nurtured by the mud of the Nile, created a respectable civilization among a very inferior race. It was because the Egyptians, says Mr. Craufurd, besides the date, possessed wheat, barley, pulse, and the ox, and that nature dressed and irrigated their country, that the Egyptians became numerous and civilized.

The Lowest Civilization.

The South Sea Islanders who scalded their fingers in Captain Cook's tea-kettle, and to whom pottery and warm water were luxuries also, were certainly low in the scale of civilization, but they were not nearly so low as the Terra del Fuegans at this moment. Mr. Darwin describes the state of these wretched creatures as the extreme of misery, and as affording him the most curious and interesting spectacle he had ever beheld. "I could not have believed," says he, "how wide was the difference between savage and civilized men." Their land, we should remember, is a land of rain, sleet, snow, and storms, unsheltered from the cold of the South Pole, and one thick murky mass of forest. The "climate (where gale succeeds gale, with rain, hail, and sleet) seems blacker than anywhere else. In the Straits of Magellan, looking due south from Port Famine, the distant channels between the mountains appear, from their gloominess, to lead beyond the confines of the world." In this terrestrial limbo live human beings who are clad, for this inclement temperature, in a single otter-skin, which they lace across their breast by strings, and, according as the wind blows, shift from side to side. He pictures the state of these poor creatures at night, some half-a-dozen of them sleeping together naked on the wet ground coiled up like animals. "Whenever it is low water they must rise to pick shellfish from the rocks; and the women, winter and summer, either dive to collect sea-eggs, or sit patiently in their canoes, and with a baited hair-line jerk out small fish. If a seal is killed, or the floating carcass of a putrid whale is discovered, they are feasts. Such miserable food is assisted by a few tasteless berries and fungi." Mr. Snow, who brings us our latest reports from the Fuegans, visited them in 1855. At present, however, their condition in the scale of humanity is almost as low as it can be ; for though they possess the capacity of kindling a fire by the friction of two sticks (an accomplishment of which, by the way, all savages that we know of are capable), and though they can form canoes by hollowing out logs of wood, they cultivate no plant and domesticate no animal, and have, as we see, no other art of civilized life.—*Times journal.*

Why do we shake Hands?

"It is," replies Dr. Humphry, in his clever volume, *The Human Foot and the Human Hard*, "a very old-fashioned way of

indicating friendship. Jehu said to Jehonadab, 'Is thine heart
right as my heart is with thine heart? If it be, give me thine
hand.' It is not merely an old-fashioned custom; it is a strictly
natural one, and, as usual in such cases, we may find a physio-
logical reason, if we will only take the pains to search for it. The
animals cultivate friendship by the sense of touch, as well as by
the senses of smell, hearing, and sight; and for this purpose they
employ the most sensitive parts of their bodies. They rub their
noses together, or they lick one another with their tongues. Now,
the hand is a part of the human body in which the sense of touch
is highly developed; and, after the manner of the animals, we
not only like to see and hear our friend (we do not usually smell
him, though Isaac, when his eyes were dim, resorted to this sense
as a means of recognition), we also touch him, and promote the
kindly feelings by the contact and reciprocal pressure of the sensitive hands. Observe, too, how this principle is illustrated by
another of our modes of greeting. When we wish to determine
whether a substance be perfectly smooth, and are not quite satisfied
with the information conveyed by the fingers, we apply it to the
lips and rub it gently upon them. We do so, because we know
by experience that the sense of touch is more acutely developed
in the lips than in the hands. Accordingly, when we wish to re-
ciprocate the warmer feelings, we are not content with the contact
of the hands, and we bring the lips into the service. A shake of
hands suffices for friendship, in undemonstrative England at
least; but a kiss is the token of a more tender affection."

Dr. Humphry is no friend to Palmistry; for, he observes:
" You will estimate the value of the science of Cheiromancy
when you hear that equal furrows upon the lower joint of the
thumb argue riches and possessions; but a line surrounding the
middle joint portends hanging. The nails, also, come in for
their share of attention: and we are informed that, when short,
they imply goodness; when long and narrow, steadiness but
dulness; when curved, rapacity. Black spots upon them are un-
lucky; white are fortunate. Even at the present day Gipsies .
practise the art when they can find sufficient credulity to encourage them."

Various Modes of Salutation.

Of all the different modes of salutation in various countries,
there is none so graceful as that which prevails in Syria. At New
Guinea the fashion is certainly picturesque; for they place upon

their hands the leaves of trees as symbols of peace and friendship. An Ethiopian takes the robe of another and ties it about his own waist, leaving his friend partially naked. In a cold climate this would not be very agreeable. Sometimes it is usual for persons to place themselves naked before those whom they salute as a sign of humility. This custom was put in practice before Sir Joseph Banks when he received the visit of two Otaheitan females. The inhabitants of the Philippine Islands take the hand or foot of him they salute, and gently rub their face with it, which is at all events more agreeable than the salute of the Laplanders, who have a habit of rubbing noses, applying their own proboscis with some degree of force to that of the person they desire to salute. The salute with which you are greeted in Syria is at once most graceful and flattering; the hand is raised with a quick but gentle motion, to the heart, to the lips, and to the head, to intimate that the person saluting is willing to serve you, to think for you, to speak for you, and to act for you.—*Farley's Syria.*

What is Comfort?

Could any one really be satisfied with the attainment and diffusion of any conceivable amount of Comfort? Or do the whole series of influences which the popular sentiment almost deifies really affect very deeply the standing calamities and the standing complaints of life? It is not difficult to bring the question to a fair test. If all the causes which we see at work around us were to continue to operate for an indefinite length of time in the utmost vigour, they would probably not raise the average standard of comfort for the whole population above the point at which the average of the better-paid professional classes stands at present. The wildest dreams of the most sanguine believer in progress on Christian principles would be more than realized if he ever saw ordinary day-labourers as well off and as intelligent as ordinary lawyers, doctors, and merchants are at present. Take, then, one reasonably prosperous person of this kind, and see whether he is in such an entirely satisfactory condition. It is clear that he is not. He neither knows whence he comes nor whither he is going, nor for what purpose he lives; or at least his knowledge upon these subjects is so indefinite, so much involved in metaphors and mysteries, that it is little more than enough to make visible the darkness in which he stands. He passes through life in a round of occupations which often fatigue and hardly ever satisfy large portions of his mind; and the very comforts which have been provided for him by so infinite a multiplicity of social devices, as often as not operate to choke and strangle his energies. We need not detail the features of a familiar picture. Every one knows the gloomy side of life, and though it is not the whole truth, it is right that its existence should be recognised. It is an insulting affectation to keep it out of sight, and to persist in crying up progress and improvement as if there was no undying worm and unquenchable fire.—*Saturday Review*.

What is Luxury?

Luxury is the indefinite and comprehensive term of reproach with which the vulgar, in all ages, brand whatever is beyond their own tastes and habits. What is luxury to one is but refinement and civilization to others.   The higher orders mingle up with their disgust at the boorish and noisy pastimes of the lower, a kind of latent feeling of their immorality: the lower revenge themselves by considering as things absolutely sinful the more splendid entertainments and elegant festivities of their superiors in wealth and refinement.—*Quarterly Review*.

What do we know of Life?

The condition of our life is that we stand on a narrow strip of the shore, waiting till the tide, which has washed away hundreds of millions of our fellows, shall wash away us also into a country of which there are no charts, and from which there is no return. What little we know about that unseen world comes to this— that it contains extremes of good and evil, awful and mysterious beyond all human expression or conception, and that those tremendous possibilities are connected with our conduct here.   It is surely wiser and more manly to walk silently by the shore of that silent sea, than to boast with puerile exultation over the little sand-castles which we have employed our short leisure in building up.   Life can never be matter of exultation, nor can the progress of arts and sciences ever really fill the heart of a man who has a heart to be filled.   In its relation to what is to be hereafter, there is, no doubt, no human occupation which is not awful and sacred, for such occupations are the work which is here given us to do— our portion in the days of our vanity.   But their intrinsic value is like that of schoolboys' lessons.   They are worth just nothing at all, except as a discipline and a task.   It is right that man should rejoice in his own works, but it is very wrong to allow them for one instant to obscure that eternity from which alone they derive their importance. Steam-engines and cotton-mills have their greatness, but life and death are greater and older. Men lived, and died, and sorrowed, and rejoiced before these things were known, and they could do so again. Why mankind was created at all, why we still continue to exist, what has become of that vast multitude which has passed, with more or less sin and misery, through this mysterious earth, and what will become of those vaster multitudes which are treading and will tread the same wonderful path?—these are the great insoluble problems which ought to be seldom mentioned, but never for an instant forgotten. Strange as it may appear to popular lecturers, they really do make it seem rather unimportant whether, on an average, there is or is not a little more or less good nature, a little more or less comfort, and a little more or less knowledge in the world. Men live and die in India, and China, and Africa, as well as in England and France; and where there is life and death there are the great essentials of existence, and the eternal problems which they involve. This page of beautiful philosophy is from the *Saturday Review*.

The truest Patriot the greatest Hero.

Is he not in reality the truest *patriot* who fills up his station in private life well; he who loves and promotes peace both public and private, who knowing that his country's prosperity depends much more on its virtues than its arms, resolves that his individual endeavours shall not be wanting to promote this desirable end? And is he not the greatest *hero* who is able to despise public honour for the sake of private usefulness, he who has learnt to subdue his own inclinations, to deny himself those gratifications which are inconsistent with virtue and piety, who has conquered his passions and brought them low even as a child that is weaned: is not such a man greater than he that taketh a city, sheddeth blood as it were water, or calls for the thundering applause of assembled multitudes? But if persons in general held these sentiments, if utility were substituted for show, and religious usefulness for worldly activity, how very little our public men would have to do! Truly they would be driven to turn their swords into ploughshares, and study the Gospel instead of the statutes.

The old Philosophers.

Horace Walpole, who possessed great knowledge of life, though himself disfigured by arrogant conceits, has left this satirical view of the wisdom of the ancient philosophers:

" I thought that philosophers were virtuous, upright men, who loved
wisdom, and were above the little passions and foibles of humanity.   I
thought they assumed that proud title as an earnest to the world, that they
intended to be something more than mortal; that they engaged themselves to be patterns of excellence, and would utter no opinion, would
pronounce no decision, but what they believed the quintessence of truth;
that they always acted without prejudice and respect of persons.   Indeed,
we know that the ancient philosophers were a ridiculous composition of
arrogance, disputation, and contradictions! that some of them acted against
all ideas of decency; that others affected to doubt of their own senses; that
some, for venting unintelligible nonsense, pretended to think themselves
superior to kings; that they gave themselves airs of accounting for all that
we do and do not see—and yet, that no two of them agreed in a single
hypothesis; that one thought fire, another water, the origin of all things;
and that some were even so absurd and impious as to displace God, and
enthrone matter in his place.   I do not mean to disparage such wise men,
for we are really obliged to them : they anticipated and helped us off with
an exceeding deal of nonsense, through which we might possibly have
passed if they had not prevented us."

Glory of the Past.

To be honoured and even privileged by the laws, opinions,
and inveterate usages of our country, growing out of the prejudice of ages, has nothing to provoke horror and indignation in any
man.   Even to be too tenacious of those privileges is not absolutely a crime.   The strong struggle in every individual to preserve possession of what he has found to belong to him, and to
distinguish him, is one of the securities against injustice and despotism implanted in our nature.   It operates as an instinct to
secure property, and to preserve communities in a settled state.
What is there to shock in this?   Nobility is a graceful ornament
to the civil order.   It is the Corinthian capital of polished society.
Omnes boni nobilitati semper favemus was the saying of a wise
and good man.   It is, indeed, one side of a liberal and benevolent
mind to incline to it with some sort of partial propensity.   He
feels no ennobling principle in his own heart who wishes to
level all the artificial institutions which have been adopted for
giving a body to opinion and permanence to fugitive esteem.
*It is a sour, malignant, and envious disposition, without taste
for the reality, or for any image or representation of virtue, that
sees with joy the unmerited fall of what had long flourished in
splendour and in honour.*   I do not like to see anything destroyed,
any void produced in society, any ruin on the face of the land.
—*Burke.*

Wild Oats.

We are more familiar with Wild Oats in a moral than in a botanical sense; yet in the latter it is an article of no small curiosity. For one thing, it has a semi-inherent power of moving from one place to another. Let a *head* of it be laid down in a moistened state upon a table, and left there for the night, and next morning it will be found to have walked off. The locomotive power resides in the peculiar hard *awn*, or spike, which sets the grain a-tumbling over and over sideways. A very large and coarse kind of wild oats, brought many years ago from Otaheite, was found to have the ambulatory character in uncommon perfection. When ordinary oats is allowed by neglect to degenerate, it acquires this among other characteristics of wild oats.— *R. Chambers.*

How Shyness spoils Enjoyment.

Mr. Arthur Helps writes upon this everyday hindrance to happiness: " I believe if most young persons were to tell us what they had suffered from shyness upon their entrance into society, it would well deserve to be placed next to·want of truth as a hindrance to the enjoyment of society. Now, admitting that there is a certain degree of graceful modesty mixed up with this shyness, very becoming in the young, there is at the same time a great deal of needless care about what others think and say. In fact, it proceeds from a painful egotism, sharpened by needless self-examinations and foolish imaginations, in which the shy youth or maiden is tormented by his or her personality, and is haunted by imagining that he or she is the centre of the circle—the observed of all observers. The great cause of this shyness is not sufficiently accustoming children to society, or making them suppose that their conduct in it is a matter of extreme importance, and especially in urging them from their earliest youth by this most injurious of all sayings, ' If you do this or that, what will be said, what will be thought of you?' Thus referring the child not to religion, not to wisdom, not to virtue, not even to the opinion of those whose opinion ought to have weight, but to the opinion of whatever society he may chance to come into. I often think the parent, guardian, or teacher, who has happily omitted to instil this vile prudential consideration, or enabled the child to resist it, even if he, the teacher, has omitted much good advice and guidance, has still done better than that teacher or parent

who has filled the child to the brim with good moral considerations, and yet has allowed this one piece of arrant worldliness to
creep in."

" *Custom, the Queen of the World.*"

Sir William Hamilton, in his *Metaphysical Essays,* has the
following passage characterizing this universal rule :—

"Man is by nature a social animal. 'He is more political,' says
Aristotle, 'than any bee or ant.' But the existence of society, from a
family to a state, supposes a certain harmony of sentiment among its
members; and nature has, accordingly, wisely implanted in us a tendency
to assimilate in opinions and habits of thought to those with whom we live
and act. There is thus, in every society great or small, a certain gravitation of opinions towards a common centre. As in our natural body, every
part has a necessary sympathy with every other, and all together form, by
their harmonious conspiration, a healthy whole; so, in the social body,
there is always a strong predisposition, in each of its members, to act and
think in unison with the rest. This universal sympathy, or fellow-feeling,
of our social nature, is the principle of the different spirit dominant in
different ages, countries, ranks, sexes, and periods of life. It is the cause
why fashions, why political and religious enthusiasm, why moral example,
either for good or evil, spread so rapidly and exert so powerful an influence. As men are naturally prone to imitate others, they consequently
regard, as important or insignificant, as honourable or disgraceful, as true
or false, as good or bad, what those around them consider in the same light.
They love and hate what they see others desire and eschew. This is not
to be regretted; it is natural, and consequently it is right. Indeed, were
it otherwise, society could not subsist, for nothing can be more apparent
than that mankind in general, destined as they are to occupations in-
compatible with intellectual cultivation, are wholly incapable of forming
opinions for themselves on many of the most important objects of human
consideration.

"If such, however, be the intentions of nature with respect to the unen-
lightened classes, it is manifest that a heavier obligation is thereby laid on
those who enjoy the advantages of intellectual cultivation, to examine with
diligence and impartiality the foundations of those opinions which have any
connexion with the welfare of mankind. If the multitude must be led,
it is of consequence that it be led by enlightened conductors. That the
great multitude of mankind are by natural disposition only what others are,
is a fact at all times so obtrusive that it could not escape observation from
the moment a reflective eye was first turned upon man. 'The whole
conduct of Cambyses,' says Herodotus, the father of history, 'towards the
Egyptian gods, sanctuaries, and priests, convinces me that this king was in
the highest degree insane, for otherwise he would not have insulted the
worship and holy things of the Egyptians. If any one should accord to all

men the permission to make free choice of the best among all customs, undoubtedly each would choose his own. That this would certainly happen can be shown by many examples, and among others by the following. The King Darius once asked the Greeks who were resident in his court, at what price they could be induced to devour their dead parents. The Greeks answered, that to this no price could bribe them. Thereupon the king asked some Indians who were in the habit of eating their dead parents, what they would take not to eat but to burn them; and the Indians answered even as the Greeks had done.' Herodotus concludes this narrative with the observation, that 'Pindar had justly entitled Custom—the Queen of the World.'"

Ancient Guilds and Modern Benefit Clubs.

The guilds in our mediæval towns, in the opinion of Mr. T. Wright, F.S.A., were derived from the municipal system of the Romans. We know that such guilds existed in the Roman towns, and with much the same objects. All people have, at all times, placed great importance in the ceremonies attending the interment of the dead; and the process of burial among the Romans was one of great expense, which could be met by families which were wealthy, but it must have been very onerous, falling all at once, on men of very limited means; to avoid the inconvenience of which they *clubbed together*, in a spirit which exists to the same degree in modern times; so that the expense on each occasion, instead of falling upon one, was distributed among the members of the club. This was the great object of the Roman guilds, and the second seems to have been drinking and sociality. People clubbed together to be merry while alive, and to be buried when dead. While they still remained attached to their old customs in burial, they were now taught the duty of investing money in the foundation of obits, or perpetual prayers for the dead; but this being looked upon as a superstitious usage, was the cause of their dissolution after the Reformation. In the successive changes of society, they embraced from time to time other objects; but the two grand objects of the Roman, Saxon, or Mediæval guilds, seemed to have been alike the respectable burial of their deceased members, and the promoting of convivial intercourse—the leading features of a modern Benefit Society.

The Oxford Man and the Cambridge Man.

If stated very briefly, the chief difference may be said to be that the Cambridge man is more practical. Whether there is something in the method of training pursued, or whether the different degrees of importance assigned to the various branches of education may be the cause, or whether the pitting of man against man in examination may operate still more powerfully, the fact soon forces itself on the attention of all close observers. If two school-friends part, and meet again after spending a year at the respective universities, they are soon conscious that they no longer work exactly in the same way. The Cambridge student has learned to regard everything as a task which he must honestly and steadily get through. To do it, and not to think about it, is his aim. Still less does he occupy himself with thinking about doing it. He is too busy and methodical for the agreeable but delusive pleasure of secondary reflection. He has to master a subject, and all he cares is to master it, and to go through it, so that he may satisfy the practical test of being examined in it and answering creditably. When he leaves college and commences a profession, he works in the same way. A law student from Cambridge, for instance, has generally no very romantic views either of his profession or of himself. Here is a very complex, confused, various piece of learning which he has undertaken to acquire. To do the thing well, he must work hard, and must utterly disbelieve that any knowledge will come unless it is painfully obtained. He must cultivate a legal memory, note carefully up all that he thinks he ought to know, and prepare himself to be able to pass an imaginary examination at the shortest possible notice. The Oxford student, on the other hand, is more inclined to speculate about law, to dally with its details, and to despise its confusion. Cambridge men, so to speak, approach law in a humble attitude, and are consequently, perhaps, as a rule, better lawyers after the received English fashion. A boating man who has shaved through a pass at Cambridge, will probably read law precisely in the same way as a boating man who has shaved through a pass at Oxford. But if we compare the general body of men who have taken fair degrees or been accustomed to read, we shall find that there is a difference in the manner in which the one and the other set approach a subject like law, and that difference may fairly be described by saying that the Cambridge manner is the more practical.—*Saturday Review*.

"*Great Events from Little Causes spring.*"

Exemplifications of this poetic saw are very numerous in the highways and byeways of History, ancient and modern; all tending to show the springs which have set the world in motion, and how the most trivial circumstances have occasioned the subversion of empires, and erected new ones in their stead. Infinite are the consequences which follow from a single, and often apparently a very insignificant, circumstance. Paley himself narrowly escaped being a baker; here was a decision upon which hung in one scale, perhaps, the immortal interests of thousands, and in the other, the gratification of the taste of the good people of Giggleswick for hot rolls. Cromwell was near being strangled in his cradle by a monkey; here was this wretched ape wielding in his paws the destiny of nations. Then, again, how different in their kind, as well as in their magnitude, are these consequences from anything that might have been, à priori, expected. Henry VIII. is smitten with the beauty of a girl of eighteen, and ere long—

"The Reformation beams from Bullen's eyes."

The Mission of St. Augustine is one of the most striking instances in all history of the vast results which may flow from a very small beginning,—of the immense effects produced by a single thought in the heart of a single man, carried out conscientiously, deliberately, and fearlessly. Nothing in itself could seem more trivial than the meeting of Gregory with the three Yorkshire boys in the market-place at Rome; yet this roused a feeling in his mind which he never lost; and through all the obstacles which were thrown first in his own way, and then in that of Augustine, his highest desire concerning it was more than realised. From Canterbury, the first English Christian city—from Kent, the first English Christian kingdom—has by degrees arisen the whole constitution of Church and State in England, which now binds together the whole British empire. And from the Christianity here established has flowed, by direct consequences, first, the Christianity of Germany—then, after a long interval, of North America—and, lastly, we may trust, in time, of all India and all Australasia.—*Stanley's Historical Memoirs of Canterbury.*

Wars have frequently been brought about by trivial causes. In the cathedral of Modena, in the marble tower called " La Ghirlandina," is kept the old worm-eaten wooden bucket which was the cause of the civil war, or rather affray, between the Modenese and Bolognese, in the time of Frederic II., Nov. 15, 1325. It was long suspended by the chain which fastened the gate of Bologna, through which the Modenese forced their passage, and seized the prize, which was deposited in the cathedral by the victors, the Geminiani, as a trophy of the defeat of the

Petronii, with wonderful triumph. The event is the subject of Tassoni's Secchia Rapita, or Rape of the Bucket, the first modern mock-heroic poem.

When the palace of the Trianon was building for Louis XIV., at the end of the park of Versailles, the monarch went to inspect the work, accompanied by Louvois, secretary-at-war, and superintendent of the building: Louis remarked that one of the windows was out of shape, and smaller than the rest, which Louvois denied. The king had the window measured, and finding that he had judged rightly, treated Louvois with contumely before the whole court. This treatment so incensed the minister, that when he returned home, he was heard to say, that he would find better employment for a monarch than that of insulting his favourites. Louvois was as good as his word, for by his insolence and haughtiness he insulted the other powers, and occasioned the bloody war of 1688.

An instance pregnant with mightier results could not, perhaps, be quoted than the following:—When many Puritans emigrated, or were about to emigrate, to America, in 1637, Cromwell, either despairing of his fortunes at home, or indignant at the rule of government which prevailed, resolved to quit his native country, in search of those civil and religious privileges of which he could freely partake in the New World. Eight ships were lying in the Thames, ready to sail: in one of them, says Hume, (quoting Mather and other authorities,) were embarked Hazelrig, Hampden, Pym, and Cromwell. A proclamation was issued, and the vessels were detained by Order in Council. The King had, indeed, cause to rue the exercise of his authority. In the same year, Hampden's memorable trial—the great cause of Ship-money —occurred. What events rapidly followed!

At the beginning of the reign of Elizabeth, when the Protestant religion was restored, the question whether there should be Saints' Days in the Calendar was considered by the Convocation, and sharply and fully debated. The Saints' Days were carried only by a single vote: 59 members voted for Saints' Days, 58 for omitting them.—*Literary Remains of H. Fynes Clinton.*

Bishop Burnet relates that the Habeas Corpus Act passed by a mere mistake; that one peer was counted for ten, and that made a majority for the measure.—*Earl Stanhope's Speech,* 1856.

The House of Brunswick and the Casting Vote.—Sir Arthur Owen, bart., of Orielton, in the county of Pembroke, is the individual who is asserted to have given the casting vote which placed the Brunswick dynasty on the throne of England. A lady, in 1856, residing at Haverfordwest, remembered her grandmother, who was staying at Orielton, at the time when Sir Arthur Owen rode to London on _horseback;_ for the purpose of recording his vote: he arrived at the precise juncture when his single vote caused the scale to preponderate in favour of the descendants of the Electress Sophia. (*I. Pavin Phillips, Haverfordwest.—Notes and Queries*, 2nd S. No. 31. Another account, which Mr. Phillips thinks the correct one, states that Sir Arthur Owen made the number even; and that it was Mr. Griffith Rice, M.P. for Carmarthenshire, who gave the _casting vote._ (See Debrett's *Baronetage*, 1824.)

The Discovery of America is referred to by Humboldt as a "wonderful concatenation of trivial circumstances which undeniably exercised an influence on the course of the world's destiny:"

Washington Irving has justly observed that if Columbus had resisted the counsel of Martin Alonzo Pinzon, and continued to steer westward, he would have entered the Gulf Stream and been borne to Florida, and from thence, probably, to Cape Hatteras and Virginia,—a circumstance of incalculable importance, since it might have been the means of giving to the United States of North America a Catholic Spanish population, in the place of the Protestant English one by which those regions were subsequently colonised. "It seems to me like an inspiration," said Pinzon to the Admiral, "that my heart dictates to me that we ought to steer in a different direction." It was on the strength of this circumstance that in the celebrated lawsuit which Pinzon carried on against the heirs of Columbus, between 1513 and 1515, he maintained that the discovery of America was alone due to him. This inspiration Pinzon owed, as related by an old sailor of Moguez, at the same trial, to *the flight of a flock of parrots* which he had observed in the evening flying towards the south-west, in order, as he might well have conjectured, to roost on trees on the land. *Never has a flight of birds been attended by more important results.* It may even be said that it has decided the first colonization in the New Continent, and the original of the Roman and Germanic races of men.

The Act to recharter the first Bank of the United States was defeated by the casting vote of Vice-president Clinton (*ex-officio* President of the Senate), and the Tariff Act of 1846 was ordered to be engrossed by the casting vote of Vice-president Dallas.

That *the Past is the Guide for the Present* is thus argued:—Every political treatise referring to events which have engrossed the attention of the day, either as modifications or as changes of our social system, must be valuable in later years. It must necessarily recommend or condemn measures on account of their probable operation in the time to come; it must in some degree be a prophecy, or else it is practically worthless. The politician studies the past merely as his guide for the future. If he is learned, wise, and at all an adept in the science which he professes—than which no other is of so momentous an import— he will consider past history as the barometer which must guide him in predicating the approach either of a tempest or a calm. Temporary clamour or occasional obstruction will not lead him to forsake clear principles of action, or to recommend a grand constitutional remedy in the case of a trifling local disease. He must look forward beyond the sphere of immediate action—resolute in this belief, that one false step, however small, may upset the equilibrium of the State.—*Blackwood's Magazine,* 1850.

Great Britain on the Map of the World.

We see two little spots huddled up in a corner, awkwardly shot off to a side, as it were, yet facing the great sea, on the very verge of the great waste of waters, with nothing to protect them: not like Greece, or Italy, or Egypt, in a Mediterranean bounded by a surrounding shore, to be coasted by timid mariners, but on the very edge and verge of the great ocean, looking out westward to the expanse. If she launch at all, she must launch with the fearless heart that is ready to brave old ocean,—to take him with his gigantic western waves—to face his winds and hurricanes—his summer heats of the dead-still tropics—his winter blasts—his fairy icebergs—his fogs like palpable darkness—his hail-blasts and his snow. Britain has done so. From her island-home, she has sailed east and west, north and south. She has gone outwardly, and planted empires. The States themselves, now her compeer, were an offshoot from her island territory. Her destiny is to plant out nations, and the spirit of colonization is the genius that presides over her career. She plants out Canada, Australia, New Zealand, and the Cape. Ceylon and the Mauritius she occupies for trade. India she covers with a network of law, framed and woven in her Anglo-Saxon loom. She clutches China, and begins at last to break up the celestial solecism. She lays hold of Borneo, and straightway piratical prahus are seen wrecked and stranded on the shore, or blown to fragments in the air. She raises an impregnable fortress at the entrance of the Mediterranean, and another in its centre, as security to her sea-borne trade. She does the same in embryo at the entrance to the Red Sea. Westward from Newfoundland, she traverses a continent, and there, in the Pacific, Vancouver's Island, which may one day become the New Great Britain of new Anglo-Saxon enterprise, destined to carry civilization to the innumerable islands of the great sea—bears the union-jack for its island banner, and acknowledges the sovereignty of the British Crown. At Singapore, she has provisionally made herself mistress of the Straits of Malacca ; and thousands of miles away on the other hand, at the Falkland Islands, near to the Land of Fire, the British mariner may hear the voice of praise issuing in the Anglo-Saxon tongue. In addition to this, she has representatives at every court, and consuls at every sea-port. Her cruisers bear her flag on every navigable sea. Europeans, Asiatics, Africans, Americans, and Australians, are found wearing her uniform, eating her bread bearing her arms, and contributing to extend her dominion.— *North British Review.*

Ancient and Modern London.

It is interesting, beyond a merely antiquarian point of view, to trace the progress of London from a walled town, covering about 700 acres, with a population half mercantile, half military, living in a labyrinth of courts and alleys, the majority being, as appears from an old proclamation, "*heaped up together, and in a sort, half smothered.*" Let us compare this with the majestic city of our day, spreading over more than 120 square miles, and containing 2600 miles of streets, flanked by 360,000 inhabited houses, with a population of 3,000,000, and an assessed rental of 13,000,000*l.*

Modern London embraces important portions of the four adjacent counties, and has swallowed up not only the old district, which is still designated "the City," and its ancient suburbs, but numberless places formerly existing as distinct towns, villages, and hamlets, which in days gone by had their separate systems of local government. Under the present regulations, the Central Criminal Court district extends over an area of more than 700 square miles, including all Middlesex, and parts of Surrey, Kent, Essex, and Hertfordshire; which is also about the area of the Metropolitan Police District.—*Alexander Pulling; Law Magazine*, N.S., No. xxviii.

Potatoes the national food of the Irish.

There is one instance, and only one, of a great European people possessing a very cheap national food. In Ireland the labouring classes have for more than two hundred years been principally fed by potatoes, which were introduced into their country late in the sixteenth or early in the seventeenth century. . Now, the peculiarity of the potato is, that until the appearance of the late disease, it was, and perhaps still is, cheaper than any other food equally wholesome.   If we compare its reproductive power with the amount of nutriment contained in it, we find that one acre of average land sown with potatoes will support twice as many persons as the same quantity of land sown with wheat. The consequence is, that in a country where men live on potatoes, the population will, if other things are tolerably equal, increase twice as fast as in a country where they live on wheat.   And so it has actually occurred: until a few years ago, the population in Ireland, in round numbers, increased annually three per cent.; the population of England, during the same period increasing one and a half per cent.—*Buckle's History of Civilization.*

Irish-speaking Population.

There were in Ireland at the time of the Census of 1861, 1,105,536 persons who spoke Irish.   163,275 of them spoke Irish only; the other 942,261 spoke both Irish and English.   Of those who spoke Irish only, 3,075 were in the civic districts and 160,200 in the rural districts.   That the number is declining is obvious from the circumstance that the proportion under 20 years of age was less than a third.   77,818 were in Connaught (in a population of less than a million), 62,039 in Munster, 23,180 in Ulster, only 238 in all Leinster.

Our Colonial Empire.

The Colonies of Great Britain comprise altogether 3,350,000 square miles, and cost us for management 3,350,000*l.* per annum, or just about a pound a mile.   They have an aggregate revenue of 11,000,000*l.*, and owe among them 27,000,000*l.*, or just two years and a half's income.   They import goods to the amount of 60,000,000*l.* yearly —half from ourselves, and half from all the rest of the world.   They export produce to the value of 50,000,00c*l.*, of which three-fifths come to this kingdom; and all this is done by a population which is under 10,000,000 in the aggregate, and of which only 5,000,000 are whites.   Add to these figures, says the *Spectator*, 900,000 square miles for India, and 200,000,000 of people with a trade of 71,000,000*l.*, and we have a result that *the Queen reigns over nearly one-third of the land of the earth, and* *nearly a fourth of its population.* If a British vizier under the Emperor should, as it seems probable, rule China, Englishmen will directly control *more than half the human race!*

Our Colonies may be grouped or classed as North American, Australian, Mediterranean, Atlantic, West Indian, Eastern, and African. In extent of territory no Colonies approach those of Australia. The palm of debt belongs to Canada, that of cost to the Mediterranean settlements, that of commerce to the Australian Colonies again. This great show of trade is owing to the precious character of their produce. Of the gross exports of 50,000,000*l.* they claim 22,000,000*l.*, and cost little or nothing for garrisons all the while. In 1860, 250,000*l.* paid the entire military expenditure on this group of our dependencies; but New Zealand, which only stood at 100,000*l.* then, is probably not managed for that figure now. We can see but little trace of its gold-fields in the return before us, which throws all the weight upon New South Wales and Victoria. The former of these settlements exported in 1860 produce to the value of 5,000,000*l.*; the latter (and here come the gold-ships) no less than 13,000,000*l.* worth of goods. Three-fourths of this, too, came to England, whereas in the export-trade of New South Wales three-fourths went to foreign countries. Victoria also imported very largely from us, as did the other Colonies of the group, standing, in the whole, for more than half the sum total of this column.

Taking population and area into consideration, the trade done by the West Indies is not a bad one. There are but 54,000 white people in all these islands, yet they export goods to the value of 6,000,000*l.*, and import about the same. Most of the settlements are somewhat in debt—Jamaica above the others; but even Jamaica does not owe three years' income, whereas Canada owes eight. The total revenue of the West Indian Colonies in 1860 was not quite a million; the total debt was not quite a million and a half. But the most curious specimen in the return is Heligoland. The area of this British Colony is one-third of a square mile. On that territory a population of 2,172 souls maintains itself, and buys 13,000*l.* worth of foreign produce every year. Heligoland has also a revenue; but Heligoland has a public debt likewise, and is behind the world to the extent of nearly 5,000*l.*

The contrast of the statistics of India with these Colonial totals will develope some remarkable facts. The mere area of India, large as it is, scarcely exceeds one-fourth of the gross area of the Colonies, but it is infinitely more populous and wealthy. Its 900,000 square miles contain fifteen times as many inhabitants as all the rest of the Colonies together; its annual revenue is four times as great; its public debt four times as heavy. But its commerce is wonderful. The exports of all the Colonies, even including the produce of the gold-fields, amount to 50,000,000*l.* only, and to no more than 27,000,000*l.* apart from the exports of Australia. India, however, exported in 1860 goods to the value of 34,000,000*l.*, of which 15,000,000*l.* worth came to us; and purchased in return 22,000,000*l.* worth from us, and 12,000,000*l.* worth from other countries. Add to this, that its cost is nothing. Under every item of charge, military as well as civil, the return in the case of India is *nil.* Where the rest of the Colonies figure for upwards of 3,000,000*l.* in the way of cost, India makes no demand whatever. That great Empire could supply us with almost everything we want. It could send us tea and silk when China fails; and if there can be any adequate substitute for the American cotton-fields, it is in India that we must seek it. It supplies us, too, with the invaluable advantage of a sphere of action and an honourable career for our adventurous youth, and all this it does without costing us a farthing, and without costing its own people more than they receive in value.—*Parliamentary Return,* 1863.

The English People.

Mr. Craufurd, the ethnologist, has, in these few sentences, described the people of England: " They are," he tells us, " among the most mixed people in the world: but the admixtures always having been of high order, no deterioration has resulted. Teutonic invasions appear to have been early made on the coasts of Britain, and the people who offered so brave a resistance to Cæsar were probably German settlers. The Romans, for four centuries, occupied all the best parts of the land, leaving the remains of the primitive peoples in the sterile and mountainous districts, which it would have been difficult to subdue, and unprofitable to keep in subjugation. The Romans, accompanied by few women, necessarily intermarried with the British. After them came the Teutonic Jutes, Saxons, Angles, Frisians, Danes, and Norwegians—the latter came over by mere boatloads; but in the course of several generations they attained, by their superior valour—for in number they never approached that of the original inhabitants—to the position of invaders, and spread their own language and institutions over the land. The Normans came next, but they were too few in number to overthrow the Saxon element; and all they have accomplished has been to add considerably to the Saxon vocabulary. We are not then, as a race, exclusively Britons, or exclusively Saxon, but a great deal more of the former than the latter."

Dignities and Distinctions.

Worth of Heraldry.

THE only individuals who affect to sneer at heraldic pursuits and studies are those of apocryphal gentility, or whose ancestral reminiscences are associated with the rope sinister, or some such distinctive badge. Heraldry is, however, a branch of the hiero-glyphical language, and the only branch which has been handed down to us with a recognised key. It in many cases represents the very names of persons, their birth, family, and alliances; in others it illustrates their ranks and titles; and in all *is*, or rather *was*, a faithful record of their illustrious deeds, represented by signs imitative and conventional. Taking this view of the ques-tion, it is evident that it is capable of vast improvements: in fact, a well-emblazoned shield might be made practically to represent, at a single glance, a synopsis of biography, chronology, and history. Insignia of individuals and races, which are of a kindred character with heraldry, at least in its original form and design, may be recognised among the nations of antiquity, and may perhaps be carried back to the primeval ages of Egyptian history. The Israelites, from their long captivity familiarized with such objects, naturally adopted them as distinguishing characteristics; and Sir W. Drummond believed that the twelve tribes adopted the signs · of the zodiac as their respective ensigns; "nor," as has been observed, "does the supposed allusion to those signs by Jacob imply anything impious, magical, or offensive to the Deity."

The heraldry (?) of the heroic ages may be traced in the pages of Homer and Æschylus; and in the succeeding generations we have testimony of the adoption of a sort of armorial bearings by the princes of Greece. Omitting Nicias, Lamachus, Alcibiades, and others on record, we will merely observe that the arms of Niochorus, who slew Lysander, were a dragon, thus realizing the prediction of the oracle,

> Fly from Oplites' watery strand;
> The earth-born serpent too beware.

Nor were mottos by any means unfrequent. The shield which Demosthenes so pusillanimously threw away was inscribed "To good Fortune."

The animals which are frequently represented within shields on
the Roman vases sufficiently establish the fact, that this usage
was common amongst that great people; and the striking example
of a goat, on a specimen in the British Museum, might, by
analogy, without any great stretch of imagination, be ascribed to
the family of *Caprus!*

Students of heraldry are commonly great enthusiasts; so that,
in its pursuit, they are apt to depreciate more important subjects.
We remember to have heard an amateur herald, who had filled
all his windows with arms of his own painting, condemn Mr.
Salt's collection of Egyptian Antiquities in terms of unmistakeable
contempt!

Heralds' College.

The corporation of the College of Arms consists of 13 officers
—namely, three Kings of Arms (Garter, Clarenceux, and
Norroy), and, we believe, six heralds and four pursuivants.
According to a Parliamentary Return, the most onerous of their
duties is the preservation and safe custody of the vast mass of
records and evidences which relate to the genealogical history,
pedigrees, and arms of the nobility and gentry of England, from
the earliest period to the present time. These officers have no
Government grant, but they are household servants of the Crown,
under the Earl Marshal; and their duty as such- consists in the
ordering and conducting all public funerals, such State ceremonials as coronations, and other ceremonials where the person of the
Sovereign is more immediately concerned. For these services
they receive salaries, the aggregate amount of which to the 13
officers is 252*l.* 18*s.* per annum. In their capacity of household
servants they also receive certain fees on the creation of dignities
and upon the installation of Knights of the Garter, paid by the
persons on whom such honours are conferred. A herald and a
pursuivant answer all public inquiries, make such searches as may
be required, and give official extracts from records; the fees received for such searches and extracts amounted to 94*l.* in 1861.
From all these sources, therefore, they received 600*l.* in that year.
The officers of arms are the agents through whom applications
are made to the Earl Marshal (acting in this behalf on the part of
the Crown) for the registration of armorial bearings, or the soli-
citation of the Royal licence for a change of name, or change of
name and arms. For the one case it becomes the duty of the
officers of arms to see that no memorial be presented to the Earl
Marshal by any individual not occupying a fit station in life for
such distinction; and in the other that no petition be, through

them, presented to the Crown, the allegations of which have not been, before such presentation, fully established, inasmuch as the Crown accepts and endorses such allegations, and directs the Earl Marshal to make them matter of record. The number of these patents and grants of arms or change of name or arms has been 869 in the period from 1850 to 1862 inclusive. The fees taken upon them are:—For grants on voluntary applications, 66*l.* 10*s.* and 10*l.* stamp duty; under Royal licences, 66*l.* 10*s.* and 48*l.* 17*s.* 6d. for exemplifications, 3*l.* 10s. of which goes to the Home-office; for grants of supporters, 55*l.*; for grants to wives or spinsters, 53*l.* and 10*l.* stamp duty; for grants of quarterings, 42*l.* 10*s.* and 10*l.* stamp duty; for grants of crests, 42*l.* 10*s.* and 10*l.* stamp duty; and for change of name, 44*l.* 13*s.*, whereof 10*l.* 2*s.* 6d. goes to the Home-office.

The Shamrock.

Mrs. Lankester describes the Wood-sorrel (*Oxalis acetosella*) as easily recognised by its three delicately-green leaflets with longish stalks, marked with a darkish crescent in the centre, veined, and its lovely white flowers which at first sight resemble the wood-anemone. There are few walks or shady woods where, in the early spring, the bright half-folded green leaves of this pretty little plant may not be found. The tiny white flowers with their delicate purple veins are called, by the Welsh, " fairy bells," and are believed to ring the merry peals which call the elves to " moonlight dancing and revelry." Among the Druids its triple leaflets were regarded as a mysterious symbol of a Trinity, the full meaning of which was involved in darkness. So, too, St. Patrick chose this leaf as his symbol to illustrate the doctrine he sought to teach, and converted many by the apt use of an illustration derived from a plant already sacred in the eyes of his hearers. The original shamrock was undoubtedly the Oxalis, though the name became applied to all sorts of trefoiled plants.

It is, however, suspected that any three-leaved plant may be called the shamrock, the wood-sorrel no more undoubtedly than the Dutch clover, all leaves of this kind having been beheld with superstitious veneration, as possessing—

The holy trefoil's charm.

Irish Titles of Honour.

Titles of honour are still borne by the representatives of some of the old Milesian families in Ireland. Some of these titles have become extinct in course of time, such as the M'Carty More, the White Knight, the O'Sullivan Bear, the O'Moore, &c., and some have been merged in peerages. The O'Bryens in the titles of Thomond (now extinct) and Inchiquin, the O'Neills in an Earldom (extinct), the O'Callaghan in Lord Lismore, and the descendant and representative of the O'Byrnes in Lord de Tabley. But the following titles are still preserved and generally acknowledged:—

These are the O'Donoghue of the Glens, the O'Conor Don, the Knight of Kerry, the Knight of Glen, the O'Grady, the M'Gillicuddy of the Reeks; and the M'Dermot, Prince of Coolvain. The two first of these represent Irish constituencies, and it is believed are the only Irish chieftains who have adhered to the national religion; all the others are Protestants. Indeed, it is a curious circumstance that while we see the O'Neills, the O'Briens, the O'Callaghans, the O'Byrnes, indeed almost all the lineal descendants of the old Irish families, staunch Protestants (some of them even Orangemen; the late Lord O'Neill was Grand Master of the Orangemen); we find, on the other hand, that the leading Roman Catholic nobility and gentry in Ireland are mostly of English and Protestant extraction. Thus the Brownes, Earls of Kenmare, came over originally in the reign of Queen Elizabeth; and being Protestants obtained large grants of the O'Donoghue property in Kerry, forfeited by Roderick O'Donoghue, in the reign of Elizabeth, and by Geoffrey O'Donoghue, "dead in rebellion," in the reign of her successor. The Earls of Kenmare are now, as is well known, at the head of the Irish Roman Catholic peerage, and so of the Dillons, Plunkets, Burkes, Nugents, Prestons, and other Irish Roman Catholic families of importance; they are all, with few exceptions, of English and Protestant descent, while we have seen that the descendants of the native Irish are almost all Protestants.

The Scotch Thistle.

Many different species have been dignified with the name of Scotch Thistle. It is probable, say some authorities, that a common species, such as *Carduus lanceolatus*, is most deserving the name. Some have fixed on doubtful native species, such as *Silybum Marianum* and *Onopordum Acanthium*. Neither of these is, however, reconcilable with history. *S. Marianum* is appropriated by the Roman Catholic Church, who say the white marking on the foliage is commemorative of the milk of the Virgin Mary. *O. Acanthium* is not only, like the last, a doubtful original species to Scotland, but, like *C. lanceolatus*, of much too great a height; for one historian says that, after the landing of Queen Scota, she reviewed her troops; and, being fatigued, retired; and, on sitting down, was pricked by a thistle; from which circumstance she adopted it as the arms of her new country, with the motto, *Nemo me impune lacessit*. Another says, on the eve of an attack by the Danes, one of the enemy having trod on a thistle, cried out with pain, which gave intimation to the Scots of their near presence; and hence the thistle became dignified as the arms of the country. With these two exceptions, we meet with no other reference to a matter of equal importance, in an historical point of view, with that of the legends in connexion with the Coronation Stone, which all historians have treated on with great minuteness.

However, if any reliance may be placed on the authorities above given, it is quite clear that it must have been a low-growing species like *Cnivus acaule*; for, whether we take into consideration the accident to the Queen or the bare-footed Dane, or the configuration of the flower-head itself, it more closely resembles the representations we find on many of the sculptured stones than either of the others. Some have supposed it to be *Carduus acanthoides*; but this, as well as all the rest, is less formidably furnished with those strong spiny scales with which the receptacle of *Silybum Marianum* is so amply provided. This circumstance agrees with the sculptured representations found on the oldest parts of Stirling Castle, Linlithgow Palace, or Holyrood House, especially with one on the top of a garden doorway opposite the new fountain, in front of the entrance to the latter, which is more like the head of *Cynara Scolymus*, the globe artichoke, a native of the South of Europe, than any thistle in the world. Uncertain as the Scotch are regarding the species of their national emblem, or even of its being a native, they are no more so than the English are regarding the species of rose they have adopted. No double rose existed in Britain at the period it was introduced into the national escutcheon; therefore, it must have been borrowed from the French; who even, in their turn, cannot now tell what species of iris their *fleur-de-lis* is meant to represent. Nor are the Irish agreed as to whether their shamrock is derived from a series of Trifolium, or from *Oxalis acetosella*. The ancient Britons, as the Welsh call themselves, have adopted the leek, *Allium porum*, a native of Switzerland.—*Scottish Farmer.*

King and Queen.

It is curious to find Lord Buckhurst and Recorder Fleetwood engaged in a conversation on the excellency of the regal dignity of a King, as they rode from London to Windsor in the reign of Elizabeth, (1575,) in the company of the Earl of Leicester, who travelled according to his own pompous notions, with divers

knights and noble gentlemen, and a princely cavalcade of attendants.   Mr. Recorder, riding between my Lord of Leicester and
Lord Buckhurst, as they passed " alonge by Saint James's walles,"
began the debate; when the great lawyer laid down :*

"I doe read that this worde Kinge is a Saxon terme, and doe originallye
comme and growe out of this ould Saxon word cyning, which doth signefie
a cuninge, a wyse, a virtuous, a polleticque, and a prudent person, fitt to
governe as well in peace as in warres; and this word Queene, in the same
tongue, is in effect of the same force, referringe the same to the female
sex, and therefore it is to be noted that the crowne of England is not
alwayes bound especiallye to be governed by the male ; but yf there wante
heyres males, then ought it to descend to the heyres females, as it appeareth
by the judgmente given touchinge the dawghters of Zelophehad (xxvi.
33 Numbers), and as it did in the tyme of the Bryttons descend upon
Queen Cordeila, who was queene of this realme before the Incarnation of
Christ 805 years, even at that tyme that the good King Ozias did repayer
the cittye of Jerusalem, which was in the yeare of the worlde 3358.   This
Cordeila was dawghter of Kinge Leire, who buylded the auntient cittye of
Leicester; yea, and is it a most true and playne matter, that the crowne of
England maye descend and come to the female dawghter, where there
lacketh heyre male, as it did unto Mawde the Empresse, who was dawghter
to Kinge Henrye the First, and by the meane that William, Mary, and
Richard, the children of the same King Henry the First, were drowned in
the seas by shipwracke, it soe fell out the said Mawde the Empresse became
sole heyre, and notwithstandinge an ynterruption made by Kinge Stephen
the intruder (for that is his proper addition in the antient chronicles), yett
the judgmente fell out for her parte, and she and her posteritye, even to
this daye, have justlye and most rightfullye enjoyed the crowne without
any enterclayme of anye person that ever hath bine heard of."   To this
Leicester replies : "I see that this is a greate and good proofe that the
female hath had and enjoyed the crowne of England by just and lawfull
tytle," &c.—*Archæologia*, xxxvii.

Title of Majesty, and the Royal " We."

It is a common error to suppose Charles V. to have been the
originator of this sovereign title.   Its earliest use is to denote the
dignity of the Roman people.   Thence the Emperors borrowed
it as the representatives of the people, in accordance with the
Lex Regia.   They were called " Majestas Augusta," and even
" Regia Majestas."   In later times this title was applied to the
Emperor Louis the Pious; and Charles the Bald assumes it in
one of his charters.   It is also found attributed to some of the
Popes.   Charles V. at most gave it fixity and continuance, instead

---

* In the *Itinerarium ad Windsor*.

of its being adopted and discontinued by turns. Francis I. of France, at the interview with Henry VIII. of England, on the Field of the Cloth of Gold, addressed the latter as "Your Majesty," 1520. James I. coupled with this title the term, "Sacred," and "Most Excellent Majesty."

The royal "We" represents, or was supposed originally to represent, the source of the national power, glory, and intellect, in the august power of the Sovereign. "Le Roi le veut"—the King will have it so—sounded as arrogantly as it was meant to sound in the royal Norman mouth. It is a mere form, now that royalty in England has been relieved of responsibility. In haughtiness of expression it was matched by the old French formula at the end of a decree: "For such is our good pleasure." The royal subscription in Spain is "Yo, el Re," *I, the King.* The first "King's speech" ever delivered was by Henry I., in 1107. Exactly a century later, King John first assumed the royal "We:" it had never before been employed in England. The same monarch was the first English King who claimed for England the sovereignty of the seas. "Grace," and "my Liege" were the ordinary titles by which our Henry VI. was addressed. "Excellent Grace" was given to Henry VI., who was not the one, nor yet had the other. Edward IV. was "Most High and Mighty Prince." Henry VII. was the first English Highness.

"*Dieu et Mon Droit.*"

The earliest notice that has been found of the Sovereign's present motto, "Dieu et mon Droit," is in the 13th Henry VI., 1435, when a gown, embroidered with silver crowns, and with the motto "Dieu et mon Droit," is mentioned in a roll at Carltonride.—*Sir Harris Nicolas; Archæologia,* vol. xxxi.

Plume and Motto of the Prince of Wales.

Dr. Doran, F.S.A., has thus briefly told their history, profiting in his inquiry by the researches of Sir Harris Nicolas:—"Old Randall Holmes solved the difficulty in his summary way, by asserting that the ostrich feathers were the blazon on the war-banner of the ancient Britons. The only thing that in any way resembles the triple feathers in ancient British heraldry is to be found on the azure shield of arms of King Roderick Mawr, on which the tails of that monarch's three lions are seen coming between their legs, and turning over their backs, with the gentle fall of the tips, like the graceful bend of the feathers in the Prince's badge. The feathers themselves, however, do not appear in connexion with our Princes of Wales until after the battle in which the blind King of Bohemia lost his life. The crest of the Bohemian monarch was an eagle's wing; as for the motto of *Ich dien,* it was assumed by the Prince to characterize his humility, in accordance with a fashion followed to a late period even by princesses—Elizabeth of York, for instance, took that of "Humble and Reverent." Edward of Woodstock, therefore, did not adopt either the badge or the legend of the dead King of Bohemia; such is the conclusion at which nearly all persons who have examined into this difficult question have arrived. Nevertheless, John, Count of Luxemburg, was the original style and title of him who was elected King of Bohemia, and fell so bravely and unnecessarily at Cressy. Now, the ostrich feather *was* a distinction of Luxemburg; and it is from such origin that the Princes of Wales derive the graceful plumes, which are their distinguishing badge, but not their crest. This much is stated by Sir H. Nicolas, in the *Archæologia* (xxxi. 252); and Mr. D'Eyncourt (*Gent. Mag.* xxxvi. 621) suggests that the King of Bohemia's crest looks more like ostrich feathers than a vulture's wing. The question may be considered as having been set at rest by John de Ardern. He was a physician, contemporary with the Black Prince; and in a manuscript of his in the Sloane Collection (76 fo. 61), Ardern distinctly states that the Prince derived the feathers from the blind King. In the directions given in this will for the funeral procession, banners bearing the arms of France and England quarterly, and others with the ostrich-plume, are respectively described as those of war and peace. The ostrich symbolised Justice, its feathers being nearly all of equal length."

Victoria.

The first time this name occurs in English history is as belonging to a "Mastres (Mistress) Victoria," who was one of the attendants, "Gentylwomen," upon Queen Katherine, when she accompanied her husband, Henry VIII., to the gorgeous meeting of the Field of the Cloth of Gold (June, 1520). Each gentylwoman was allowed "a woman, ij men servantes, and iij horses." And the Queen had 265 of all ranks, and they in turn had 999, making the total number 1260 persons. The King's retinue amounted to 4544; Wolsey had above 400.

English Crowns.

The crowns worn in former times by the kings of England have varied much in form and material. The Saxon kings had a crown consisting of a simple fillet of gold. Egbert improved its appearance by placing on the fillet a row of points or rays; and after him, Edmond *Ironside* tipped these points with pearl; William the Conqueror had on his coronet points and leaves placed alternately, each point being tipped with three pearls, while the whole crown was surmounted with a cross. William Rufus discontinued the leaves. Henry I. had a row of *fleur-de-lis*; from this time to Edward III. the crown was variously ornamented with points and fleur-de-lis, placed alternately; but this monarch enriched his crown with fleur-de-lis and crosses alternately, as at present. Edward IV. was the first who wore a close crown, with two arches of gold, embellished with pearls; and the same form, with trifling variations, has been continued to the present day. The English crown, called the " St. Edward's crown," was made in imitation of the ancient crown said to be worn by that monarch, kept in Westminster Abbey till the beginning of the Civil Wars in England, when, with the rest of the regalia, it was seized and sold in 1642. A new crown was prepared for the coronation of Charles II.: it is set with pearls and precious stones, as diamonds, rubies, emeralds, sapphires; it has a mound of gold on the top, enriched with a fillet of the same metal, covered also with precious stones; the cap is of purple velvet, lined with white silk, and turned up with ermine.

The Imperial State Crown.

Professor Tennant, the well-known mineralogist, thus minutely describes the Imperial State Crown of Her Majesty Queen Victoria, which was made by Messrs. Rundell and Bridge in the year 1838, with jewels taken from old Crowns, and others furnished by command of her Majesty:

The Crown consists of diamonds, pearls, rubies, sapphires, and emeralds, set in silver and gold; it has a crimson velvet cap with ermine border, and is lined with white silk. Its gross weight is 39 oz. 5 dwts. troy. The lower part of the band, above the ermine border, consists of a row of one hundred and twenty-nine pearls, and the upper part of the band a row of one hundred and twelve pearls, between which, in front of the Crown, is a large sapphire (partly drilled), purchased for the Crown by His Majesty King George the Fourth. At the back is a sapphire of smaller size, and six other sapphires (three on each side), between which are eight emeralds.

Above and below the seven sapphires are fourteen diamonds, and around the eight emeralds one hundred and twenty-eight diamonds. Between the emeralds and sapphires are sixteen trefoil ornaments, containing one hundred and sixty diamonds. Above the band are eight sapphires surmounted by eight diamonds, between which are eight festoons consisting of one hundred and forty-eight diamonds.

In front of the Crown, and in the centre of a diamond Maltese cross, is the famous ruby said to have been given to Edward Prince of Wales, son of Edward the Third, called the Black Prince, by Don Pedro, King of Castile, after the battle of Najera, near Vittoria, A.D. 1367. This ruby was worn in the helmet of Henry the Fifth at the battle of Agincourt, A.D. 1415. It is pierced quite through after the Eastern custom, the upper part of the piercing being filled up by a small ruby. Around this ruby, to form the cross, are seventy-five brilliant diamonds. Three other Maltese crosses, forming the two sides and back of the Crown, have emerald centres, and contain respectively one hundred and thirty-two, one hundred and twenty-four, and one hundred and thirty brilliant diamonds.

Between the four Maltese crosses are four ornaments in the form of the French fleur-de-lis, with four rubies in the centres, and surrounded by rose diamonds, containing respectively eighty-five, eighty-six, and eighty-seven rose diamonds.

From the Maltese crosses issue four imperial arches composed of oak-leaves and acorns; the leaves containing seven hundred and twenty-eight rose, table, and brilliant diamonds; thirty-two pearls forming the acorns, set in cups containing fifty-four rose diamonds and one table diamond. The total number of diamonds in the arches and acorns is one hundred and eight brilliants, one hundred and sixteen table, and five hundred and fifty-nine rose diamonds.

From the upper part of the arches are suspended four large pendent pear-shaped pearls, with rose diamond caps, containing twelve rose diamonds, and stems containing twenty-four very small rose diamonds. Above the arch stands the mound, containing in the lower hemisphere three hundred and four brilliants, and in the upper two hundred and forty-four brilliants; the zone and arc being composed of thirty-three rose diamonds. The cross on the summit has a rose-cut sapphire in the centre, surrounded by four large brilliants, and one hundred and eight smaller brilliants.

The following is the summary of jewels comprised in the Crown:—

1 Large ruby, irregularly polished.	1363 Brilliant diamonds.
1 Large broad-spread sapphire.	1273 Rose diamonds.
16 Sapphires.	147 Table diamonds.
11 Emeralds.	4 Drop-shaped pearls.
4 Rubies.	273 Pearls.

It is difficult to declare what is the precise value of the jewels in the Queen's crown; but it is confidently affirmed that, unlike most other princely crowns in Europe, whether of kings, emperors, or grand dukes, all the jewels in the British crown are really precious stones; whereas in other state crowns valuable stones have been replaced by coloured glass, and the consequence is that their estimated value is far beyond what such crown jewels are really worth.

Queen's Messengers.

The Queen's foreign-service Messengers are fifteen in number. The first three for service are obliged to be in attendance at the Foreign-office. Formerly there was no distinction between them and the home-service messengers; they were all under the Lord Chamberlain, and their connexion with his office is said to be the origin of the silver greyhound pendent from their badge. At a later period they were transferred to the Secretaries of State, and took journeys abroad indifferently in their turn, but in 1824 there was a separation into home and foreign service. Lord Malmesbury reduced the number of foreign-service messengers from eighteen to fifteen; and these are found quite sufficient, owing to the greater speed with which journeys are now performed, and the introduction of the electric telegraph rendering many journeys unnecessary. The Queen's messengers formerly had very small salaries, only 60*l.* a year, but made large profits by mileage and other allowances when employed. The situation was worth 800*l.* or 900*l.* a year; it has been altered to a salary of 525*l.* and the travelling expenses. This was considered by the messengers too great a reduction of their income. Earl Russell has introduced a new plan, giving them salaries of 400*l.* a year and 1*l.* a day for their personal expenses while employed abroad, besides their travelling expenses. Queen's messengers are treated with great kindness and consideration abroad; they are usually invited to the Minister's table. They are examined on appointment by the Civil Service Commissioners: the qualifications required are an age between twenty-five and thirty-five, some knowledge of French, German, or Italian, and ability to ride on horseback. The home-service messengers occupy a very inferior position.

Presents and Letters to the Queen.

The resolution of the Royal Family to decline all presents was conveyed, in 1847, to a gentleman at Sheffield, in the following official letter from Sir Denis Le Marchant:—" Whitehall, Oct. 5, 1847: In the absence of Secretary Sir George Grey, I have to acknowledge the receipt of a small box, containing a gold bijou, sent by you to the Queen, as a present for his Royal Highness the Prince of Wales; but, in consequence of the very great number of presents of this nature which have been offered to her Majesty, it has been found absolutely necessary, to avoid the possibility of giving individual offence, that her Majesty should decline presents generally, and the box is therefore declined." [This rule is not, however, invariably observed.]

Again, it is contrary to established rule for the Lord Chamberlain to receive any letter addressed to Her Majesty, *if the same be sealed.*

Sir C. B. Phipps explains in a letter the absence of her Majesty's name from the subscription-list for the widow of the late Captain Harrison, of the *Great Eastern.* He states: " It is contrary to established rule for her Majesty the Queen, or the Prince Consort, to join a subscription for a private individual."

The Prince of Waterloo.

It will be recollected that, in 1815, the Duke of Wellington received the grant of Prince of Waterloo, which was understood to have been given to his Grace and to his direct descendants. After the death of the Duke in 1852, the question of succession to the title was discussed in the Belgian House of Representatives, when, in reply to a request for information upon the subject, M. Frère-Oban stated that, upon inquiry, he had learned that the direct line of the Duke of Wellington was not extinct ; for although the rights claimed by his son were contested, because at the time of his birth the system of registration was imperfect or irregular, yet it had subsequently been proved by other means, and particularly by an inscription in a family Bible, that the present Duke was the legitimate offspring of the first Prince of Waterloo, and as such was entitled to be recognised as one of the d rect lineal descendants who were included in the original g.ant.

The See of London.

It may not be generally known that the See of London was archiepiscopal in the time of the ancient Britons, before the mission of August ne. In the thousand years which intervened between his era and that of the Reformation, the See of London numbered no less than eighty prelates, the most distinguished of whom were St. Dunstan, Warham, Courtenay, and Bonner, the last of whom was deprived by King Edward VI., and again, after his temporary restoration under Queen Mary, by Elizabeth. The reformed list commences with Bishop Ridley, who was burnt at Oxford under Queen Mary ; and from whom the present occupant of the See, Dr. Tait, is twenty-eighth in descent. Among those prelates occur the names of Grindal, Bancroft, Abbott, Laud, Juxon, and Sheldon, all of whom were eventually promoted to arch-bishoprics—Grindal to York, and the rest to Canterbury. One prelate before the Reformation, Bishop Tonstal, and one since that time, Bishop Montaigne, were translated from London to the wealthier See of Durham ; but from Dr. Sheldon, who held the See after the Restoration, down to Dr. Howley, the imme-diate predecessor of Bishop Blomfield, not a single instance occurs either of a translation from the See of London, or of a direct ap-pointment to the bishopric, except by translation from another see. The Diocese of London, until the last few years, com-prised the counties of Essex and Middlesex. By a recent enact-ment, however, the former county has been transferred to the diocese of Rochester, in exchange for the parishes of Charlton, Woolwich, Deptford, Greenwich, and other suburban d.stricts in the county of Kent. To these at the next avoidance of the See of Winchester will be added the whole of Southwark, Lam-beth, Clapham, Wandsworth, Tooting, and Battersea, together with one or two adjoining districts in the county of Surrey.

Expense of Baronetcy and Knighthood.

The fees chargeable on a Baronetcy in the Heralds'-office are reported by Sir C. G. Young, Garter King-at-Arms, to amount to 21*l.* 2s. 3d. (payable to the Heralds' College), besides which there is a sum of 15*l.* 2s. 4d., "incidental to the creation of a baronet," and payable for the necessary certificate of his arms and pedigree registered in the college, so that the sum total pay-able to the Heralds'-office is 36*l.* 4s. 7d. The newly-created baronet, it would appear, is further mulcted by the Crown-office in the sum total of 257*l.* 9s. 1d., of which 120*l.* is for stamps, nearly 58*l.* for the royal household, and 21*l.* for the heralds. The Knight Bachelor is required to pay a fee of 9*l.* 8s. 3d. if the dignity is conferred by the Sovereign; 9*l.* 13s. 6d. if it is conferred by patent ; and 18*l.* 15s. 2d. when the knighthood is conferred prior to the admission into the Order of the Bath as a G.C.B. This is in the Heralds'-office. In the Crown-office a sum of 155*l.* 12s. 10d. is exacted, of which 30*l.* is for stamps and 69*l.* 19s. 4d. for the royal household. As regards the Order of the Bath, there are no fees chargeable by the Heralds' College, except on the preliminary grade of common Knighthood already described. The robes, collars, and badges for the Knights of the several Orders are also very costly. The sum of 4625*l.* 10s. 7d. was charged for items, including four silver boxes for the great seal of

H

the Order of the Garter for the Sultan and the King of Sardinia, repairs of collars, ribands, stationery, &c. The complete robes, of the Order of the Garter for the King of Sardinia cost 346*l*., and the same for the Sultan (excepting the silver under-dress), 279*l.* Two mantles of the Garter and one of the Thistle cost 190*l.* The banner of the King of Sardinia in St. George's Chapel is charged by the herald painter at 27*l.* 17s. 6d. The gold-smith charges 2378*l.* for 140 new military companions' badges, at 16*l.* 9s. 9d. each; 195*l.* for fifteen new civil commanders' badges, at 13*l.* each; 302*l.* for 130 new civil companions' badges at 10*l.* 1s. 9½d. each; 157*l.* for nine new silver enamelled stars (G.C.B.), at 17*l.* 10s. each; 261*l.* for eighteen new military K.C.B. stars, at 14*l.* 10s.; and 295*l.* for re-enamelling and "making as new" twelve collars and eighty-eight badges, besides other items. These honours have, on some occasions, been made as profitable to the Sovereign as to his officers of State. James I. became the subject of much ridicule, not quite unmerited, for putting honours to sale. He created the order of baronet, which he disposed of for a sum of money; and it seems that he sold common knight-hood as low as *thirty pounds*, at least it was so reported. In the old play of *Eastward Hoe*, one of the characters says: "I know the man well: he is one of my thirty-pound knights."

The Aristocracy.

Mr. Lothair Bucher, in the *Transactions of the Philological Society*, Berlin, 1858, writes:

"One may safely affirm beforehand that the word ARISTOCRACY has been part and parcel of the English language from a very early period. But the Attorney-General in Horne Tooke's trial (1795) in enumerating the new opinions propagated by the friends of the accused, and the new terms in which they conveyed those opinions, says—'To the rich was given the name *Aristocracy;*' and in considering this application of the term as a new one, he is evidently quite correct."

"Now," writes a critic in the *Saturday Review*, "Aristocracy is the name of a particular form of Government; it is an abuse of language to apply it to a class of people. Yet, when one says—'the Government of Berne was an aristocracy,' it is a very slight change to speak of 'the aristo-cracy of Berne,' meaning the patrician order, or its members. The word was doubtless brought into use in England because the class which it was intended to stigmatize as an 'aristocracy' was a class more extensive than the 'nobility,' in the English use of that word. Now the name has ceased to be a stigma. The words 'aristocrat,' 'aristocratic,' 'aristocracy,' are often used in a complimentary way. But, to our taste at least, there is always a smack of vulgarity about them."

Precedence in Parliament.

To the readers of the reports of parliamentary debates, in the newspapers, it may be useful to state, upon the authority of Mr. May, that " in the Commons no places are particularly allotted to members ; but it is the custom for the front bench on the right hand of the (Speaker's) chair to be appropriated for the members of the Administration, which is called the Treasury or Privy Councillors' Bench. The front bench on the opposite side is usually reserved for the leading members of the Opposition who have served in high offices of State ; but other members occasionally sit there, especially when they have any motion to offer to the House. And on the opening of a new Parliament, the members for the city of London claim the privilege of sitting on the Treasury or Privy Councillors' Bench."—May, on the *Practice and Law of Parliament.*

Sale of Seats in Parliament.

The smaller boroughs having been from the earliest period under the command of neighbouring peers and gentlemen, or sometimes of the Crown, were first observed to be attempted by rich capitalists in the general elections of 1747 and 1755: though the prevalence of bribery in a less degree is attested by the statute-book, and the journals of Parliament from the Revolution, it seemed not to have broken the flood-gates till the end of the reign of George II., or rather perhaps the first part of the next. The sale at least of seats in Parliament, like any other transferable property, is never mentioned in any book that the writer remembers to have seen of an earlier date than 1760. The country gentlemen had long endeavoured to protect their ascendancy by excluding the rest of the community from Parliament. This was the principle of the Bill, which, after being repeatedly attempted, passed into a law during the long administration of Anne, requiring every member of the Commons, except those for the Universities, to possess, as a qualification for his seat, a landed estate, above all incumbrance, of 300*l.* a-year. The law was, however, notoriously evaded; and was abolished in 1858, by the Act 21 Vict. cap. 26.

Placemen in Parliament.

In 1694 a bill passed both Houses "touching free and impartial proceedings in Parliament," against the eligibility of Placemen. On its discussion Mr. Harley, afterwards Earl of Oxford, remarked, that "in the 1st of James I., the Chancellor, studious of the good of the kingdom, sent down to the House of Commons a list of the members in office, and they were turned out of the House, and new members chosen." King William, however, refused his sanction to this Act. "A Dutchman (says Mr. Burgh) comes over to Britain on pretence of delivering us from slavery, and makes it one of his first works to plunge us into the very vice which has enslaved all the nations of the world that have ever lost their liberties. When the Parliament passed a bill for incapacitating certain persons who might be supposed obvious to Court influence, our *glorious Deliverer* refused the royal assent."

New Peers.

Nothing is more plausible than to talk of strengthening an order by making it more popular in its constitution, &c.; but *practically*, we know that in early days in England nothing was so *un*popular as a batch of bran-new potentates. The proofs are abundant. When James I. began scattering coronets (" *crownets*," they called them in old times), a wag issued a pamphlet which professed to teach people " How to remember the names of the Nobility."—*Hannay.*

The Russells.

Hereditary likeness is one of the commonest phenomena in th world, and is an index of the moral resemblance which makes character of a particular class run through a line, and thus, in free countries like ours, produces hereditary politics and affects the fortunes of the State, as was the case at Rome. " A Russell," says Niebuhr, very justly, "could not be an absolutist; the thing would be monstrous." This conviction is, no doubt, one excellent reason why Liberals glorify the race with such constancy.— *Hannay.* [Is not this the reason why Lord John Russell, when raised to the Peerage in 1861, preferred to the Earl of Ludlow the title of Earl *Russell?* He would not part with the glory.]

Political Cunning.

The obtaining of the same ends by opposite means is exemplified as follows:—Jack Cade, when he wanted to be *popular*, called himself a Mortimer, and said his wife was a Lacy! The great Napoleon, to win the Continent, on the contrary, professed that he belonged to the *canaille*, though he knew, and his brother Joseph, and all of them well knew, that the Buonapartes were good Italian nobility.—*Hannay.*

The Union-Jack.

The term "Union-jack" is one which is partly of obvious signification, and in part somewhat perplexing. The "Union" between England and Scotland, to which the flag owed its origin, evidently supplied the first half of the compound title borne by the flag itself. But the expression "jack" involves some difficulty. Several solutions of this difficulty have been submitted, but, with a single exception only, they are by far too subtle to be considered satisfactory. A learned and judicious antiquary has recorded it as his opinion, that the flag of the Union received the title of "Union-jack" from the circumstance of the union between England and Scotland having taken place in the reign of King James, by whose command the new flag was introduced. The name of the king in French, "*Jaques*," would have been certainly used in heraldic documents: the union flag of king "Jaques" would very naturally be called after the name of its royal author, *Jaques' union*, or *union Jaques*, and so by a simple process we arrive at *union-jack*. This suggestion of the late Sir Harris Nicolas may be accepted without any hesitation; and the term "jack" having once been recognised as the title of *a* flag, it is easy enough to trace its application to *several* flags. Thus the old white flag with the red cross is now called the " St. George's jack;" and English seamen are in the habit of designating the national ensigns of other countries as the "jacks" of France, Russia, &c.

We quote this sensible view from the *Art Journal*. The paper by Sir Harris Nicolas above referred to will be found in the *Naval and Military Magazine* for 1827; and with engravings, in Brayley's *Historic and Graphic Illustrator*.

Field-Marshal.

The title of Field-Marshal is one of comparatively modern date, having been first created only so far back as the reign of George I. In the *London Gazette* for the month of January, 1736, we find it announced that " His Majesty has been pleased to erect a new post of honour, under the title of Marshal of the Armies of Great Britain, and to confer the same on the Duke of Argyll and the Earl of Orkney, as the two eldest generals in the service." The corresponding title up to that time would seem to have been that of "captain-general," which was subsequently revived, as a distinction, in the person of William Duke of Cumberland, just previous to the Rebellion of '45, and again in that of the late Duke

of York in 1799. The title of field-marshal has been but spar-
ingly conferred—only about thirty individuals, exclusive of royalty,
having been gazetted as field-marshals during upwards of 120 years.

Change of Surname.

The *usage* at the Home Office in dealing with applications for
Change of Name has been thus stated by the Secretary, Sir
George Grey, there being no written law on the subject:

"About two hundred years ago, the practice of applying for permission to
change names arose; and in 1783, in consequence of the frequency of the
request, it was deemed necessary to put some check on it. A regulation was, therefore, made that all cases should be referred to the College of
Arms. That reference is not, however, necessarily decisive, as it is intended only for the information of the department. That usage has been
universally adopted, subject to the modification introduced by Sir Robert
Peel, that where there are no plausible grounds for an application, and it is
obviously the mere result of whim or caprice, it should be at once declined,
without any reference to the College of Arms, leaving it to the applicant to
change his name on his own responsibility."

Now, Sir Robert Peel died in 1850, in which year a gentleman named
Laurie obtained two royal licences to change his name; first to Northdale,
and then to Nuthall, "in compliance with the will of the late Catherine
Jack, spinster, of Sloane-street." In 1851 a lady named Braham was permitted by royal licence to assume the name of Medows, on the plea that
she was "the co-heiress expectant" of her aged grandmother, who was
so called. In 1852 a gentleman named Rust was granted a royal licence
to assume his wife's maiden name, D'Eye, "out of respect to her memory."
In 1853 a Mr. Penny was allowed to assume the name of Harwood, "by
wish of his mother, out of respect to his grandmother." In 1854 Thomas
Clugas, of Guernsey, was permitted by royal licence "to use his paternal
name of Clucas." In 1855 a Miss Galston was allowed to assume the
name of Stepney, "out of respect to her maternal ancestors in general."
It is difficult to conceive more trifling grounds than these on which royal
licences have been granted in the above-quoted instances.

The authorities are, however, divided in their opinions. The
Lord Chancellor (in 1863) refused to recognise officially a change
of name, because the applicant had not obtained the royal licence
to bear that name, and the arms connected with it; while, on the
other hand, the Secretary of State for the Home Department has
declared that such a licence is unnecessary, and that a name can
be legally assumed without it. But the claim to the new name
assumed can only be established "by usage of such a length of
time as to give the change a permanent character," a reservation
which has clogged the undoubted right of every Englishman to
assume any name he pleases, provided the assumption be made

bonâ fide, and with reasonable publicity, while it has the effect of placing everybody at the mercy of any ill-conditioned official who may take pleasure in obstructing him and opposing him.

Reference to the *London Gazette* proves that Royal licences have hitherto been constantly issued from capricious motives, and on no fixed principle whatever. Doubtless, in many cases, they have been granted in furtherance of testamentary conditions connected with property; but they have been quite as often granted merely to enable applicants to avoid names which were distasteful to them, and to assume others which were more agreeable to them.

As the qualification which Sir George Grey and the Lord Chancellor appear desirous of affixing to the right to change name, without the assistance of a Royal licence, virtually cancels that right altogether in a vast number of cases, it becomes, in consequence, highly important that the rules by which those indulgences are obtainable, and the amount of the fees which must be paid for them, should be exactly made known.

A Parliamentary Return states that since 1850 415 applications have been made for royal licence for a change of name, and 398 licences have been granted. There is a stamp duty of 50*l.* on every such licence if the change of name is made in compliance with the injunction of any will or settlement, and of 10*l.* if the application is voluntary. The fees payable are stated to be 10*l.* 2s. 6d. on a change of name only ; 13*l.* 12s. 6d. on a change of name and arms ; and 1*l.* 7s. 6d. for every additional name inserted in a licence ; which fees are paid into the Exchequer. But the return is described as being made only " so far as relates to the Home Secretary's office," and therefore does not appear to include fees at the Heralds' College.

To conclude—it does not appear that the Queen either claims or exercises any special prerogative whatever connected with the subject of change of surname ; or that a Royal licence is anything more than the recognition in the highest quarter of a voluntary act already accomplished. Its recipient is not even compelled to bear for a day the surname which it authorizes him to assume ; nor are other people enjoined by it to recognise him by that name, if they are not inclined to do so. The case of the Right Hon. R. C. Dundas, who in 1836 obtained a Royal licence, in compliance with the conditions of a Will by which he inherited a considerable estate, to bear the name of Christopher *only*, and who, in spite of that licence and without either procuring its revocation or obtaining the grant of a fresh one, has since sat in Parliament under the surname of Nisbet, and who now bears the surname of Hamilton, assumed *proprio motu*, completely establishes this point.

Changes in Laws.

The Statute Law and the Common Law.

Lord Chancellor Westbury, in the House of Peers, in the Session of 1863, made the following statement with reference to the revision and expurgation of the Statute Law, from the earliest commencement of our legislation down to the beginning of the 17th century—the legislation, in fact, of about 500 years.

The Laws are divided into Written and Unwritten law. The written is the statute law, and the decision of the judges constitutes the unwritten law of the land. The Statute Law* is in a great measure supplemental to the Common Law, and a knowledge of the common is necessary in order to enable a man to read and understand the statute law. The Common Law is only traditionary—it is supposed to reside in the breasts of the judges; accordingly, when it is necessary to ascertain it in the House of Lords, their lordships require the attendance of the judges, who are called upon to declare what that law is. In like manner, in the great court of equity to which belongs that large portion of natural justice which is repudiated by the common law, the judges have the power of determining what constitutes the rudiments of that law. This is, undoubtedly, a dangerous and a difficult trust. It is little less than legislative power, because the sources of common law are of the most varied character. It is probably derived in a great measure from customs and usages, recorded only in the memory of man; it is partly derived, no doubt, from old rules embodied in acts of which no record now exists. It is partly made up of relics of the old Roman jurisprudence which remained so long throughout the land; and it is partly the result of customs and maxims, handed down from one generation to another. The sources were so varied in ancient times that the custom of declaring the law also varied. In the old time it was impossible to know what the law was. The judges were not only legislators, but the worst of legislators—legislators *ex post facto*. Accordingly, at an early period, it became necessary for the protection of liberty, in order to get some kind of approach to uniformity, constancy, and

---

* The Statutes were inscribed in Latin to the time of Edward I. (1272); in Norman-French to about the time of Richard III. (1483); and subsequently in the English language.

regularity in the law, that the grounds and reasons of the judges' decisions should be given. At first an attempt was made to do so by entering the reasons for the judgments in the rolls of the court; and our court rolls, preserved from the time of Richard I., contain repeatedly the reasons for the decisions and sentences. At the latter end of the reign of Edward II., or in the beginning of the reign of Edward III., the practice of reporting the decisions of the judges began, and from that period down we have a series of judicial reports of those decisions. That was a great security for the people, because it was an approach to certainty in the law. The origin and reason of it was a distinctive peculiarity in the English mind—namely, the love of precedent, a love of appealing to precedent rather than indulging in abstract reasoning. This was the only mode in which the law was recorded, and the only mode in which it became known. These reports were kept for a considerable period of time under the superintendence of the judges themselves, and great care was taken in sifting and ascertaining the grounds of the decision. The evil was, therefore, comparatively little; but in course of time, as the reports multiplied and as the personal superintendence and care of the judges were withdrawn, great complaints began to arise; and so much inconvenience was felt that, as early as the time of Lord Bacon, it became a subject of general dissatisfaction which attracted his attention, and led to his compiling and publishing his celebrated book for the amendment of the law of England. The Lord Chancellor, in his revision and expurgation, proposed to do little, if anything at all, more than revive the proposal of Bacon. "The wisdom and excellence of that proposal has been admitted from age to age; and the fact that nothing has been done to give effect to it we must attribute to the singular *inertia* that characterized the English Legislature."

*Curiosities of the Statute Law.**

Most people have a confused idea that as new laws are made old ones are repealed; and that the Statute-Book, bulky as it is, contains nothing but what every Englishman is bound to know and observe. Such, however, is not the case: for the old laws, instead of being cleared away to admit the new ones, have been allowed to remain, so that nine-tenths of this Statute-Law is really not law at all; and if the Statute-Book were freed from the enactments which have become obsolete, or ceased to be in

* Selected and condensed from the *Times*, June 13, 1863.

force without being specifically repealed, it would be reduced from forty to four or five volumes. Enough of confusion, prolixity, and repetition would still remain within this compass to exercise the wits and fill the pockets of the lawyers; but the perusal of it would no longer occupy a lifetime, and this excuse for our ignorance of it would be very much weakened.

To show the necessity of the revision of our Statute-Book, we shall quote from the schedule of the Bill presented by the Lord Chancellor to the House of Lords in the Session of 1863, a few samples of useless or inoperative enactments, to show how curiously the history of a bygone age is reflected in its legislation.

Here in the midst of provisions confirming or modifying feudal privileges and liabilities is, "The Sentence of Curse given by the Bishops against the Breakers of the Charters." No less out of place in the Statute-book, according to modern notions, is "The Award made between the King and his Commons at Kenilworth." Next, we light upon enactments prescribing "The Remedy if a Distress be impounded in a Castle or Fortress," and prohibiting the custom of distraining upon one foreigner for the debt of another. By the famous Statute *Circumspectè Agatis* laymen are restrained from laying violent hands on a clerk, while other Acts warn "men of religion" against aggression on their lay neighbours. Then we come to a whole series of sumptuary laws, and laws for the encouragement or discipline of particular trades. Bread and ale are placed under special protection; butchers and cooks are forbidden to buy flesh of Jews, and sell the same to Christians; exporters of wool are to give surety to import silver in return; iron is not to be exported at all; "no shoemaker shall be a tanner, nor any tanner a shoemaker;" yet (by a later Statute) "shoemakers may tan leather till the next Parliament;" all merchandises of a certain kind are to be carried to Calais; gowns and mantles are to be worn of a specified length; salmon, herring, and eels are to be packed in a specified manner; long-bows are not to cost more than a specified sum; calves are not to be killed at the will of their owners; the "breade of horsys" is subjected to State control; and "the stuffynge of feather-beds" does not escape the vigilance of Parliament. Most of these Acts, and a very large per-centage of all those which are proposed for repeal, have reference to a state of society which has little in common with our own. Instead of enacting that "every one may put his child to school," we debate now-a-days as to whether he should not be compelled to do so; and, instead of fixing the rate of workmen's wages by Act of Parliament, we tolerate a liberty of combination which sometimes enables them to exact more than the market value of their labour. If the habit of "telling slanderous Lyes of the Great Men of the Realm" is not quite extinct, it is no longer checked by penalties, and we are content to leave "fonde and fantasticale Prophesies" to refute themselves.

The expurgation by which it was proposed to rid the Statute-book of this lumber was originated some 250 years ago, by Bacon, as stated in pp. 104—105; but the statutes which he marked, before the Restoration or the Revolution, before the Union of Scotland or Ireland, before the abolition of the feudal tenures, before the passing of the Habeas Corpus Act, still encumber the Statute-book; and the plain, sensible, and unanswerable suggestions which he threw out for the heroic work of consolidating the statutes have remained without effect. Each succeeding generation has employed itself in adding something more to that mass of evil which the great philosopher felt and denounced. If the mind of Bacon was shocked at the tangled labyrinth of our Statute Law in the reign of James I., if Sir Matthew Hale occupied his mind with the same subject in the reign of Charles II., what would they have said could they have foreseen the 10,000 statutes passed in the reign of George III., and the Ossa which the industry of the last forty-five years has piled upon the shoulders of that mighty Pelion?

Secret of Success at the Bar.

Sir Thomas Buxton relates that he once asked Sir James Scarlett what was the secret of his pre-eminent success as an advocate He replied that he took care to press home the one principal point of the case, without paying much attention to the others. He also said that he knew the secret of being short. "I find," said he, "that when I exceed half an hour I am always doing mischief to my client; if I drive into the heads of the jury important matter, I drive out matter more important that I had previously lodged there."

Queen's Serjeants, Queen's Counsel, and Serjeants-at-Law.

To remove certain doubts of very recent growth (cast upon a matter previously deemed plain enough), the following statement is the result of a very careful inquiry:—Queen's serjeants are sworn to " serve and counsel the Queen and duly to minister the Queen's affairs, and sue the Queen's process after the course of the law and after their cunning, and they are to take no fee of any one against the Queen." Queen's counsel, as distinguished from Queen's serjeants, are appointed by Letters Patent under the Great Seal, giving them precedence " in our courts as elsewhere." The oath administered to Queen's counsel is precisely the same as the oath administered to Queen's serjeants. Next after Queen's counsel come serjeants-at-law, who, on taking their degree, swear that they shall " serve the Queen's people and truly counsel them that retain them, after their cunning." Sometimes a serjeant-at-law,

applies for a " Patent of Precedence," which gives him precedence
next after the last of the Queen's counsel previously appointed.
No oath is administered on the grant of a patent of precedence, as
it implies no special service or duty to the Crown.

Do not make your Son an Attorney.

Apart from the heavy expenses which must, even under the
most favourable circumstances, attend the introduction of a youth
into the legal profession, the fact must never be lost sight of that
the examination which articled clerks are now called upon to pass
before they can be admitted is of such a rigorous nature that perhaps not one in ten of the established practising attorneys could
undergo the ordeal.   Then, if we consider that the legal profession is at the present moment vastly overstocked, and reflect upon
the fact of numbers of clever young men, who finding it impossible to beat out a connexion for themselves, either make for one
of the colonies, or settle down at home in managing clerkships,
at salaries scarcely equal to the remuneration paid to skilled mechanics, there is quite enough to make us hesitate before placing
our sons in law offices.   Nor must the fact be overlooked, that
the tendency of our legislation has been, and will continue to be,
to simplify legal procedure as much as possible; to lower the
scale of fees payable to attorneys and solicitors, and even to dispense in many instances, with the necessity for employing professional men at all.—*S. Warren, Q.C.*

Appellate Jurisdiction of the House of Lords.

The proper constitution of the Supreme Court of Appeal
justifies the utmost solicitude of the legislature and the country.
The difficulties surrounding its reconstruction were found too
great to admit of solution during the session of 1856, unexpectedly complicated as they were by the creation of that very
distinguished judge, Baron Parke, a peer for life only, as Lord
Wensleydale.   The greatest constitutional lawyers in the House
of Lords, supported by a considerable majority of peers, declared
that the Crown had no power to create a peer for life only, with
a right to sit and vote in that house ; that such an act was illegal,
and that the very essence of the British peerage consisted in its
hereditary character.   Issuing out of these discussions a Bill for
reconstructing the appellate jurisdiction was sent down from the
Lords to the Commons, but so late in the session that they declined then to entertain it.   Whatever may be the ultimate fate
of this measure, it is still practicable, even without adopting its

special machinery, to preserve the appellate jurisdiction of the House of Lords—itself an object of the highest importance—by providing for more assistance from the legal and equitable judicial force of the country. In the meantime a well-earned hereditary peerage was conferred on Lord Wensleydale, under which he took his seat before the session closed.—*Blackstone's Commentaries,* edited by Warren.

Payment of an Advocate.

In 1863, Chief Justice Erle gave judgment in the case of Kennedy *v.* Broun, which involved the right of the plaintiff, a barrister, to recover the sum of 20,000*l.*, alleged to have been promised by Mrs. Broun, then Mrs. Swinfen, for professional services rendered in the matter of the Swinfen estates; the trial at Warwick having been compromised by Lord Chelmsford, then Sir Frederick Thesiger. An action was brought by Mr. Kennedy to recover the 20,000*l.* in question, and a verdict was given in his favour. A rule was obtained to set aside that verdict and enter it for the defendant. The Chief Justice, in a most elaborate judgment, said that the relation of the parties, as advocate and client, incapacitated the latter from making any promise of remuneration which could be recovered as a debt. The payment to an advocate was as *honorarium,* not *merces*—and the opinion of all the judges, from the days of Justinian to the present time, supported that view. The rule for a new trial to enter the verdict for the defendants was therefore absolute. This of course quashed Mr. Kennedy's claim.

Utter-Barristers.

"The term 'Utter-Barrister' occurs for the first time in the reign of Henry VIII. It is mentioned in the 'Orders and Customs' of the Middle Temple, where it is applied to one who, having continued in the house for five or six years, and profited in the study of the law, has been called by the benchers 'to plead, argue, and dispute some doubtful matter before certain of the benchers,' which 'manner of argument or disputations is called *motyng;* and this making of Utter-Barristers is as a preferment or degree given him for his learning.'"

Fifty years ago no junior barrister presumed to carry a bag in the Court of Chancery, unless one had been presented to him by the King's counsel, who, when a junior was advancing in practice, took an opportunity of complimenting him on his increase of business, and giving him his own bag to carry home his papers. It was then a distinction to carry a bag, and a proof that a junior was rising in his own profession.

What was Special Pleading?

From a period of very remote antiquity down to the passing of the Common Law Procedure Act, 1852, the pleadings in our Law Courts were of a highly artificial character, and had been elaborated, by the care of judges and practitioners during many successive centuries, into a regular system or science, called *pleading*, or more properly, *special pleading*, which constituted a d.s-tinct branch of the Law, with treatises and professors of its own. It was a system highly rated by our ancient lawyers, and had at least the merit of developing the point in controversy with the severest precision. But its strictness and subtlety were a frequent subject of complaint; and one object of the Common Law Procedure Act, 1852, was to relax and simplify its rules. Whether the effect of this will be to impair its value or not in other respects, experience alone can decide.—*Stephen's Commentaries*, note.

Lord Campbell studied, at Lincoln's Inn, the mysteries of special pleading, under the guidance of Mr. Tidd, through whom he traced his legal pedigree up to the celebrated Tom Warren, father of this wondrous art. Tom Warren begat Serjeant Runnington, Serjeant Runnington begat Tidd, Tidd begat Campbell, and Campbell begat Dundas and Vaughan Williams. "Tidd," writes his grateful pupil, "lived to see four sons sitting together in the House of Lords—Lord Lyndhurst, Lord Denman, Lord Cottenham, and Lord Campbell. To the unspeakable advantage of having been three years his pupil, I chiefly ascribe my success at the bar."

What is Evidence?

Mr. Stephen, in his able Treatise on the Criminal Law of England, gives the follow definitions of Evidence:

All the facts with which we are acquainted, visible or invisible, internal or external, are connected together in a vast series of sequences which we call cause and effect; and the constitution of things is such, that men are able to infer from one fact the existence, either past or future, of other facts. For instance, we infer from a footmark on soft ground that a foot has been impressed upon it. From the fact that a man is planting his foot on soft ground, we infer that if he completes that motion a footmark will appear. Any specific fact, or set of facts, employed for the purpose of inferring therefrom the existence of any other fact, is said to be evidence of the fact. Suppose the question is whether John Smith is living or dead: A says, "I knew John Smith, and I saw him die." B says, "I knew

John Smith. I saw him in bed; he looked very ill. I shortly afterwards heard he was dead, and saw a funeral procession, which I attended, and which every one said was his funeral, leave his house and go to the church-yard, where I saw a coffin buried with his name on it." C says, " Z told me that he heard from X that John Smith was dead." D says, "I had a dream that John Smith was dead." Each of these facts, if used for the purpose of supporting the inference that John Smith was really dead, would be evidence of his death. The assertions of A and B would, under ordinary circumstances, be convincing ; that of C far from satisfactory, and that of D altogether idle, except to a very superstitious person. This would be usually expressed by saying that the assertions of A and B would be good evidence, that of C weak evidence, and that of D no evidence at all of the fact of the death. But this is not quite a correct way of speaking ; whether one fact is evidence of another, depends on the way in which it is used. If people usually believed in dreams, the assertion that a man had dreamt of John Smith's death would be evidence of his death. Whether or not it would be wise to allow it to be evidence of his death, would depend on the further question, whether in point of fact the practice of inferring the truth of the dream from the fact of its occurrence, usually produced true belief.

It would, unquestionably, aid the ends of justice if the real nature of evidence were better understood ; which can only be assisted by the right use of reason.

What is Trial?

The decision of fact, which constitutes in every civilized country the chief business of courts of justice; for experience will abundantly show that above a hundred of our lawsuits arise from disputed facts, for one where the law is doubted.

About twenty days in the year, says Blackstone, are sufficient in Westminster Hall to settle, upon solemn argument, every demurrer or point of law that arises throughout the nation; but two months are annually spent in deciding the truth of facts before six distinct tribunals, exclusive of Middlesex and London, which afford a supply of causes much more than equivalent to any two of the largest circuits. (3 Bl. Com. 320.) The state of things in our own days is substantially the same.—*Stephen's Commentaries.*

Trial by Jury.

In England, when the aspect of the French Revolution divided our public men into factions—in the evil time, when statesmen had talked complacently "of a vigour beyond the law," when judges had tortured free speech into sedition, and when open violence and secret art were sapping the liberties we prize most dearly, English juries, with the approbation of the country, interposed frequently against political wrong, and vindicated the good cause that elsewhere had been abandoned. As for the loyalty and good sense of the nation as a whole, the mode in which it obeyed the Government attests this in a remarkable way; and though, of course, the Revolution in France stirred up some elements of disorder here, they were as nothing among the great mass of Englishmen. This truth is urged by Mr. Massey with more force than by any other historian, and it deserves to be put prominently forward, as several writers have asserted the contrary. In his very instructive summary of the state of English opinion at this period, he says:

" Because freedom had been abused at Paris, the liberties of Englishmen were assailed. The press was put under restraint; legions of spies were let loose upon the country, and no man could speak his mind in safety, or even do the most harmless act without fear of question. It is no wonder that the old English feeling was aroused, and that the State trials of 1794 were regarded with an intensity of interest which had not been equalled since that of the Seven Bishops. The public safety at that time depended on the trial by jury, and men were satisfied that their liberties were safe when it appeared that the great institution which had so often sustained them was still sound and unshaken. . . . Happily the prosecutions failed, and from their failure was derived that security which but for these trials would not have been ascertained.—*Times review of Massey's History of England.*

That sound and experienced judge, Sir John Coleridge, in a lecture delivered by him at the Athenæum, Exeter, stated that

He had been a judge for an unusually long period, and he should ever regard with admiration the manner in which juries discharged their duties. Again and again he had reason to marvel at their patience, and again and again he had observed questions put by a jury which had been omitted by counsel and judge, the answer to which had thrown a light that had guided them to the truth of the whole matter. He had often thought if he had the appointment of the magistrates in the country, that he would appoint those gentlemen who had served on petty juries on the Crown side for two assizes at least; for he was sure that a more practical knowledge of criminal law was learnt in that way than could be acquired by several months of careful reading. One thing should always be remembered, that stupid verdicts were no arguments against the institution, for no human institution, however wise in itself, could be expected to work perfectly. Let them improve their jurymen by raising the character of their national education; let them introduce into their panels all classes who by law were liable to serve; and when they had done that, and not till then, if they found it to fail, let them condemn the institution. They lived under a law which, though far from perfect, was framed in a wise and just spirit. They could not possibly overrate the blessing which they possessed, yet it was so much a matter of course that they were apt to think as little of it as they did of the sun that shone upon them from Heaven.

Attendance of Jurors.

The law on this subject has been thus concisely explained by Mr. Under-Sheriff Burchell. At the present period, persons who claim to be excused from attending as jurors should get their names removed from the jury-list. In July, within the first week, the Clerk of the Peace is to issue his warrant to the high constable for the overseers to prepare and make out a list of persons qualified as jurors. For three weeks in September the list is to be exhibited on the doors of churches and chapels, with a notification where objections are to be heard. Within the last seven days of September the justices are to hold a petty sessions to hear objections. If persons having exemptions do not attend to the subject, they may be returned and be liable to serve until the list is corrected in the September following. Some complaints are made of persons being returned by parish officers who had either removed or been dead for years. The law as stated prevails throughout the counties of England.

The Law of Libel.

It would be useless to attempt to define, within our limit, the principles of the Law of Libel—it would be attended with fruitless results; but we may be permitted to give such an outline of the subject as may be useful for reflection and research, if not for immediate practice. Now that the old saying, "The greater truth the greater libel," is no longer applicable even to indictments for defamation, the popular idea of what is and what is not actionable is correct, so far as it goes. It is now generally understood that a false and malicious attack upon another man's character is in all cases illegal; that a somewhat less offensive imputation than would support an action for mere words will render its author liable in damages if it be conveyed in writing, but that the law deems all statements of this kind to be justifiable which can be shown to be true. For the ordinary intercourse of life these rules and cautions are sufficient. No one can speak ill of his neighbour with impunity, unless he is prepared to make good his words to the letter; or, at least, to prove that they were spoken without malice or on a lawful occasion. With regard to the Press, it has been proclaimed again and again from the judicial Bench, that "fair comments" in a journal or periodical are not within the Law

I

of Libel; but, then, what is to be the test of "fairness"? It is quite possible that a journalist's comments may be made *bonâ fide* and out of a regard for the public welfare, and yet may be incapable in their very nature of legal proof. In the case of Campbell v. Spottiswoode, the former obtained a verdict against the printer of the *Saturday Review* for an alleged calumny against himself as editor and part-proprietor of the *British Standard and Ensign.* The defendant's counsel relied at the trial, and in his argument before the Court of Queen's Bench, on the "general privilege" of all who discuss public questions without actual malice. The Lord Chief Justice and the Court decided against him, on the ground that there is no such general privilege; and that the imputation of base motives throws upon a public critic, as it would upon a private detractor, the necessity of bringing them home to the party maligned. According to this doctrine, the jury is not to be allowed to compare the comments with the evidence before the writer, and to say whether they were "fair" and justified by appearances. Nothing short of their being strictly true in fact, and proved to be so in open court, will relieve the latter of his liability.

Nevertheless, we have the authority of the Lord Chief Justice (Erle) of the Common Pleas (Turnbull v. Bird, 1861), for the principle that very strong and injurious language, if provoked and employed "for the purpose of maintaining the truth," "without any corrupt motive," may be innocent in the view of the law. We have the sanction of the same eminent Judge that "a man may publish defamatory matter in defence either of his private or his public rights. Every subject of this realm has a right to comment upon the acts of public men, for they concern him as such subject; but he must not make his commentary a cloak for malice. Such a commentary, however libellous, is justifiable if the defendant honestly believes that he is writing what is fair and just; but if he makes wilful misrepresentation, or misstatement that might have been avoided by ordinary care, his protection ceases." We find it assumed by Chief Justice Erle, and stated in plain terms by Mr. Justice Willes, that there is such a thing as a "*privilege* of fair discussion on a matter of public interest," though two of the learned Judges of the Queen's Bench were at much pains to show that a right belonging to all her Majesty's subjects cannot properly be called a "privilege." Moreover, we have the general but most emphatic testimony of Lord Ellenborough, that where the "object" is "to correct misrepresentations of fact, to refute sophistical reasoning, to expose a vicious taste in literature, or to censure what is hostile to morality," there can be no libel.

In a case against the *Lincolnshire Chronicle,* the Judge, Mr. Justice Coleridge, laid down the law as follows:

· "In discussing the public conduct of a public man, a journalist might certainly use the most unceremonious freedom, and juries should not be nice in criticising the language in which the censure might be conveyed, if they could see that the motive and spirit of the whole were public and honest. On the other hand, no newspaper was justified in commenting upon the private life even of a public man; but the present appeared to be an intermediate case. The plaintiff filled a public situation, but it could hardly be said that the paragraph was merely a comment upon his conduct as alderman, neither did it relate to a strictly private matter. The most objectionable paragraph appeared to him to be that which imputed to the plaintiff ' confused notions on the important matters of *meum* and *tuum*,' but the jury must look at the whole, and say whether in their opinion it exceeded the bounds of fair comment upon the conduct of a person filling the position which the plaintiff filled. The jury found a verdict for the defendant."

But, by the judicial *dicta* in Campbell v. Spottiswoode, no greater latitude is allowed in comments on public topics than in remarks on private affairs. Any theoretical indulgence to the former, whether it be called privilege or not, is a worthless boon if truth, or rather legal demonstration, is to be the only test of " libel or no libel" for literary critiques. As Mr. Bovill well pointed out, no privilege is wanted where truth can be successfully pleaded. On the other hand, no privilege is demanded where malice can be established against the writer, or inferred by the jury from the tone and spirit of the composition. It is where a public critic, with the best and purest intentions, has injured the good name of a public man that the question arises. The great difficulty is to render the Press harmless to individuals, and yet to leave it powerful for good.—*Abridged from the Times.*

With regard to the propagation of Libel, " it may be some doubt in the eye of morality, whether the purchaser of a satirical libel does not share in the guilt of the author ; and whether the pleasure in reading it is not of a criminal sort, and a proof of the malignity of human nature. There would be no thieves nor stolen goods, experience tells us, if there were no receivers ; and no scurrilous writings nor libellous prints would be published, to corrupt the ear or gratify the impudence of the eye, if there were no purchasers." These sentiments are from Bayle's *Essay on Defamatory Libels ;* and we remember Lord Brougham to have once expressed himself in almost the identical words of Bayle, in a speech on the Newspaper Stamp Duty.

Induction of a Rector.

The ceremony of inducting a clergyman to his benefice is briefly as follows: the instance being the induction of the Rev.

Pascoe Grenfell Hill, Feb. 9, 1863, to the benefice of the united parishes of St. Edmund the King and St. Nicholas, Lombard-street. The Rev. Mr. Hill brought with him the Rev. J. Lupton, who performed the office of induction. The reverend Chaplain, therefore, accompanied by the Rev. Mr. Hill, proceeded to the church-door in Lombard-street, and the Clerk having put the key into the lock of the door, the Chaplain took Mr. Hill's right hand, and placing it on the key thus inserted in the lock, said, holding the archdeacon's mandate in his hand, "By virtue of this instrument, I, James Lupton, Rector of St. Michael's, Queenhithe, induct you into the real, actual, and corporal posses-sion of the United Rectory of St. Edmund the King and Martyr with St. Nicholas Acons, with all its fruits, members, and appur-tenances." The new Rector then opened the church door, and having entered the church, shut himself in, and then pulled one of the bells, so as to assure the public that he was in the church and had taken possession of it. He then returned to the church-door, opened it, and let his friends and the officials in.

Benefit of Clergy.

The privilege of Benefit of Clergy,—*Privilegium Clericale*—arose in the pious regard paid by Christian princes to the Church in its infant state, and consisted of—1st, an exemption of places consecrated to religious duties from criminal arrests, which was the foundation of sanctuaries; 2nd, exemption of the persons of clergymen from criminal process before the secular judge, in par-ticular cases, which was the original meaning of the *privilegium clericale*. In the course of time, however, the *benefit of clergy* ex-tended to every one who could read, for such was the ignorance of those periods, that *this* was thought a great proof of learning; and it was enacted, that from the scarcity of clergy in the realm of England, there should be a prerogative allowed to the clergy, that if any man who could read were to be condemned to death, the bishop of the diocese might, if he would, claim him as a clerk, and dispose of him in some places of the clergy as he might deem meet; but if the bishop would not demand him, or if the prisoner could not read, then he was to be put to death. 3 Ed-ward I., 1274.—Benefit of Clergy was abolished by statute 7th and 8th George IV., c. 28.

The King's Book.

"The King's Book," so frequently mentioned in connexion with the value of church livings, is the Return of the Comm.ssioners appointed under 26 Henry VIII., c. 3, to value the first-fruits and tenths bestowed by that Act upon the King. The valuation then made is still in force, and the record containing it is that commonly known as the Kings' Book (the *Valor Ecclesiasticus*, &c.) which has been printed by the Record Commission.

Compulsory Attendance at Church.

We do not find any very early regulations made to enforce the observation of festivals among Christians. The Middle Ages are somewhat more prolific. Attendance at church on the principal festivals was made a subject of inquiry, about A.D. 900, in Abbot Regino's articles; and by that of Clovishoff, in 905, the clergy are enjoined to be more diligent in teaching, and the people to be more regular in their attendance. This observance is also enjoined by the laws of Canute, about 1032, which decree "all divine rites and offices, let every one studiously keep and observe; the feast-days and the fasts, let him celebrate with the utmost ceremony." After the Conquest, the synod of Exeter, 1287, includes the "festival days," with the Lord's days, among those when the people ought specially to attend the churches. And Ascension Day, the feast of Corpus Christi, the high feast of the Assumption of our blessed Lady, and All Saints' Day, are included with the Lord's days, in the 27th Henry VI. (1450) in the list of days whereon the holding of fairs is prohibited.

The Acts by which at the Reformation it was attempted to secure the due attendance of the people upon the remodelled services include "the other days ordained and used to be kept as holidays." But the application of their provisions to the attendance upon other holidays than Sundays, seems to have been pretty soon dropped. The statute of James the First, re-enacting the penalty of 1s. for default in attendance at church, is limited to Sundays; and the latter day alone is mentioned in the Acts of William and Mary, and George III.; by which exceptions in favour of dissenters from the Church of England were introduced. Mr. Neale, however, cites several cases which appear to settle that the ecclesiastical courts have not the power to compel any person to attend his parish church, because they have no right to decide the bounds of parishes.

The repeal of the Act enjoining attendance at church on the 5th of November, so far as Roman Catholics are concerned, by the 7 and 8 Victoria, c. 102, removing the penalties to which they stood exposed up to the year 1844, must be looked upon more as a piece of consistency in legislation than as the removal of a possible grievance. And a somewhat similar remark may be made in respect to members of the Church of England, upon the total repeal of the 1st of Elizabeth, so far as concerns the penalty of 1s., for non-attendance at church on holidays. As the statute of James applies solely to Sundays, there is now no civil punishment left for this neglect: though it would appear to remain punishable, under the 5th and 6th of Edward VI., by ecclesiastical censures.—*Neale's Feasts and Fasts*, p. 307.

Among the recent cases of prosecution, in a Treatise on Sir Matthew Hale's *History of the Pleas of the Crown*, by Professor Amos, the following passage occurs under "Repealed Statutes:"

" In the year 1817, at the Spring Assizes for Bedford, Sir Montague Burgoyne was prosecuted for having been absent from his parish church for several months: the action was defeated by proof of the defendant having been indisposed. In the *Report* of Prison Inspectors to the House of Lords, in 1841, it appeared that in 1830, ten persons were in prison for recusancy in not attending their parish churches. A mother was prosecuted by her own son."

The Mark of the Cross.

The old Danish laws made it obligatory upon those who could not write to affix their *bomærke* (house-mark); and the Russians required a mark, or a cross. The probable reason why the cross was always used in the Middle Ages in the testing of ecclesiastical charters was not only that it was a sacred symbol, but that Justinian had decreed it should have the strength of an oath.—*B. Williams, F.S.A.*; *Archæologia*, xxxvii. p. 384.

Sir Henry Spelman tells us that " The Saxons in their deeds observed no set forme, but used honest and perspicuous words to express the thing intended with all brevity, yet not wanting the essential parts of a deed: as the names of the donor and donee, the consideration, the certainty of the thing given, the limitation of the estate, the reservation if any were, and the names of the witnesses, which always were many, some for the one part, and some for the other. As for dating, it was not usual amongst them. Seals they used not at all, other than (the common seal of Christianity) the sign of the Cross, which they, and all nations following the Greek and Roman Church, accompted the most solemn and inviolable manner of confirming."

Marriage-Law of England.

On the 17th of March, 1835, Dr. Lushington, in the House of Commons, stated the history and principle of the Marriage Law of England thus—" By the ancient law of this country as to marriages, a marriage was good if celebrated in the presence of two witnesses, though without the intervention of a priest. But then came the decision of the Council of Trent rendering the solemnization by a priest necessary. At the Reformation we refused to accept the provision of the Council of Trent; and in consequence, the question was reduced to this state—that a marriage by civil contract was valid. But there was this extraordinary anomaly in the law, that the practice of some of our civil courts required, in certain instances and for some purposes, that the marriage should be celebrated in a particular form. It turned out that a marriage by civil contract was valid for some purposes, while for others—such as the descent of the real property to the heirs of the marriage—it was invalid. Thus, a man in the presence of a witness, accepting a woman for his wife, *per verba de præsenti*, the marriage was valid, as I have said, for some purposes, but for others to make it valid it was necessary that it should be celebrated *in facie ecclesiæ*. This was the state of the law till the passing of the Marriage Act in 1754."

"Marriage, in its origin, (says Lord Stowell,) is a contract of natural law: it may exist between two individuals of different sexes although no third person existed in the world, as happened in the case of the common ancestors of mankind. In civil society it becomes a civil contract, regulated and prescribed by law, and endowed with civil consequences. In most civilized countries, acting under a sense of the force of sacred obligations, it has had the sanction of religion superadded. It then becomes a religious as well as a natural and civil contract; for it is a great mistake to suppose that, because it is the one, it may not likewise be the other."—(2 *Hagg. Cons. Rep.* 63.)

Marriage Fines.

In the feudal times, the lord might object to the marriage of a bondman's daughter with a stranger, even of her own condition; and by marriage with a freeman she became free during coverture, if not free for ever; this and the lord's approval of her marriage being purchasable by fine. At Swincombe, in Oxfordshire, the bondman could not get a husband for his daughter, and could not take to himself a wife, without the lord's permission.

Although a fine used to be paid by a freeman in the occupation of bond-land, on the marriage of his daughter, there was no more degradation in such a fine than there now is in the Archbishop of Canterbury's charge for a marriage-licence. At Southfleet, Friendsbury, Wouldham, and other places in their neighbourhood, a tenant who wished to give his daughter in marriage had to an-

nounce the marriage to the warden or bailiff of the village, and
to invite him to the wedding; the girl could not be married to
any one out of the manor without the lord's good-will; an heiress
could not be married even to a neighbour without the lord's consent. A tenant at Headington, Oxon, paid no fine on the marriage of his daughter within the manor—he paid two shillings for
leave to give her in marriage to a stranger; but we are told that
payment was on account of the chattels which might be removed
out of the manor with her. When we consider the lord of a
manor to be the patron and protector of all within it, there seems
to be nothing very offensive in this arrogation of assent to the
marriage of his tenant's daughter.

Irregular Marriages.

Little more than a century ago, a common notion prevailed
that the performance of the marriage ceremony by a person in
holy orders rendered it sacred and indissoluble, without regard
to any other condition: Hence arose the scandals and indecencies
of the Fleet Marriages, *i.e.*, marriages performed in the Fleet
prison, and its neighbourhood, by a set of drunken, swearing
parsons, and their myrmidons, who wore black coats, and pretended to be clerks and registrars to the Fleet. Those malpractices
were put an end to by the Marriage Act of 1754: the register-
books were purchased by Government in 1821, and deposited in
the Bishop of London's Registry. A similar abuse flourished
at May Fair, until it was abolished by the Act of 1754, when the
register-books were deposited in St. George's church, Hanover-
square.

The "Border Marriages" were also of this class of abuses,
and arose from nothing formerly having been necessary in Scotland to constitute a man and woman husband and wife save a
declaration of consent by the parties before witnesses, or even
such a declaration in writing without any witnesses: a marriage
which was considered binding in all respects. Still, a marriage in
Scotland, not celebrated by a clergyman, except these "Border
Marriages," was rarely or never heard of. They were performed
at Lamberton toll-bar, about three miles north of Berwick-upon-
Tweed; and at Gretna Green, the nearest locality accessible to
strangers actually within the territory of Scotland.* The pre-
liminaries of such a marriage used to be a long purse in hand or
in prospect, for the purpose of meeting heavy posting expenses,
and bribes to secure speed. In the course of time, facility of tra-

---

* See *Things not generally Known*, First Series, pp. 120—121. *Popular
Errors Explained*, p. 207.

velling by railway, and of obtaining licensed carriages from the stands in towns, increased; and the farm-servants and the servants generally in the Border counties began to avail themselves of what was deemed a lawful practice by their superiors from other places. During the holidays for farm-servants, at Whitsuntide and Martinmas, the times of the statute-hirings, parties generally under the influence of drink, and too often tipsy, would hire carriages in Carlisle, and drive, by the two or three couples in a carriage, over the Border to get married in Scotland; they would live together for two or three days, then go to their services, and perhaps never again think of their having been married at all; or not till circumstances might arise making it worth the while of one of the parties to claim conjugal rights, with a view to participation in an inheritance of property—a not uncommon accident among the natives of the Border Counties.

Under this state of affairs, at the Spring Assizes at Carlisle, in 1856, there were three trials for bigamy; upon the increase of which crime the Judge made some serious remarks to the Grand Jury, in his charge. A magistrate of Cumberland, having leisure time, and a sufficient acquaintance with the Marriage Laws of England and Scotland, to avoid falling into any gross error, set to work to frame Petitions to Parliament and the Home Secretary, reciting that such petitions were from the Magistrates of Cumberland, charged with the suppression of vice and immorality in their county; that a state of irregularity which had formerly been permitted in the Law of Marriage had grown into an abuse, under a change of circumstances; that the Petitioners thought that the young people of their county acted more out of levity and under excitement, than from any real want of good principle; and that they submitted the exigencies of the case might be met by requiring all parties, *not being natives of Scotland,* and wishing to be married in Scotland, to acquire *domicile* in Scotland, by a residence of a fixed number of days, prior to being considered entitled to the privilege of the laws relating to marriage in Scotland; and prayed that the parties petitioned would authorize such measures, &c. The Bench of Magistrates mostly approved of the petitions, one alone declining to sign. The clerical magistrates generally abstained from signing, urging that if they did sign, it might be objected that they had been instigated through interested motives. The petitions were signed by all the lay magistrates attending the Session at Whitehaven, and were forwarded to London for presentation; the Hon. Charles Howard taking charge of the petition to the Commons, but with misgivings as to its success; his only hope being that the substance of it might be passed in a clause of the Dissenters' Marriage Bill, then before the House.   Nor was the Home Secretary, Sir George Grey, more sanguine: he promised to look over the petition, adding the state of the feeling of the House was such that it could not be made a Government measure.

The petition to the Lords was taken charge of by Lord Brougham, who was selected because, at the commencement of the Session squibbing speeches had passed between him, with Lord Campbell on his side, and Lord Aberdeen joined by Lord Minto, relative to the laws of Scottish marriages.   Such had also been the case in several sessions prior to the one of 1856: bills had been threatened to be introduced for *altering* the laws of marriage *in Scotland* entirely; but always, after Easter, the matter had been dropped.

At the above interview, Lord Brougham entered upon the state of the case with the Cumberland magistrate, who knew before-hand that a civil marriage between English in Scotland was not deemed valid for the inheritance of the offspring of real estate in England.*   Lord Brougham confirmed this knowledge by citing instances in which real estates in England had not passed to the issue by marriages in Scotland; and he also mentioned that chil-dren born before marriage could be legitimized to the inheritance of estate and title in Scotland, by the subsequent marriage of the mother to the father; and Lord Brougham named, in the House of Lords, an instance of the fact.   His Lordship added that the Law of *Scotland* ought to be changed, and must be changed, when it was replied that his Lordship would find that the object of the magistrates of Cumberland was not to change the Laws of Scotland, but to oblige natives of England to obey the Laws of England.   We mention this to show how widely the ideas were astray from the real object in view.

A Bill founded on the principle of the petitions was introduced by Lord Brougham: it was quickly supported by petitions signed at large meetings convened in the Border Counties; at one of which, in Carlisle, a solicitor mentioned an instance wherein clients of his own had not only been married, but, in the woman's opinion (she having succeeded to some property), *had been divorced* in the course of two or three days, by one of the officiating *marriers* of Gretna.   One of these *marriers*, Murray, of Gretna, admitted that he had married between 700 and 800 couple in a recent year; and as there were two or three other *marriers* in good practice, the number of couples married at Sark toll-bar,

---

* In some cases where parties had been married at Gretna, the marriage used to be repeated, as soon as they returned to England, *in a church.*

and at Gretna, may safely be estimated at upwårds of 1000 in the year.*

When the Bill came to its critical point in the House of Commons, the Lord Advocate for Scotland stated that " seeing that it did not interfere with the Law of Scotland, he should not object to its progress." Thus, the Bill went through its third reading, and passed, within three months from its introduction ; and thus was a stop put to a state of affairs threatening the rapid demoralization of the lower classes in the Border Counties and North-Western parts of England.†

Solemnization of Marriage.

The great facilities for Marriage afforded by the present state of the law will be apparent from the following recapitulation of the various forms and authorities, from the 20th Annual Report of the Registrar-General :

" Marriages may be solemnized—

Authority.

1. According to the rites of the Established Church.
1. Special licence from the Archbishop of Canterbury.
2. Licence from a Surrogate, &c.
3. Publication of banns.
4. Certificate from the Superintendent Registrar.

2. In registered places of worship not of the Established Church.
1. Licence from the Superintendent Registrar.
2. Certificate from the Superintendent Registrar.

3. In the District Register Office.
1. Licence from the Superintendent Registrar.
2. Certificate from the Superintendent Registrar.

4. Between Quakers and between Jews.
1. Licence from the Superintendent Registrar.
2. Certificate from the Superintendent Registrar.

" By the English law as it stood before the passing of the Act of 6 and 7 Will. IV., c. 85, no marriage could be lawfully solemnized (except where both the parties were Quakers or Jews respectively) in any other place than

---

* In 1815 the number of marriages celebrated at Gretna was stated in Brewster's *Edinburgh Encyclopædia*, at 65, which produced about 1000*l*. at the rate of fifteen guineas each : Murray, however, charged as low a fee as sixpence each.

† For the details of these successful steps for the abolition of the Gretna Green marriages, the writer is indebted to the obliging courtesy of a Correspondent who took an active part in the measure.

a church or public chapel wherein banns might be published, unless by special licence from the Archbishop of Canterbury. This law was enforced by severe penalties; and if any persons intermarried without licence from a competent authority, or without the previous publication of banns, the marriage was null and void to all intents and purposes. Thus all persons (with the exception of Jews and Quakers), whether conforming to the Church of England or not, were compelled to resort to the Established Church in order to have their marriages lawfully solemnized. The boon conferred upon Roman Catholics and Dissenters generally by the amended law of 1836, which enables them to marry in their own places of worship and according to their own forms, may well be appreciated. The Act of 1856, besides abolishing the objectionable practice of reading notices of marriage before boards of guardians, has sanctioned marriage out of the district in the 'usual place of worship' of one of the parties, and reduced the interval between the giving of notice of marriage by licence and the grant of the licence from seven days to one clear day."

The Law of Copyright.

The *Publishers' Circular* gives the following summary of facts respecting the Copyright Laws :—In our own country, the copyright lasts 42 years absolutely for the author's life, and seven years after his death. In Greece and in Sardinia it lasts only 15 years from the date of publication. In the Roman States it extends to 12 years after the author's death. In Russia it lasts for 25 years after the author's death, and for ten years more if a new edition has been published in the last five years of the first term. In Belgium and Sweden it lasts 20 years after the author's death, with a provision in Sweden, that, should the representative of the author neglect to continue the publication, the copyright falls to the State. In France it lasts for the benefit of children or widow (that is, to the widow if she be what is called in France *en communauté de biens*, a peculiar arrangement in French marriage settlements, which establishes between husband and wife a perfect community in each other's property) 30 years after the author's death, but to other representatives only 10 years. In Spain it lasts 50 years, reckoning from the author's death. In Austria, Bavaria, Portugal, Prussia, Saxony, the Kingdom of the Two Sicilies, Wurtemberg, and the States of the Germanic Confederation, it lasts 30 years from the author's death, to all his heirs and assigns without distinction; and in Denmark, so recently as 1858, it lasted an indefinite period, provided the work was kept in print; now, however, it is restricted to a period of 30 years after the author's death, with a provision that republication by others is permitted when five years have elapsed in which a work has been out of print. In the United States, copyright lasts for

28 years, and an extension of 14 years granted to the author if he lives, or to his widow, children, and grandchildren. With regard to lectures, sermons, &c., the law of France appears to be that professors and preachers have the sole right of reproducing their lectures and sermons in print; but that advocates and political speakers, while they alone have the right to publish their speeches in a collective or separate form, cannot prevent their being published in the journals of the time as news.

Holding over after Lease.

The doctrine is well established—viz., that where a tenant by lease holds over after the determination of the term, and pays rent, he becomes a tenant from year to year, *under all the conditions of the expired lease consistent with such a tenancy.* Baron Watson remarks—" It is important that no doubt should be thrown upon a question of such very general importance, as a great many of the houses in London and throughout the country are occupied by tenants holding over."

Abolition of the Hop Duty.

The 15th September, 1862, dates the freedom of English Hops from Excise impost, and the abolition of Customs duties upon foreign Hops. Time alone can show the effect so serious a change will have on the average prices of a produce of increasing importance throughout the world. The general opinion is that under perfect freedom of trade hops will vary in price in each d.strict of production only in proportion to their quality and the cost of transport; and that consumers will find prices more uniformly even than has hitherto been known, since the simultaneous failure in the crop at home and abroad is beyond probability. This tax was first imposed by Mr. Harley in the year 1711; and its removal will make the hopgrower in future free from those heavy losses which the Duty inflicted on him in years of large crops and small prices. Hopgrowing has now become a simple farming operation, left to natural causes. It might be that, owing to the costly nature of the production and the precarious nature of the crop, it would always remain a somewhat more speculative branch of business than any other branch of farming. It is, however, thought that the supply of hops will be more abundant, and, above all, more steady and uniform from year to year. The consequence will be that the beer we drink will be more wholesome. Burton, in his *Anatomy of Melancholy,* says: " Beer made without hops is productive of heaviness and melancholy; but that well hopped is an antidote to it."

Customs of Gavelkind.

The well-known treatise, entitled "The Common Law of Kent; or the Customs of Gavelkind, with the Decisions concerning Borough-English," by Thomas Robinson, with additions by J. D. Norwood, comprehends everything relating to the subject, embracing all that is useful in Somner, Tayler, and Lambarde, as well as a full account of both tenure and custumal. The work contains chapters on the etymology and significations of the word Gavelkind; on the antiquity and universality of partible descents in England; on the places out of Kent where the custom of gavelkind may be alleged and maintained; on the manner of pleading the custom, and the difference between that and other counties, and between the general and special customs; on what lands and tenements in Kent are of the nature of gavelkind; of the effect of the alteration of the tenure and of the disgavelling statutes; on the nature of gavelkind in reference to descent and partition, and the remedy for and against parceners by the custom; on the special customs incident to gavelkind lands in Kent, tenancy by the courtesy; of dower, of customary wardship, and of alienation by any infant tenant in gavelkind; the father to the bough and the son to the plough, and the custumal of Kent with precedents. The principal peculiarities which distinguish socage lands subject to the custom of gavelkind from free or common socage are—1. That the lands descend to all males in equal degree, in equal shares. 2. That the husband is tenant by the courtesy of his deceased wife's lands, whether there were issue born alive or not. 3. That the widow is dowable of one-half instead of the third. 4. That an infant may alien by feoffment at the age of fifteen. 5. That upon a conviction of felony, there is no escheat by reason of corruption of blood; corruption of blood only occurs now in cases of treason, petit treason, and murder—see 54 G. 3, c. 145. These peculiarities do not recommend themselves as possessing so great advantages as to induce us to continue a system of law in Kent different from the rest of England. One of its great disadvantages is the difficulty of deducing the title, on account of the complicated subdivisions of the estate.

Treasure Trove.

Treasure Trove (from the French *trouver*, to find, *trouvé*, found) is the law by which money, or other treasure, found hidden, is adjudicated to the legal claimant.

In 1863, Mr. F. Peel, (one of the Secretaries to the Treasury,) stated in Parliament :

It was by no means an unreasonable or absurd law that when an article of gold or silver, belonging to an unknown owner, was found, it should be held to be the property of the Crown. The rights of the Crown in that respect were not, however, rigidly enforced. The articles found were usually returned to the person who was declared to have the best claim to them; or, if they were of historical interest, they were deposited in the British Museum or some local collection, and their intrinsic value was paid to the finder. What the Treasury desired was to obtain speedy information of the discovery of any treasure trove. The Circular which was issued some time ago was intended to instruct the finders of any treasures how to communicate with the Crown on the subject.* That Circular was subsequently withdrawn because it laid claim to antiquities which were not exactly treasures and did not belong to the Crown, and because it directed a reference to the wrong tribunal in cases of dispute. The draught of another circular was prepared ; but so many difficulties beset the subject that it was not deemed advisable to issue it. If occasion should arise for a new order it would of course be made, but there appeared to be no necessity for one at present.

Sometimes, the right to the property is confirmed by the special conditions of the holding of the property whereon it is found. Thus, at the above date, Lord Palmerston related in Parliament that about two years ago some workmen, when digging a drain on one of his farms, found a gold torque, which his Lordship purchased of the man who discovered it, the value being about 30*l.* Lord Palmerston, however, had an investigation made of the original grant of the farm several centuries ago, and ascertained that it conferred on the grantee all the treasure-trove on the property; wherefore his Lordship felt entitled to keep the relic in question.

In January, 1863, eleven pounds' weight of ancient gold ornaments were ploughed up in the neighbourhood of Hastings, and

---

* This Treasury Minute of July 16, 1861, directs that the superintendents and inspectors of police shall be authorized to receive treasure-trove from the finders, and shall transmit it to the Solicitor of the Treasury, who will ascertain at the Mint the real intrinsic or metallic value of the treasure, and the amount will then be remitted to the finder. Cases will no doubt occur in which rare and valuable coins will be disposed of at a higher price than their bullion value, but they will then find their way into some collection, either public or private, and will not be melted down. It should be generally known that treasure-trove is not claimed peremptorily by the Crown, nor is there any occasion for the finder to sell it to the nearest silversmith under the apprehension that it would have to be given up without compensation.

were sold as old brass, to a man who had been a Californian gold-digger, and recognised the metal as solid gold. He was taken into custody, but discharged, the magistrates having no jurisdiction in the matter, the power of making such an investigation being vested, according to an old statute, (4th Edward I.) in the coroner ; the jury returning a verdict that the gold, (value about 530*l*.) the owner or owners not being known, was the property of the Queen, and that the persons accused had concealed the finding from the Queen and the coroner. This discovery of gold orna-ments, and their almost total destruction, render it desirable that the law of Treasure-trove should be made clear to popular com-prehension : that if it is not just, as seems to be the common impression, it should be amended, and the practice of the Crown, in exercising its conventional rights, defined. At any rate, so long as finders do not know that they will receive full value for dis-coveries, and have not confidence in their appraisement, it is in vain to expect country-folk will yield Treasure-trove to an authority they contemn. In some parts a belief is held that such discoveries entail condign punishment upon the finders : it was formerly a capital offence ; it is now a misdemeanour, punishable by fine and imprisonment.

It is difficult to make the peasantry comprehend manorial rights. A man who finds a treasure in his own ground, and that treasure one which can have no living owner, naturally looks on himself as its rightful possessor. He has probably never heard of King Edward's law of Treasure-trove, and a natural sense of justice does not guide him rightly in the matter. If a liberal reward were given—nearly the *metal* value of the *trouvaille*—it is quite possible that we might have become possessed of many precious relics which now are broken up and consigned to the melting-pot.

In France, the right is more practically understood. Thus, in July, 1863, a pot of louis-d'ors was found in the Rue Lafayette, in Paris, when the following adjustment was made.

One of the labourers while at work, struck his pick on to an earthen jar, which broke, and out of which rolled several pieces of gold. The other workmen hearing the sound, rushed round the spot, probably to ob-tain a share of the treasure, when the latter cried out " Stop ! Form a ring around me, and then let no one move." The others obeyed. He then quietly picked up the pieces of gold, which he placed in his hat, and, taking up the broken jar which contained the remainder, he stood in the midst of the circle, and said, " Now call a sergent-de-ville to accompany me to the nearest police-office, where I will deposit the money." This was done, and the prize was found to consist of 978 gold louis-d'or of twenty-four livres each, bearing the effigies of Louis XV. and XVI., the whole amount-ing to more than 23,000f. The whole was forwarded to the Prefecture of Police, where it was to remain during the inquiry to discover the legitimate owners of the property. It is only after that has been done that the share, attributed by law to the finder of a treasure, will be paid to the lucky workman.

Principal and Agent.

There is a well-known case involving this point, in which the late Lord Abinger differed from the rest of the Court of Exchequer: a plaintiff had employed an agent to let a house for him, and the defendant asked the agent " if there was any objection to the house;" to which the agent in perfect good faith answered, there was not. It turned out, however, that the adjoining premises were of a disreputable character, of which the plaintiff was aware, although his agent was not. The defendant, on the discovery of the objection, refused to fulfil his written contract to take the house; and the question was, whether he was liable for a breach of the agreement. Lord Abinger thought he was not, but the rest of the Court thought he was, and so judgment was given for the plaintiff. Upon merely technical grounds, perhaps, the majority of the learned Barons were right; but no one can read the masterly opinion of Lord Abinger without feeling that the law *ought to be* as he laid it down, and on the broad and simple ground that in such a case the knowledge of the principal should be held to be the knowledge of the agent.

Legal Hints.

Although no book ever was or ever can be written to enable a man to dispense with the assistance of a lawyer in cases where a knowledge of the law is practically required, attention to certain hints may save him from many a scrape. Of this kind are the following from Lord St. Leonards's *Handy-Book:* You should be cautious whom you employ as an auctioneer, for any loss by his insolvency would fall upon you; he is your agent. We may add, however, that he is the agent of both parties, buyer and seller; and for that reason his signature satisfies the Statute of Frauds, and binds both. Again, you may employ *one* person to bid for you at an auction when you sell property, to prevent its going beneath its value; but you must not employ *more than one*, for that would be considered unfair puffing. Never bid for a leasehold estate clogged with the condition that the production of a receipt for the last half-year's rent shall be accepted as proof that all the lessee's covenants were performed up to that period; for there may have been a prior breach of covenant, and the landlord may not have waived his right of entry for the forfeiture. Do not take possession of an estate until objections to the title are

removed, for such a step would in some cases be held to be an
acceptance of the title.   Before you enter an auction-room make
up your mind as to price, and do not be led away by the per-
suasions of the auctioneer, who is the agent of the seller, or the
biddings of others.   Do not sign a contract tendered to you by
the auctioneer, unless a reciprocal contract is signed and delivered
to you at the same time by him.   In writing about the sale or
purchase of an estate, you should always cautiously declare your
offer not to be final, lest the other party should, by accepting the
terms you mention in your letter, not intending them to be final,
entrap you into a binding contract.   Mind your fire insurances.
Very few policies against fire, says Lord St. Leonards, are so
framed as to render the company legally liable. If you have added
an Arnot's stove, or made any other important change in your
mode of heating your house since your policy, you should call
upon the Company to admit the validity of your policy by an
endorsement on it.   •

Vitiating a Sale.

It is rather startling to hear an ex-Lord Chancellor saying,
"Thus I have told you what truths you must disclose.   I shall
now tell you what falsehoods you *may* utter in regard to your
estate."   Of course it is not meant that morally any falsehood
may be told, but only that there are some which do not, at Law
or in Equity, vitiate the contract of sale.   And it is curious to
see the distinctions taken in these falsehoods.   They remind us
of the difference in Roman Catholic theology between venial and
mortal sins.   Thus, you may falsely praise, that is, *puff*, your
property.   You may describe it as uncommonly rich water-
meadow, although it is imperfectly watered.   In selling an
advowson you may falsely state that an avoidance of the living
is likely to occur soon.   You may say, as a mere puff, that your
house is fit for a respectable family; but you may not say, in
answer to inquiries, contrary to the fact, that the house is not
damp.   And you must disclose a right of sporting or of common
over your estate, or a right to dig mines under it.   The reason
of such distinctions as given by the law —*valeat quantum*—is,
that some statements are cautions to purchasers to make inquiries
for themselves, and that concealments, to be material, must be of
something that the party concealing is bound to state.   Although
Lord St. Leonards (in his *Handy-Book of Property Law*) does not
allude to the point, we might, had we space, while upon this
subject, enlighten our readers by a set of cases in which the law
relating to bugs is elaborately laid down, and explain to them in

what instances the presence of these domestic nuisances in inconvenient numbers does or does not affect a contract for taking a house. But we must be content to refer them to the leading authorities in the pleasant volumes of Meeson and Welsby, where they will find the law fully expounded.—*Saturday Review.*

Law of Gardens.

Some persons, when leaving a place, finding they could not remove the trees and shrubs, have them cut down; but they were actionable, for the law prohibits waste with malevolent intentions. The decision given in the case of Buckland *v.* Butterfield establishes this point; for "a tenant is liable to pay for the waste, if he cuts down or destroys," &c. And it has also been decided by Lord Denman, Mr. Justice Littledale, and Mr. Justice Parke, that a tenant could not remove a border of box, planted in the garden by himself; but that it belonged to the landlord, in the absence of any agreement to the contrary. In the course of the argument the counsel for the tenant asked, " Could not the tenant remove flowers which he had planted in the ground ?" Mr. Justice Littledale instantly said, " No."

Giving a Servant a Character.

The giving a Character to a Servant is one of the most ordinary communications which a member of society is called on to make; and, as the learned Mr. Starkie observes, is a duty of great importance to the interests of the public ; and in respect of that duty a person offends grievously against the interests of the community in giving a good character where it is not deserved, or against justice and humanity in either injuriously refusing to give a character, or in designedly misrepresenting " one to the detriment of the individual."

The following Rules are suggested for the consideration of masters and mistresses not acquainted with the law in such cases:

Rule 1. No magistrate has any jurisdiction touching the character of a domestic servant; and the common threat of a master or mistress being summoned for not giving a character is absurd.

Rule 2. It has been clearly decided that a character honestly and *bonâ fide* given by a master or mistress to any person making the usual inquiry, is a privileged communication ; and unless inconsistent with truth, or actual malice can be proved by evidence, no damages can be sustained. But it must be carefully borne in mind that, however truly or honestly the character may be given, an action at law can be brought against the master or mistress, and the ladies of the family put to the anxiety of appearing in court, as well as the lady to whom the character was given. And, although the servant may be immediately defeated, and the case stopped by the judge, you will find yourself some fifty or sixty pounds out of pocket by your victory.

Rule 3. The only safe course, when a master or mistress cannot in sincerity and truth recommend a servant, is to decline answering any questions on the subject, and the following form of written answer may prove useful : " Mrs. A. presents her compliments to Mrs. B., and in reply to her note requesting the character of Ann C——, trusts she will kindly excuse Mrs. A. declining to answer any questions on the subject." Address and date. A copy should be kept.

In the case of Carrol *v.* Bird, the courts of law have decided that neither master nor mistress is bound to give a character, and that no action will lie against them for refusing. The cases also of Taylor *v.* Hawkins are well worthy of notice. It must, however, be repeated, that both justice and humanity claim from a master and mistress their kindest care and consideration for the character of their servants, more particularly female servants ; but it is confidently believed that if the above rules were better known and more generally acted on, all good and honest servants would be gainers.—*Times*, April 19, 1860.

It may be useful to mention here that in the Court of Exchequer, a cook, formerly in the service of Col. Sibthorp, M.P., brought an action against him for an alleged libel in a letter to a lady who had applied to him for the character of the cook, but which was not satisfactory to the lady. It was submitted the Colonel's letter being proved a privileged communication, the action could not be maintained without proof of express malice on the part of the defendant, of which there was not the slightest evidence ; the judge concurred in this view, and the plaintiff was accordingly nonsuited.

Deodands.

Within memory, when an accident occurred, it was customary to inflict a kind of fine or penalty thus : supposing a boy was run over by a vehicle, the verdict was recorded " Accidental death, with a deodand of one shilling upon the cart." In the *Liber Albus* (27 Henry III.), we read that a man fell from a boat into the Thames, and was drowned ; no one was held in suspicion as to the same ; the judgment was " Misadventure," and the value of the boat, 4s. 7d., was exacted as a deodand, payable to the king. [See *Things not generally known*, First Series, p. 173.] The *deodandum* (Deo dandum, given to God) of our jurisprudence may be reckoned among the mysterious things of history. The deodand is philanthropic, it is religious, and it is so far clerical, that its value, when levied, was handed over to the clergy. Fleta,

a commentator on English law, *temp.* Edward I., says that the
deodand is to be sold, and the price distributed to the poor, for
the soul of the king, his ancestors, and all faithful people departed
this life.   Yet it was not *ecclesiastical:* it cannot be recovered by
suit in the courts of canon law, but only in the courts of the king's
coroner, either for counties, or for all England.   This ancient
custom was abolished by act 9th and 10th Vict., cap. 62, which
enacts that subsequent to September 1st, 1846, there shall be no
forfeiture of chattels in respect of homicide.

Arrest of the Body after Death.

It was long erroneously believed that the body of a debtor
might be taken in execution, in this country, after his or her death.
Such, however, was the practice in Prussia, till its abolition by the
Code Frédérique.
The above idle notion we remember to have been repeated in
connexion with the pecuniary embarrassments of Sheridan, at the
time of his death, in 1816.   It may have been fostered through the
mis-reading of an account of a sheriff's officer arresting the dying
man in his bed ; " he would have carried him off in his blankets,
had not Dr. Bain assured him it was too probable his prisoner
would expire on the way to the lock-up house !" After Sheridan's
death, the removal of his remains from Savile-row to Mr. Peter
Moore's house, in George-street, Westminster, to be near the
Abbey for interment, more probably led to the story that the
body was removed to escape arrest.

The Duty of making a Will.

When in 1859, Lord Northwick's collection of pictures **was**
about to be disposed of by auction, at Thirlestane-house, Cheltenham, we paid a visit to the gallery, and great was our regret at
the thought of the dispersion of so extensive a collection, which
had long been the pride of Cheltenham, and had been to that
thriving town what the National Gallery is to the metropolis.
Lord Northwick had collected these pictures during a life extending for nearly a quarter of a century beyond the average
term allotted to man.   Until within a year or two of Lord Northwick's death, in 1859, he spent much of his time every day among
his pictures, and took great delight in pointing out their beauties
to any intelligent visitor. The collection, and another at Campden,
were swept away by sale, which realized nearly 100,000*l.*   Upon
our visit to the Thirlestane Gallery, much as we were gratified
with the pictures, we became impressed with the futility of de-

voting a long life to their collection, without providing against their dispersion ; and subsequently to the sale, there appeared in the *Morning Post* the following remarks, which more fully bespeak our own feelings upon the subject:

> We contemplate the dispersion of these pictures with two painful reflections, which, by way of caution or suggestion to other collectors, we wish to impress upon the public. The first is the comparative uselessness of collecting works of art without some provision for their preservation. The purpose of a life is dissipated, and a new illustration is given to the preacher's moral, "*Vanitas vanitatis est omnia vanitas.*" Undoubtedly, he who collects treasures of art in the way Lord Northwick did, and gives the public the benefit of them during his life, does a great service in his day and generation ; but it is impossible not to remember how much greater a service he renders who not only forms a collection but provides for its perpetuity. In the next place, see the duty of making a Will. These collections are dispersed because they form a portion of the personalty of the deceased, and there being no instructions as to their disposal, there is no choice but to sell them, and appropriate their proceeds among the heirs-at-law. Next to the mischief of making an unfair Will is that of making none at all. Had Lord Northwick ordered by Will the sale of his pictures, however disappointed the world might have been, it would have been felt that he had a right to do as he liked. But dying intestate, the sale follows as a matter of course, and the results of a long life and large fortune devoted to works of art are just nowhere. A gallery of pictures left to a family or to the public is an offering at the shrine of art ; but, sold by auction, and dispersed among innumerable private purchasers, is sheer vanity and labour lost.

Don't make your own Will.

Lord St. Leonards, in his *Handy-Book of Property Law*, says : " I am somewhat unwilling to give you any instructions for making your Will, without the assistance of your professional adviser ; and I would particularly warn you against the use of printed forms, which have misled many men. They are as dangerous as the country schoolmaster or the vestry-clerk. It is quite shocking to reflect upon the litigation which has been occasioned by men making their own Wills or employing incompetent persons to do so. To save a few guineas in their lifetime, men leave behind them a Will which it may cost hundreds of pounds to have expounded by the courts before the various claimants will desist from litigation. Looking at this as a simple money transaction, lawyers might well be in despair if every man's Will were prepared by a competent person. To put off making your Will until the hand of death is upon you, evinces either cowardice or a shameful neglect of your temporal concerns. Lest, however, such a moment should arrive, I must arm you in some measure against it

" If you wish to tie up your property in your family you really must not make your own will. It were better to die without a will, than to make one which will waste your estate in litigation to discover its meaning. The words "children," "issue," "heirs of the body," or "heirs," sometimes operate to give the parent the entire disposition of the estate, although the testator did not mean any such thing. They are seldom used by a man who makes his own will without leading to a lawsuit. And now an operation has been given to like words by the new statute, which I could not explain to you without you possessed more know-ledge of law than I give you credit for. It were useless for me to show how to make a strict settlement of your property, and therefore I will not try. I could, without difficulty, run over the names of many judges and lawyers of note, whose wills made by themselves have been set aside, or construed so as to defeat every intention which they ever had. It is not even a profound know-ledge of law which will capacitate a man to make his own will, unless he has been in the habit of making the wills of others. Besides, notwithstanding that fees are purely honorary, yet it is almost proverbial that a lawyer never does anything well for which he is not fee'd. Lord Mansfield told a story of himself, that feel-ing this influence, he once, when about to attend on some profes-sional business of his own, took several guineas out of his purse and put them into his waistcoat pocket, as a fee for his labour."

Bridewell.

This name, from a well dedicated to St. Bridget, or St. Bride, between Fleet-street and the Thames, was given to a palace built there, and which, soon after, became a House of Correction, in the reign of Queen Mary. Hence, places of confinement in other parts, in which employment and penitentiary amendment were leading objects, were called *Bridewells.*

The greater part of the City of London Bridewell was taken down in 1863; committals are now made to the City prison at Holloway, but re-fractory City apprentices are still committed to Bridewell by the Chamber-lain, this jurisdiction being preserved by the Court of Chancery. The number of committals rarely exceeds 25 annually; nevertheless the power of committal which the present Chamberlain has most praiseworthily as-serted and successfully maintains, acts as a terror to evil-doers, and keeps in restraint 3000 of these lads of the City.

By a document lately discovered in the State-Paper Office, it appears that in the Bridewell of London were imprisoned the members of the Congregational Church first formed after the accession of Elizabeth; they were committed to the custody of the gaoler, May 20, 1567.

Cockfighting.

British cocks are mentioned by Cæsar; but the first notice of English cockfighting is by Fitzstephen, in the reign of Henry II.; and it was a fashionable sport from *temp.* Edward III. almost to our time. Henry VIII. added a cockpit to Whitehall Palace, where James I. went to see the sport twice a week. There were also cockpits in Drury-lane, Shoe-lane, Jewin-street, Cripplegate, and " behind Gray's Inn ;" and several lanes, courts, and alleys are named from having been the sites of cockpits. The original name of the *pit* in our theatres was the *cock-pit*, which seems to imply that cockfighting had been their original destination. One of our oldest London theatres was called the *Cockpit ;* this was the Phœnix in Drury-lane, the site of which was Cockpit-alley, now corruptly written Pitt-place. Southwark has several cockpit sites. The cockpit in St. James's-park, leading from Birdcage-walk into Dartmouth-street, was only taken down in 1816, but had been deserted long before. Howell, in 1657, described " cockfighting, a sport peculiar to the English, and so is bear and bull baitings, there being not such dangerous dogs and cocks anywhere." Hogarth's print best illustrates the brutal refine-ment of the cockfighting of the last century; and Cowper's " Cockfighter's Garland," greatly tended to keep down this modern barbarism, which is punishable by statute. It was, not many years since, greatly indulged in through Staffordshire ; and " Wednesbury (Wedgbury) cockings" and their ribald songs were a disgrace to our times.

Cockfighting was, in fact, the great national amusement, par-ticularly in the north of England, and Berwick-upon-Tweed was among the places most celebrated for it. Some ninety years ago, in the north of England, when a cockfighting was about to take place, the parties were in want of an adept in putting on the spurs : a person present was recognised by an acquaintance, who ex-claimed, " Here comes a Berwick man; he knows how to do it." Cockfighting is now legally a misdemeanor ; and on the 15th of April, 1857, at the Liverpool Police Court, James Clark, a publican, in Houghton-street, was fined 5*l.* and costs for permitting cockfighting in his house.

In the autumn of 1862, several persons were convicted by the magistrates at Barnsley, for cockfighting, under the Act, which inflicts a fine on any one assisting at a cockfight, *in a place used for the purpose.* This is an absurd condition, and is a blunder of the Act-framer. Now, the *place* used for the purpose of *this fight* was an old quarry ; but the magistrates held that any place where a cockfight took place was a place used for the purpose, the fact of the fight being the evidence of the use. The case came by appeal before the Court of Queen's Bench, when the Judges decided, in accordance with a ruled case, there must be some evidence of general use, if on a piece of waste ground, and that one act would only prove the use when it was a place over which a man had some control. The judgment was therefore reversed. At Bradford, within a few days of this decision, William Speight and J. Holroyd were fined 3*l.* each for cruelty in having set game-cocks to fight; twelve other persons, resident in various parts of the Riding, were fined 10s. each.

On June 24th, 1863, before a bench of magistrates at Loughborough, the Marquis of Hastings, and three of his gamekeepers, were charged, on behalf of the Society for the Prevention of Cruelty to Animals, with causing a cock to be cruelly tortured. It was proved in evidence that three weeks before, the Marquis of Hastings had " some good cockfighting" at Donington Hall, *on a Sunday !* They fought six pairs of cocks, six cocks were killed, all had steel spurs on, and the Marquis was one of the persons who put the cocks together to fight; the other persons accused being spectators. Lord Hastings admitted that the fight had taken place, but denied that there had been any cruelty used in the sense of the words of the information. His Lordship was, however, convicted in the penalty of 5*l.*, and his three keepers in 2*l.* each.

Ignorance and Irresponsibility.

Sir John Bowring states that he remembers a murder occurring in Ceylon, and on the murderer being brought to trial, it was found utterly impossible to make him comprehend that he had committed any sin whatever in revenging himself upon one by whom he thought he had been injured. The consequence was that the Judge came to the conclusion that the murderer could not be held responsible for his crime. So ignorant was this man that he could not count up to the number of five, losing himself always at three.

Ticket-of-Leave Men.

Archbishop Whately, who always handles a practical subject in a masculine way, annihilates the English Ticket-of-leave system with a single sentence:—" What should we think of a right, encouraged by a Secretary of State, to go every day to a menagerie and let out by mere rotation one animal from a cage without inquiring whether he released a monkey or a tiger ?" The Archbishop proposes that all sentences beyond fifteen years should be irreversible, except by an Act of Parliament, specifying the names, offences, and previous committals of the prisoners pardoned.

Cupar and Jedburgh Justice.

It is an odd circumstance that Lord Campbell, to whom both as judge and legislator the law of England owes so much, was born at a place which gives its name, " Cupar justice," to the peculiar system of law which hangs a man first and tries him afterwards ; and that he had his country residence (Hartrigge-house, Roxburghshire) in the neighbourhood of another town which gave the name of " Jedburgh justice" to an equally summary code, the great principle of wh.ch is, " Hang all or save all."

What is to be done with our Convicts.

Transportation having had a fair and patient trial, and having altogether failed as a punishment, and having no colony fitted and willing to receive the sweepings of our gaols, the alternative to which we are compelled is to keep our convicts at home, and to make the best of them, by making them self-supporting. Or, in the forcible words of the late Mr. Charles Pearson, City Solicitor:

If the honest millions, as they pass through life, can, and do, during what is recognised as the producing age, not only provide for their own wants, but create a large surplus, by which the non-producing classes are supported and the institutions of society are maintained, it surely ought not to be endured that any portion of the same race and of the producing age . . . . . should be permitted to renounce their allegiance to the fundamental law of their existence, and declare in practice, that by the sweat of the face of other men, they will eat of earth's choicest fruits.

The only rational, merciful, and effectual corrective of such offenders against all laws, human and divine, is to classify and place them in secure prisons, surrounded by lofty and substantial walls ; to subject them, week by week, to seventy, or at least sixty, hours of useful and profitable work ; to allow them sixty, or at most seventy, hours for food, rest, cleanliness, and their other bodily requirements ; to give them twenty-eight hours with means and opportunities for mental and spiritual instruction, and for the public and private worship of God. . . . . . If any Government, having thus placed at its disposal annually the hundred millions of hours of confiscated labour, which 30,000 criminals would yield, cannot make the class not only self-supporting, but productive of a surplus for the future benefit of those who produce it, such a Government would be pronounced by men of business unfit to be at the head of a great manufacturing and commercial people.

The Game Laws.

In 1834, Mr. Henry Warburton, in Parliament, denounced the Game Laws as they then existed, in this remarkable illustration:—" I have read in Mariner's account of the Tonga islands, that there the rats were preserved as game; and, though everybody might eat rats, nobody was allowed to kill them but somebody descended from their gods or their kings. This is the only country and the only case I know of which furnishes anything like a parallel to our game laws."

The Pillory.

The Pillory (Fr. *pilori*, probably from Lat. *pila*, a pillar) was a mode of punishment by a public exposure of the offender long used in most countries of Europe. No punishment has been inflicted in so many different ways as that of the pillory. Sometimes the machine was constructed so that several criminals might be pilloried at the same time; but it was commonly capable of holding but one at once. Francis Douce, in his *Illustrations of Shakespeare*, vol. i., p. 146, gives six representations of distinct varieties of this instrument. These varieties are all reducible, however, to the simplest form of the pillory. It consisted of a wooden frame or screen raised on a pillar or post several feet from the ground, and behind which the culprit stood supported on a platform, his head and hands being thrust through holes in the screen, so as to be exposed in front. This screen, in the more complicated forms of the instrument, consisted of a perforated iron circle or *carcan* (hence the name given to the pillory in French), which secured the hands and heads of several persons at the same time.

The Pillory seems to have existed in England before the Conquest, in the shape of the stretchneck, in which the head only of the criminal was confined; but it was usually constructed for the head and hands. It was used for punishing all sorts of cheats; as, bakers for making bread of light weight; fraudulent corn, coal, and cattle dealers; cutters of purses; sellers of sham gold rings; forgers of letters, bonds, and deeds; users of unstamped measures, &c. It was also a Star Chamber punishment; and from the time of Titus Oates to its abolition, the pillory was a common punishment for perjury. The usual places where the pillory was pitched were the Royal Exchange, the Old Bailey, Temple Bar, Lincoln's-Inn Fields, Charing Cross, New Palace Yard, and Tyburn. About the year 1812, the writer remembers to have seen four men in the pillory, at the north end of Fleet-market

(Holborn-bridge). The last person who stood in the pillory in London, was Peter James Bossy, for perjury, in the Old Bailey, June 23, 1830. A pillory is still standing at Coleshill, in Warwickshire; and in an unused chancel of Rye church, Sussex, is a pillory, last used in 1813. The pillory was abolished in Great Britain in 1837, by stat. 1 Vict., c. 23; and in France in 1832.

Death-Warrants.—Pardons.

Although we occasionally read in the public journals of the issue of the usual Death-warrant for the execution of a criminal, there is (except in the case of a peer of the realm) no such thing as a death-warrant ever signed by the Crown or by any one or more of the officers of the Crown; the only authority for the execution of a criminal convicted of a capital crime being the verbal sentence pronounced upon him in open court, which sentence the Sheriff is bound to take cognizance of and execute without any further authority. It is true that a written calendar of the offences and punishments of the prisoners is made out and signed by the Judge, of which a copy is delivered to the Sheriff; but this is only a memorandum and not an official document, and it is optional with the Judge to sign it or not.

The false notion of there being such a document as a Death-warrant for the execution of a criminal has been fostered to our own time by the frequent reference of writers of note to its existence. Sir Nathaniel Wraxall says of Dr. Dodd's case in 1777—

"*I have heard* Lord Sackville recount the circumstances that took place in the council held on the occasion, at which the King assisted. To the firmness of the Lord Chief-Justice, Dodd's execution was due: for, no sooner had he pronounced his decided opinion that no mercy ought to be extended, than the King, taking up the pen, signed the death-warrant."

This is flatly contradicted in the *Quarterly Review*, No. 57, as follows:—Lord Sackville never could have told him any such thing—the King *never* signs any death-warrant—his pleasure on the Recorder's report is in ordinary cases *verbally*, and in fatal cases *silently*, signified—and it is *always* guided by the opinion of the legal members of the Privy Council.

This popular error of the Death-warrant is fully explained, from an accredited legal source, in *Things not generally known*, First Series, p. 172.

It is erroneously supposed that the Sovereign can save a life that has been declared forfeit by the law; but the Sovereign's sign-manual to a pardon is of no effect unless it be countersigned (that is, sanctioned) by a responsible minister.—*J. Doran, F.S.A.; Last Journals of Horace Walpole*, vol. i.

Origin of the Judge's Black Cap.

The practice of our Judges in putting on a Black Cap when they condemn a criminal to death will be found, on consideration, to have a deep and sad significance. Covering the head was in ancient days a sign of mourning. " Haman hastened to his house, mourning and having his head covered." (Esther vi. 12). In like manner Demosthenes, when insulted by the populace, went home with his head covered. " And David . . . wept as he went up, and had his head covered ; . . . and all the people that was with him covered every man his head, and they went up, weeping as they went up." (2 Samuel xv. ·o.) Darius, too, covered his head on learning the death of his Queen. But among ourselves we find traces of a similar mode of expressing grief at funerals. The mourners had the hood " drawn forward over the head." (Fosbroke, *Encyc. of Antiq.*, p. 951). Indeed, the hood drawn forward thus over the head is still part of the mourning habiliment of women when they follow the corpse. And with this it should be borne in mind that, as far back as the time of Chaucer, the most usual colour of mourning was black. Atropos also, who held the fatal scissors which cut short the life of man, was clothed in black. When, therefore, the Judge puts on the black cap, it is a very significant as well as solemn procedure. He puts on mourning, for he is about to pronounce the forfeit of a life. And, accordingly, the act itself, the putting on of the black cap, is generally understood to be significant. It intimates that the Judge is about to pronounce no merely registered or suppositious sentence; in the very formula of condemnation he has put himself in mourning for the convicted culprit, as for a dead man. The criminal is then left for execution, and, unless mercy exerts its sovereign prerogative, suffers the sentence of the law. The mourning cap expressly indicates his doom.—*Notes and Queries.*

The last English Gibbet.

In March, 1856, the last Gibbet erected in England was demolished by the workmen employed by the contractors making docks for the North-Eastern Railway Company upon the Tyne. The person who was gibbeted at that place was a pitman, convicted at the Durham Midsummer Assizes of 1832. So great was the horror and disgust of all parties with the sight of the body of the poor wretch dangling in chains by the side of a public road, that great gratitude was expressed when the pitmen took it down one dark night. It is a gratifying fact, showing the progress of civilization among the mining population, that, though there have been several strikes among them since 1832, none of those strikes have been marked by a repetition of the fearful acts of violence of that year. At one of the great meetings of pitmen held in the spring of 1832 the Marquis of Londonderry attended on horseback to remonstrate with them. But he had a company of soldiers with him, which were hiding in the valley. This was known to the pitmen, and the pitman that held his horse's head as he spoke had a loaded pistol up his sleeve, in case the Marquis should wave the soldiers to come up, to blow the Marquis's brains out. Fortunately, the good feeling and kind heart of the nobleman prevailed, and that emergency did not arise.

Public Executions.

It is the grossest and most illogical of assumptions to conclude, without a particle of attempted proof, that Public Executions produce only brutalizing effects upon the spectators. It is just as fair to assume that their results even on the spectators are edifying. But these results are only remote and indirect, and comparatively unimportant. Public executions are to be justified on other grounds than their effects on bystanders. They are designed not only to prevent possible murder but to avenge actual murder. They are great retributive acts; they represent and embody the last and most solemn and weightiest impersonation of Eternal Justice. An execution is retaliatory, and is to be defended as such. As we no longer hang men for other crimes than that of murder, life for life becomes a social necessity. Any other punishment than that of death is incommensurate with the crime; and we cannot afford to place the sanctity of human life and the safety of our spoons under the same sanctions.—*Saturday Review.*

On the other hand, it is maintained that executions ought never to be made a spectacle for the multitude, who, if they can bear the sight, always regard it as a pastime; nor for the curiosity of those who shudder while they gratify it.

In neither of these views is the effect of a public execution upon the criminal taken into account. This effect, as instanced at the execution of the Mannings for murder, in 1849, was thus forcibly urged by Sir Francis Head:

The merciful object of every punishment which the law inflicts, is not so much to revenge the past crime as to prevent its recurrence. Now, Mrs. Manning's last moments clearly explain, or rather indisputably prove, the benefit which society practically derives from a public execution. She had courage enough—as she sat smiling by his side—to plan the murder of "her best friend;" to dig his grave; to prepare vitriol and lime to burn his body; to blow his brains out; to bury him in her own kitchen. She had resolution enough—almost before he was cold—to go to his lodgings to obtain his property. Her self-possession before the police authorities at Edinburgh was unexampled; her hardness of heart on her trial, as well as in prison, most extraordinary. And yet this bold, courageous woman, who after the murder, and with her hands stained with blood, had said to her husband, "I think no more of what I have done than if I had shot the cat that is on the wall!" afterwards triumphantly adding, "I have the nerve of a horse!" did not dare to face the indescribable terrors of a public execution! She did not fear death in private; on the contrary, she almost succeeded in gradually, with her own hands, strangling herself; but her obdurate heart quailed at the idea of beholding in fearful array before her, the uplifted horrid faces of the London mob; and accordingly, as her last act, "she drew from her pocket a black silk handkerchief, requested that she might be blindfolded with it; and, having a black silk veil fastened over her head, so as completely to conceal her features from public gaze, she was conducted in slow and solemn procession towards the drop;" and as for a few fleeting moments she stood with bandaged eyes beneath the gibbet, how unanswerably did the picture mutely expound the terror which the wicked very naturally have of being publicly hanged before the scum and refuse of society! "The whistlings—the imitations of Punch—the brutal jokes and indecent delight of the thieves, low prostitutes, ruffians, and vagabonds," so graphically described by Mr. Charles Dickens, were— by her own showing—not only the most fearful portion of her sentence, but, under Providence, these coarse ingredients may possibly have effected that momentary repentance which the mild but fervent exhortations of the chaplain had failed to produce.

Many men, neither sentimental nor enthusiastic, nor even philanthropists, however, conclude that though public executions under the present system are deterring, to a certain extent, yet they are exceedingly brutalizing and calculated to harden and deprave the spectators. Sir George Bowyer, M.P., has said:

The problem remains unsolved how the terror of capital punishments is to be purified from the abominable accessories and consequences which Dickens and Thackeray have so vividly and usefully described. I am not one of those who think that capital punishments are either unlawful or inexpedient. The passage in Holy Writ which says that the civil ruler bears the sword to be a terror to evil-doers, points out with infallible authority both the lawfulness and the use of the extreme penalty. But still I must admit that this dreadful prerogative of Sovereignty—the power of life and death—may be, and is in this country, exercised in such a way, that one might almost doubt whether the moral pestilence which it spreads did not counterbalance the security that it affords to society.

The Committee of the House of Lords on Capital Punishment were so convinced of the evil effects of the present mode of carrying into effec capital punishments, that they recommended that executions should in future take place within the prison, and in the presence only of official and selected witnesses. But this opinion does not solve the difficulty. Mr. George Augustus Sala truly says that private executions would not be tolerated in the present state of society. Besides, certainly the terror produced by the sight of death cannot be equalled by the sound of a bell or the hoisting of a black flag, which the Lords' Committee propose; and these forms would soon lose any impressiveness. The sight of death is, indeed, most awful to human nature :

> " ———— O sight
> Of terror, foul and ugly to behold,
> Horrid to think—how horrible to feel !"

The knowledge that a criminal had been put to death would no doubt be less terrible to the criminal and dangerous population if they were prevented from seeing the execution. If the plan of private executions be rejected, what can be done to give a character to public executions more wholesome than that justly condemned by the committee?

The cold, business-like formality of a public execution is then referred to: beyond a glimpse of the chaplain's surplice there is nothing to remind the spectators of the awful and sacred character with which the Christian religion invests death. The people see a man strangled, and that is all.

Archdeacon Bickersteth evidently felt this when he said before the Lords' Committee, " I would suggest that the churches might be opened. . . . There might be a service at the time, and perhaps a prayer for the criminal." This is a very pregnant hint. At the execution of three men at Dundalk a few years ago, when the criminals came on the scaffold, all the people knelt and prayed for them at the request of the priest. Those who were there describe the scene as most solemn and honourable to the Irish character. The prisoners confessed their guilt and declared their penitence. An account describing a late execution for murder at Ancona, says that the prisoner knelt on the scaffold and repeated the Litany, the crowd making the reponses. A friend of mine who was at an execution for murder in Rome, told me that the thousands of spectators round the scaffold recited the *Miserere* and *De Profundis* in a loud voice. How different this is from "levity, jeering, laughing, hooting, whistling, low jesting, and indecent ribaldry" described before the Committee! This contrast surely suggests that the people in England should be better taught than they are, and that it is by religious influences that executions can be purified from their abominable and loathsome effects. The people should be made to feel that they are, so to speak, attending a death-bed scene of the most frightful and appalling kind, and not the mere slaughter of a biped without feathers.

Sir George Bowyer then relates how the problem is solved in Italy, where, in every city is a religious society of laymen, called "the Confraternity of Death," or of Mercy, whose duty it is to attend criminals before and at their execution:

The exposition of the blessed sacrament for the forty hours' prayer commences in the churches, and the people attend in great numbers during the whole day, and even sometimes during the night. The prisoner is taken to the place of execution (usually outside the town) in the following manner :—First the great black cross and banner of the Confraternity is seen slowly advancing, followed by the members walking two and two in their black cassocks and their hoods over their faces, with apertures for their eyes. As they proceed along the streets they recite the Penitential Psalms aloud. They are followed by the litter for the dead body, carried by four of their number; and then comes the convict, assisted by the clergy and brethren. At the scaffold the Confraternity stand round and continue their devotions until the prisoner is dead, and then they remove the body in the same funeral procession.

These facts, it must be admitted, are very suggestive ; but, how far such ceremonies are adapted for a Protestant country is extremely questionable.

That experienced judge, Baron Alderson, in his answers given to a Committee of the House of Commons, looked on the deterring effect of punishment, such as it was, as more indispensable than the reforming :—

" It is desirable—I do not know whether it is the duty of the State—to make all criminals better if possible ; but I think this object is to be held subservient to that of preventing crime by the example of punishment ; and on no other principle that I can perceive is it possible to defend capital punishments, which can hardly be said to have any tendency to make the individual criminals better, though I think they have a strong effect in repressing crime."

The latest evidence upon the subject is—that in September, 1863, the Association for the Promotion of Social Science, holding its second session at Ghent, discussed at great length the subject of punishment of death. The abolition was finally voted by a great majority. In the course of the debate a member read a list of 167 convicts sentenced to death, of whom 161 had been present at capital executions; and he concluded from this fact, that the witnessing capital punishment is not efficacious in the suppression of crime.

Measure and Value.

Numbers descriptive of Distance.

BEFORE the introduction of railways we scarcely possessed any standard by which an idea could be formed of the distances and movements of the planets by comparison with those which exist on the terrestrial globe. Thus, the mean distance of the moon from the earth is about 237,000 miles. A steam-carriage on a railway, proceeding uninterruptedly, at the rate of 25 miles an hour, would run 237,000 miles in 1 year, 4 weeks, and 2 days. This falls within the limits of our conception. We may imagine something analogous to this, supposing a carriage, or rather a succession of carriages, to be kept constantly at work for rather more than two years, and working 12 hours per day. But our powers of imagination fail us in estimating a distance equal to that of the earth from the sun, namely, *ninety-five millions of miles.** Our steam-carriage illustration is here no longer available, since it falls far beyond the boundaries of probability. Proceeding uninterruptedly at twenty-five miles an hour, it would require 433 years to move over a space equal to ninety-five millions of miles.—*Dr. Lardner.*

Precocious Mental Calculation.

A rare exceptional instance of this faculty being cultivated and matured for a highly-useful purpose, is presented in the case of Mr. Bidder, the eminent civil engineer, known in his childhood as "the Calculating Boy." (See a portrait in the *Boy's Own Book.*)

George Parkes Bidder, when six years old, used to amuse himself by counting up to 100, then to 1000, then to 1,000,000: by degrees, he accustomed himself to contemplate the relations of high numbers, and used to build up peas, marbles, and shot, into squares, cubes, and other regular figures. He invented processes of his own, distinct from those given in books of arithmetic, and could solve all the usual questions mentally more rapidly than other boys with the aid of pen and paper. When he became eminent as a civil engineer, he was wont to embarrass and baffle the parliamentary counsel on contested railway bills, by confuting their statements of figures almost before the words were out of

---

* It is now shown to be 91,328,600 miles.

their mouths. In 1856, he gave to the Institution of Civil Engineers an interesting account of this singular arithmetical faculty —so far, at least, as to show that *memory* has less to do with it than is generally supposed: the processes are actually worked out *seriatim*, but with a rapidity almost inconceivable. They are accomplished mentally by occupying the mind simultaneously with the double task of *computing* and *registering*. The first—computing—is executive, or reasoning, and is that portion of the process, which, whilst it is the most active, is not that which causes the greatest strain upon the mind. The result is recorded by the second faculty, registering, which is the real strain upon the mind, and that by which alone the power of Mental Calculation is limited.

Experience has shown that, up to a certain point, the power of registering is as rapid as thought; but the difficulty increases, in a very high ratio, in reference to the number and extent of impressions to be registered, until a point is reached, the registering of which, in the mind and by writing, are exactly balanced. Below that point, mental registration is preferable; above it, that by writing will be as quick, and more certain.

All the rules employed by Mr. Bidder were invented by him, and are only methods of so arranging calculation as to facilitate the power of registration: in fact, he thus arrives at a sort of natural algebra, using actual numbers in the place of symbols. When he first began to deal with numbers (in his 6th year), he had not learned to read, and certainly long after that time he was taught the symbolical numbers from the face of a watch.

A brief outline of Mr. Bidder's method is given in the *Year-Book of Facts*, 1857, pp. 149-152. The paper, *in extenso*, has been edited and published by Mr. Charles Manby, F.R.S., Honorary Secretary to the Institution of Civil Engineers.

The Roman Foot.

The late celebrated architect and antiquary, Luigi Canina, made a great number of inquiries as to the length of the ancient Roman foot. He measured very carefully the Antonine and Trajan columns, and found them (exclusive of their pedestals and some pieces let in to repair them) exactly alike. This height, which was known to have been 100 Roman feet, was measured with extreme care by means of rods of wood carefully dried, and found to be exactly 29·635 French mètres. Measuring chains were then constructed of this length, and the Roman miles (*mille passuum*) carefully measured down the Appian Way as far as the twelfth mile, and were found to correspond with the traditional sites of the milestones. The great length of these measurements being such an extensive check, their accuracy was at once accepted by the Roman archæologists as the best authority known. This would make the ancient Roman foot 11·66753 English inches; and the mile 4861·41 English feet; being about one-eleventh less than our English mile of 5280 feet. For rough reckoning the antiquary may deduct one-eleventh from Roman miles to bring them into English; or may add one-tenth to English miles to bring them into Roman; the ratio being 10 : 11, but inversely. There is a common error in supposing the Roman mile, or *mille passuum*, was 1000 paces, or single steps. This is not the case : the military *passus* consisted of *two* steps (*gressus*), or about 5 feet Roman.—*Notes and Queries.*

The Peruvian Quipus.

The well-known contrivance of the Quipus, or method of counting and even recording events by means of cords, was equally ingenious and original. The quipus of the Peruvians were of twisted wool, and consisted of a thick cord, with threads more or less fine, attached to the main part. The smaller lines were covered with knots, either single or double. The size of the quipus varies much, sometimes the main cord being five or six yards long, and at others not more than a foot; the branches rarely exceeding a yard in length, and being sometimes shorter. In the neighbourhood of Lurin, on the coast of Peru, a quipu was found which weighed twelve pounds. The different colours of the threads had different meanings : thus, the red signified a soldier, or war; the yellow gold; the white, silver, or peace, &c. In the system of arithmetic, a single knot signified 10, two single knots 20, a double knot 100, a triple knot 1000, and so on to higher numbers. But not only the colour and mode of combining the knots, but also the laying-up of the strands of the cord, and the distances of the threads apart, were of great importance in reading the quipus. It is probable that in the earliest times this ingenious contrivance was merely used for enumeration, as the shepherd notches the number of his sheep on a stick; but in the course of time the science was so much improved that the initiated were able to knot historical records, laws, and decrees, so that the great events of the empire were transmitted to posterity; and, to some extent, the quipus supplied the place of chronicles and national archives. The registry of tributes, the census of populations, the lists of arms, of soldiers, and of stores, the supplies of maize, clothes, shoes, &c., in the storehouses, were all specified with admirable exactness by the quipus; and in every town of any importance, there was an officer, called the quipu camayoc, to knot and decipher these documents.—*Markham's Visit to Peru.*

Distances measured.

Many people hear of distances in thousands of yards—a usual measure of artillery distances—and have very little power of reducing them at once to miles. Now, four miles are ten yards for each mile above 7000 yards, whence the following rule : the number of thousands multiplied by 4 and divided by 7 give miles and sevenths for quotient and remainder, with only at the rate of ten yards to a mile in excess. Thus 12,000 yards is 48 7ths of a mile, or 6 miles and 6 7ths of a mile: not 70 yards too great. Again, people measure speed by miles per hour, the mile and the hour being too long for the judgment of distance and time. Take half as much again as the number of miles per hour, and you have the number of feet per second, too great by one in 30. Thus 16 miles an hour is 16 + 8, or 24 feet per second, too much by 24-30ths of a foot.—*Athenæum,* No. 1854.

Uniformity of Weights and Measures.

A collection of the Weights and Measures of the various countries of the world, made, under the auspices of the International Association, for obtaining a uniform Decimal System of Measures, Weights, and Coins, was among the curiosities of the International Exhibition of 1862. Few persons are perhaps aware of the extraordinary diversities in weights and measures, and in their use, which exist in our own country. The price of corn, for instance, will be quoted in at least fifteen different ways in as many different localities; at so much per *cwt.,* per *barrel,* per *quarter,* per *bushel,* per *load,* per *bag,* per *weight,* per *boll,* per *coomb,* per *hobbet,* per *winch,* per *windle,* per *strike,* per *measure,* per *stone.* The word *bushel* is in some places used for a measure, in others for a weight, and this weight is by no means the same in all places. In different English towns the bushel means— 168 lbs., 73½ lbs., 62 lbs., 80 lbs., 75 lbs., 72 lbs., 70 lbs., 65 lbs., 64 lbs., 63 lbs., 5 quarters, 144 quarts, 488 lbs., and in Manchester, while a bushel of English wheat is 60 lbs., a bushel of American wheat is 70 lbs. The meaning of a *stone* is almost equally various. An acre of land expresses seven different quantities. These variations in measurement must be highly inconvenient, and prejudicial to trade ; and the labours of the above-named Association are directed to bringing about a uniformity, which seems greatly called for. The metrical system employed in France is that which is advocated. This has been already established in Belgium, Holland, Sardinia, Lombardy, Greece, Spain, Portugal, and many other parts of the world. Great Britain and the American States still adhere to their old systems.

Trinity High-water Mark.

Trinity High-water Mark is placed in various parts of London, as described in the *Register of Tides in the River Thames*, printed by order of the Honourable Court of Commissioners, of the 26th of October, 1849 ; and every bench-mark in London is shown in feet and decimals of feet above an oblate spheroidal datum plane, decreasing in radii towards the north pole from the centre of gravity between the parallels of latitude at London and Liverpool, about 2·02 feet, or 24$\frac{1}{4}$ inches, which is evidently worthy of consideration, at a rate of 2 feet to the mile in 40 miles of sewer. The difference at Liverpool is also given in the aforesaid Report ; and this may prove of public utility if reported on by the engineer employed in the levelling of the main drainage of London.   The Ravensbourne drainage is a specimen of such levelling.   The approximate mean water at Liverpool is 12$\frac{1}{2}$ feet below the level of Trinity High-Water at London, as described identical with the level of the datum plane of the Ordnance survey of London, which is also 12$\frac{1}{2}$ feet below the level of Trinity High-Water mark.

Origin of Rent.

The want of intelligent workmen, without the concurrence of other causes, might have destroyed the old English predial polity, if that system had not failed through its own nature ; having been essentially rude and awkward and uncommercial.   Under the Plantagenets, service could in general be reduced to money at the discretion of the lord or the option of the tenant.   The service often cost the tenant more than it was worth—he found it cheaper to pay than to work : on the other hand, money must have been at all times welcome to the lord, and he did not at all times require labour.   In the course of time agricultural service went out of use altogether, and money was regularly tendered and accepted instead of it : so that the improved rent, as it has been called, now paid by a farmer, appears to be a compound—historically considered—of the ancient mail or gable, and of a great variety of petty charges, which were originally compensations for tributes of corn, malt, poultry, bacon, and eggs—or fines for the non-performance of acts of tillage, carriage, porterage, and the like.   The elements of rent were recognised in Scotland longer than in England, because petty charges subsisted in Scotland for some time after they had been abandoned in England. At the beginning of the eighteenth century, David Deans—the tough true-blue Presbyterian farmer—still paid "mail duties, kain, arriage, carriage, dry multure, lock, gowpen, and knaveship, and all the various exactions now commuted for money, and summed up in the emphatic word RENT."—*Heart of Mid-Lothian*, chap. viii.; *Law Magazine*, N. S., No. 27.

Curiosities of the Exchequer.

Mr. Foss, in his *Lives of the Judges*, tells us that the Court of Exchequer was anciently sometimes called *Curia Regis ad Scaccarium ;* and its name was derived from the table at which it sat, which was "a four-cornered board, about ten feet long and five feet broad, fitted in manner of a table to sit about, on every side whereof is a standing ledge or border, four fingers broad. Upon this board is laid a cloth bought in Easter Term, which is of black colour, rowed with strokes, distant about a foot or span, like a chess-board. On the spaces of this Scaccarium, or chequered cloth, counters were ranged, with denoting marks, for checking the computations."

In the old Court of Exchequer, at Westminster, before the coronation of King George IV., might be seen the chequered cloth which covered the table of that Court. This table, at which sat the officers of the Court, and the king's counsel, was ten or twelve feet square, and was covered with a woollen cloth, the groundwork of which was white, with a very dark blue chequered pattern over it ; the dark stripes being about three inches wide, leaving between them white squares of about four inches across.

Again, the cover on the table of the Exchequer Court in Dublin is composed of a thick woollen substance made in squares of black and white, resembling a chess-board.

The origin of the word *Scaccarium* (whence Exchequer) is not certain. Madox, the historical authority upon the subject, considers the most likely derivation to be from *Scaccus,* or *Scaccum,* a chess-board, or the *ludus Scaccarium*, the game of chess. He then refers to the chequered cloth mentioned by Foss; adding, "from the Latin *Scaccarium* cometh the *French Eschequier,* or *Exchequier,* (*Exchiquer,*) and the English name from the French."

Mr. G. A. Sala, in a communication to *Notes and Queries*, 3rd S. No. 81, however, traces exchequer to the Italian *Zecca,* treasury or mint ; whence, also, he derives the word cheque ; remembering that in old time our goldsmiths were Lombards and Venetians.

However this may be, the forms by which accounts were kept in the Exchequer, and receipts given for moneys paid by "the King's debtors" in those days, when few persons knew how to write and cipher, and "double entry" was unknown, were strictly observed down to a period scarcely thirty years ago. The rude wooden "tallies" that were prepared as quittances for payment, and stowed away in the Exchequer as entries of receipt, were still maintained in their sham employment until finally abolished by an Act passed in 1834. The officials who superintended, or were supposed to superintend, the operation of cutting, delivering, and keeping the tallies were paid by fees on all receipts; and as the national revenue augmented their incomes became enormous. A "Tallier," or, as the name became latterly, "Teller," of the Exchequer enjoyed at last an income from his sinecure office of more than 30,000*l.* per annum.

The Tally was a slip of willow-wood, cut to a length proportioned to the magnitude of the pecuniary transaction it was intended to record. Its indications were rendered by notches, which signified various sums, according to their size and shape.[*]

When fabricated the instrument indicated this meaning. A large notch of an inch and a half in width signified 1000*l.*; a smaller notch, one inch in width, signified 100*l.*; one of half-an-inch signified 20*l.*; a notch in the wood slanting to the right signified 10*l.* (in combination this notch was placed before the 20*l.* notch); small notches signified 1*l.* each; a cut sloping to the right signified 10s. (in combination placed before the 1*l.* marks); slight indentations, or jags, in the wood signified shillings; strokes with ink on tally signified pence; a round hole, or dot, signified a halfpenny; a farthing was written in figures.

When split in two lengthwise across the notches, each section of the tally, of course, corresponded exactly. One half was then delivered to the party paying money, as a receipt, and the other kept by the officers of the department, as a check or record of the transaction. On neither side was the slightest value attached to the tally; but down to 1834 no payment could be made into the Exchequer without summoning the officers of the Tally, who gravely notched and split the willow wand, and handed over the Exchequer half to be placed in careful custody. The absurdity came to an end in that year; but by way of farewell ceremony, is reported to have burnt down the Parliament Houses; certain furnace flues having become overheated by burning a lumbering mass of Exchequer tallies. Nor was the tally the only idle formality observed when payments were made into the Exchequer. Centuries ago the Royal moneys were actually received and kept in that department; but for a long while past the actual cash has been lodged in the Bank of England, where it is more safely guarded, and more conveniently administered. Nevertheless, every sum received on

---

[*] Abridged (with interpolations) from a communication to the *Illustrated London News*, 1857.

Exchequer account was still nominally brought to the Exchequer Office; and for that purpose a Bank clerk regularly attended every day with a bundle of cancelled notes, which were solemnly counted over and checked, and deposited as a precious trust in a massive iron chest secured with three keys, each in the custody of different officers.

The tally in course of time failed to satisfy the payers of money to Exchequer account, and a written quittance became necessary. This also in its turn grew obsolete in form and language, but was in like manner preserved in all its antique unintelligibility until the Act of 1834.

Such was the "tally" system of olden time, and, undoubtedly, it in some way is involved in the origination of what is known as the "tally shop" system ōf to-day.

Formerly, in the Exchequer business, the collectors and receivers charged with the receipt of public moneys from the taxpayers were required to find sureties for their honesty. These security bonds were valid only for a year, and, therefore, annually renewed, to the great profit of the law and other officers of the Crown. When each collector had duly settled his account, and paid-in all the proper moneys into the Exchequer, for any year, he received back his bond, signifying a discharge from all further liability, and this was called getting his *quietus*. The practice and the term are now disused, but they evidently constituted the point of *Hamlet's* allusion:—

> When he himself might his quietus make
> With a bare bodkin.

What becomes of the Public Revenue.

Of the seventy millions of the Revenue more than one-third is disposed of by the interest of the National Debt, a charge not liable to any important variation. It was less by 89,412*l.* in 1862 than in the year before. But the difference is very slight on such a sum as 26,142,606*l.* The armed force of the country is the next great channel of expenditure. The Army in 1862 absorbed 15,570,869*l.*, an increase of 399,000*l.* over its cost in the previous year. The Navy required 12,598,042*l.* in the same period, or 733,626*l.* less than in 1861. Together they account for more than 28,000,000*l.* of the public expenditure. The naval and military operations in China figure in both years of this return. In 1861 they drew from the Exchequer 3,043,896*l.*; and in 1862 a further sum of 1,230,000*l.* The votes of money for fortifications rose suddenly from 50,000*l.* in 1861 to 970,000*l.* in 1862. There are small variations, both of reduction and increase, dispersed through an immense number of items, but when the gross sum they absorb is reckoned up, the difference between one year and another is scarcely worth noting.

Queen Anne's Bounty.

The origin of this revenue, which is considered to effect little compared with what might be accomplished under improved management, is as follows. We know that in olden times the Romish Pontiff had the "tenths" of the net annual income of good livings, as well as first-fruits. When the Pope and Henry VIII. quarrelled, and the Papal supremacy was subverted, not only was the supremacy in ecclesiastical affairs transferred from the Pope of Rome to England's supreme ruler, but also the tenths and first-fruits likewise. At length Queen Anne came to the throne, when (with the consent of her Parliament) she nobly refused to receive what the Church should enjoy, and placed the income under the direction of a Board called "the Governors of Queen Anne's Bounty." Their revenue for the improvement of poor livings is considerable, but it might be largely increased. The Pope would have had the real present value, and not that of centuries since; yet, strange to say, while some old benefices have been freed from payment no new rich livings have since been included, and all the old ones are rated according to the absurd scale of assessment made in the time of Henry VIII. To illustrate this the writer compiled the following, some time since:—

Benefice.	Diocese.	Value in King's Books.			Value in Clergy List.		
1. Stanhope	Durham	£67	6	8	£4848	0	0
2. Whitchurch	Lichfield ...	8	17	0	1458	0	0
3. Halsall	Chester	24	11	5	3500	0	0
4. Croston	Manchester .	31	11	0	1050	0	0
5. Edgmond	Lichfield......	46	8	0	2600	0	0
6. Houghton-le-Spring	Durham	124	0	0	1600	0	0
7. Bingham	Lincoln	44	7	0	1503	0	0
		£347	1	1	£16,559	0	0

Thus, seven benefices which now pay only 34*l.* as tenths to the fund, would, if rated according to the present net value, furnish 1600*l.* annually. If this were altered, and a graduated scale of taxation upon all valuable livings adopted, we should soon see a more equitable and less objectionable management of ecclesiastical affairs. If all the rich clergy regularly assisted the poor benefices, would not the rich laity do the same?

We quote the above from a communication to the *Times,* 1862. It has been significantly remarked that a Report of the Receipts and Expenditure of the Bounty is desirable.

Ecclesiastical Fees.

A Return issued in 1863, gives a curious list of Fees payable by members of the sacred profession. The Bishop of Lichfield had to pay 624*l.* on his appointment to that see; the Bishop of Bath and Wells 450*l.* on his translation from Sodor and Man. To this prelate the Attorney-General, or " his office," presented a demand for nearly 30*l.*; the Secretary of State (including stamp), 23*l.*; a mysterious impersonality, " the Petty Bag-office," absorbed 167*l.* When the Bishop had his audience of Her Majesty the homage fees were 94*l.*, and the *Court Circular* charged a guinea for its line and a half of history. The bill winds up with an item of 21*l.* for " passing documents through the various offices." Bishop Baring's " homage" on translation from Gloucester to Durham cost him only 21*l.* 6s. 8d. The Bishops of Chester and Lichfield add an item of 11*l.* 2s. and 12*l.* for gloves. The fees on the consecration of a church or churchyard are heavy, but it is noticeable as a rule that the bishops waive the customary payment to themselves.

Burying Gold and Silver.

The practice of burying treasure in the earth has uniformly prevailed in all countries harassed by intestine commotions, or exposed to foreign invasions. Of sums so deposited a very considerable proportion has been altogether lost; and this has, no doubt, been one of the principal means by which the stock of the precious metals has been kept down to its present level. Every one is aware that, during the Middle Ages, *treasure-trove*, or money dug from the ground, formed no inconsiderable part of the revenues of this and other countries. And though the burying of money has long ceased in Great Britain, such has not been the case with our neighbours. Wakefield tells us that, down to 1812, the practice was common in Ireland; and though much fallen off, it still continues to this day to be occasionally resorted to in that part of the kingdom. It has always prevailed, more or less, in almost every part of the Continent. The anarchy and brigandage that accompanied the Revolution of 1789 made the practice be carried to an extraordinary extent in France; and there, owing to various causes, it still maintains a broad and firm footing. Dupuynode, in 1853, estimated the sum at 40 millions thus rendered sterile. Yet, we doubt whether the burying of treasure be at present as prevalent in France as in many parts of Germany, and in Hungary, Russia, Italy, Spain, and European Turkey. The feeling of insecurity that has prevailed in all these

countries, especially since 1848, has given a stimulus to this practice. Of the many millions that were distributed among the
countries round the Black Sea, during the late campaigns in that
quarter, the greater portion is believed to be as much withdrawn
from circulation as if it had never been dug from the mine.

It is impossible, of course, to form any estimate of the sums
that are thus annually, as it were, placed in mortmain. They are
always greater when wars or revolutionary disturbances are in
progress; when their occurrence is anticipated, or but little confidence is placed in the permanence of existing institutions. There
can, at all events, be no question that the sums which have been
disposed of in the way now stated in the different Continental
countries of late years have been enormous—greater, perhaps,
than those absorbed by any of the usual channels of expenditure.
But the practice has been carried to a greater extent in India,
Persia, Turkey in Asia, and other eastern countries, than anywhere
in the western world. Despotism and a want of security have
always prevailed in these countries. The inhabitants have been,
in consequence, accustomed to regard the money they have committed to the earth as their only real wealth, and have availed
themselves of every opportunity to place portions of their means
beyond the grasp of their avaricious and tyrannical masters. And
as many of the hoards so deposited will never be brought to light,
the practice has, undoubtedly, been a principal cause of the constant flow of bullion to the East.

Bernier, "that most curious traveller," as he is called by Gibbon,
has some remarks on this subject, in which he calls the empire of
the Mogul an abyss of gold and silver, which the people buried
to escape the injustice and exactions to which they were exposed.
At a later date, Mr. Luke Scrafton refers to the same practice.
"In India," he says, "the Hindoos bury their dead under-ground,
often with such secresy as not to trust their own children with
the knowledge of it; and it is amazing what they will suffer
rather than betray it. When their tyrants have tried all manner
of corporal punishments upon them, and that fails, resentment
prevailing over the love of life, they frequently rip up their bowels,
or poison themselves, and carry the secret to their graves. And
the sums lost in this manner in some measure account why the
silver of India does not appear to increase, though there are such
quantities continually coming into it, and none going out."

The comparative security that was lately enjoyed by the natives
in most parts of India may have done something to lessen this
habit, in the countries directly under the Company's government;
but there was in Oude, and many other parts of India, previous
to the late insurrection, a good deal of disorder, oppression, and

robbery. And since that unfortunate outbreak, insecurity and disorders of all sorts have immeasurably increased, and have proportionally stimulated the practice of hoarding. The rebellion in China led to similar effects; and we have been assured by those who, from experience and observation are well qualified to form an opinion on such a subject, that it may be moderately estimated that in India and China, during the half-dozen years ending with 1857, a sum of not less than 100,000,000l. sterling has been consigned to the earth.—*J. R. Macculloch; Ency. Brit.*, 1859.

Thirty years ago, *hoarding* coin went on in England to a considerable extent, and greatly augmented the scarcity, and consequently the value, of the precious metals. Even the old practice of *making a stocking* was by no means given up in rural districts. A writer in the *Quarterly Review*, 1832, states, " We ourselves, but a few days back, personally witnessed an old crone, the wife of a small and apparently poor farmer, in a wild pastoral district, bring no less than three hundred sovereigns in a bag to a neighbouring attorney, to be placed by him in security; her treasure having accumulated till she was afraid to keep it longer at home. Such examples are by no means so rare as may be imagined. The failures of so many country banks in 1825 destroyed the confidence of country-people in the bank-notes of the present banks, and causes their preference for gold. The failure of many attorneys, as well as of country banks, which received and gave interest on deposits, and, (with the exception of the savings'-banks, which are very limited in the amount of the deposits they allow,) the total absence, in the rural districts of England, of any safe and accessible depositaries for the savings of the economical, such as the invaluable Scotch banks, have tended most injuriously to discourage economy; and where that principle was strongly ingrafted, have converted it into a practice of hoarding—have caused it to stagnate in unprofitable masses, which, spread through proper channels, would have stimulated new industry and new accumulations, and added both to the wealth of the owner, and to the general stock."

Results of Gold-seeking.

The question as to the probable continuation, increase, or diminution of the Supply of Gold is of the greatest interest; though nothing but the vaguest conjectures can be offered respecting it. Though gold be very generally distributed, it is extremely doubtful whether there be many places in which the deposits are so rich and so extensive as in California and Australia; and even in these the produce is either stationary, or has begun to decline. The

myriads of adventurers that are attracted to prolific diggings can
hardly fail, in no very lengthened period, to rifle the richest beds.
And when this is done—when the excitement caused by the
original discovery is worn off, and the great prizes in the gigantic
lottery recur only at distant intervals,—then, unless some new and
equally promising discoveries should be made, a serious check
will be given to the gold-seeking mania.   The process of quartz-
crushing is believed to produce only moderate profits, and is not
of a kind to collect crowds of competitors.   The few fortunes
that have been realized in California and Australia have not been
made by the diggers, but by the merchants and others who have
supplied their real or imaginary wants, or bought their gold-dust
and nuggets on advantageous terms.   Of those engaged on their
own account in the search of gold, very few have retired from
the pursuit with anything like a real competence.   The great
majority have hardly realized the wages current in the districts
before the deposits were discovered ; and the conviction seems to
be everywhere gaining ground, that more is to be made by cultivating the surface of the earth than by digging in its bowels, or
crushing its rocks.—*J. R. Macculloch ; Ency. Brit.,* 1859.

What becomes of the Precious Metals ?

The indestructibility of Gold is one of its many characteristics,
and some very curious questions arise from the fact.   We know
that at a very early period of the history of the human race,
gold was discovered in very large quantities, and was used for
a variety of ornamental and useful purposes.   Among the latter
may be named its employment as a medium of exchange, not
exactly in the form of money, but nearly approaching to it.
Pieces of the precious metal were cut into certain lengths and
were stamped with figures denoting their weight, and these circu-
lated freely among the buyers and sellers of those remote and
primitive times.   What was known as a talent of gold weighed,
it is supposed, 125 lbs., and Dr. Adam Clarke estimates that the
revenue of King Solomon in gold, was equal in value to about
4,683,375*l.* sterling.   To some extent this estimate is confirmed
by the Bible ; for it is stated in the book of Kings that " the weight
of gold that came to Solomon in one year, was six hundred and
three score and six talents of gold," without reference to silver,
which the same authority states, "was nothing accounted of in
the days of Solomon."   According to Calmet, the precious metals
expended by the same monarch in building Jerusalem and the
Temple, amounted in value to eight hundred millions of pounds
sterling, and the questions naturally suggest themselves as to

where this enormous amount of material came from, and what has become of it also.

It is sufficient for our purpose to know that the precious metals did actually exist in very large quantities ; and there is little doubt that they had been accumulating almost from the period of the creation of man. The early history of the Jews abounds with statements as to the uses to which gold was put. The subsequent conquests of Rome doubtlessly led to its absorption at one time of a very large proportion of the accumulated mineral wealth of the world.

It is also plain that the Romans could not employ the precious metals for domestic purposes, or at least not to any considerable extent. Watches, spoons, and plate were the inventions of much later times. Since it is clear that many hundreds of tons of gold found their way to Rome during its prosperous time, and equally clear that gold is indestructible, we may well inquire, " What has become of the vast treasures ?" Was it, after the decline and fall of Rome, distributed among other nations ? Were large quantities of the precious metals buried in the earth, which still holds them in its keeping?

Amidst a multitude of suggestive replies there remains the un-doubted fact that gold is indestructible. Who shall say, in short, in the presence of the certain knowledge we have, that war, con-quest, and spoliation have been the rule among nations for centu-ries past, that some of the "talents" of King Solomon, are not existing at this moment in the shape of sovereigns, in the pockets of the subjects of Queen Victoria ? Or, who will have the hardi-hood to assert that the very watch-guard, or trinket he or she may wear, is not a *bonâ fide* part of the treasure forwarded by the Queen of Sheba to Solomon the wise ?

The fact seems to be clearly demonstrable that much of the gold and silver spoken of in Scripture and in ancient profane his-tory is in active circulation at this hour amongst the inhabitants of the globe.—*Mechanics' Magazine.*

Tribute-money.

The coins of the British Prince Cunobelin were not only stamped with the figures of animals, but with the word TASCIO, which signified TASK, TAX, and TRIBUTE. The pay-ment of them into the Exchequer acquitted the subject of duties on merchandise, and was also a commutation of personal ser-vices. " I have thought," says the learned Camden, " that in old time there was a certain sort of money coined on purpose for this use, seeing, in Scripture, it is called *tribute-money ;* and I am the more confirmed in this opinion, because, in some of the British pieces, there is the Mint-master stamping the money with TASCIO, which among the Britons meant the tribute-money."

The First Lottery.

The first Lottery in England of which we have any account, took place in 1569, the proposals for which were published in 1567 and 1568. It consisted of 10,000 lots of ten shillings each: there were no blanks, and the prizes consisted chiefly of plate. There were then only three lottery-offices in London. The lottery was drawn at the west door of St. Paul's Cathedral; and the profits were intended for the repair of the havens of the king-. dom, and other public works. M. Greillier considers this number of lots much underrated, and raises them to 400,000; and he arrives at that conclusion because the drawing was continued uninterruptedly *both day and night*, between the 11th of January and the 6th of May. The first Lottery for sums of money took place in 1630.

Coinage of a Sovereign.

The number of operations necessary for the conversion of an ingot of Gold into Sovereigns is greater than most persons are aware of. In the first instance it is melted; in the second it is cast into bars; in the third the bars are rolled; in the fourth they are cut into short lengths; in the fifth they are annealed in copper pans; in the sixth they are flattened into fillets; in the seventh the fillets are adjusted; in the eighth they are punched, and blanks produced; in the ninth the blanks are weighed singly by automaton balances; in the tenth the blanks are marked, or have their edges raised; in the eleventh they are annealed in cast-iron pans; in the twelfth they are blanched in an acid bath; in the thirteenth they are washed in cold water; in the fourteenth they are dried in hot beech-wood saw-dust; in the fifteenth they are muffled; and in the sixteenth stamped on both sides, milled on their edges, and made perfect for circulation! Thus sixteen operations, separate and distinct from each other, have to be performed in the production of sovereigns from an ingot. But the ingot will be after all only partly converted; the perforated "fillets," amounting in weight to nearly half that of the original ingot, must be returned to the crucible, recast into bars, and these bars passed through the routine processes above enumerated. The fillets resulting from this second crop of sovereigns will again have to be melted, and yet again and again, if the ingot is to be made to yield all its value in coin; and thus the sixteen operations will be multiplied before the last sovereign is obtained from the precious wedge of gold.—*Mechanics' Magazine.*

Wear and Tear of the Coinage.

It has been discovered by the Mint authorities that the intelligent or intelligible life of coins is much shorter than it was prior to the introduction of the railway system and cheap travelling. People move about now more frequently than they used, and so does money. Whether the former wear out sooner from their greater activity is a problem for social economists, but that the latter does is certain. Towards the close of the last century careful experiments deduced the fact that deterioration among ten-year-old silver coins of the various denominations was as follows:—Crowns, 3½ per cent.; half-crowns, 10 per cent.; shillings, 24½ per cent.; and sixpences, 38 2-10ths per cent. Now, the loss is nearly as follows on coins of the same age:—Crowns, 5 per cent.; half-crowns, 12 per cent.; shillings, 30 per cent.; sixpences, 45 per cent.; and threepences, over fifty per cent. This increase is evidently due to " fast living," so to speak, and the weakest individuals; or, at any rate, the smallest, suffer most from its consequences. The gold coinage does not deteriorate in anything like the same ratio, and this from obvious causes. It is not subjected to anything like the same course of treatment. It moves in higher and more circumscribed circles, is only a legal tender when of legal weight, and is therefore nursed with more care under the porte-monnaie system. Of copper and bronze moneys, pence and half-pence suffer the most rapid deterioration, farthings being the longest lived of the three denominations. They are all tokens of value merely, and their shortcomings are less noticed, and, indeed, of far less consequence to the public.—*Mechanics' Magazine.*

Counterfeit Coin.

There is little doubt that the method first employed in the manufacture of money was that of pouring fluid bullion into earthen moulds previously impressed by some rude artist with the device intended to be represented on the coin; and that (as now in some remote localities of Central India) a small cylindrical vessel, forming a smelting-furnace, a pair of tongs, a cutting-tool or file, and a pair of scales, constituted the entire apparatus for a mint. It is not a little singular that the casting process is that resorted to by counterfeiters up to this day. The customary mode adopted for the production of spurious money at present is precisely identical, indeed, with that employed in the manufacture of genuine coin by the monarchs and the *moneyers*—as the fabricators of money were then termed—of the Heptarchy, only that

M

the coiners of to-day use appliances superior to those of the tenth
century.   A private coiner of the nineteenth century, whether in
Birmingham or London, expends very little in the purchase of his
plant of machinery.   He provides himself with a pennyworth of
plaster of Paris, which he converts into a mould; making a genuine
coin serve as the medium for impressing the material when in a
soft state with the devices—the obverse and reverse. If he cannot
steal pint measures from a publican, he will have to invest a
portion of his capital in Britannia-metal spoons at a shilling a
dozen, and these he will break up and melt in an earthen pipkin,
purchasable for another penny.   With a tobacco-pipe for a ladle
he will take up sufficient of the fused metal to create a florin, say,
and this he will pour into the moulds. As soon as these are filled,
and the base compound has become solidified, the moulds are
separated, and any defects observable in the graining or milling of
the edge are made good with a file or some other implement
adapted to the nefarious purpose.   If, after this, a clever confede-
rate can finish the work by depositing a coat of silver (by galvanic
agency), so much the better for the manufacturer, his chance of
uttering being thus much enhanced.—*Mechanics' Magazine.*

Standard Gold.

In 1855, an alteration was made in the quality of gold marked
in Goldsmiths' Hall, it being represented to the President of the
Board of Trade that it would be advantageous alike to the manufacturer and the public: instead of there being only two different
standards, there are now five—viz., 22, 18, 15, 12, and 9 carats.
If, on the purchase of a watch, the cases, instead of having the
mark of " 18 carat," the gold of which would be worth 67s. per
oz., should be marked only " 12 carat," the gold is worth only
45s. per oz., and the purchaser has been legally robbed of the difference in value, which, supposing the cases to weigh 1 oz. 10 dwts.,
would be 33s.

When purchasing a gold watch, therefore, see that the cases
are marked " 18 carat ;" if they are not so marked, do not make
the purchase.

Interest of Money.

Among the curiosities of the Exchequer, it may be mentioned
that about the year 1857, there were paid into its account the proceeds of a lottery prize, drawn in the reign of George II., but
which had remained unclaimed for 102 years. The original
amount of the prize was 490*l.*, to which in the course of a century there had been added 1499*l.* 8s. for interest. The sum of

1989*l.* 8s. was therefore handed over for the public service; but even now we have no doubt that if the purchaser of the ticket, warned by this announcement of the fact, can come forward and prove his claim, the money will be honourably refunded to him from the Exchequer.

Interest of Money in India.

In the *Institutes of Menu,* which were drawn up about B.C. 900, the lowest legal interest for money is fixed at 15 per cent., the highest at 60 per cent. Nor is this to be considered a mere ancient law now fallen into disuse. So far from that, the *Institutes of Menu* are still the basis of Indian jurisprudence; and we know, on very good authority, that in 1810, the interest paid for the use of money varied from 36 to 60 per cent.; Ward places it at 75 per cent., and this without the lender incurring any extraordinary risk.

Origin of Insurance.

Mr. G. F. Smith, in a paper read to the Institute of Actuaries, is of opinion that the earliest direct mention of Marine Insurance is in an ordinance of the City of Barcelona, of the year 1433, in which it is ordered that no vessel should be insured for more than three-quarters of its value; that no merchandise belonging to foreigners should be insured at Barcelona, unless freighted on board a ship belonging to the King of Arragon; and that merchandise belonging to Arragonese subjects on board vessels belonging to other countries should only be insured for half its value. It appears most probable that the inventors of Marine Insurance were the Italians, who, as is well known, were the leading commercial nation in the fourteenth and fifteenth centuries. It was in Venice that the first Bank was established, and that a funded debt, transferable from hand to hand, was first introduced. Bills of exchange, if not invented in Italy, were used extensively by the Lombard merchants and money-dealers; and book-keeping by double entry is of Italian origin; as is also the phrase, "Policy of Assurance."

After the Great Fire, Assurance Offices were set up. One of these is described, in Phillips's *World of Words,* under the heading "Phœnix Insurance Office, the first office that was set up in London for the insuring of houses from accidents by fire, so called from its emblem or device: the rate for ensuring 100 pounds on a brick house, is 6 shillings for 1 year, 12 shillings for 2 years, 15 shillings for 3 years, 19 shillings and sixpence for four years, 1 pound 10 shillings for seven years, and 2 pounds 1 shilling for eleven years: the number of houses so insured since Anno Dom. 1681 is ten thousand." A second is mentioned as the "Friendly Society, one of the offices settled in London for the insuring of houses from casualties by fire: the reward or consideration-money paid for insuring to the value of 100 pounds in this office, is 1 shilling 4 pence per annum for seven years. The device of it is a sheaf of arrows, and the number of houses insured since A.D. 1684 is 12,500."

Stockbrokers.

Stock-jobbing or broking was contemporaneous with the creation of our National Debt, in the reign of William III., 1695, and gave rise to that class of money-dealers who have the exclusive *entrée* to the Royal.Exchange. "William," says Mr. Francis, in his work on the Stock Exchange, "had already tried his power in the creation of a national debt: jobbing in the English funds and East India stock succeeded; and the Royal Exchange became what the Stock Exchange has been since 1700—the rendezvous of those who, having money, hoped to increase it, and of that yet more numerous and pretending class, who, having none themselves, try to gain it from those who have."

In the course of the Session of 1771, a Bill was brought into the House of Commons, "for the more effectually preventing the infamous practice of Stock-jobbing." It passed the committee, but was not further proceeded in.

Lord Chatham, in the previous year, 1770, had, in Parliament, denounced "the Monied Interest as a set of men in the City of London, who are known to live in riot and luxury upon the plunder of the ignorant, the innocent, the helpless. Whether they be the miserable jobbers of 'Change-alley, or the lofty Asiatic plunderers of Leadenhall-street, they are equally detestable. . . . . By the monied interest I mean that blood-sucker, that muck-worm, which calls itself the friend of Government— that pretends to serve this or that administration, and may be purchased on the same terms by any administration—that advances money to Government, and takes special care of its own emoluments. Under this description I include the whole race of commissaries, jobbers, contractors, clothiers, and remitters."

In the South Sea year, patriots were made or marred by jobbing: "from the Alley to the House," said Walpole, "is like a path of ants."

Yet, it is an established fact, that, abroad and at home, all parties having large financial operations, approach the London Stock Exchange with more confidence than any other money-market in the world.

Tampering with Public Credit.

Thirty years ago, it was wisely said by a writer in the *Quarterly Review*: " It is physically impossible to carry on the commerce of the civilized world by the aid of a *purely* metallic currency —no, not though our gold and silver coins were every tenth year debased to a tenth ! Why, in London alone, five millions of money are daily exchanged at the clearing-house, in the course of a few hours. We should like to see the attempt to bring this infinity of transactions to a settlement in coined money. Credit money, in some shape or other, always has, and must have, performed the part of a circulating medium to a very considerable extent. And (by one of those wonderful compensatory processes which so frequently claim the admiration of every investigator of civil as well as of physical economy,) there is in the nature of credit an elasticity which causes it, *when left unshackled by law*, to adapt itself to the necessities of commerce, and the legitimate demands of the market. Well may the productive classes exclaim to those who persist in legislating on the subject, and are not content with determining who may and who may not give credit to another, what kind of monied obligations shall, or shall not, be allowed to circulate—that is, to be taken in exchange for goods at the option of the parties,—well might they exclaim, as the merchants of Paris did to the minister of Louis, when he asked what his master could do for them—" Laissez-nous faire,"—" Leave us alone, to surround ourselves with those precautions which experience will suggest, and the instinct of self-preservation put in execution."

Over-speculation.

During the prevalence of a speculative mania there is not one person in ten among the English public that can be induced to weigh any arguments or facts that run counter to their fancies ; but by the small proportion capable of giving heed, the following *résumé* of British banking experience during the twelve years from 1846 to 1857 will be considered valuable.

In 1858 an interesting paper was published by Messrs. Waterlow and Sons, under the ominous title of *British Losses by Bank Failures*, and extending from 1820 to 1857. In the great mania for the establishment of new banks, it may not be out of place to call attention to the general facts proved in this document. Omitting, then, the years previous to 1846, which may perhaps be considered to be out of date, and taking the twelve years from 1846 to 1857 inclusive, it appears that the liabilities of the private banks which suspended payment amounted to 6,700,000*l.*, and those of the joint-stock banks to 40,800,000*l.*, making a grand total of 47,500,000*l.* To this, moreover, must be added another 1,500,000*l.* for some banks, the liabilities of which are not mentioned.

Value of Horses.

As an example of the large sums produced by the sale of first-rate Horses, we may quote the following prices from the sale of the stud of the late Earl of Pembroke, at Paris, in 1862. The condition of the horses was so good that, in spite of their being aged, some of them sold for more money than Lord Pembroke paid for them years previously. Thus, a pair of bay carriage-horses, aged respectively 13 and 14, bought at Anderson's seven years ago for 400*l.*, fetched 600*l.*; and another pair, which had been bought at the same place for 600*l.*, fetched 1088*l.*! Never was the policy of buying a good thing, and taking care of it, more practically proved than at this sale. Elis, a brown carriage-horse, more than 16 years old, sold for 100*l.*; Pilot, a bay, upwards of 15 years old, fetched 220*l.*; Papillon, 14 years old, 384*l.*; Abeille, 13 years old, 200*l.*; Grasshopper, a chestnut cob, 13 years old, 128*l.*; Zouave, a grey carriage-horse, 12 years old, 304*l.*; Calthorpe, a bay carriage-horse, 12 years old, 280*l.*; Sebastopol, a grey carriage-horse, 11 years old, 240*l.*; Pigeon, a brown phaeton-horse, 9 years old, 140*l.*; Solferino, a bay carriage-horse, 16 hands high, and 7 years old, 640*l.*; and Glaucus, a bay carriage-horse, 6 years old, 448*l.*

Friendly Societies.

The repeated failures of Friendly Societies to effect the object for which they were projected, prove how the best intentions may be defeated through want of proper foresight and calculation of probabilities, which so often reduce to certainty results which, to unthinking minds, appear mere chances.

In 1863, Mr. Tidd Pratt, the Registrar, reported: Sixty-five societies have been dissolved in the course of the year. The causes of such societies not being able to meet the claims of the members are to be found in incorrect tables for the contributions, small number of members, insecure investment of funds, and unnecessary expenses of management, which actually, in some instances, take 10s. out of every 1*l.* subscribed. Most of these societies still hold their meetings at public-houses, with the landlords for treasurers; and the members are required by the rules of most of the old societies to spend a monthly sum in beer " for the good of the house," which amount is generally taken from the box, whether the members have or have not paid their contributions; and in many instances the money is not repaid to the society. In the correspondence of the year it is stated, in a letter to the Registrar respecting the affairs of a society, that it has spent nearly 1300*l.* of the funds "for the good of the house." There is generally a strong party in favour of it. One letter states that a female friendly society will be obliged to break up unless they are allowed to have an annual feast and music; and an objector who is contending with the managers against any such application of the trust-funds writes:—"I can do nothing with them unless you assist me by sending a very saucy letter to the stewards." Sometimes the law is evaded by paying an extravagant rent for the room, the excess being really allowed in beer.

The Registrar considers it to be proved by thirty-five years' experience that some further provisions are necessary to secure to working men that they shall not be required to subscribe to these societies more than is necessary, and that they shall be certain of obtaining the benefits paid for. Returns which have been obtained from only 128 unions show about 1150 inmates in their workhouses who have been members of friendly societies which have been broken up or dissolved.

Wages heightened by Improvement in Machinery.

It is stated, in a Report of the Commissioners appointed in 1832 to inquire concerning the employment of women and children in factories, that "in the cotton-mill of Messrs. Houldsworth, in Glasgow, a spinner employed on a mule of 336 spindles, and spinning cotton 120 hanks to the pound, produced in 1823, working 74½ hours a week, 46 pounds of yarn, his net weekly wages for which amounted to 27s. 7d. Ten years later, the rate of wages having in the meantime been reduced 13 per cent., and the time of working having been lessened to 69 hours, the spinner was enabled by the greater perfection of the machinery to produce on a mule of the same number of spindles, 53½ pounds of yarn of the same fineness, and his net weekly earnings were advanced from 27s. 7d. to 29s. 10d." Similar results from similar circumstances were experienced in the Manchester factories. The cheapening of the article produced by help of machinery increases the demand for the article; and there being consequently a need for an increased number of workmen, the elevation of wages follows as a matter of course. Nor is this the only benefit which the workingman derives in the case, for he shares with the community in acquiring a greater command over the necessities which machinery is concerned in producing.—*G. R. Porter.*

Giving Employment.—Indirect Taxation.

Mr. Babbage relates the following illustrative anecdote: An Irish proprietor, whose country residence was much frequented by beggars, resolved to establish a test for discriminating between the idle and the industrious, and also to obtain some small return for the alms he was in the habit of bestowing. He accordingly added to the pump, by which the upper part of his house was supplied with water, a piece of mechanism so contrived, that at the end of a certain number of strokes of the pump-handle, a penny fell out from an aperture to repay the labourer for his work. This was so arranged, that labourers who continued at the work obtained very nearly the usual daily wages of labour in that part of the country. The idlest of the vagabonds of course refused this new labour-test; but the greater part of the beggars, whose constant tale was that "*they could not earn a fair day's wages for a fair day's work*," after earning a few pence, usually went away cursing the hardness of their taskmaster.

Never sign an Accommodation Bill.

Nothing is more deceptive than imaginary wealth. "We are apt," says Sir E. B. Lytton, "to rely upon future prospects, and become really expensive while we are only rich in possibility. We live up to our expectations, not to our possessions, and make a figure proportionable to what we may be, not what we are. We outrun our present income, as not doubting to disburse ourselves out of the profits of some future place, project, or reversion we have in view."

By no means is this artificial state of living more nourished than what are familiarly called "bill transactions." This has been illustrated in novels and tales, but never more to the purpose than in the following passage in *Pisistratus Caxton.* "To sign an Accommodation Bill, and still more, tò renew one when due, is opening an account with ruin. One always begins by being security for a friend. The discredit of the thing is familiarized to one's mind by the false show of generous confidence in another. Then, what you have done for a friend, *a friend* should do for you—a hundred or two would be useful now—you are sure to repay it in three months. To youth the future seems safe as the Bank of England, and distant as the peaks of Himalaya. You pledge your honour that in three months you will release your friend. The three months expire. To release one friend, you catch hold of another—the bill is renewed, premium and interest thrown into the next pay-day—soon the amount multiplies, and with it the honour dwindles—your *name* circulates from hand to hand on the back of doubtful paper,— your name, which, in all money transactions, should grow higher and higher each year you live, falling down every month like the shares in a swindling speculation. You begin by what you call trusting a friend, that is, aiding him to self-destruction—buying him arsenic to clear his complexion,—you end by dragging all near you into your own abyss, as a drowning man would catch at his own brother."

A Year's Wills.

The Registrar-General has drawn from a calendar of the Wills and Adminstrations of the year 1858, the following interesting calculations. 210,972 adults died in the twelvemonth, and 30,823 persons left personal property behind them; 21,653 had made their Wills; the other 9170 had made none, and letters of administration had to be taken out. 89 persons with more than 10,000*l.* (one worth 100,000*l.*) died without making a Will. The aggregate amount of property left by all these persons is estimated at 71,860,792*l.*, averaging 2331*l.* each. Distinguishing between the men and the women, we find that 102,049 adult men died in the year, and 21,454 left personal property—for one who left any, four leaving none; 108,923 adult women died, and 9369 left personal property. The average amount left by the men was 2751*l.*; by the women, 1371*l.* Omitting now any estimate for the first ten days of the year, and dealing only with the actual Wills and administrations of the rest of the twelvemonth, the personal property of those who died leaving any, 29,979 in number, amounted to 69,893,380*l.*, of which 57,396,350*l.* was left by the men, and 12,497,030*l.* by women. The stream of wealth flowed thus :—

Persons.	Dying worth	Left
22,513	............Less than 1000*l.*	5,762,880*l.*
6277	.... 1000*l.* but less than 10,000*l.*	20,010,500*l.*
1020	............10,000*l.* but less than 50,000*l.*	21,960,000*l.*
102	............50,000*l.* but less than 100,000*l.*	7,100,000*l.*
67	............Above 100,000*l.*	15,060,000*l.*
29,979		69,893,380*l.*

Only one property was sworn as high as 900,000*l.* and under 1,000,000; 1935 were under 20*l.* The property divides nearly equally at 20,000*l.* About 35,000,000*l.* belonged to 29,392 persons, none having more than 20,000*l.*, and the other 35,000,000*l.*

belonged to 587 persons, fifty times fewer than the former company. Of those who left above 100,000*l*, 37 were described as esquires, a term which would include men who had made their fortunes by trade or commerce; ten were titled personages, five were bankers, four merchants, three clergymen, one cotton manufacturer, one corn merchant, one hotel-keeper; one was in the navy, one in the Indian army, one in the Indian Civil Service, one was a spinster. Three medical men left more than 50,000*l*. A person described when he made his will as a commercial clerk left above 30,000*l*.; 17 "labourers and mechanics" above 1000*l*. Of 75 lawyers, 15 died without making their Wills. The foregoing statements, which must be taken as approximations rather than an absolute accuracy, relate to England alone. In the year ending March 31, 1859, legacy-duty was paid in the United Kingdom on 62,441,611*l*., but that does not include property passing from husband to wife or the converse, no legacy-duty being then payable; succession-duty on real property was paid upon 29,242,630*l*., and, estimating that to be taxed to the next successor at half its saleable value, it will amount to 58,485,260*l*. On this assumption 123,926,871*l*. passed by death to another generation of successors. It is certainly a remarkable fact, that (upon an average) on every death, including alike men, women, and children, more than 100*l*. of property paying legacy-duty, and perhaps 187*l*. of property of every kind, is left for the benefit of successors in the United Kingdom.— *Times.*

The extraordinary circumstances under which Wills are sometimes made have given rise to the following suggestive remarks by an able writer in the *Saturday Review* :—

"If the matter is considered in reference to general principles, there is no more curious power in the world than the right which people exercise by Will of legislating after they are dead and gone, without restraint and without appeal; and it is perhaps even more singular that they exercise this power without being subject to any formalities whatever except the presence of two witnesses. To sell a house or a field is a matter which requires care and inquiry, and the circumstances ensure a certain degree of notoriety. But property of any amount may be disposed of in any way that caprice may dictate by an instrument which may be executed under any circumstances, and kept in any custody. No one but the testator need know its contents, and he may, and often does, prepare it with the most wanton caprice, and leave it in the most absurd depository to take its chance of loss or discovery as it may happen. It is well worth consideration whether the unlimited power which the law of England confers of making whatever Wills a testator chooses ought not to be qualified by some special provisions as to the manner in which such wills should be made."

Progress of Science.

What human Science has accomplished.

IF we reflect on the extreme feebleness of the natural means by the help of which so many great problems have been attacked and solved; if we consider that to obtain and measure the greater part of the quantities now forming the basis of astronomical computation, man has had greatly to improve the most delicate of his organs, to add immensely to the power of his eye; if we remark that it was not less requisite for him to discover methods adapted to measuring very long intervals of time, up to the precision of tenths of seconds; to combat against the most microscopic effects that constant variations of temperature produce in metals, and therefore in all instruments; to guard against the innumerable illusions that a cold or hot atmosphere, dry or humid, tranquil or agitated, impresses on the medium through which the observations have inevitably to be made; the feeble being resumes all his advantage: by the side of such wonderful labours of the mind, what signifies the weakness, the fragility of our body; what signify the dimensions of the planet, our residence, the grain of sand on which it has happened to us to appear for a few moments !—*Arago.*

Changes in Social Science.

The conquests of science over the realms of matter in our day would scarcely have affected Bacon with greater surprise than the change in what we may call the social position of science. There was a time, not so very far removed from his own, when scientific truth was worshipped, if at all, with closed doors and in muffled accents. Science, like religion, had her age of persecution and her "church in the catacombs;" she, too, had heroes, and martyrs, and confessors of her own, and won her way to popularity through an ordeal of shame and suffering, the history of which remains to be written. The philosopher of the Middle Ages shunned the haunts of men; his crucible was heated in some secret or underground chamber; his knowledge was a forbidden lore, and if it showed itself in the command of new powers, was ascribed, not to inspiration from on high, but to dealings with an agent which even modern credulity so often proclaims as the source of intellectual mastery. From these fiery trials science has emerged without even a scar upon her.   Militant she still is, but she is also triumphant, and vies with the learning of "letters," which was never branded with the like infamy, in the number and dignity of her votaries.   The change which has come over her social status has reacted on her doctrines.   There are no longer any "mysteries" of science; "problems," and even "apparent contradictions," remain, but mysteries, with everything else that savours of the occult and esoteric, are exploded, and not many difficulties are admitted.—*Times.*

Discoverers not Inventors.

Although Galileo only discovered the moons of Jupiter, we often and unconsciously think of him as if he had been their creator, and had first set them to play their untiring game of hide-and-seek round the stately planet; and so also in no irreverent spirit we call the laws which Kepler divined to regulate certain movements of the heavenly bodies, "Kepler's Laws," although he disclaimed the title, grandly affirming that God, whose laws they were, had waited some thousand years before one man, even Kepler, had discerned them.   And so again, notwithstanding our conviction that the star Neptune has been shining in the sky since what we shall be content to call "the beginning," and that all the tiny planets which have so rapidly been added to our astronomical catalogues are probably as old as the sun, we cannot help feeling as if Adams, Leverrier, Hind, and their brethren, had just planted those lights in the sky, and that midnight should be sensibly less dark because of their addition to the heavens.

When we work as transformationalists we are like sculptors, not evolving a pre-existent statue from a concealing mass, but bestowing a statue on a block of marble.   The hollow screw is Archimedes' screw; the condensing steam-engine, Watt's engine; the railway locomotive, Stephenson's locomotive; the electric telegraph, Oersted's telegraph; the Crystal Palace, Fox and Paxton's palace.   Yet as implied in what has been already said, we treat discoverers as if they were inventors, and to make amends we call inventors discoverers.   And although, in strictness of speech, it is inadmissible to speak of Watt, as accomplished men are frequently found doing, as the *discoverer* of the steam-engine, and only Sancho Panza thought of invoking blessings on the man who first *invented* sleep, still the popular confusion between the discoverer and the inventor shows how difficult it is to assign the one higher praise than the other.—*Prof. George Wilson.*

Science of Roger Bacon.

Roger Bacon, writing about the year 1260, that is, six hundred years ago, says:—" I call that Experimental Science which neglects argumentation; for the strongest arguments prove nothing as long as the conclusions are not verified by experience. Experimental science does not receive truth at the hands of superior sciences. It is itself mistress, and other sciences are its servants. It has, in truth, the right to command all sciences, since it alone certifies and sanctions their results. Experimental science is, therefore, the queen of sciences and the limit of all speculation." The features in Bacon's writings that have caused his name to be handed down as a founder of physical science are very obvious. He doubts wisely and has a profound reverence for facts. The theory of a vacuum has come to him on the highest authority, but its difficulties distress him. He speaks of experimental philosophy as more perfect than all the natural sciences; "for it teaches us to test by trial the noble conclusions of all the sciences, which, in the others, are either proved by logical arguments or are examined into on the imperfect evidence of nature; and this is its prerogative."

" As a workman in the laboratory, and with lenses, he himself discovers the existence of explosive compounds, confirms the tradition of history as to the effect of burning glasses, and understands the principle of the camera. He points out the faultiness of Cæsar's calendar. His views of the limits of medicine are excellent. ' For, whereas a healthy rule of life depends upon what is eaten and drank, on the hours of sleep and waking, of exercise and rest, on climate and the temper of the mind, and that all these should be observed from childhood in the constitution they fit, scarcely any man cares to take thought of these things, nay, not even physicians, such at least as we have met with.' Contrast this and his critical approval of the use of charms to delude credulous patients into health with the science ridiculed in the *Malade Imaginaire*, and the advantage will not be found on the side of the seventeenth century. But, even in physical science, Bacon's splendid powers of generalization prevail over the habit of analysis, and he is rather a prophet than a teacher. He believes that the period of human life may be prolonged many years by a sound system of dietetics; and the averages of life in our own century confirm him. He believes that 'engines of navigation may be made without oarsmen, so that the greatest river and sea-ships with only one man to steer them, may sail swifter than if they were fully manned. Moreover, chariots,' he thinks, 'may be made so as to be moved with incalculable force without any beast drawing them.' 'And such things might be made to infinity, as, for instance, bridges to traverse rivers without pillars or any buttress.' He even knows a wise man who has determined to construct a flying machine; but Bacon's tone on this subject is a little less confident. That he himself hoped for much that has since been proved impossible—for the art of increasing gold, and for the discovery of an elixir of life—cannot of course be questioned. Bacon summed up the science of his times, and the analogies which guided him in his estimate of the laws of motion could not teach him to antici- pate by five hundred years the individuality of the elements, or to under- stand the texture of the human body.   His error, after all, was chiefly that he believed in Thought as a conqueror, and expected to establish her kingdom on the ruins of the thrones of the visible world."—*Saturday Review.*

The One Science.

In an able summary in the *Times* of the contents of Sir Henry Holland's *Essays on Scientific and other Subjects,* we find the fol- lowing suggestive passages:—" The sciences are so interlacing and coalescing that it would seem as if in a year or two we should only have one huge science embracing all; or, at least, what are now regarded as separate sciences should be considerably reduced in number. This is more or less implied in the controversy on the " Correlation of Forces." The question is,—Are there really " Forces" in nature ?   Or should we not rather say that there is but one force appearing under different forms?   Among these forces may be mentioned light. The undulatory theory of the transmission of light is as old as Huyghens, but its universal acceptance is an incident of our own day; and it is in our own day that radiant heat has been discovered to be subject to those great physical laws which are the basis of the undulatory theory. Here, then, we find in our time, within the last few years, that the three great sciences of optics, of acoustics, and of heat, reduce their principal facts to the same formula. Or again, take this science of optics in another relation. It has within the last few years proved itself to be the most delicate instrument of chemistry. By the aid of a little starch the chemist can detect the millionth part of iodine in solution. Mr. Faraday has found that a strong ruby tint is given to a fluid by a proportion of gold not exceeding the half-millionth part in weight. These are wonderful results of ordinary chemical analysis; but what are they in comparison with the results obtained through the analysis of the spectrum ? By means of it chymists have been able to detect in a compound 1-$70,000,000$th part of a grain of lithium, and the 1-$180,000,000$th part of a grain of sodium, the metal of common salt. The method of the analysis is very simple. If a little sodium, for instance, be burnt in a flame, and during the process of this burning the rays be made to pass through a prism, then in a certain defined portion of the spectrum beyond there will appear a thin yellow line, so vivid that it will show even when the sodium has been reduced to the 1-180,000,000th part of a grain. By help of the same analysis we pass on to astronomy, and discover the chemistry of the sun, the moon, and the stars. In the photosphere, or luminous atmosphere surrounding the body of the sun, there has in this way been discovered no less than six known metals.

" In these few examples we indicate roughly but sufficiently the intimate connexion of the physical sciences, and the necessity which is imposed on the student in the present day to know all if he would understand one. It has been said that he who has seen but one work of ancient art has seen none, while he who has seen all has seen but one. We may say the same of science. To know one is to know none, and to know all is to know but one."

Sun-force.

Daily the conviction deepens among those who have studied the matter, that with a few exceptions all the physical powers which man wields as movers or transformers of matter are modifications of Sun-force. It was bestowed upon antediluvian plants, and they locked it up for a season in the woody tissue which it enabled them to weave, and afterwards time changed that into coal; and the steam-engine which we complacently call ours, and claim patents for, burns that coal into lever-force and steam-hammer power, and is in truth a sun-engine. And the plants of our own day receive as liberally from the sun, and condense his force into the charcoal which we extract from them, and expend in smelting metallic ores. With the smelted ·metals we make voltaic batteries, and magnets, and telegraph wires; and call the modified sun-force electricity and magnetism, and say it is ours, and ask if we may not do what we like with our own.

And again, the plants we cultivate concentrate Sun-force in grass, hay, oats, wheat, and other fibres and grains, which seem only suitable to feed cattle and beasts of burden with. But by and by a Spanish bull-fighter is transfixed by this force, through the horns of a bull, and dies unaware of his classical fate, pierced to the heart by an arrow from Apollo the Sun-god's bow. On English commons prizes are run for, by steeds which are truly coursers of the sun, for his force is swelling in their muscles and throbbing in their veins, and horse-power is but another name for sun-power. Nor is it otherwise with their riders; for they too have been fed upon light, and made strong with fruits and flesh which have been nourished by the sun. His heat warms their blood, his light shines in their eyes; they cannot deal a blow which is not a *coup-de-soleil*, a veritable sun-stroke; nor express a thought without help from him.

In grave earnestness, let me remind you, that as force cannot be annihilated any more than matter, but can only be changed in its mode of manifestation, so it appears beyond doubt that the force generated by the sun, and conveyed by his rays in the guise of heat, light, and chemical power, to the earth, is not extinguished there, but only changes its form. It apparently disappears when it falls upon plants, which never grow without it; but we cannot doubt that it is working in a new shape in their organs and tissues, and reappears in the heat and light which they give out when they are burned. This heat, which is sun-heat *at second hand*, we again seem to lose when we use plants as fuel in our boiler-furnaces; but it has only disguised itself, without loss of power, in the elasticity of the steam, and will again seem lost, when it is translated into the momentum of the heavy piston, and the whirling power of a million of wheels.

The second-hand heat of the sun appears equally lost when vegetable fuel is expended in reducing metals; but oxidize these metals in a galvanic battery, and it will reappear as chemical force, as electricity, as magnetism, as heat the most intense; and, in the electro-carbon light, will return almost to the condition of sunshine again.—*Prof. George Wilson.*

"*The Seeds of Invention.*"

Sir William Armstrong maintains, as a half-truth, that Invention is the fruit of the circumstances that call for it almost more than of the mind from which it springs. In a sense it is true, as Sir William Armstrong says, that "the seeds of invention exist, as it were, in the air, ready to germinate whenever suitable conditions arise;" but it depends not the less on the genius of individual inventors to determine whether the germination shall happen in one century or the next. The history of the locomotive is itself the strongest argument against relying too much on these floating seeds of invention and favouring circumstances, and taking too little account of inventors. If the Killingworth brakesman had died in his youth, it is scarcely too much to say that we should probably not yet be travelling by steam. We owe it to George Stephenson's keen insight and resolute temper that the locomotive was forced upon an unbelieving world, no one can say how long before circumstances would otherwise have called it into existence. The seed had been floating, it is true, and had been in a manner detected centuries before; but it remained without life, not because the occasion had not called it forth, but because the right man had not arisen.

The Object of Patents.

The recklessness with which Patents are issued, and the dishonesty on the part of the State in selling the same article to two or more persons, and then coolly leaving them to litigation for the possession of it, cannot be too strongly reprehended. The common sense of the question is summed up by Dr. Percy, in these words: " I cordially subscribe," says the Doctor, " to the opinions expressed by Mr. Grove, Q.C.—namely, that the real object of Patent Law was ' to reward not trivial inventions, which stop the way to greater improvements, but substantial boons to the public; not changes such as any experimentalist makes a score a day in his laboratory, but substantial practical discoveries, developed into an available form.' "

The law with respect to Patents has been greatly simplified and improved by the statute 15 and 16 Vict. c. 83: the fees payable for a Patent have been reduced, and the payment of spread over several years. One Patent now suffices for the United Kingdom, and is no longer void, as formerly, for trifling inaccuracies in the Specification, as these may be now disclaimed.

Before quitting the subject of Patents it may, perhaps, be serviceable to call attention to the admirable Abridgments of Specifications now publishing by the Patent Commissioners. In a few minutes one can get exact information there which cannot otherwise be obtained in as many hours. These Abridgments are in the form of small 8vo volumes.

Hereafter we hope to see provided out of the revenues of the Patent-office, a public library and museum, to constitute a historical and educational institution for the benefit and instruction of the skilled workman of the kingdom. Exact models of machinery are to be exhibited in the subjects, showing the progressive steps of improvement.

Theory and Practice.—Watt and Telford.

James Watt was a highly accomplished theorist, on every point on which he worked; yet his name has been frequently cited, as a proof that theory could be dispensed with. And his career, when compared with that of Telford, will illustrate *theory applied to practice*, as distinguished from practice alone, however acute. It is impossible to contemplate the career of Telford without a feeling of high interest, created by the comparison of his apparently inadequate education with his startling successes. Looking at the individual himself, there is everything for his age to admire; and as long as his structures last, each of them is the *monumentum*, but not *ære perennius.* The time will come when his name shall be like that of the builder of the old London bridge, who was, no doubt, the Telford of the day,—a stimulus to his contemporaries, useful and honoured, but not the remembered of succeeding ages. On the other hand, the discoveries of Watt, though equally startling in what is called the practical point of view, have the mind of the discoverer impressed upon them, and have been, and must be, the guide of his successors, not merely to repetitions of what he did himself, but to the enlargement of ideas, and the conversion of principles into forms useful in art. Take away the honourable qualities which enabled the two men to outstrip their contemporaries, each in his line; qualities which are the properties of the individual minds, and consider what is left, namely their modes of proceeding : consider the effect of these two modes on men in general, and there is nothing in that of Telford which would raise a workman above a workman; while in that of Watt there is the vital principle to which we owe all the mechanical triumphs of civilization, and all the theoretical successes of philosophy.— *Penny Cyclopædia.*

Practical Science.—Mechanical Arts.

It seems impossible to exclude from a review, however slight, of contemporary progress in the exact Sciences, the advantages which have accrued to them, both directly, and as it were reflexively, by the astonishing progress of the Mechanical Arts. The causes, indeed, which called them forth are somewhat different from those which are active in more abstract, though scarcely more difficult, studies. Increasing national wealth, numbers, and enterprise, are stimulants unlike the laurels, or even the gold medals, of academies, and the quiet applause of a few studious men. But the result is not less real, and the advance of knowledge scarcely more indirect. The masterpieces of civil engineering—the steam-engine, the locomotive-engine, and the tubular bridge—are only experiments on the powers of nature on a gigantic scale, and are not to be compassed without inductive skill, as remarkable and as truly philosophic as any effort which the man of science exerts, save only the origination of great theories, of which one or two in a hundred years may be considered as a liberal allowance. Whilst, then, we claim for Watt a place amongst the eminent contributors to the progress of science in the eighteenth century, we must reserve a similar claim for the Stephensons and the Brunels of the present; and whilst we are proud of the changes wrought by the increase of knowledge during the last twenty-five years on the face of society, we must recollect that these very changes, and the inventions which have occasioned them, have stamped perhaps the most characteristic feature—its intense practicalness—on the science itself of the same period.

It has long been the fashion of one party to lament "the Decline of Science" in England; whilst another section has gravely declared that Science in this country is but the growth of yesterday, having been imported from Germany, and tenderly nurtured by the magnates of the realm. In the House of Commons, in the Session of 1863, a member stood up, and, with exultation, announced that Science had at length found its way into that democratic assembly through the individual exertions and influence of one now no more. From the language which this scion of a great house employed it might be inferred that Science had been previously almost unknown in England. The member, no doubt, spoke according to his knowledge; but it possibly escaped his memory that a man named Isaac Newton once existed. Without justly exposing ourselves to the charge of presumption, we might also boast of a few other names of distinction among the dead as well as the living.

There is another point upon which the public appear to be much misinformed—namely, that Science is in the receipt of large sums from the State. The annual amount voted out of the taxes for Science and Art is unquestionably large; but it should be borne in mind that, comparatively, only a small portion is really devoted to Science, while Art takes the lion's share. Let it be so by all means. True Science to be worth anything must never become the creature of State bounty. We want no Institute with its salaried members and its eternal jobbing. We need no patronizing Mecænas, whether from the high-born or the self-exalted. What Science earnestly desires is to be let alone, that she may follow her destined course quietly, modestly, and without molestation. She especially loathes the Pythonic embrace of meddlesome persons who, knowing nothing of her, yet profess an intimate acquaintance with her and a tender regard for her welfare, solely with the object of puffing themselves into notoriety. She disdains them utterly.—*Times journal.*

We hear much, too, of "Science and Art" now-a-days coupled together, as if the strongest affinity existed between them; although no two things can be more unlike each other. The Arctic Circle and the Torrid Zone cannot be wider apart or in stronger contrast; for Science is frigidly logical, and Art hotly emotional.

N 2

Force of Running Water.

It has been proved by experiment, that the rapidity at the bottom of a stream is everywhere less than in any part above it, and is greatest at the surface. Also, that in the middle of the stream the particles at the top move swifter than those at the sides. This slowness of the lowest and side currents is produced by friction, and when the rapidity is sufficiently great, the soil composing the sides and bottom gives way. If the water flows at the rate of three inches per second, it will tear up fine clay; six inches per second, fine sand; twelve inches per second, fine gravel; and three feet per second, stones of the size of an egg.—*Lyell's Geology*.

Correlation of Physical Forces.

Of late years experimental philosophers have been occupied with the investigation of a profound problem. Formerly, the most brilliant phenomena of nature were attributed to the existence of imponderable fluids. But the Correlation of heat, light, electricity, magnetism, and chemical affinity, as varying manifestations of force, attributable to modifications of motion in matter, now employs our subtlest thinkers—Faraday and Grove, Wheatstone and De la Rive. These researches extend even to the confines of the moral phenomena. The chemistry of nature differs from that of the laboratory, and the difference has been attributed, not simply to organization, but to the vital force—a power found only in living organisms. Yet, at length, the laboratory of Hoffman imitates the processes of nature, especially in plants, and produces some of the most delicate of the perfumes of flowers and fruits, and even seems on the very verge of the manufacture of some of its greatest treasures—such as quinine. Some are staggered by the steady march of scientific research into the most sacred sanctuaries of life, and recoil from investigations which trace the growth of the cell in the ovary into the perfect man; as though mystery were essential to faith; or, if it were so, as though there is the slightest risk that in ages to come man will have so stolen the sacred fruit that no mystery will remain to be solved.—*Sir James Kay Shuttleworth on Public Education*.

The Effect of Oil in stilling Waves.

It was thought that this old idea had been completely disproved by experiment; but, according to the *Saturday Review*, the very contrary has been the result of recent experiments, in course of which, at all events, waves on a pond, generated by the wind, were completely stilled to a " glassy smoothness" by means of a film of oil scarcely more than the 7,000,000th part of an inch in thickness, and exhibiting the most brilliant zones of iridescent colours from its extreme thinness. The *modus operandi* is believed to consist simply in the wind ceasing to have a hold upon the water by the intervention of the oil, which slips along the surface *with* the wind, so that the oil must be applied to windward, and it moves to leeward, smoothing the surface as it goes!

Spontaneous Generation.

Of all errors upon the formation of beings, the most absurd is Spontaneous Generation. Yet it is one of the most popular. If this theory is admissible for inferior beings, such as intestinal worms, infusoria, or polypi, why not for superior beings? The difficulty becomes an impossibility in both cases. Can it be imagined that an *organized* body, of which all the parts are intimately connected, with an admirably contrived correlation, so full of profound wisdom, is produced by a blind assemblage of physical elements? The organized body must have derived its existence from elements of which it was destitute! Then motion might proceed from inertia, sensibility from insensibility, life from death!

Guano.

In Mr. Ross' translation of Dr. Tschudi's *Travels in Peru*, 1847, we are informed that the correct orthography is *Huanu*, and not Guano. He states that it is a term in the *Quichua* dialect, meaning " animal dung." As the word is now generally used it is an abbreviation of *Pishu Huanu*, bird dung. " The Spaniards," he says, " have converted the final syllable *nu* into *no*. The European orthography *Guano*, followed also in Spanish America, is quite erroneous, for the Quichua language is deficient in the letter G, as it is in several other consonants. The H, in the common formation of the word, is strongly aspirated, whence the error of the orthography of the Spaniards, who have sadly corrupted the language of the Autochthones of Peru.

What is Perspective?

Perspective is the science which furnishes us with the laws by which we can give the apparent, as geometry those by which we can give the real, forms of objects. These laws are obvious without rules to thoughtful, artistic common-sense—but, to many, books on the subject will always be useful, if not indispensable. The science was called perspective, or *seeing through*, from an impression that the correct foreshortening of objects could be gained by viewing and tracing them through a pane of glass. This plan only ensures correctness when the plane of the eye is parallel to that of the medium upon which the drawing is made. A picture in perspective is simply a plane parallel to the plane of the eye intersecting the rays that come from the surface of the objects represented. The points of these rays at the places of their several intersections combine to form the true perspective representation. This was the art that Mantegna made so much of at Padua; and that with which Bellini, the painter of the National Gallery " Doge," delighted the Venetians. Without much semi-scientific pedantry, the whole science may be understood by balancing a half-crown on the top of the forefinger of your right hand. Hold it up so that its broad plane is parallel to the eye's plane; put it nearer or further, and it seems to increase or diminish in size. Turn it obliquely, and it appears an oval; put the edge on a line with the eye, and it appears a mere thin straight line. A sphere is the only geometric form that undergoes no perspective changes. The eye is able to take in any given space set at an angle of under sixty degrees. When both eyes view a scene, instead of the circle one eye sees, we have an ellipse formed by the continuation of the two circles of vision,—the point of sight being opposite the centre of the space between the two eyes. Perspective is of great use in Art; but the books upon it are too abstruse, and imply a knowledge of mathematics. [This common-sense explanation is from the pen of Professor Wallace, M.A., in the first number of a journal edited by him and entitled *The Public Instructor.*]

The Stereoscope.

Till the discovery of the Stereoscope, naturalists were puzzled to account for *a single image resulting from double vision;* and Gall and Spurzheim endeavoured to explain it by the supposition that one eye only was active at a time, the other only admitting light, and that Nature had given us two merely to provide against the accidental loss of one.—*Leslie's Handbook.*

Burning Lenses.

The danger from Lenses, when the heat of the sun is powerful, is well known. As an illustration, we may relate an instance which occurred on the premises of Messrs. Negretti and Zambra, philosophical instrument makers, in Hatton Garden. There was a smell of fire, but it could nowhere be detected, until a person entered the shop from the street with the startling information that the window was on fire, and such was really the fact: a large reading-lens hanging in the window exposed to the sun, its focus happening to be just within range of the woodwork of the window fittings, set fire to them, and no doubt in a very few seconds some serious damage would have been caused. Is it not possible that in tropical climates, when vessels are becalmed, they may be set on fire by the eye-deck lights everywhere observable on ships' decks; or, nearer home, in warehouses, &c., where such means of lighting is resorted to? The matter merits serious consideration and should serve as a caution.

How to wear Spectacles.

In the proper use of Spectacles there is no circumstance of more importance than their position on the head. They should be worn so that the glasses may come as close to the eye as possible without touching the eyelashes; they must also be placed so that the glasses may be parallel to the paper when held in an easy position. To accomplish this, let the sides of the spectacles bear upon the swell of the head, about midway between the top of it and the ear; the eyes will then look *directly* through the glasses to the paper, and make the most advantageous use of them, instead of looking *obliquely* through them to the paper, as in numerous cases, where persons place the sides of their spectacles in contact with, or very near, their ears—in which position they produce a distorted image on the retina. The sides of the spectacles should also be placed at an equal height upon the head; and the hands being applied to the *points* of the sides, will generally direct their equal height, as well as allow of their opening to the full extent without injury.—*Adams on the Human Eye.*

Vicissitudes of Mining.

Although the thoughts of men have been turned to the mineral conditions of these islands for more than two thousand years; and in that period the *art* of Mining has improved; and the engineering appliances which have been brought to bear upon the ventilation and the draining of mines, are fine examples of mechanical ingenuity,— the *science* of Mining, however, can scarcely be said to have, as yet, any existence. In 1856, Mr. John Taylor, who must be regarded as a good authority, stated before a Committee of the House of Commons, "That there were no greater facilities for ascertaining

the productive character of a mine now than formerly. The difference was simply in improved machinery. Our knowledge was
not greater than that of our forefathers." Whatever was said in
1856, is true at the present moment.

The psychological influences of subterranean toil form a strange
but interesting subject of study. These and the effects of that
continued uncertainty as to the reward which labours of the
severest kind are to receive, are distinguishingly marked on every
miner. In occult powers they are believers; and when, about a
century since, the " Divining Rod" was introduced into Cornwall
as a means for finding mineral lodes, it was eagerly seized upon;
and, to the present day, several families are supposed to possess
remarkable powers as diviners, or, as they are commonly called,
"dowsers."

Mr. Rawlinson observes that the existence of " diviners," or
"dowsers," for finding out the mineral lodes was a serious reflection upon the present age; yet it was a curious fact, that a
French adventurer, who was supposed to have been successful in
finding water-beds in Africa, was introduced to the Government
during the Crimean war, and was sent out to trace, by the
divining-rod, water in that locality.

The most elementary laws of science are still a book sealed to
the large majority of miners, and while they are, of all men, themselves the most theoretical, they always meet any attempt to explain phenomena upon the evidences of inductive research, by
pronouncing the explanation to be a " theory," which is of no
value to a "practical."

Mr. Wallace, himself a miner, says: " The impossibility of
arriving at any knowledge of practical value respecting ore deposits
in veins, is avowed by those who, with singular inconsistency,
attach the greatest importance to individual experience. Even
some occupying high distinction as directors or proprietors of
mines, affirm, without qualification, that it is impossible to see
through solid rocks.

It must be admitted that amongst the miners there is an entire
absence of any method by which a knowledge may be obtained
of the causes leading to the production of mineral deposits; while
the speculations of those philosophers who will not endure the
toil of subterranean investigations are wild, and are consequently
valueless.

The natural consequence of this imperfect knowledge is, that
all mining speculations are necessarily attended with much uncertainty. From time to time a most productive mine is discovered. The Devon Great Consols, first known as Huel Maria,
has paid 826l. dividends upon every share, one pound only being

paid for shares now worth 490*l.* each. Upon the shares of South Caradoc, near Liskeard, the trifling sum of 25*s.* only was ever paid; the price of these shares, in 1862, was 390*l.*; and 391*l.* profit had been paid on every share.

There are other examples of great success in mining. Such results as these are laid hold of by designing men, and used to bait the hooks by which those who are in a hurry to be rich are caught. Permission to search for minerals is obtained from the possessor of the land near to some productive mine. A few trials are probably made, and then comes the formation of a company to work "Huel Chance" (or some more attractive name is adopted), through which the lodes from the fortunate neighbour are shown, by the aid of a parallel ruler, to run.

Mr. Rawlinson states, with regard to the pecuniary losses incurred in mining speculations, that some years ago, whilst holding an official inquiry in Cornwall, he was brought into connexion with several of the large mining adventurers of that district; and they stated it as their opinion that, if the value of all the ore mines in Cornwall, and the cost of working them were compared, the statement would stand as something like 25*s.* paid for every pound's worth of ore obtained.

Statistics show that about 350,000 persons are employed in the production of minerals, to the value of nearly 35 millions per annum, which gives, as the production of each miner, not more than 2*l.* per week, an amount so small that we can hardly conceive it possible that it would remunerate the large capital which is invested in these mines.—See Mr. Robert Hunt's valuable *Report,* 1862.

Uses of Mineralogy.

Professor Tennant states there have been already described 500 minerals, more than half which number are found in the British Isles; whilst more than 450 are found in our colonies. In the International Exhibition of 1862, our vast colonial mineral wealth was shown in remarkable specimens of gold, silver, copper, precious stones, &c., many of which had been found by working miners who had been sent out from this country. Yet, miners are generally ignorant of the value of minerals, which they reject as not worth collection: now, the gold they collect is worth 4*l.* per ounce; but rough stones are often rejected, which are worth 50*l.* per ounce, and some 500*l.* per ounce—they are diamonds. Mr. Tennant believes that, in many of our colonies, these minerals are thrown away, whereas a little knowledge of the use of the blowpipe would enable miners to distinguish one substance from another.

Our Coal Resources.—The Deepest Mine.

Professor Morris describes the carboniferous series of rocks in England which contain Coal as deposited above the old red sandstone, or what have been called the Devonian rocks, and several thousand feet in thickness, though the coal measures are of much more limited depth, and the mines of coal vary from thirty feet to only two inches thick.   The distribution of Coal in England is much greater than in any country in Europe; though in the United States of America, near Pittsburg, the beds of coal extend over a vast area, and one is of great thickness.   The quantity of coal that is raised from the pits in this country, however, exceeds that from all the other coal-fields in the world.*   The probable duration of coal in England has formed an interesting subject of speculation with some geologists, who have estimated the period variously at from 300 to 1000 years.   Sir William Armstrong, at the Meeting of the British Association, in 1863, estimated the minimum period of the northern coal-field at 200 years; but Mr. N. Wood, the great coal-viewer of the North, is of opinion that of the northern coal-field no conjecture, of practical utility, can yet be formed, as more than one half of the basin, lying under the sea, has not yet been explored.

Sir William Armstrong's remark, however, was misunderstood,

---

* There are two distinct theories respecting the formation of coal, though all agree that it is of vegetable origin.   This is proved by the trees and plants found in the substance of coal, by the vegetable remains imbedded in the accompanying strata, and by microscopical examination.   The plants most abundant are ferns, some of which were of gigantic size.   These are supposed to have composed two-thirds of the mass of most coal.   Large trees are sometimes discovered growing upright in the shale that lies beneath and above a seam of coal.   The vegetation from which coal has been formed, according to the views of some geologists, grew on the places where it is found, and they consider it to have been composed of decayed beds of peat which grew in succession one over the other, and that by the compression of the whole, when submerged, and by the accompanying action of heat, these vegetable beds were converted into coal.   Other geologists imagine that it was produced by the accumulation of drift wood brought down by great rivers, similar to the present accumulation of drift wood on the coast of Mexico brought down by the great American rivers. There are geological facts adduced in support of both theories.   Ireland presents the remarkable geological feature of an immense area of carboniferous rocks without coal, that valuable portion of the deposit having, it is supposed, been swept away by some of the denudations to which the surface of the globe has been exposed in the early periods of its history.— *Prof. Morris.*

and thought to refer to the coal supply of the whole kingdom, whereas he limited the remark to the coal-field of Durham and Northumberland. This misapprehension re-opened the question of the exhaustion of our coal resources, and led to the communication of some valuable evidence to the *Times* journal. Thus, Mr. E. Hull, of the Geological Survey, states as the result of a series of investigations of the British coal-fields, that adopting the limit of depth at 4000 feet, he found there to be enough workable coal, at the rate of consumption for that year, (about 71,000,000 tons,) for nearly 1000 years ; and even if the consumption should ultimately reach 100,000,000 of tons, that supply could be maintained for 700 or 800 years.

With respect to the assumed depth, 4000 feet, Mr. Hull adds:

" Already a depth of nearly 1000 yards has been reached in a Belgian colliery, and coal is now being extracted from depths of 700 and 800 yards in Lancashire. Even with the vertical limit of 4000 feet, I have since found reason to believe that the estimate I arrived at in the case of the South Wales coal-field was rather under than over the truth. In that coal-basin alone, with an area of 906 square miles, I calculated that the rate of consumption for 1859, of $9\frac{1}{2}$ millions of tons, could be maintained for 1600 years ; but it is only right to state, that Mr. H. Vivian, M.P., in a pamphlet published by him in 1861, controverts this view, and arrives at the conclusion that ' South Wales could supply all England with coal for 500 years, and her own consumption for 5000.'

" As regards the absolute quantity of mineral fuel in this island, it may be considered as practically inexhaustible. The seams of coal outcrop in our coal-fields, and descend under the Permian and Triassic formations to depths exceeding 10,000 feet. The question of the available supply is therefore one depending on the rapidity of production and the limit of depth."

Dr. Buckland, in 1841, dwelt upon the wanton waste of coal at the pits, which, in 1836, he had maintained would finally "exhaust the Newcastle coal-field at a period earlier by at least one-third than that to which it would last if wisely economized." The waste has, however, been much abated.

Mr. Robert Hunt, however, maintains the *consumption* to be greatly understated. He says:

" All calculations on the probable duration of our coal-fields have been founded on the very erroneous data which supposes that not more than 36,000,000 of coals are raised annually. We know that more than *sixty-six* millions of coals are now annually produced, and the demands upon our resources are rapidly increasing.

Sir William Amstrong himself quotes Mr. Hunt as showing " that at the end of 1861 the quantity of coal raised in the United Kingdom had reached the enormous total of *eighty-six* millions of tons, and that the average annual increase of the eight preceding years amounted to 2¾ millions of tons."

If, therefore, Dr. Buckland's remarks were important in 1836 (when his *Bridgewater Treatise* was first published), and of " greater force" in 1858, how much more must they be worthy of most serious consideration in 1863.—*Communication to the Times by Mr. Frank Buckland.* Another Correspondent, however, adds this consolation:

" There may yet remain plenty of coal in the world.   Three-fourths of the globe are covered with water, and what geologist shall presume to declare that there are no vast deposits of coal deep below the ocean bed ? We have been up and down below the waters several times, and we shall probably sink again ; but then the bed of the Atlantic may become dry land and peopled with our successors. Change is the law of the universe. The moon is stated to be approximating to the earth at the rate of a fraction of an inch in a century or so, and may one day come tumbling upon us. The whole of the solar system seems to be travelling—some report at the slow rate of 47,000 miles an hour—towards an unknown region of infinite space.   Great Britain, therefore, has no reason to complain if she shares the common fate of all things, whether in the heavens above or on the earth beneath."

Monkwearmouth, Sunderland, is the deepest coal-mine in all England ; the coal being won at nearly two miles' distance from the shaft, and upwards of 1900 feet, or more than five times the height of St. Paul's, below the surface of the green fields and trees above. The pit employs nearly 300 hands, and yields between 500 and 600 tons of domestic coal per day ; every few seconds, the tall cage shoots up out of the gloom of the shaft, and the tubs, like miniature railway-waggons, holding nearly half a ton each, are brought to the bank, and wheeled away in different directions. Not for a single instant does the work stop: it is coal—coal everywhere beneath and around ; the very atmosphere is made gloomy with its fine particles ; and all this, seen amid clanking of chains, roaring of steam, and the rapid activity and whirl of hurried business, make it one of the most curious and interesting scenes imaginable.

The dangers of the working are thus detailed. The boys in charge of the trams carry the " Davy," the wire-gauze of which is far less liable to injury than the glass shade of the " Geordie," or Stephenson lamp ; and with these the lads may safely pass the " goafs" or worked-out seams, in which, though built up as far as possible, gas always lurks, though the invisible enemy around them is so thick that the gas will light inside their lamps and burn with a ghastly blue flame. Beyond this steep incline or bank there is still nearly a mile to be traversed to the " in-bye"—

the face of the working, the spot from which the coals are actually won: where, too, the gas has its head-quarters, and has to be watched and guarded against every hour and minute of the day and night, for the work of a mine never stops, and day and night are meaningless terms in such eternal gloom and silence. The heat at the bottom of the bank, indeed in all parts of the mine, is very great in the extreme depths of Monkwearmouth. It is seldom less than 84 or 85 deg., and at the workings often over 90 deg. So great is the heat, in fact, that the men nearly always work almost naked, and in some cases absolutely so. The heat certainly does not arise from want of proper ventilation, which seems ample. Not much bratticing is used to convey the a r through the workings, and it is almost entirely confined to the places where the coal is won. In fact, as far as human ingenuity, skill, or experience can go, the pit is made safe from gas at least. Its only risk seems to be from shaft accidents or inundation, to both of which more or less all colleries in this district and near to the sea are, to say the least, equally exposed and equally pro-tected against, as far as it is possible to do it.

Iron as a Building Material.

The late Professor Cockerell, in a lecture on Architecture, at the Royal Academy, observed upon the early employment of this material in building:

The progress of architecture depends as much on discovery of new materials and new methods of build.ng as on taste. Iron was used by Tubal Cain as a subsidiary material. It has been employed in build.ng ever since; but never in solid and in the gross as a constituent part of the substance of building before Mr. Rennie employed it as voussoirs in the Southwark Bridge. Sir Robert Smirke has nobly followed in applying iron in trabeation, and so has Mr. S. Smirke in the new reading-room of the British Museum, and others; but the engineers have kept ahead of the architects, from Mr. Rennie to Messrs. Stephenson, in displaying the powers of iron.

Iron has been cited in Deuteronomy as the essential and last fruit of the promised land. Our interiors, as halls and churches, will assume new development and grandeur by iron, since we have seen 200 feet span at Birmingham without abutment, and 150 feet at Paris in still more enduring structure. The Pantheon of Rome, Sta. Sophia, St. Peter's, the Baths, and the great Rid.ng-house at Moscow, will hide their glories; and iron will hence-forward dispense with pillars and clerestory, flying-buttresses and abutments, and roof our churches in bold and single spans. With all due reverence for antiquity and precedent, we ought to open our eyes to the reconciliation of this new material and its peculiar faculties with the laws of proportion and taste; and this is a problem worthy of the best spirits, both as to the form of roofs or ceilings, and the form of supports, which, in iron, with 1-40th part of substance of stone, will give equal strength of support.

Iron may be termed the osteology of building. Hitherto the architectural system has proceeded on statics and equipoise of molecules, as if the human frame were built without bones. Now our buildings will have bones, giving unity and strength which never before existed. The nervures of the Gothic will now be in uniform and single arcs, erected at once: the library at St. Géné-viève, by Mons. Arbruste, exhibits an experiment in this way.

Concrete, not new.

Professor Cockerell observes:—Concrete is a novelty charac-teristic of the nineteenth century, or rather a resuscitation of ancient practice, as shown by quoting Philibert de l'Orme; but in the bridge of Alma, at Paris, concrete has taken a new and admirable development, where three arches of about 140 feet span are cast on the centreing, forming one vast stone from pier to pier. The only voussoirs used are in the face of the arches. A peculiar cement and hard fragmented stone has effected this with vast economy of cost and time, and promises well. The so-called Temple of Peace at Rome is ceiled and vaulted with a similar concrete. The coffering was previously moulded in all its detail upon the centreing, and then covered with grosser concrete, so that on removal of centreing all was finished. A vast fragment now lies in the middle of the Temple, and at Tivoli we find that Adrian employed the same simple process.

Sheathing Ships with Copper.

From an old pamphlet we learn that :—" Mr. Pepys, a scientific man, in the reign of Charles the Second, suggested the great im-portance of Sheathing Ships with Copper, and urged the advan-tages with sound and persuasive arguments; and says, in some despair, ' I wish it were tried on one ship.' But this experiment was delayed for nearly a century; and when it was tried, al-though it answered beyond expectation, yet the prejudice against innovation was so strong, that in Admiral Keppel's fleet, 1778, there was only one coppered ship."

Copper-smelting.

A prodigious quantity of copper is obtained from Lake Superior. Mr. Petherick, the well-known mining engineer, informed Dr. Percy that at Minnesota, in 1854, not fewer than forty men were engaged during twelve months in cutting up a single mass of native copper, weighing about 500 tons! The native copper at Lake Superior in some places occurs curiously intermingled, but generally not alloyed, with native silver. The following anecdote is recounted of the value of the gold in the residue from some South American copper-ores, and which was communicated to Dr. Percy by Dr. Lyon Playfair. At certain large chemical works where sulphate of copper was prepared by dissolving copper in sulphuric acid, an insoluble residue was produced in the process, which had been put aside from time to time, and had fortunately not been thrown away. A small sum was offered by certain persons for this residue, which had not previously been regarded as of much value. Suspicion was excited, especially by the quarter from which the offer proceeded, and it was declined; whereupon the residue was examined, and was found to contain 700*l.*-worth of gold!

Antiquity of Brass.

Dr. Percy, the able metallurgist, extracts from history the remarkable inference that the *orichalcum* of Cicero, and which closely resembled gold, was really Brass; this alloy of copper and zinc being the only metallic substance which it is possible to conceive the ancients could have so mistaken. The modification of brass which is termed "Muntz's metal," has been the subject of one of the most lucrative patents known: when its well-known proprietor died, his property was sworn under 600,000*l.*

Brilliancy of the Diamond.

The cause of the wonderful *Brilliancy* of the Diamond is not popularly known. It has no inherent luminous power; it is simply transparent, like common glass, and yet, if the latter were cut into the form of a brilliant, it could no more be mistaken for a real one than for a sapphire or an emerald. The secret, therefore, of the brilliancy of the diamond must lie in something other than its clearness or its transparency. It is owing to its great *refractive* power. When rays of white light pass through transparent substances they are refracted, or bent out of their former course, and under certain circumstances are separated into their constituent elements, and dispersed in the form of the well-known prismatic colours. The cut drops of glass chandeliers show a familiar example of these properties. Now, the degree in which this effect is produced by any substance depends on the refractive power it possesses, and it so happens that the diamond has this power in an extraordinarily high degree, its index of refraction being 2·47, while that of glass, or rock crystal, is only about 1·6, and of water 1·3. The effect of this great refractive capability, particularly when aided by judicious cutting, is, instead of allowing the light to pass *through*, to throw it about, backwards and forwards in the body of the stone, and ultimately to dart it out again in all sorts of directions, and in the most brilliant array of mingled colours; and this is the marvellous effect that meets the eye. Sir David Brewster has shown that the play of colours is enhanced by the small *dispersive* power of the diamond, in comparison with its refractive properties.

The general value of diamonds has been rising of late years; for, though the production is not scanty, the demand, owing to general prosperity, and the extension of ornament to wider classes in society, is largely on the increase.—*Mr. Pole; Macmillan's Magazine.*

Philosophy of Gunpowder.

It may be well to have one word, as *transmutation*, to indicate chemical molecular change, and another, as *transformation*, to indicate mechanical molecular change; but, as industrialists, we must hesitate to marvel more at the one than the other. How cheerfully they labour to a common end, like twin brother and sister; the one strong by measurable strength, the other by immeasurable fascinating power, we see in the case of that great world-changer, that emblem of war, and minister of peace, Gunpowder. It needs the strong brother to fell the oaks, and with a hint from his twin to burn them into charcoal. It needs his stout arms to quarry the sulphur, and bring the saltpetre from India; to crush them into grains, and grind them together. But it also needs his weird sister, in whose palm he lays the innocent dust, to breathe upon it before the Alps are tunnelled, or Sebastopol lies in ruins.—*Prof. George Wilson.*

New Pear-flavouring.

The new *Pear*-flavouring is derived from an alcoholic solution of pure acetate of amyloxide, considerable quantities of which are manufactured by some distillers, and sold to confectioners, who employ it chiefly in making *Pear-drops*, which are merely barley-sugar, flavoured with this oil. There is, also, an Apple-oil, which, according to analysis, is nothing but valerianate of amyloxide.

Methylated Spirit.

Methylene is a highly volatile and inflammable liquid produced from the destructive distillation of wood; whence *Methylated* Spirit, or wood spirit. It is permitted to be used, duty free, in arts and manufactures. Hitherto, no effort to obtain a potable spirit from methylated alcohol has succeeded. A patent has been granted for a process which professes not only to accomplish this object, but to render wood spirit itself potable, and that, too, at a cost almost nominal; and it has afforded matter for earnest discussion among some of our leading pharmacologists, who, anxious to preserve the integrity of medicinal preparations, have not unreasonably been alarmed by the assertion that wood spirit can be so far defecated as to render it almost indistinguishable from vinous alcohol, and by the exhibition of specimens of such spirit which might be used, instead of spirits of wine, for pharmaceutical purposes. But after a series of experiments, Mr. Phillips, of the Revenue Laboratory, has not been able by the process indicated to render either methylated or wood spirit potable, although it was submitted to numerous successive distillations, which from their costliness could not be applied profitably on a commercial scale.

One of the latest Acts passed, Session 1863, was to reduce the duty on rum. It recites that by the Act 18th and 19th Victoria, cap. 38, spirit of wine was allowed to be methylated duty free; and that it is expedient to allow foreign and colonial rum to be methylated, on payment of reduced duty. Rum may now be " methylated " in the Customs' warehouse; but the wood naphtha, or methylic alcohol, or other article to be mixed with the rum, is to be provided by the Inland Revenue Commissioners; and the mixture is to be denominated " methylated spirits," and such spirits may be exported.

Meanwhile, the Inland Revenue returns in 1863 showed a decreased consumption of spirit, from the fact of methylated spirit taking the place of duty-paid or pure spirit. Of the one article of spirit of nitre, very little is sold which is not distilled from " methylated finish." This increased quantity of sweet spirit of nitre sold is not taken medicinally, but is extensively used in the adulteration of potable spirits.

What is Phosphate of Lime?

Phosphate of Lime, a minute constituent of all fertile soils and of most waters, is of great value to the ivory-turner, the manure-maker, the potter, the silver-assayer, the drug-manufacturer, the dyer, and the lucifer-match maker.   It reaches all of them in the shape of the bones of dead animals; dead cattle from our farms, dead horses from the Pampas of South America, dead walrusses from the Arctic icebergs, dead whales from the Pacific Ocean, dead men even from fields of battle.   Land and sea-plants have, as it were, milked this essential constituent of their frames, drop by drop, from the breast of nature.   Animals of all classes, from the lowest to the highest, have robbed plants of their hard-gotten gains, and made their bones strong with the precious substance. Finally, the chartered robber man has robbed them all, claiming even the relics of his brethren, and obtaining in a handful of bone-dust the phosphate of tons of rock and water.—*Prof. G. Wilson.*

What is Wood?

Its chief ingredients, charcoal and water, are uncostly and abundant; but in themselves they are useless to the carpenter, and he cannot change them into timber.   So he calls to remem-brance that his great grandfather planted an acorn, which has turned its first small capital to so excellent account that now it is a timber-merchant on a large scale, and will contract with you to build a ship of war out of oak of its own making.   It is with other trees as with this ancestral oak.   Each, with its republic of industrious roots and leaves, is a joint-stock company with limited liability, engaging to furnish you with pine-stems for masts, fir-wood for planking, logwood for dyeing, cork-bark for bottling, oak-bark for tanning, walnut for tables, rosewood for picture-frames, satinwood for looking-glasses, willow for cradles, mahogany for wardrobes, ebony for will-chests, elm-tree for coffins.—Those trees form the Worshipful Company of Wood-makers, an ancient guild.—*Ibid.*

How long will Wood last?

Cedar-wood will last 1000 years.   The oil of cedar-wood, mixed with oil of creosote and forced into timber by means of a pump, will be found highly preservative of all timber for ship-building and breakwaters.   In very old buildings, the timbers where they have been whitewashed, are often found in the highest state of preservation. In *olden* days they cut the timber in the winter season, when the sap was most out of it; but now, for the use of tanners, it is felled in summer; the result of which is, that it shrinks, chaps, and decays, sooner than it otherwise would. The wood of the walnut-tree is very durable, and so is that of the horse-chesnut-tree. Many very ancient barns about Gravesend are built entirely of the last. In preparing wood for ship-building, &c., it is best to lay it in a " running stream" for a few days only, to extract the sap that remains in it, and then dry it in the sun or air, by which it neither chaps, casts, nor cleaves. The use of linseed-oil, tar, or such oleaginous matter, tends much to the preservation of wood. Hesiod prescribes " smoking" timber in order to preserve it :—

> "Temonem in fumo poneres."

Virgil advised the same method :—

> " Et suspensa focis exploret Robora fumus."

Others have advised the oil of smoke! [pyroligneous acid?] The solid stems of trees most subject to decay, are commonly found in the Irish " peat-bogs," in such excellent preservation, that they are esteemed equal to any timber for substantial buildings; the peat being highly antiseptic and preservative. Larix (which can be procured in blocks of any size from Dantzig) is the best kind of wood for breakwaters, harbours, &c. It is capable of resisting the weather for a length of time in those situations.—*Correspondent of the Builder.*

The Safety Match.

The statistics of London Fires in one year (1858) show that, out of the 1114 fires forming the total of serious conflagrations, the following proportion was occasioned by the usual contrivances for procuring flame, viz.:

Children playing with lucifers .			12
Lucifer matches accidentally ignited .			7
,, ,, making			3
,, ,, careless use of			17
			39

In the first of these instances the sacrifice of life and wholesale destruction of property were traced principally to the fact of children inserting lucifer matches into various nooks and crevices, where an accidental concussion had produced their ignition. The next in the series of casualties are accidents resulting from the sudden ignition of boxes or bundles of phosphorized matches. The

necessity as well as the possibility of removing the fatal cause of
these accidents has long been felt ; and by the following contrivance such occurrences, which hitherto have led to so many
terrible disasters, may be completely obviated.   This invention,
which has reached us from France, consists of a match which
cannot ignite by friction with ordinary substances, but which
bursts into flame when struck upon a chemically-prepared substance, owing to the peculiar action occurring between the two
bodies which are thus brought into contact.   Without the prepared strip, the matches may be struck or trodden upon without
the possibility of ignition.   The advantage of having these articles
tipped with a material which is not inflammable *per se* is sufficiently obvious, not only to careful housewives, but to the owners
of large establishments where the ordinary " lucifers " are now
used, and, we are afraid, often left carelessly about.

The reputed inventor of the Lucifer Match died in 1859, in
Stockton, aged seventy-eight.   The *Gateshead Observer* adds to
this announcement:—" In the year 1852 (August), correcting
the history of ' matches' in the ' Jurors' Reports' (Great Exhibition), we stated, says our authority, that ' A quarter of a century
ago, Mr. John Walker, of Stockton-upon-Tees, then (as now)
carrying on the business of chemist and druggist in that town, was
preparing some lighting mixture for his own use.   By the accidental friction on the hearth of a match dipped in the mixture, a
light was obtained.   The hint was not thrown away.   Mr. Walker
commenced the sale of friction-matches : this was in April, 1827.'
Dr. Faraday, it is said, first brought the discovery into general
notice."

Pottery.—Wedgwood.

There are three conditions locally necessary to the manufacture
of Earthenware : the first is the presence of coals, the second is
the existence of beds of clay and the accessibility of other materials
of minor importance, and the third is the requisite labour.   The
great Wedgwood found these conditions to be mainly fulfilled in
the part of North Staffordshire now called Stoke-upon-Trent, and
with an enterprise, an industry, and a perseverance which is appreciated there, set on foot a manufacture which has now become a
staple, and employs, directly or indirectly, upwards of 100,000 of
the population of this country, and which is at this time one of
the most important articles of our commercial interchange.

Where there is coal there is generally iron, and iron works and
earthenware manufactories naturally and unavoidably engender
smoke ; but although the inhabitants of the Potteries have refused
to accept any compulsory measure, which, if recklessly carried

out, might completely annihilate their trade and deprive of employment the vast number of the inhabitants of the district, yet
there is no place where greater efforts have been made by private
individuals voluntarily to adopt measures for the suppression of
what they admit to be an evil, not in any degree to the extent set
forth.

The first use of flint in pottery has been thus explained. A
potter named Astbury, travelling to London, perceived something
amiss with one of his horse's eyes, when an ostler at Dunstable
said he could cure him, and for that purpose put a common black
flint into the fire. The potter observing it when taken out to be
of a fine white, immediately conceived the idea of improving his
ware by the addition of this material to the clay.

Imposing Mechanical Effects.

Mechanical force, when exerted even as a motive-power, can
be employed by man on many a grand scale. The movements of
massive pieces of machinery, even though moving aimlessly, still
more when working for a purpose, always awaken in us the idea of
power; and often also create emotions of awe and sublimity akin
to those which are begotten by the spectacle of great natural
phenomena. The sweep of a railway train across the country,
and the dash of a war-steamer against the waves with which it
measures its strength, never become paltry pageants, even though
we are ignorant of the errands on which these swift coursers are
bound. Still more striking are those actions of machinery which
involve not only swift irresistible motion, but also transformation
of the materials on which the moving force is exerted. Take, for
example, a cotton-mill, which some never tire of representing as
dreary and prosaic. In the basement story revolves an immense
steam-engine, unresting and unhasting as a star, in its stately,
orderly movements. It stretches its strong iron arms in every
direction throughout the building; and into whatever chamber
you enter, as you climb stair after stair, you find its million hands
in motion, and its fingers, which are as skilful as they are nimble,
busy at work. They pick cotton and cleanse it, card it, rove it,
twist it, spin it, dye it, and weave it. They will work any pattern you select, and in as many colours as you choose; and do
all with such celerity, dexterity, unexhausted energy, and skill,
that you begin to see what was prefigured in the legend of Michael
Scott, and his "sabbathless" demons (as Charles Lamb would
have called them), to whom the most hateful of all things was
rest, and ropemaking, though it were of sand, more welcome than
idleness. For our own part, we gaze with untiring wonder and ad-

miration on the steam Agathodæmons of a cotton-mill, the embodiments, all of them, of a few very simple statical and dynamical laws; and yet able, with the speed of race-horses, to transform a raw material, originally as cheap as thistle-down, into endless useful and beautiful fabrics. Michael Scott, had he lived to see them, would have dismissed his demons and broken his wand.—*Prof. George Wilson.**

Horse-power.

In speaking of the power, or force which an engine exerts, it is necessary to have some measure of force, or standard of inference. That used in this country is *a Horse-power*, a force equal to that which the average strength of a horse was believed capable of exerting. This has been estimated at 33,000 lb. avoirdupois weight, raised one foot high in a minute. There have been different estimates as to the real power of horses; and it is now considered that taking the most advantageous rate, for using horse-power, the medium power of that animal is equal to 22,000 lb. raised one foot high per minute. However, the other 33,000 lb. is taken as the standard, and is what is meant when a horse-power is spoken of. In comparing the power of a steam-engine with that of horses applied to do the same work, it must be remembered that the engine horse-power is 33,000 lb. raised one foot per minute; the real horse-power only 22,000 lb.; and that the engine will work unceasingly for twenty-four hours, while the horse works at that rate only eight hours. The engine works three times as long as the horse; hence, to do the same work in a day as the engine of one horse-power, 4·5 horses would be required (33,000 × 3 = 99,000; 99,000 ÷ 22,000 = 4·5). The power of a man may be estimated at one-fifth of the real power of a horse, or 44,000 lb. raised one foot per minute.—*Hugo Reid on the Steam-Engine.*

The First Practical Steam-boat.

Mr. Macquorn Rankine, in supporting the opinion of Mr. Benet Woodcroft, that the title of the " first practical steamboat" is due to that vessel in which the double-acting cranked steam-engine—in short, Watt's rotative engine—was first applied to drive the propeller,—proceeds on the principle, that to constitute a " practical" machine, that machine must be capable, not merely of working well during a series of experiments, but of continuing to

* This and the other abstracts in the present section by Prof. George Wilson, are from a valuable paper by that able writer, on the Physical Sciences which form the Basis of Technology.

work well for years, with ordinary care in its management and repairs. Such certainly never was, and never could have been the case, with any steam-boat in which the wheels were made to turn by means of chains and rachet-work—a sort of mechanism which may answer its purpose during an experiment, but which must rapidly wear itself out by shocks and rattling. Such an engine is not a " practical steam-engine ;" and a vessel driven by it is not a " practical steam-boat." Hence the importance which Mr. Rankine is disposed to ascribe to the first actual use of a permanently efficient rotative steam-engine to drive a vessel.

It may be true that as an original inventor, Symington ought to be ranked below his predecessors; because his steam-boat of 1801 was only a new combination of parts which had previously been invented separately by others—the paddle-wheel, by some unknown mechanic of remote antiquity ; the application of steam to drive vessels, by a series of inventors, comprising Papin, Hulls, D. Bernouilli, Jouffroy, Miller, and Taylor ; and the rotative steam-engine by Watt: still, the merit of having first used a " practical steam-engine" to drive a vessel is due to Symington.—*Communicated to the Literary and Philosophical Society of Manchester*, 1863.

Effect of Heavy Seas upon Large Vessels.

Professor Tennant, in considering the effect of heavy seas upon vessels of 400 to 600 feet long, remarks that the waves of the Atlantic are stated, by some captains of American ' liners," to attain an elevation of 20 feet, with a length of 160 feet, and a velocity of 25 to 30 miles per hour. Dr. Scoresby, in his paper on Atlantic waves, gives about the same mean elevation for the waves in rather a hard gale a-head ; on one occasion, with a hard gale and heavy squalls, some few waves attained a height of 43 feet, with a length of nearly 600 feet, and a velocity exceeding 30 miles an hour. Other authorities assume even more than those heights and distances. The amount of strength, to resist the impact of such waves, must vary with the length and size of a ship, and the materials of which it was constructed; and as the experience of the Britannia Bridge shows, that a weight of 460 tons, at a velocity of 30 miles per hour, could be borne by a cellular tube of 460 feet span, it was demonstrated, that by the use of iron, almost any amount of strength could be given to a vessel ; and as stability could be imparted by proper proportions, efficient vessels could be built of any dimensions, as has been exemplified by the *Great Britain*, which after remaining ashore on rocks for several months, had been got off without serious injury. .

The Railway.

" Depend upon it, whenever this new mode of travelling comes into operation, we shall become altogether a *faster* people," was the vaticination of a common-sense observer some thirty years since ; and experience has proved the soundness of the opinion. Increased facility of moving from place to place must, more or less, affect every one except the recluse shut up in his chamber from choice, or the less fortunate one prostrated on the bed of suffering, or age—

> "Lies he not bedrid ? And again does nothing
> But what he did, being childish."—*Shakspeare.*

This quickening of locomotion has multiplied our desires by adding to the means of gratifying them; a greater number of incidents and opportunities of observation is thus gained ; but, being crowded into the same length of existence, the wear and tear becomes greater ; the knife wears out the sheath ; and men grow old before they reach mid-age ; or rather, the finer portions of existence are lost, and the residue approaches a *caput mortuum*.

Meanwhile, the Railway is yet an incomplete invention ; and it is contended that our passenger-trains are deficient in the requisite accommodation for the comfort and even health of the passengers, who are still exposed to an unnecessary vibration which, in the course of continual travelling, produces nervous diseases. Mr. Bridges Adams, the engineer, and therefore a practical authority upon the subject, maintains that the railway companies are so fettered in their operations as to be unable to make feasible improvements : were these restrictions removed, Mr. Adams contends the public would receive the advantage in many forms, in easier and cheaper transit, and in reciprocal relations of town and country, such as involve a revolution in our national ecomies.   The same acute writer anticipates the time when our towns shall have their railway-streets, which may become a fact at no very distant future.   London has already its subterranean railway ; above, the air is grilled with the electric-wire railway ; and the street-system is being commenced upon the banks of the Thames, and the stream is already bridged with viaducts.

Accidents on Railways.

The question of Railway Accidents involves the whole question of railway management in detail.   Accidents may be called the weak points of the system, where imperfection is manifested, where failure crops out, and where the line of demarcation may be drawn between the practicable and the impracticable.   " If the road is perfect," says Captain Huish, " if the engine is perfect, if the carriages are perfect, and I will go on to say, if the signalman is perfect, and if everything about the railway is perfect, almost any amount of speed that can be got out of an engine may be done with safety. But we deal not with theoretical excellence, but with practical facts, and none of these things are perfect ; and in a large machine like a railway they cannot always be kept perfect."

Safety to life and limb is of course the most important consideration in the working of railway traffic. Yet the problem is substantially this:—There are upwards of one hundred and forty millions of passengers and seventy million tons of goods per annum conveyed over our railways ; assumed that all these must be transported by railway, what is the best way to do it ? It must at the best be by a species of compromise ; there must be a limit to tentative measures, there must be a risk. " If you do not go at all," says Mr. Seymour Clarke, " there is no risk of an accident ; if you go one mile an hour it is more risky than if you stand still ; it is a natural attendant upon all travelling, that there is a liability to accident of some sort." And, again, Mr. Locke thinks " that where you have the certainty of inflicting an inconvenience on the public by a prospective advantage in the saving of an accident, you should be very careful how you entail perpetually recurring inconvenience for the sake of preventing an accident which may never arise."

The Evidence adduced before the Select Committee of the House of Commons on railway accidents in 1858, from which the foregoing extracts have been made, has led the committee to the conclusion, that accidents on railways arise from three causes—inattention of servants; defective material, either in the works or the rolling stock ; and excessive speed.

Of the accidents reported to the Board of Trade that happened in 1857, there appears to have been twice as many by collision between trains as by running off the rails ; and of the accidents by collision, five-sixths took place between passenger-trains and goods trains; and only about one-sixth between passenger-trains one against another. It further appears that a very small proportion, not above one in twenty, of the accidents reported, have directly arisen from excessive speed, but in every case in conjunction with imperfections in the permanent way. It may be observed that the greater proportion, if not all of these accidents, may be traced primarily to the crowding of trains, timed for unequal speeds, and the want of punctuality, which involve the risk of every kind of accident as a consequence :—by a want of perfect manifestation or apprehension of signals, or by excessive speeds. As tentative measures, the free use of the electric telegraph for giving intelligence of the exact relative positions and circumstances of trains on the line, and the use of the most powerful brakes for bringing up the trains in the shortest practicable distance, are probably of the most urgent necessity. Perfect brakes are also indisputably promotive of safety in working traffic and in compensating for unavoidable irregularities. With the usual amount of braking power, a train at 50 miles per hour may not be stopped within 900 or 1200 yards. An instantaneous brake is not of course what is wanted; on the contrary, a length of 200 yards appears to be the shortest desirable space within which a train at 50 or 60 miles per hour should be stopped, so that the process of retardation should not be accompanied by risk of carriages riding over each other, or of violence to the passengers. This appears to have been accomplished by powerful systems of train-brakes. Steam-brakes applied to the locomotives and extended to the tenders, and even to the brake-vans, have been found beneficial and capable of stopping a train within half the usual distance.— *Encyclopædia Britannica*, 8th edit.

Railways and Invasions.

The Volunteer Review at Brighton, in 1862, afforded a good practical demonstration of the facility with which troops might be moved towards a threatened point on the particular railway which would be most likely to be required for such a duty in an actual case of emergency. On the morning of the review, 6922 Volunteers were despatched from London-bridge in 2 hours and 41 minutes, and 5170 from the Victoria Station in 2 hours and 20 minutes, without difficulty. They were conveyed in 16 trains, each composed of an engine and tender and 22 vehicles, and each carrying on an average 20 officers and 735 men; and they reached Brighton in an average of 2 hours and 28 minutes from the time of starting. The Company had also to provide for the Easter Monday traffic, and to convey upwards of 2000 Volunteers along the south coast from the several stations on their own line. Indeed, the total number of passengers who travelled upon the London, Brighton, and South Coast Railway on that day was 132,202, including Volunteers and the holders of season and return tickets.

The vast power which the railways of this country place at the disposal of the Government for the transport of troops is little known. It is in practice limited only by the number of troops that are forthcoming; and railway organization is highly favourable for the concentration of all its energies upon this object whenever it is worth while to interfere with the ordinary traffic.

Connected with the Brighton Railway system alone there are 145 locomotive engines, 1858 carriages or passenger vehicles, and 2588 waggons and trucks or merchandise vehicles, for working 240 miles: on the South-Eastern there are 179 engines, 972 carriages, and 2535 waggons, for 286 miles; and on the South-

Western, 177 engines, 850 carriages, and 3488 trucks, for 444 miles. These numbers might be increased to any amount, if increase were required, at a day's notice, by aid from the gigantic resources of the more extensive systems north of London. Excursion traffic is more difficult to manage in many respects than military traffic. A word from the commanding-officer procures an amount of order in the one case which barriers and policemen fail to do in the other. A hundred thousand men may at any time be conveyed without fatigue from London to Brighton in a single day, and they may further be transported along the coast from point to point, to Portsmouth and Weymouth on the west, and to Dover on the east, without break of gauge. They may also be brought from the north through London, and from the north, *viâ* Reading, without coming to London at all; and, indeed, the means of communication thus afforded are of so much importance to successful defence, that the railway system determines to a great extent in this country, as it has notably done in America, the strategic lines along which offensive operations must be carried on, and defensive movements effected.—*Quarterly Review*, No. 223.

What the English owe to naturalized Foreigners.

The industry of England owes much to the foreigners who have from time to time become settled and naturalized amongst us. Dr. Percy has stated, in his *Metallurgy*, that we are indebted to German miners, introduced into England by the wisdom of Elizabeth, for the early development of our mineral resources. It also appears that the Dutch were our principal instructors in civil and mechanical engineering ; draining extensive marsh and fen lands along the east coast in the reign of James I., and erecting for us pumping-engines and mill-machinery of various kinds. Many of the Flemings, driven from their own country by the Duke of Alva, sought and found an asylum in England, bringing with them their skill in dyeing, cloth-working, and horticulture ; while the thousands who flocked into the kingdom on the revocation of the Edict of Nantes by Louis XIV., introduced the arts of manufacturing in glass, silk, velvet, lace, and cambric, which have since become established branches of industry. The religious persecutions in Belgium and France not only banished from those countries free Protestant thought, but at the same time expelled the best industrial skill, and England eventually obtained the benefit of both.

Our mechanical proficiency, however, has been a comparatively recent growth. Like many others of our national qualities, it has come out suddenly and unexpectedly. But, though late learners, we have been so apt that we have already outstripped our teachers; and there is scarcely a branch of manufacture in which we have not come up to, if indeed we have not surpassed, the most advanced continental nations.

The invention of the steam-engine, towards the end of last century, had the effect of giving an extraordinary impetus to improvement, particularly in various branches of iron manufacture; and we began to export machines, engines, and ironwork to France, Germany, and the Low Countries, whence we had before imported them. Although this great invention was perfected by Watt, much of the preliminary investigation in connexion with the subject had been conducted by eminent French refugees: as by Desaugliers, the author of the well-known *Course of Experimental Philosophy*, and by Denis Papin, for some time Curator of the Royal Society, whose many ingenious applications of steam-power prove him to have been a person of great and original ability. But the most remarkable of these early inventors was unquestionably Thomas Savery—also said to have been a French refugee, though very little is known of him personally—who is entitled to the distinguished merit of having invented and constructed the first working steam-engine. All these men paved the way for Watt, who placed the copestone on the work of which the distinguished Frenchmen had in a great measure laid the foundations.

Many other men of eminence, descendants of the refugees, might be named, who have from time to time added greatly to our scientific and productive resources. Amongst names which incidentally occur to us are those of Dollond the optician; and Fourdrinier, the inventor of the paper-making machine. Passing over these, many were the emigrés who flocked over to England at the outbreak of the great French Revolution of 1789, and who maintained themselves by teaching the practice of art, and by other industrial pursuits. Of these, perhaps, the most distinguished was Marc Isambard Brunel, who for the greater part of his life followed the profession of an engineer, leaving behind him a son as illustrious as himself,—Isambard Kingdom Brunel, the engineer of the Great Western and other railways, the designer of the Great Eastern steam-ship, and the architect of many important public works.—Abridged from the *Quarterly Review*, No. 223.

Geological Growth.

Geologists who are familiar with the idea of Geological phenomena worked out through periods of inconceivable duration will, perhaps, be able to appreciate Mr. E. B. Hunt's argument on the growth and chronology of the great Florida reef. After stating the dimensions of the reef, Mr. Hunt proceeds: "Taking the rate at twenty-four years to the foot, we shall have for the total time $24 \times 250 \times 900$, on the data, as stated; or we find the total period of 5,400,000 years as that required for the growth of the entire coral limestone formation of Florida."

"Implements in the Drift."

We have already, at page 59, referred to these important evidences, in connexion with the mode of life of the present inhabitants of Tierra del Fuego. The geological inference must, however, be drawn with extreme caution, which induces us to return to the subject.

The period of time long before history was, for convenience we designate the "Stone Age." We gather from manifold evidence that during this period metals were unknown. Wherever their use was introduced, there the "Stone Age" virtually ended. The recent discovery of the flint instruments of the drift seems to carry the "Stone Age" back to a period of which, till very lately, we had no idea. The interval between the time when men fashioned these thousands of implements already found in the drift, and the earliest examples of the second "Stone Age" so to speak, as the Danish "kjökkenmödding," or the oldest Swiss "pfahlbau," must be long indeed.

It by no means follows that all the men who have used stone weapons must necessarily have been savages. At least, a consideration of the every-day life of the Swiss "pfahlbauten" would refute such a proposition. There was progress even in the "Stone Age," and the iron swords of the Gauls of Brennus probably differed less from the finest-tempered Damascus blade than do the flint implements of the drift from those of Denmark; or, to come nearer home, from the stone relics of our Channel Islands. There may have been an all-pervading "Stone Age," but universality is not implied in the term. The people of the lands now Hungary and Transylvania seem to have used copper implements, preceding those of bronze, when the men of the West were fashioning their flints.

The present state of the tribes of Tierra del Fuego is their "Stone Age," and, if ever they become a nation hereafter, they will probably collect in their museums the humble implements of their earliest culture.

The above observations were communicated to the *Times*,

April 30, 1863: it is but a glimpse of a great subject, but is so suggestive as to be entitled to attention.

The Earth and Man compared.

If it were possible for man to construct a globe 800 feet, or twice the height of St. Paul's Cathedral, in diameter, and to place upon any one point of its surface an atom $\frac{1}{4380}$th of an inch in diameter, and $\frac{1}{720}$th part of an inch in height, it would correctly denote the proportion man bears to the earth upon which he stands.

Why the Earth is presumed to be solid.

Besides the confirmation of some of the most material points of the theory of gravitation which results from the experiment of "Weighing the Earth,"* it furnishes a presumption of the strongest kind that the *earth is solid to the centre*, and not, as many have supposed in every age, a hollow shell. The mean density, $5\frac{2}{3}$, is very much greater than that of the substances which abound at the surface. All common rocks are under 3, and nothing under the ores of the heaviest metals comes up to $5\frac{2}{3}$. The earth is as massive as if it were all composed of silver ore, from the centre to the circumference, so that there must be an increase of density towards the centre. If those who think the earth to be a shell were to presume that its solidity ceased at 500 miles below the surface, they would then be compelled to give to the terrestrial matter, one part with another, a density greater than that of mercury, in order that the whole shell, the hollow part included, might have the mean density which is found by this experiment.—*Penny Cyclopædia.*

The Centre of the Earth.

Lt.-Col. Sir Henry James writes to the *Athenæum* as follows:— In verifying on a globe the interesting fact stated by Sir John Herschel, in his *Outlines of Astronomy*, and by Sir Charles Lyell, in his *Principles of Geology*, that the central point of the hemisphere which contains the maximum of land, falls very nearly upon London, or more exactly upon Falmouth, our most western port of departure for all parts of the habitable globe, it occurred to me to inquire what would be the central point of that portion of the globe which should include the whole of Europe, Asia,

---

* Described and illustrated in *Things not generally Known.* First Series.

Africa, and America; and I found that the point lies in lat. 23° 30′ on the northern tropical line, and in 15° E. long., near a place called Ghad in Africa, about 700 miles south of Tripoli. But the portion of the globe which, from this point as a centre, includes the so-called four quarters of the world is as near as possible two-thirds of the surface of the sphere; and I found that by projecting this portion of the sphere upon a plane drawn parallel to the great circle of which the above defined centre was in the pole and at 20° from it, and from a point in the prolongation of the axis of this great circle distant one-half of the radius from the surface of the sphere, that the whole of the four quarters of the globe could be represented on one strictly geometrical projection. I have had this projection made by Mr. J. O'Farrell, one of the highly intelligent assistants of the Ordnance Survey. I believe this is the first time that two-thirds of a sphere has been presented to the eye at one view.

The Cooling of the Earth.

It is a generally received belief among geologists, that the centre of the earth is occupied by incandescent fluid matter, which is gradually but constantly losing its heat. Adopting this theory, which rests on mere conjecture, Professor William Thomson, in a paper published in the Transactions of the Royal Society of Edinburgh, endeavours to fix the date of the first consolidation of the globe, supposed to have been once in a state of perfect liquefaction. It is estimated that the temperature increases as we descend towards the centre of the earth, at the average rate of one degree of Fahrenheit per 50 British feet, or 105 degrees per mile. Our author admits the temperature of melting rock to be 7000 degrees; supposing, therefore, the surface of the earth to have been in a fluid state, its consolidation, he thinks, cannot have taken place less than 20,000,000 years ago, since we should otherwise have more underground heat than we actually have; nor more than 400,000,000 years ago, because in that case we should have much less. This, it must be allowed, is rather a wide range, and is a curious instance of the strange results which calculation affords when applied to a gratuitous hypothesis. Compared with the earth's radius, which is 3958 miles, the depths to which we have been able to penetrate are utterly insignificant, and can afford no reliable data whatever; the more so, as by Professor Thomson's own admission, the rate of increase of temperature decreases progressively.

Our author, moreover, in the course of his arguments, meets with difficulties, the importance of which does not seem to have escaped him, since he endeavonrs to remove them by some rather doubtful assertions. To those, for instance, who would object to the supposition that any natural action could possibly produce at one instant, and maintain for ever after, a 7000 degrees' lowering of the surface temperature of the earth, he replies :—" I answer by saying, what I think cannot be denied, that a large mass of rock exposed freely to our air and sky will, after it once becomes crusted over, present in a few hours, or a few days, or at the most a few weeks, a surface so cool that it can be walked over with impunity." Now we do confess ourselves very much inclined to deny such a proposition. What kind of mass does our author mean? Is it a small mass? then he need but visit a gun foundry, where he will find pieces of ordnance still hot though cast several days before. Or is it a large mass, like a mountain? The nearest approach to it would be lava, which remains hot for weeks after the eruption, and for any larger mass there is no evidence either in existence or possible. But the immense difficulty of the subject may be inferred from the fact, that Professor Thomson himself further down makes an admission which is fatal to his own view, viz., that " if at any time the earth were in the condition of a thin solid shell of, suppose, 50 or 100 feet thick of granite, enclosing a continuous melted mass of 20 per cent. less specific gravity in its upper parts, where the pressure is small, this condition cannot have lasted many minutes, since the rigidity of a solid shell of superficial extent so vast in comparison with its thickness must be as nothing, and the slightest disturbance would cause some part to bend down, crack, and allow the liquid to run out over the solid." What then, we may ask, becomes of the liquid theory altogether?—*Galignani's Messenger.*

Identity of Heat and Motion.

George Stephenson's remark, that the sun is the agent that drives our locomotives, has attained a wider and more definite meaning from modern investigations. It is now known, not only that heat and motion are mysteriously related, but that they are the same thing. From the researches of Mayer and Joule, Thomson and Rankine, it is ascertained that so much heat can be converted into so much motion, and the motion reconverted into the original quantity of heat. Sir William Armstrong says that a degree of Fahrenheit in a pound of water is the same thing as the force required to lift 772 pounds a foot high, thus testifying to the final and exact establishment of the largest generalization which modern science has made; and among the many fruits which cannot but flow from the discovery, one of the earliest is its application, by

Sir William Armstrong himself, to test the waste of power in artillery practice, by observing the heat called forth in the shot. Every degree of temperature added to the projectile is part of the force intended to destroy the target ; and if it is asked what material makes the most effective cannon-ball, it is only necessary to ascertain what substance will keep coolest when it strikes the mark. It is observable that the convertibility of heat and motion opens up a new light into the ultimate constitution of matter. The marvellous experiments of Professor Tyndall on the power of the minutest films of gas and vapour to absorb heat, as a dark glass stops light, are equally interesting as valuable contributions to meteorology, and as a new mode of probing the molecular condition of the gases themselves. The laws of the variation of atmospheric temperature were unfathomable until it was discovered that the habitable quality of the earth depends on the floating vapour which clothes it, and which keeps it warm in exactly the same way as the coverings by which we protect our bodies from the inclemency of the weather ; but the significance of these experiments goes far beyond the limits of a single branch of science, and again we seem to be hovering on the verge of large revelations as to the ultimate arrangement of the particles of matter.

It is in the development of new powers of testing the infinitesimal, and carrying research immeasurably beyond the coarse limits of microscopic vision, that the strength of recent effort has been displayed. The most startling result of this form of investigation is the insight which has been gained into the materials and the condition of the luminous atmosphere of the sun. It could scarcely have been anticipated that the nature of a body separated from us by millions of miles should have been discovered by experiments which deal with qualities hidden in the inconceivably minute dimensions which express the form and distances of what, for want of better knowledge, may still be termed the ultimate atoms of material substances ; and yet it was by testing the light-stopping power of thin films of different vapours, that philosophers have felt themselves entitled to say that some of the same substances which we are familiar with on earth have contributed to the atmosphere of the sun.—*Saturday Review*.

Universal Source of Heat.

Dr. Percy, in his very able Treatise on Metallurgy, gives an explanation of the principle that the sun is really the source of the heat-producing power of all fuel; and we are inevitably reminded of the question with which George Stephenson puzzled

P

Buckland. " Now, Buckland," said Stephenson, as they were looking at a train in motion, " can you tell me what is the power that is driving that train ?" " Well," said the other, " I suppose it is one of your big engines." " But what drives the engine ?" " Oh! very likely a canny Newcastle driver." " What do you say to the light of the sun ?" " How can that be ?" asked the Doctor. " It is nothing else," said the engineer : " it is light bottled up in the earth for tens of thousands of years ; light, absorbed by plants and vegetables, being necessary for the condensation of carbon during the process of their growth, if it be not carbon in another form, —and now, after being buried in the earth for long ages in fields of coal, that latent light is again brought forth and liberated, made to work, as in that locomotive, for great human purposes." Dr. Percy explains the process by which this light or heat is stored, and discusses the question of fuel in all its forms and branches. We find under this head, *inter multa alia,* an account of the manufacture of the peat-bricks in South Bavaria, which have for some years past been used for the boilers of locomotives; again, an explanation of the failure of Mr. Vignoles's process of manufacturing iron in Ireland by means of peat charcoal, in consequence of the value of the raw material so much exceeding his estimate; besides an elaborate discussion on that litigated question so differently judged by different tribunals, and still undecided—" What is or is not coal ?"

Inequalities of the Earth's Surface.

The earth is a spherical body, or, more correctly, an elliptic spheroid. Its surface, therefore, may be considered equidistant from its centre point within, and of uniform curvature. This is so as regards the ocean, which is

" Unchangeable save to *its* wild waves' play ;"

but the surface of the land is very diversified. In parts it is spread out into plains; in others, into easy undulations. Here and there it rises into hills, with valleys and extensive basins between them ; while at places chains of mountains appear at varying altitudes, some of which penetrate the clouds.

Although the irregularities of the small portion of land which we can see at one view seem very considerable, and more especially the largest mountains, yet these protuberances are insignificant when compared to the magnitude of the earth itself.

Mount Everest, in Nepaul, is the loftiest point of the Himalaya chain, and the highest mountain in the world. It rises 29,002 feet—equal to 5·49 miles,—above the level of the sea. This height is only $\left(\dfrac{7912\cdot40}{5\cdot49}\right)\dfrac{1}{1441}$ part of the earth's diameter; or equal to 1 inch placed on a globe $\left(\dfrac{1441}{12}=\right)$ 120 feet in diameter. It therefore bears the same proportion to the diameter of the earth that a grain of sand, the ninetieth part of an inch in diameter, does to a globe $\left(\dfrac{1441}{90}=\right)$ 16 inches in diameter.

" If we would construct a correct model of our earth, with its seas, continents, and mountains, on a globe 16 inches in diameter, the whole of the land, with the exception of a few prominent points and ridges, must be comprised on it within the thickness of thin writing paper; and the highest hills would be represented by the smallest visible grains of sand."*

Astronomers have measured the distances and weighed the masses of the planets, yet the height of the atmosphere and the depths of the ocean are unsolved problems. The bottom of " blue water" is almost as unknown to us as the interior of the earth. It is a common opinion that the greatest depths of the sea are about equal to the greatest heights of the mountains. Attempts have been repeatedly made to sound out its depths, but no reliance can be placed on any reports of soundings beyond 8000 or 10,000 feet. One ran out his sounding-line 34,000 feet, and did not touch bottom; another 39,000 feet with the same result; one reported bottom at 49,000 feet, another at 50,000 feet. But there are no such depths. There are currents and counter-currents in the ocean, as in the air, which operate upon the bight of the sounding-line, and cause it to run out after the weight has reached the bottom, so that the shock cannot be felt.

The oceanic circulation is as complete as that of the atmosphere, and is possibly subject to, or governed by, the same laws; and there appears to be a law of descent through " blue water," the same as there is a law of ascent through " blue air." The one increases in density downwards as the other decreases in density upwards; and the development of this law proves that the sea is not so deep as reports made it.

There is a set of currents in the sea by which its waters are conveyed from place to place through regular and certain channels, traversing from one ocean to the other with the regularity of the machinery of a watch. The chief motive power of marine currents is caused by heat. But an active agency in the system of circulation is derived from the salts of the sea-water, by winds,

* Herschel's *Outlines of Astronomy*.

marine plants, and animals. These give the ocean great dynamical force.

The only reliable deep-sea soundings are those obtained by Brooke's plummet; and the greatest depths at which the bottom of the sea has been reached with this plummet are in the North Atlantic Ocean, and do not show it to be deeper than 25,000 feet, the deepest place being immediately to the south of the Grand Banks of Newfoundland. Thus, from the top of Mount Everest to the deepest reliable sea bottom reached by sounding, we have a vertical height of nearly $10\frac{1}{4}$ miles, equal to $\left(\dfrac{7912\cdot40}{10\cdot23}\right)\dfrac{1}{773}$rd part of the earth's diameter.—*The Builder.*

Chemistry of the Sea.

The specific gravity of Sea-water varies of course with the proportion of salts and the degree of heat it receives from the sun, or by the intermixture of currents of various temperatures; but in our own latitudes it is about 1·028—that is, a given volume of pure distilled water weighing 1000 grains, the same volume of sea-water weighs 1028 grains. Many useful substances are daily extracted from the sea for the use of man, among which we may mention pure water for the use of ships, salt, iodine, bromine, &c. Many attempts have been made to purify sea-water in order to render it potable, not only for supplying ships, but for the use of maritime towns and villages, where pump-water is often brackish, and where the inhabitants are frequently obliged to have recourse to rain-water. Now, when sea-water is submitted to congelation, it abandons its salt almost completely—a fact which appears to have been discovered many years ago by Chevalier Lorgna, who found that a mixture of three parts of pounded ice and two parts of common salt produced a cold of about 4° below the zero of a Fahrenheit thermometer, and that such a mixture caused sea-water to freeze rapidly. A mixture of various chemical salts in proper proportions produces a similar degree of cold. Lately, the cold produced by the evaporation of ether has been proposed for the same purpose. The purification is complete if the ice thus formed be melted and frozen again. In the Polar regions the ice formed from salt-water is more or less opaque, except it be in very small pieces, when it transmits light of a bluish green shade. When melted, it produces sometimes perfectly fresh water, and at other times water slightly brackish. The fresh-water ice resulting from rain or melted snow, as seen floating in the Arctic seas, is distinguished from the salt-water ice by its black appearance, especially when in small pieces, and by its transparency when removed from the water into the air. Its transparency is so great, when compared with sea-ice, that Dr. Scoresby used to amuse his sailors by cutting large lenses out of this fresh-water ice, and using them as burning-glasses to light the men's pipes. Their astonishment was increased by observing that the ice did not melt, while the solar rays emerging from it were so hot that the hand could not be kept more than a second or two at the focus.—*Macmillan's Magazine.*

The Sea : its Perils.

On the surface of the globe there is nowhere to be found so inhospitable a desert as the " wide blue sea." At any distance from land there is nothing in it for man to eat, nothing in it that he can drink. His tiny foot no sooner rests upon it, than he sinks into his grave : it grows neither flowers nor fruits ; it offers monotony to the mind, restless motion to the body ; and when, besides all this, one reflects that it is to the most fickle of the elements, the wind, that vessels of all sizes are to supplicate for assistance in sailing in every direction to their various destinations, it would almost seem that the ocean was divested of its charms, and armed with storms, to prevent our being persuaded to enter its dominions.

But though the situation of a vessel in a heavy gale of wind appears indescribably terrific, yet, practically speaking, its security is so great, that it is truly said that ships seldom or never founder in deep water, except from accident or inattention. How ships manage to get across that still region, that ideal line, which separates the opposite trade-winds from each hemisphere ; how a small box of men manages, unlabelled, to be buffeted for months up one side of a wave and down another ; how they ever get out of the abysses into which they sink ; and how, after such pitching and tossing, they reach in safety the very harbour in their native country from which they originally departed—can and ought only to be accounted for, by acknowledging how truly it has been written, that " the Spirit of God moves upon the face of the waters."

It is not, therefore, from the ocean itself that man has so much to fear : the earth and the water each afford to man a life of considerable security, yet there exists between these two elements an everlasting war, into which no passing vessel can enter with impunity ; for of all the terrors of this world, there is surely no one greater than that of being on a lee-shore in a gale of wind, and in shallow water. On this account it is natural enough that the fear of land is as strong in the sailor's heart as is his attachment to it ; and when, homeward bound, he day after day approaches his own latitude, his love and his fears of his native shores increase as the distance between them diminishes. Two fates, the most opposite in their extremes, are shortly to await him. The sailor-boy fancifully pictures to himself that in a few short hours he will be once again nestling in his mother's arms. The able seaman better knows that it may be decreed for him, as it has been for thousands, that in gaining his point he shall lose its object—that England, with all its virtue, may fade before his eyes, and,

"While he sinks without an arm to save,
    His country blooms, a garden and a grave."

Nor can it be regarded as improbable that in the beds of the present seas the edifices and works of nations, whose history is altogether unknown to existing generations, are embedded and preserved:

"What wealth untold,
    Far down and shining through their stillness lies;
They have the starry gems, the burning gold,
    Won from a thousand royal argosies.
Yet more—the depths have more—their waves have roll'd
    Above the cities of a world gone by;
Sand hath fill'd up the palaces of old,
    Sea-weed o'ergrown the halls of revelry."

Limitations of Astronomy.

These limitations are great. Ages before the existence of scientific astronomy, the question was put to the patriarch Job, " Canst thou bind the sweet influences of Pleiades, or loose the bands of Orion; canst thou bring forth Mazzaroth in his season? or canst thou guide Arcturus with his sons?" And when Job in his heart, if not with his lips, answered the Almighty, No, he answered for all his successors as well as for himself. Astronomical problems accumulate unsolved on our hands, because we cannot, as mechanicians, chemists, or physiologists, experiment upon the stars. Are they built of the same materials as our planet? Are they inhabited? Are Saturn's rings solid or liquid? Has the moon an atmosphere? Are the atmospheres of the planets like ours? Are the light and heat of the sun begotten of combustion? and what is the fuel which feeds his unquenchable fires? These are but a few of the questions which we ask, and variously answer, but leave in reality unanswered, after all. A war of words regarding the revolution of the moon round her axis may go on to the end of time, because we cannot throw our satellite out of gearing, or bring her to a momentary stand-still;

and the problem of the habitability of the stars awaits in vain an *experimentum crucis.*

The astronomer, accordingly, must be content to be the chronicler of a spectacle, in which, except as an on-looker, he takes no part. Like the sailor at the mast-head in his solitary night-watch, he must see, as he sails through space in his small earthly bark, that nothing escapes his view within the vast visible firmament. But he stands, as it were, with folded arms, occupied solely in wistfully gazing over the illimitable ocean, where the nearest vessel, like his own, is far beyond summons or signal, and the greatest appears but as a speck on the distant horizon. His course lies out of the track of every other vessel; and year after year he repeats the same voyage, without ever practically altering his relation to the innumerable fleets which navigate those seas.— *Professor George Wilson, on the Physical Sciences, &c.*

Distance of the Earth from the Sun.

Mr. Hind, the astronomer, in a communication to the *Times,* September 17, 1863, observes: " It may occasion surprise to many who are accustomed to read of the precision now attained in the science and practice of Astronomy, when it is stated that there are strong grounds for supposing the generally received value of that great unit of celestial measures —the mean Distance of the Earth from the Sun—to be materially in error; and that, in fact, we are nearer to the central luminary by some 4,000,000 miles than for many years past has been commonly believed. The results of various researches during the last ten years appear, however, to point to the same conclusion."

Mr. Hind then proceeds to describe the actual state of our knowledge respecting it, extending through two entire columns of the above Journal. We have only space for the results:

" To recapitulate briefly: a diminution in the measure of the sun's distance now adopted is implied by—1st, the theory of the moon, as regards the parallactic equation, agreeably to the researches of Professor Hansen and the Astronomer Royal; 2nd, the lunar equation in the theory of the earth, newly investigated by M. Le Verrier; 3rd, the excess in the motion of the node of the orbit of Venus beyond what can be due to the received values of the planetary masses; 4th, the similar excess in the motion of the perihelion of Mars, also detected within the past few years by the same mathematician; 5th, the experiments of M. Foucault on the velocity of light; and 6th, the results of observations of Mars when near the earth about the opposition of 1862.

" Subjoined are a few of the numerical changes which will follow upon the substitution of M. Le Verrier's solar parallax (8″·95) for that of Professor Encke, on which reliance has so long been placed. The earth's mean distance from the sun becomes 91,328,600 miles, being a reduction of 4,036,000. The circumference of her orbit, 599,194,000 miles, being a diminution of 25,360,000. Her mean hourly velocity, 65,460 miles. The diameter of the sun 850,100 miles, which is smaller by nearly 38,000. The distances, velocities, and dimensions of all the members of the planetary system of course require similar corrections if we wish to express them in miles; in the case of Neptune, the mean distance is diminished by 30 times the amount of correction to that of the earth, or about 122,000,000 miles. The velocity of light is decreased by nearly 8000 miles per second, and becomes 183,470 if based upon astronomical data alone. These numbers will illustrate the great importance that attaches to a precise knowledge of the sun's parallax, in our appreciation of the various distances and dimensions in the solar system.

" The evidence which has been adduced since the publication of M. Le Verrier's investigations, would rather induce us to adopt a diminished measure of the earth's distance from the sun, as the most probable solution of the difficulty.

" M. Léon Foucault, of Paris, has succeeded in measuring the absolute velocity of light by means of the 'turning mirror'—an experimental determination of no little interest and significance. He concludes that it cannot differ much from 298,000,000 of French metres per second, or 185,170 English miles, which is a notable diminution upon the velocity previously derived from astronomical data alone. The time which light requires to travel from the sun to the earth is known with great precision; at the mean distance of the latter it is rather less than 8′ 18″, and if this number be combined with M. Foucault's measure of the velocity, it will be evident that the received distance is too great by about one-thirtieth part—that light, in fact, has not so far to travel before it reaches the earth as generally supposed. The corresponding solar parallax is 8′ 86″, which approaches much nearer to M. Le Verrier's theoretical value than to the one depending on the transits of 1761 and 1769. So curious a corroboration of the former deserves especial remark."

Blue Colour of the Sky.

Mr. Glaisher, in his Report of Scientific Balloon ascents made by him and Mr. Coxwell, in 1863, remarks that the Colour of the Sky in 1862 was of a deeper blue generally than in 1863. On the 31st of March the sky was of a deep Prussian blue, and on the 18th of April it was of a faint blue only, exhibiting another great contrast to the appearance of last year. Sir Isaac Newton considers this colour as a "blue of the first order, though very faint and little, for all vapours, when they begin to condense and coalesce into small parcels, become first of that bigness, whereby such an azure must be reflected." Professor Clausius considers the vapours to be vesicles or bladders, and ascribes the blue colour of the first order to reflection from the thin pellicle of water. In reference to these opinions the following facts are important:—1. The azure colour of the sky, though resembling the blue of the first order when the sky is viewed from the earth's surface, becomes, as observed by Mr. Glaisher in his balloon ascents, an exceedingly deep Prussian blue, as we ascend to the height of five or six miles, which is a deep blue of the second or third order. 2. The *maximum* polarizing angle of the atmosphere being 45 deg. is that of air, and not that of water, which is 55 deg. 3. At the greatest height to which Mr. Glaisher ascended—namely, at the height of five, six, and seven miles, where the blue is the brightest— "the air is almost deprived of moisture."

Hence it follows that the exceedingly deep Prussian blue cannot be produced by vesicles of water, but must be caused by reflection from the molecules of air, whose polarizing angle is 45 deg. The faint blue which the sky exhibits at the earth's surface is therefore not the blue of the first order, and is merely the blue of the second or third order, rendered paler by the light reflected from the aqueous vapour in the lower regions of the atmosphere."

Mr. Glaisher speaks of the curious changes in colour that he and Mr. Coxwell experienced in ascending, and remarked that they could now easily go a mile higher without turning quite so blue as before. In one descent they very nearly got into the sea, and only escaped that fate by coming down at the rate of four miles in two minutes.

Beauty of the Sky.

It is a strange thing how little in general people know about the Sky. It is the part of creation in which Nature has done more for the sake of pleasing man, more for the sole and evident purpose of talking to him and teaching him, than in any other of her works, and it is just the part in which we least attend to her. There are not many of her other works in which some more material or essential purpose than the mere pleasing of man is not answered by every part of their organization; but every essential purpose of the sky might, as far as we know, be answered, if once in three days, or thereabouts, a great black ugly rain-cloud were broken up over the blue, and everything well watered, and so all left blue again till next time, with perhaps a film of morning and evening mist for dew. But, instead of this, there is not a moment of any day of our lives when Nature is not producing scene after scene, picture after picture, glory after glory, and working still upon such exquisite and constant principles of the most perfect beauty, that it is quite certain it is all done for us, and intended for our perpetual pleasure.—*John Ruskin.*

Influence of High Temperatures in Balloon Ascents.

Professor Owen has remarked the importance of the influences of very high distances on the human frame, which is adapted of course to a very different medium. The fact which Mr. Glaisher mentions as to his feeling a greater power of resisting the influence of very high temperatures is interesting in physiology, and in relation to the series of facts with which we are acquainted. We know that our lungs adapt themselves to atmospheres of different degrees of gravity, so that there are people who live habitually on high mountains, and feel no such difficulty in breathing as is felt at once when the inhabitant of a plain or low country comes up to these elevations. Now that depends upon the greater proportion of the minute cells of the lungs which are open and receive an attenuated atmosphere, in proportion to the minute cells that are occupied by a quantity of mucus. Those on the plain do not make so large a use of their breathing apparatus as those who live at great altitudes. Hence more cells, occupied by mucus, will be taken up, and opened to free course and play; and Professor Owen has no doubt that is the solution of the interesting fact mentioned by Mr. Glaisher. Physiologists are all agreed that one condition of longevity is the capacity of the chest; and therefore it is hoped the increased breathing capacity acquired by Mr. Glaisher and Mr. Coxwell will tend to the prolongation of their lives.

Value of Meteorological Observations, Telegraphy, and Forecasts.

The establishment of a Meteorological Department by the Board of Trade is understood to have originated with the late Prince Consort, who suggested that the more methodical observation of the phenomena of the Weather might be rendered conducive to the saving of many valuable lives. The plan had worked to February, 1861, when the Secretary of the Board of Trade wrote to the Royal Society concerning the new features which the operations of the Meteorological Department had assumed; and expressing an anxiety to know whether the science of meteorology was now in such a state as to admit of a permanent reliable system of storm-signals and daily weather forecasts; also, whether the progress and useful application of meteorological science would be more efficiently promoted by devoting the money voted by Parliament to the original objects contemplated—viz., the collection, tabulation, and discussion of meteorological phenomena, or by devoting it to the system of telegraphy and weather forecasts. The Secretary of the Royal Society, after the lapse of a month, replied, on behalf of the President and Council, to the effect that they were assured by Admiral Fitzroy that the original objects for which the Meteorological Department was formed were still kept in view. " In the forewarnings of storms," adds Dr. Sharpey, " much must as yet undoubtedly be viewed as in a great measure tentative; but there is one class of cases on which such premonitory information is entitled to be regarded as resting on more assured scientific relations. Admiral Fitzroy considers that he has satisfactorily established the occasional occurrence of storms of a cyclonic character, of very limited diameter, not much exceeding perhaps that of the British islands themselves, and originating in their vicinity. The practice of forewarning is specially suited to such storms. They are characterized by great violence, and by frequent and rapid changes in the direction of the wind. The key to their comprehension is supplied by the telegraphic reports, which convey to the central office a knowledge of the various simultaneous directions of the wind in different localities; and, when once comprehended, they are particularly suited for forewarning, inasmuch as, in its general course, the advance of the cyclone is steady in direction and moderate in rate.

"In connexion with this subject the President and Council revert with satisfaction to a reply by Sir John Herschel to the Royal Commission on Lights, Buoys, and Beacons, that 'the most important meteorological information which could be telegraphed would be information first received by telegraph of a cyclone actually in progress at a great distance, and working its way towards the locality. There is no doubt that the progress of a cyclone may be telegraphed, and might secure many a ship from danger by forewarning.' It is obvious that this remark, which refers to the approach of a distant cyclone, is equally applicable to cyclones originating in or near our islands, the existence of which has been made known by the system of telegraphy which Admiral Fitzroy has established.

" With respect to the 'forecasts of the state of the weather,' which are published in the newspapers, the President and Council learn from Admiral Fitzroy that they really occasion no cost to Government, and scarcely fall, therefore, within the questions submitted for reply; moreover, the President and Council have no data whereon to rest a conclusion in regard to the degree of reliance to which these last-named forecasts may be entitled."

Weather Signs.

A few of the more marked Signs of Weather—useful alike to seaman, farmer, and gardener, are the following:

Whether clear or cloudy—a rosy sky at sunset presages fine weather:—a red sky in the morning bad weather, or much wind (perhaps rain):—a grey sky in the morning, fine weather:—a high dawn, wind:—a low dawn, fair weather.

Soft-looking or delicate clouds foretell fine weather, with moderate or light breezes:—hard edged, oily-looking clouds,—wind. A dark, gloomy, blue sky is windy;—but a light bright blue sky indicates fine weather. Generally, the *softer* clouds look, the less wind (but perhaps more rain) may be expected;—and the harder, more "greasy," rolled, tufted, or ragged,—the stronger the coming wind will prove. Also—a bright yellow sky at sunset presages wind; a pale yellow, wet:—and thus by the prevalence of red, yellow, or grey tints, the coming weather may be foretold very nearly:—indeed, if aided by instruments, almost exactly.

Small inky-looking clouds foretell rain:—light scud clouds driving across heavy masses show wind and rain, but if alone, may indicate wind only.

High upper clouds crossing the sun, moon, or stars, in a direction different from that of the lower clouds, or the wind then felt below, foretell a change of wind.

After fine clear weather, the first signs in the sky of a coming change are usually light streaks, curls, wisps, or mottled patches of white distant clouds, which increase and are followed by an overcasting of murky vapour that grows into cloudiness. This appearance, more or less oily or watery, as wind or rain will prevail, is an infallible sign.

Usually the higher and more distant such clouds seem to be, the more gradual but general the coming change of weather will prove.

Light, delicate, quiet tints or colours, with soft, undefined forms of clouds, indicate and accompany fine weather; but gaudy, or unusual hues, with hard, definitely outlined clouds, foretell rain and probably strong wind. Misty clouds forming, or hanging on heights, show wind and rain coming —if they remain, increase, or descend. If they rise or disperse, the weather will improve or become fine.

When sea birds fly out early and far to seaward, moderate wind and fair weather may be expected.

When they hang about the land, or over it, sometimes flying inland, expect a strong wind with stormy weather. As many creatures besides birds are affected by the approach of rain or wind, such indications should not be slighted by an observer who wishes to foresee weather or compare its variations. There are other signs of a coming change in the weather known less generally than may be desirable, and therefore worth notice;

such as, when birds of long flight, rooks, swallows, or others, hang about home and fly up and down or low, rain or wind may be expected. Also when animals seek sheltered places, instead of spreading over their usual range; when pigs carry straw to their sties; when smoke from chimneys does not ascend readily (or straight upwards during calm), an unfavourable change is probable.

Dew is an indication of fine weather, so is fog. Neither of these two formations occur under an overcast sky, or when there is much wind. One sees fog occasionally rolled away as it were by wind, but seldom or never *formed* while it is blowing.

Remarkable clearness of atmosphere near the horizon: distant objects, such as hills unusually visible, or raised (by refraction), and what is called "a good *hearing* day," may be mentioned among signs of wet, if not wind, to be expected.

More than usual twinkling of the stars; indistinctness or apparent multiplication of the moon's horns; halos; "winddogs," and the rainbow; are more or less significant of increasing wind, if not approaching rain, with or without wind.

Mr. Glaisher remarks, in the account of one of his recent balloon ascents:—"It would also seem that, when the sky is overcast and no rain falling, the Sun is shining on its upper surface, and both these conclusions agree with all my own experiences. That double strata or layers of clouds are indications of rain is shown by my recent observations; but it is one of those facts which have so far attracted the attention of some observers of nature as even to have passed into proverbs. My friend, Mr. Sopwith, tells me that in the mining districts, where he has resided so much, it is a common saying that 'it will be rain to-day; the clouds is twee ply thick;' by which, in their homely phrase, they clearly express that their expectations of rain are based on the observance of one range of clouds flying in the air at a higher elevation than another."

It has been well observed that the old lunar theory, still implicitly received by country-folks, and held by many ladies as a fact of direct experience—the theory that weather is apt to change at the moon's quarters, clearly applies rather to the earth than to any particular spot on it. And all the various complicated forms of that theory, invented to supply its apparent failures—such as that a change from fine to wet may be expected if the new quarter is entered on after midnight, and *vice versâ* for a post-meridian change,—are liable to the same objection.

The late Marshal Bugeaud, says the *Emancipation*, when only a captain, during the Spanish campaign under Napoleon I., once read in a manuscript which by chance fell into his hands, that from observations made in England and Florence during a period of fifty years, the following law respecting the Weather had been proved true :—'Eleven times out of twelve the weather remains the same during the whole moon as it is on the fifth day, if it continues unchanged over the sixth day; and nine times out of twelve like the fourth day, if the sixth resembles the fourth.' From 1815 to 1830 M. Bugeaud devoted his attention to agriculture; and guided by the law just mentioned, avoided the losses in hay time and vintage which many of his neighbours experienced. When Governor of Algiers, he never entered on a campaign till after the sixth day of the moon. His neighbours at Excideuil and his lieutenants in Algeria would often exclaim, 'How lucky he is in the weather.' What they regarded as mere chance was the result of observation. In counting the fourth and sixth days, he was particular in beginning from the exact time of new moon, and added three-quarters of an hour for each day for the greater length of the lunar - as compared with the solar day.

Mr. Shepherd, C.E., appears to prefer the planet Jupiter to the moon, and has discovered an elaborate law for the variations of our English weather, except so far as the principle is affected by comets.

Mr. Shepherd is not quite without even higher authority. Sir John Herschel has publicly intimated his suspicion that the periodic expansion in the Sun's spots had some close connexion with the extraordinarily wet summer of 1860, and in his article on Meteorology in the *Encyclopædia Britannica*, the same eminent authority has connected this periodic change in the Sun's spots, which takes place in about twelve years, with the periodic time of Jupiter's revolution round the sun (which is nearly the same in length), so that here we have an eminent astronomer half conceding the same very dubious principle—that causes which affect equally, if not the whole earth, at least all places which, in the diurnal rotation, are brought into the same relative position towards the sun or the planet, are the principal influences which determine our local weather.

Yet, if this be so, how does it happen that the year 1860, which was abnormally wet in Europe, was abnormally dry in many other parts of the world? If Mr. Shepherd be right in connecting this fact with the orbital position of Jupiter, or Sir John Herschel in connecting it with the large spots on the Sun, it would scarcely have merely affected the local distribution of heat; or, if it could, the means by which these causes rob England to burn India remain as dark as before.—*Paper in the Spectator newspaper.*

Barometer for Farmers.

In one of his letters, Humboldt says that a Barometer should be considered as necessary on a farm as a plough : but farmers generally prefer to trust in the moon and other exploded nonsense to purchasing a reliable instrument that would repay them tenfold. A substitute, called Leoni's Prognosticator, consists of a vial full of a clear liquid, in which swims a snowy substance. In fine weather that substance lies on the bottom, but before a storm it rises to the surface, with a tendency to the side opposite the quarter from which the storm is coming. The substances used are kept secret. An ordinary barometer indicates the density of the atmosphere. Leoni's instrument evidently indicates its electric state, and for that reason we are of opinion that it is a better instrument to prognosticate the weather. The following is a substitute that will not cost more than 1s., and for aught we know it may be the identical thing itself. Dissolve some camphor in alcohol and throw into the solution some soda; the camphor will be precipitated in snowy flakes; collect these by passing the mixture through a filter and put them in a vial with clear alcohol, in which as much camphor as it would take has been dissolved. Cork it, place it where it will not be disturbed, and examine it every morning and night. This is termed a *Storm-glass.*

Icebergs and the Weather.

The intimate relation existing between the Climates of particular seasons, and the discharge of Icebergs from the great Arctic glaciers has long been perfectly understood and described by both British and American naval officers. But the quantity of ice annually released in the shape of bergs is so insignificant, majestic as those frozen masses are, in proportion to the quantity remaining behind, and to that annually engendered over the vast area of the Arctic continental icefields, that any difference in the amount of "average" annual discharge cannot materially disturb the balance. Nor is the disengagement of the bergs, when viewed on a large scale, a process depending on variable conditions. The slow downward descent of glaciers towards the ocean (which is now fully recognised as the result of a well-known law) is dependent on forces of such vast magnitude and in such constant operation as to admit of no perceptible modification owing to local atmospheric influences.

What does materially affect climate, however, is the variation in the annual range, Equator-wards, of the great Arctic currents, which convey on their surface not only the bergs, but the vast compact fields of pack-ice, extending over areas of many thousands of square miles, and thus bringing about a reduction of temperature, infinitely in excess of that produced by the bergs.

The exceptionally boisterous and rainy summer of 1860 was

due to the much increased southward range, along the eastern and southern shores of Greenland, of the Spitzbergen drift, and was alluded to by Dr. Wallich, in some observations published by him at the close of that year.

St. Swithun: his true History.

So little is really known of this good Saint, that it is tedious to wade through a mass of more or less probable conjecture.

The facts of St. Swithun's life seem to be that he was born near Winchester about the year 800—that he became a monk, and afterwards prior of the old abbey of that city, and was chosen by King Ecgberht the Bretwalda to be tutor of his son Æthelwulf, heir to the throne of Wessex. From 852 to 863, when he died, Swithun was Bishop of Winchester. He distinguished himself as an architect by building a bridge of stone and a tower to his cathedral, and as a Minister of State both to Æthelwulf and his successor, Æthelbald. In 971, more than a century after his death, he was exhumed, and "translated" and beatified by his successor, the famous Bishop Æthelwold, in the time of Archbishop St. Dunstan. Ridiculing, with Godwin *De Præsulibus*, the idea taken up by Lord Campbell, that Swithun was Æthelwulf's "Chancellor," in the modern sense of the word, Mr. Earle (formerly Professor of Anglo-Saxon at Oxford) claims for him the credit of having had a great share in the administration of that King's policy, and especially in the education of his youngest son, the Great Alfred. Indeed, he surmises that Swithun was Alfred's companion in his journey to Rome in 853, though the *Saxon Chronicle* says nothing about it. And he also argues that Æthelwulf's much-debated dedication of the tenth of his land as tithes to religious purposes, in the year 855 (when the Northmen first wintered in England), was due to Swithun's advice. "This was," he says, "the culminating point of Swithun's policy." Equally baseless is the hypothesis that Swithun was the "intermediary," the "prudent counsellor and successful diplomat" who averted civil war when Æthelwulf returned from his pilgrimage to Rome, bringing with him as wife the Frankish Princess Judith. It is more certain, we think, that Swithun's name continued to be held in affectionate reverence among the people; and this probably led to his beatification by popular consent. The formal process of canonization had not yet been introduced.—*Saturday Review.*

Mr. Earle discusses the legend which connects St. Swithun with *forty days of rain*, and decides that it is wholly without foundation. Mr. Howard, the meteorologist, many years since, by his observations, gave a sort of currency to this notion; but it has since received its quietus in the following facts, from the Greenwich observations for 20 years:—It appears that St. Swithun's day was wet in 1841, and there were 23 rainy days up to the 24th of August; 1845, 26 rainy days; 1851, 13 rainy days; 1853, 18 rainy days; 1854, 16 rainy days; and in 1856, 14 rainy days.

In 1842 and following years St. Swithun's day was dry, and the result was, in 1842, 12 rainy days; in 1843, 22 rainy days; 1844, 20 rainy days; 1846, 21 rainy days; 1847, 17 rainy days; 1848, 31 rainy days; 1849, 20 rainy days; 1850, 17 rainy days; 1852, 19 rainy days; 1855, 18 rainy days; 1857, 14 rainy days; 1858, 14 rainy days; 1859, 13 rainy days; and in 1860, 29 rainy days. These figures show the superstition to be founded on a fallacy, as the average of 20 years proves rain to have fallen upon the largest number of days when St. Swithun's day was dry.

No event, or natural phenomenon which could be construed into such, is alluded to by any of the various authors who wrote histories of St. Swithun. On the contrary, the weather seems to have been most propitious during his translation. How then did the popular notion about St. Swithun's Day arise? Most probably, as Mr. Earle remarks, it was derived from primeval pagan belief regarding the meteorologically prophetic character of some day about the same period of the year as St. Swithun's. Such adaptations, it is well known, were frequent on the supplanting throughout Europe of heathenism by Christianity. In confirmation of this view it is to be observed, that in various countries of the European continent, the same belief prevails, though differences exist as to the period of the particular day in question. Thus, in France, St. Médard's Day, (June 8,) and the Day of St. Gervais and Protais, (June 19,) have a similar character ascribed to them. In Belgium they have a rainy saint, named St. Godelière; whilst in Germany, among others, a character of this description is ascribed to the day of the Seven Sleepers.

Rainfall in London.

Mr. G. V. Vernon has communicated to the Literary and Philosophical Society of Manchester a Paper on the number of Days on which Rain falls annually in London, from observations made during the fifty-six years, 1807-1862. Howard's *Climate of London* has been used for the years 1807 to 1831; the *Philosophical Transactions* for the years 1832 to 1840; and the *Greenwich Observations* for the years 1841 to 1862. During the entire period of fifty-six years, no month occurred in which rain did not fall.

The minimum number of days occurred in 1832, the cholera year, and 1834; the number of days being 86, 82 respectively. The maximum number occurred in 1848, the number being 223 days.

Taking the quarterly values, we find that rain falls on the greatest number of days in autumn, and the least in spring.

Taking the means of five yearly periods, there appears to be a kind of periodicity in the number of days on which rain falls;

having a maximum in 1815 to 1817, and a minimum in 1845 to 1847.

The Force of Lightning.

A person may be killed by Lightning, although the explosion takes place at the distance of twenty miles, by what is called the back-stroke. Suppose that the two extremities of a cloud, highly charged with electricity, hang down towards the earth, they will repel the electricity from the earth's surface, if it be of the same kind with their own, and will attract the other kind; and if a discharge should suddenly take place at one end of the cloud, the equilibrium will instantly be restored by a flash at that point of the earth which is under the other. Though the back-stroke is often sufficiently powerful to destroy life, it is never so terrible in its effects as the direct shot, which is frequently of inconceivable intensity. Instances have occurred in which large masses of iron and stone, and even many feet of a stone wall, have been conveyed to a considerable distance by a stroke of lightning. Rocks and the tops of mountains often bear the marks of fusion from its action, and occasionally vitreous tubes, descending many feet into banks of sand, mark the path of the electric fluid. Some years ago, Dr. Fielder exhibited several of these fulgorites in London, of considerable length, which had been dug out of the sandy plains of Silesia and Eastern Prussia. One found at Paderborn was forty feet long. Their ramifications generally terminate in pools or springs of water below the sand, which are supposed to determine the course of the electric fluid. No doubt the soil and substrata must influence its direction, since it is found by experience that places which have been struck by lightning are often struck again. A school-house in Lammer-Muir, in East Lothian, has been struck three different times.—Mrs. Somerville's *Connexion of the Sciences.*

The inquiries into the chances of refuge from lightning have been attended with saving results. Here is an instance:

A few years since an awful thunderstorm occurred in the neighbourhood of Inkpen, Berkshire. Three men, named Martin, Buxey, and Palmer, were employed in mowing grass, when a storm of thunder and lightning broke over the field, and one of them suggested that they should run beneath a tree; Martin knowing that trees generally attract lightning, immediately remarked, "We had better go anywhere than under a tree." Buxey and Palmer, however, as the storm was severe, and the hail was falling heavily at the time, ran and seated themselves beneath a large lime-tree, but Martin walked off to a cottage, and was safely sheltered. In about half-an-hour after the storm had abated, both Buxey and Palmer were found lying on the grass beneath the tree, quite dead from the lightning. The clothes of Buxey were found to be on fire, and the hair of Palmer was much scorched.

Effect of Moonlight on Vegetation.

It has been demonstrated that Moonlight has the power, *per se*, of awakening the Sensitive Plant, and consequently that it possesses an influence of some kind on Vegetation. It is true that the influence is very feeble, compared with that of the sun; but the action is established, and the question remains, what is the practical value of the fact? "It will immediately," says Professor Lindley, "occur to the reader that possibly the screens which are drawn down over hothouses at night, to prevent loss of heat by radiation, may produce some unappreciated injury by cutting off the rays of the moon, which Nature intended to fall upon plants as much as the rays of the sun."

Even artificial light is not wholly powerless. Decandolle succeeded in making crocuses expand by lamplight; and Dr. Winn, of Truro, has suggested that the oxyhydrogen lamp may be made subservient to horticulture in the dark days of winter.

An extraordinary effect of Moonlight upon the human subject occured in 1863. A boy, thirteen years of age, residing near Peckham Rye, was expelled his home by his mother for disobedience. He ran away to a corn-field close by, and on lying down in the open air, fell asleep. He slept throughout the night, which was a moonlight one. Some labourers on their way to work, next morning, seeing the boy apparently asleep, aroused him; the lad opened his eyes, but declared he could not see. He was conveyed home, and medical advice was obtained: the surgeon affirmed that the total loss of sight resulted from sleeping in the moonlight.

Contemporary Inventions and Discoveries.

Mr. Piesse, the well-known operative chemist, has thus popularly grouped some of the leading novelties of our age:

The inventions and discoveries of my time may truly be included among some of the greatest and most wonderful which the world has seen. I have not yet passed forty summers, but perfectly recollect being one of the gaping crowd that first witnessed lighting the streets with gas. Near to the Marble Arch, at the top of Oxford-street, London, stands an iron post, on which is inscribed "Here stood Tyburn Gate, 1829." Now I well remember this Oxford-street turnpike, and the oil-lamps ' dimly burning,' which enabled the University coach and the eight-horse waggons to near-side the off-side gatepost; at that time all Oxford-street and the shops therein protested against 'the light of other days,' and became illumined with Murdoch's gas: thus the oil-lamps passed away for ever. Tunneling Primrose Hill for the first railway into London was a fund of enjoyment to me; there I learned my first practical lesson in mineralogy—to distinguish iron pyrites from real gold nuggets, which it at times resembles. One morning the newspapers teemed with an account of the late Duke of Wellington witnessing the first electric telegram from Drayton, twelve miles from London. People flocked to Paddington, and paid a shilling to do the same; of course I was among them! It appears to me but the other day when every housewife kept her linen rags to make tinder. The bunch of matches, like a large fan, the flint and steel were in every house. What a change has the lucifer produced? After hearing Professor Brande one night deliver a popular lecture at the Royal Institution, the Secretary read a letter received that day from Paris, announcing the discoveries of Daguerre. The assertion that the picture of a camera could be fixed by the mere agency of light startled belief, yet from that hour photography took its rise. Strange discoveries now crowd upon the memory. The oxyhydrogen flame that burns the diamond and volatilizes platinum; then came the Drummond lime-light that is visible as a star sixty miles away; now followed Dobereiner's lamp that ignites itself when you lift a latch. Electroplating becomes one of the arts of the country. A new force of nature, actinism, was recognised. Wonderfully active principles of plants—quinine, morphia, and strychnine, are discovered. The food of plants and the balance of organic nature are developed at Giessen. New metals are discovered and are practically eliminated for the use of manufacturers; and so we thus come to the present, when I now write with an aluminium pen made from tiles laid in a wall when Constantine was crowned at York."*

The Bayonet.

Mr. Akermann, in an elaborate series of "Notes on the Origin and History of the Bayonet," has been unable to verify the statement that this weapon derives its name from Bayonne, the reputed place of its invention. Voltaire alludes to it in the eighth book of the *Henriade*. The results of the inquiry may be thus briefly recited:—That "bayonette" was the name of a knife, which may probably have been so designated either from its having been the peculiar weapon of a crossbow-man, or from the individual who

---

* What would the old Scotchman of the following anecdote say to such an age?—Sir Alexander Ramsay had been constructing upon his estate in Scotland, a piece of machinery, which was driven by a stream of water running through the home farm-yard. There were a thrashing machine, a winnowing machine, a circular saw for splitting trees, and other contrivances. Observing an old man, who had long been about the place, looking very attentively at all that was going on, Sir Alexander said, "Wonderful things people can do now, Robby?" "Ay," said Robby, "indud, Sir Alexander; I'm thinking if Solomon was alive now, he'd be thought naething o'!"—*Dean Ramsay.*

first adopted it ; that its first recorded use as a weapon of war occurs in the Memoirs of Puysegur, and may be referred to the year 1647 ; that it is first mentioned in England by Sir J. Turner, 1670-71 ; that it was introduced into the English army in the first half of the year 1672; that before the peace of Nimwegen Puysegur had seen troops on the Continent armed with bayonets, furnished with rings, which would go over the muzzles of the muskets ; that in 1686 the device of the socket-bayonet was tested before the French king, and failed ; that in 1689 Mackay, by the adoption of the ringed bayonet, successfully opposed the Highlanders at the battle of Killicrankie ; lastly, that the bayonet with the socket was in general use in the year 1703.

William Cobbett, who had been a soldier, and carried the bayonet, used to call it " King George's Toasting-fork."

Derivation of the word Loot.

This word, which so often occurs in the account of the late Indian war, is simply the Hindustani for plunder. Noun, " loot," plunder ; verb, " lootna," to plunder. This is one of the many examples of Hindustani words generally used in English conversation in India, which gradually came into use at home, amongst the oldest and most familiar of which is, perhaps, the slang term "that's the cheez," for "that's the thing," "cheez" Hindustani for "thing."

Telegram.

When this Indian term was first applied to our telegraphic messages, a considerable amount of learned disquisition was wasted in seeking its origin. Any one who has been in India must remember the curious pronunciation by natives of many English proper names, as well as of other words, for which they have no translation in Hindustani; generally abbreviating a long difficult expression, and sometimes even changing altogether the pronunciation. On the introduction of the telegraph into India, there being no Hindustani word, the natives were obliged to attempt English, and the easiest way they could manage to pronounce telegraphic message was " telegram." This being an easy abbreviation was at once picked up and adopted by the English in India, and then came home in the same way that we got " loot" from India, and now again from China.—*Correspondent of the "Daily News."*

Archæology and Manufactures.

Archæology, far from being a mere unprofitable dilettantism, has a positive money-value, one appreciable not only by the literary or scientific mind, but even by those who look exclusively to material interests—that commerce, in fine, no less than history or art, is under obligations to archæology. In the case of our pottery and earthenware manufacture,—now an important branch of our national trade—at the time when Wedgwood first began his operations, England was an importing country with regard to this article of trade, drawing her supplies from Holland, France, and Germany. About the year 1760, Wedgwood established himself in Staffordshire. The models which he selected for imitation were taken from the antique:—from the Portland Vase, Greek vases, cameos, and old coins,—but, above all, from the magnificent collection of Etruscan vases and earthenware, which was purchased about that time from Sir William Hamilton, for the British Museum. Such was the immediate improvement in classical elegance and purity of design, which the manufactures derived from these sources, that within very few years England became an exporting country in this article; and the trade was steadily developed, until, in the year 1857, the declared value of her exports nearly reached a million and a half of money. Wedgwood's own sense of his obligation to ancient models was marked by the name he gave to the new village formed around his works in Staffordshire, which he called Etruria, in honour of them. More recently the collection of Etruscan antiquities made by the Prince of Canino, and brought to England by Signor Campanari, has marked another stage of progress in this branch of industry; and, at this moment, the best silversmiths and jewellers in London resort to the British Museum, to study these models, and copy them for reproduction. Much of the well-known Minton-ware is either copied from, or due to the study and imitation of, the Majolica ware of Mediæval Italy; whilst the smaller objects of Assyrian art, brought from Nineveh by Mr. Layard, are extensively copied by artists, and reductions of them made in Parian, in marble, or in bronze.—*Address to the Cambrian Archæological Association, by Mr. C. G. Wynne, M.P.*

Good Art should be cheap.

There is no hope of the diffusion of a better taste till all classes of society are familiarized with the best works of the best artists; and English manufactures will never be generally improved in design till the purchasers as well as the producers know how to appreciate what is beautiful, and till a better intuitive taste prevails in the cottage as well as in the mansion. So long as it is *cheaper* to reproduce familiar shapes and ornaments, so long will it be vain to expect sufficient encouragement for improvements in design. Theorists may preach for ever as to abstract beauty, but *the public will buy the old-fashioned, tasteless goods, if they cost less.*

We do not believe that a beautiful thing need be more expensive than an ugly thing. At any rate, this is the lesson to impress upon such of our manufacturers as may be disposed to join the art-movement of the day. It is not enough to design a novelty in really good taste—it must be at least as cheap as the monstrosity which it is meant to supersede, and, if possible, cheaper. Is it not worth while to inquire whether there may not be some deeper reason than a supposed depraved taste for the hideous colouring, so dubious and sombre, of our Manchester goods, for example? To take an instance: we believe that Hoyle's Prints, famous throughout the world for their slates and lilacs, are dyed of those most unpicturesque hues for no other reason than that they are the most "fast" colours that can be produced. If our chemists could discover the secret of making the primitive colours equally "fast," and if the needful pigments were no dearer, we believe that cotton printing would be revolutionized. But, meanwhile, customers in every market of the world will ask for Hoyle's Fast Prints, in preference to the brightest and most beautiful colours, which, however charming to the eye when bran-new, would disappear in the first wash.—*Saturday Review.*

Imitative Jewellery.

From the profuse display of what are designated "gold chains" in the windows of jewellers' shops, there is evidently a large demand for these articles, although the purchasers are little aware of the value of the articles. The gold coin of the realm is, in technical language, 22 carats fine—that is, it consists of 22 parts by weight of fine, or pure gold, and 2 parts by weight of copper; and gold plate, &c., is 18 carats fine—that is, it contains 18 parts by weight of gold and 6 of copper in the 24. The alloy of which a large proportion of gold chains is made contains only 8 or 10 parts by weight of fine gold in the 24 parts, the remaining 16 or 14 parts being common brass. The application of brass for this purpose is of comparatively recent date, and enables the manufacturer to adulterate gold to a much greater extent than is practicable with copper alone. This depends upon the fact that brass resembles gold in colour, and copper does not. The brassy gold chains in question are far inferior in colour to chains made of gold of 18 or 22 carats fine, and they would hardly be tolerated by many persons when seen side by side with those of the latter description. They are now manufactured on a very large scale by the aid of machinery, and so great has been the decrease in their cost of production, that the value of the labour upon certain kinds of chains has been reduced from 30s. to 3s. 6d., or even less.   It is usual to deposit upon the finished chain an exceedingly thin coating of pure gold by the electrotype process. This, of course, is speedily worn off by friction, and consequently the original fine colour of the chain at the time of purchase disappears. The propriety of this practice is questionable.   If the public like cheap brassy gold chains, and are satisfied with their appearance, it is their own affair, and no one has a right to say a word ; but, in buying such articles, beware of the small value of the materials in comparison with gold.*

French Enamel.

Among the artistic triumphs in the International Exhibition of 1862 was the magnificent work in gold and enamel, by M. Payen, which is stated to have cost him several years' labour, or the sum of 6000*l*.   In this work the late Prince Consort evinced considerable interest when he was in Paris; and it was mainly to the Prince's kind interference on behalf of M. Payen, that the Great Seal of England was sent to Paris, in order that it might be copied as one of the great seals of the different nations, which form the border of the work.   The subject of the allegory is the Reward of Genius and Industry : this is shown on a large centre-piece on a ground of blue enamel ; and the border, in which the seals of different countries are emblazoned, is formed of filigree work in gold.   There was besides in the Exhibition an immense variety of works by M. Payen, including gold rings from three francs to three thousand francs each.

---

* In a book published in 1679, we find these cautions on Gold and Silver Wares :—" Can you imagine that although the buyer perceive not the deceit at first, when the work is newly sold and cunningly set off with all your skill, that he will not perceive it in the wearing like brass or copper, and when sold again be allowed but 3s. or 3s. 6d. the ounce for the silver, and but 2*l*. 10s. or 3*l*. the ounce for the gold, when he paid 5s. the ounce for the silver, and 4*l*. the ounce for the gold, besides the fashion? You may be sure he will not only repent the dealing with you, but publicly say you are a very cheating knave; and say also, ' Who would buy such sort of works, wherein is so much deceit, but rather use any other thing instead thereof?'   And thus the people are discouraged to buy your works, and your trade decays, while you vainly think to treble your profit, but instead thereof lose your trade.   When otherwise, if your gold and silver works be of standard goodness, your customers will say, 'Tis as good as money in their pockets, weight for weight; and that they know what they paid for the fashion, which is all the loss they shall be at, and the work wears creditable; and they will not repent of their bargain, but publicly commend it, whereby others will be encouraged to buy such works, and so your trade increases."

Life and Health.

Periods and Conditions of Life.

PHYSIOLOGISTS divide Human Life into four periods, the embryonic, immature, reproductive, and sterile ages : the first terminating at birth ; the second at puberty, which is achieved at 15 ; the third at 45, after which few mothers have children ; and the last at 100 and upwards.

Individual life exists on such conditions that it may at any moment cease ; and the vital tenure varies not only with every change of external circumstances, but by natural laws at every year of age. It is most insecure in infancy and old age. At the age of puberty—before the period when the growth of the body is most rapid—before the age of its greatest strength—before the age of greatest intellectual power—it is less assailable by death. The chance of living through a given year increases from birth to the age of 14 or 15 ; it decreases to the age of 55-8 at a slightly accelerating rate ; after which the vitality declines at a much more rapid rate.

Age of the People.

It is worthy of remark that the very aged have not in the ten years [1851-1861] increased in near the same proportion as the general population. In 1851 there were in England 107,041 persons who had passed the limit of "14 years;" in 1861 the number had only increased to 113,250. In 1851 215 persons were returned as being above 100 years old, but only 201 persons in 1861—one in every 100,000. Of this last number 146 were women, and but 55 men—nearly three women to one man. Only 26 had never been married. About a third were found living in large towns—21 in London, 11 in Liverpool, five in Manchester, one in Birmingham, four in Bristol, one in Leeds. As in 1851, so in 1861, these very aged persons were not found so often in the midland districts of the kingdom as in the north and the east, and most of all in the west. At the last Census, Norfolk had among its 435,000 people 11 above 100 years old ; Gloucestershire, with 485,000 people, had eight centenarians ; and Somerset, with its 445,000, had nine. Wales, with its 1,112,000, had no less than 24, the same number as Lancashire with its 2,400,000 people, and more than London with its 2,800,000 inhabitants. So far as the occupations of these long-lived persons are given, the returns show a majority engaged in pursuits that caused them to be much in the open air. Three had been farmers, 13 out-door farm servants, five labourers, three hawkers, three seamen, three soldiers; there was a fisherman, a quarrier, a waterworks man, a miller. But there was also a scrivener, four shoemakers, a baker, a grocer, a carpenter, a marine-store dealer, three persons occupied in cotton manufacture, two in woollen, one in silk, one in lace. Of the women the returns commonly state only whether the person is wife or widow, but we are told that there were six who had been domestic servants, two nurses, three charwomen, two washer-women, and a gipsy. One centenarian was a member of the Household. Fourteen are described as land or house proprietors, or independent; 19 were passing their last years in the work-house. Six were blind.—*From the Census Report.*

The Human Heart.

If we regard the construction of the blood-vessels, and other parts of the circulating system, we find that they are constructed entirely on physical laws. The Heart is the mover which propels the blood, and, after having given the stroke, its fibres become relaxed, to receive a fresh supply. In this case it is important that the fluid should not again regurgitate into its cavities; and to prevent that, a system of valves, not thicker than paper, has been contrived. Here we see a design identical with that pur-sued by man in the construction of his pump, or even, in some cases, of his floodgates. The only difference between the work of man and the work of Nature is, that the latter is executed in a manner so superior, that man feels that he sinks into insignificance beside the Creator.

That wonderful machine, the Heart, goes night and day, for eighty years together, at the rate of 100,000 strokes for every twenty-four hours, having at every stroke a great resistance to overcome. Now, each ventricle will contain at least one ounce of blood; the heart contracts 4000 times in an hour, from which it follows that there pass through the heart every hour 4000 ounces, or 350 pounds of blood. The whole mass of blood is said to be about twenty-five pounds; so that a quantity equal to the whole mass of blood passes through the heart fourteen times in one hour, which is about once in every four minutes.

The Sense of Hearing.

Mr. John Marshall, in a Lecture on the special organs of the Sense of Hearing, describes the wonderful arrangements for the protection of these organs and their adaptation to their office ; the examination of their relative duties, in distinguishing the kinds and intensities of the sounds of such exceeding variety, produced by inanimate nature, by animals, and by art (music). For the appreciation of the pitch and quality of sounds Mr. Marshall considers that we are indebted to the delicate fibrous structure of the cochlea ; for the knowledge of the intensity of sound to the tympanum or drum, which, possessing the power of tension and relaxation, thus acts a protective part ; while in our knowledge of the distance and direction of sound we are guided by the external parts of the ear and by our experience.

Care of the Teeth.

Dr. J. H. Bowditch, of the United States, having examined with a microscope the matter deposited on the teeth and gums of more than 40 individuals, selected from all classes of society, and in nearly every variety of bodily condition, has discovered, in nearly every case, animal and vegetable parasites in great numbers ; in fact, the only persons whose mouths were found to be entirely free from these parasites cleaned their teeth four times daily, using soap once. Among the agents applied, it was found that tobacco-juice and smoke did not impair the vitality of the parasites ; nor did the chlorine tooth-wash, pulverized bark, soda, ammonia, &c. Soap, however—pure white soap—destroyed the parasites instantly, and is, therefore, the best specific for cleaning the teeth.

It having been asked, "Did the Greek surgeons extract teeth ?" Mr. George Hayes, the well-known dentist, replied, that on one of the orna-ments found in an ancient building in the Crimea, is represented a surgeon drawing a tooth from the mouth of one of the barbarian royalties. "This," says Mr. Hayes, "I think, establishes the fact that there were then peri-patetics, either Egyptian or Greek dentists, who resorted to those distant countries for the purpose of practising their art. I believe this is the only representation of a surgical operation to be met with on ancient sculpture."

Sugar has been proved injurious to the teeth, from its tendency to combine with their calcareous basis.

On Blindness.

Many have been the appeals to our sympathy with the affliction of the loss of sight, but neither has, perhaps, exceeded in pathos the following from an address delivered by Sir John Coleridge, at the West of England Institution for the Blind:

" Conceive to yourselves, for a moment, what is the ordinary entertainment and conversation that passes around any one of your family tables ; how many things we talk of as matters of course, as to the understanding and as to the bare conception of which sight is absolutely necessary. Consider again, what an affliction the loss of sight must be, and that when we talk of the golden sun, the bright stars, the beautiful flowers, the blush of spring, the glow of summer, and the ripening fruit of autumn, we are talking of things of which we do not convey to the minds of these poor creatures who are born blind anything like an adequate conception. There was once a great man, as we all know, in this country, a poet—and nearly the greatest poet that England has ever had to boast of—who was blind; and there is a passage in his works which is so true and touching that it exactly describes that which I have endeavoured, in feeble language, to paint. Milton says:

> " ' Thus with the year
> Seasons return ; but not to me returns
> Day, or the sweet approach of ev'n, or morn,
> Or sight of vernal bloom, or summer's rose,
> Or flocks, or herds, or human face divine ;
> But cloud instead, and ever during dark
> Surrounds me, from the cheerful ways of men
> Cut off, and for the book of knowledge fair
> Presented with a universal blank
> Of Nature's works, to me expunged and rased,
> And wisdom at one entrance quite shut out.
> So much the rather then, celestial light,
> Shine inward, and the mind through all her powers
> Irradiate ; there plant eyes ; all mist from thence
> Purge and disperse ; that I may see and tell
> Of things invisible to mortal sight.'

The great poet when intent upon his work sought for celestial light to accomplish it. And this brings me to that part of the labours of our institution upon which I dwell the most, and which, after all, is the greatest compensation we can afford to the inmates for the affliction they suffer; and that is, the means we provide for them to read the blessed Word of God, which they can read by day as well as by night, for light in their case is not an essential."

Sleeping and Dreaming.

Mr. A. E. Durham, in a discourse at the Royal Institution, on these questions, commenced by some remarks on Sleep considered as pleasant, irresistible, and necessary. A Chinese murderer, whose punishment was total privation of sleep, died on the ninth day. The amount of needful sleep varies in different persons, eight hours being the average. John Hunter took four hours' sleep and an hour's nap after dinner. General Elliot (of Gibraltar) required only four hours. The conditions favouring sleep were referred to—*e.g.*, silence, warmth, sufficient food, and, especially, a quiet conscience and a mind at ease; and various exceptions were noticed. Considered psychologically, sleep was defined as suspended consciousness, and dreaming as a partial revival of consciousness. Torpor through cold, and coma through disease, are not sleep. After describing the structure of the brain, Mr. Durham stated that he regarded the action of sleep as analogous to a chemical process, during which the brain tissue regains from the blood what it had lost through the activity of the mind. To enable him to ascertain the condition of the brain during sleep, &c., he administered chloroform to a dog, and, while it was insensible, removed a portion of the skull, substituting for it a piece of glass. He found thus that, when the dog slept, the blood-vessels were comparatively empty, the arteries lost their bright red colour and assumed the blue colour of the veins, and the brain tissue collapsed, leaving a space within the skull which was filled with cerebral fluid. When the dog was awakened the blood-vessels resumed their functions, and the brain once more filled the cavity.

Position in Sleeping.

It is better to go to sleep on the right side. If one goes to sleep on the left side the operation of emptying the stomach of its contents is like drawing water from a well. After going to sleep let the body take its own position. If you sleep on your back, especially soon after a hearty meal, the weight of the digestive organs and that of the food, resting upon the great vein of the body, near the backbone, compresses it, and arrests the flow of the blood more or less. If the arrest is partial, the sleep is disturbed, and there are unpleasant dreams. For persons who eat three times a day it is amply sufficient to make the last meal of bread-and-butter, and a cup of some warm drink. No one can starve on it; while a perseverance in the habit soon begets a vigorous appetite for breakfast, so promising of a day of comfort. —*Hall's Journal of Health.*

The Hair suddenly changing Colour.

Dr. Davy has read to the British Association an interesting paper " On the Question, whether the Hair is or is not subject to Sudden Changes of Colour." This he decides in the negative, explaining away the evidence on which the contrary belief has become popular; and also maintaining with regard to seemingly analogous phenomena, such as the becoming white of the ptarmigan, and many animals and birds in winter, that it is through moult and not change of colour in feather or hair.

Nevertheless, in the biography of Montaigne, the celebrated French essayist, we read :—"Among others whose acquaintance Montaigne made in the bath-room, was Seigneur d'Andelot, formerly in the service of Charles V. and governor for him of St. Quentin. One side of his beard and one eyebrow were white ; and he related that this change came to him in an instant. One day as he was sitting at home, with his head leaning on his hand, in profound grief at the loss of a brother, executed by the Duke of Alva as accomplice of Counts Egmont and Horne, when he looked up and uncovered the part which he had clutched in his agony, the people present thought that flour had been sprinkled over him."

Mr. D. P. Parry, Staff-surgeon, at Aldershott, writes the following very remarkable account of a case of which he says he made memoranda shortly after the occurrence :—"On February 19, 1858, the column under General Franks, in the south of Oude, was engaged with a rebel force at the village of Chanda, and several prisoners were taken ; one of them, a Sepoy of the Bengal army, was brought before the authorities for examination, and I being present had an opportunity of watching from the commencement the fact I am about to record. Divested of his uniform and stripped naked, he was surrounded by the soldiers, and then first apparently became alive to the dangers of his position ; he trembled violently, intense horror and despair were depicted in his countenance, and although he answered the questions addressed to him, he seemed almost stupified with fear ; while actually under observation, within the space of half-an-hour, his hair became grey on every portion of his head, it having been when first seen by us the glossy jet black of the Bengalee, aged about 24. The attention of the bystanders was first attracted by the sergeant, whose prisoner he was, exclaiming, 'He is turning grey,' and I with several other persons watched its progress. Gradually but decidedly the change went on, and a uniform greyish colour was completed within the period above named."

Consumption not hopeless.

Sir Edward Wilmot, the physician, was, when a youth, so far gone in Consumption, that Dr. Radcliffe, whom he consulted, gave his friends no hope of his recovery, yet he lived to the age of ninety-three ; upon which Dr. Heberden notes : "This has been the case with some others, who had many symptoms of Consumption in youth."

The life of Sir Hans Sloane was protracted by extraordinary means : when a youth, Sloane was attacked with spitting of blood, which interrupted his education for three years ; but by abstinence from wine and other stimulants, and continuing, in some measure, this regimen ever afterwards, he was enabled to prolong his life to the age of ninety-three years ; exemplifying the truth of his favourite maxim—that sobriety, temperance, and moderation, are the best preservatives that nature has granted to mankind.

Change of Climate.

. The difference in disease produced by change to warmer or colder climate has been thus ably illustrated by Dr. Graves:

We observe that the English in India suffer greatly from liver disease; whilst, on the other hand, negroes and natives frequently die of phthisis (consumption) in England. Monkeys die of consumption, so do lions and tigers. This is a very important fact in the pathology of phthisis, as tending to prove that although phthisis is in many instances distinctly hereditary, nevertheless it may be, and is, frequently acquired. Nothing can furnish a stronger proof that phthisis may be acquired than the instances I have adduced, for I need not tell you that no lion or tiger is ever born in warm climates of a consumptive sire, or ever dies there of tubercular disease. An additional illustration of the influence heat exercises on the size of the liver is afforded by the celebrated Strasburg geese. By feeding these birds in a particular way, and keeping them in artificial heat, the liver becomes diseased, grows to an enormous size, and in this state furnishes the materials of the famous pâté. How many instances occur where our citizens, exposing themselves to the long continued operation of the very same causes, confinement, overfeeding, heat, and want of exercise, are affected by them in exactly the same way! How slight the difference between the morbid phenomena displayed in the post-mortem of a city feaster and the autopsy of an over-fed goose.

Perfumes.

A knowledge of the nature and operations of Perfumes is a very proper thing to propagate. Ignorance respecting them often leads to mischief. Dr. Capellini relates the story of a lady who fancied that she could not bear the smell of a rose, and who accordingly fainted at the sight of one, which turned out to be artificial! This is rather an extreme case; but minor mistakes, adverse to the use of perfumes, are very common. Many persons suppose that they are injurious, because flowers left in a bedroom by night, will sometimes cause headache and sickness. But this is attributable, not to the escaping aroma, but to the carbonic acid which the air imbibes from the flowers. On the other hand Mr. Rimmel contends that perfumes are beneficial and prophylactic in the highest degree. He reminds us that after the Dutch had destroyed, by speculation, the clove-trees in the Island of Ternate, that colony was visited by a series of epidemics, which had been kept off until then by the fragrant smell of the cloves; and in more modern times, when London and Paris were ravaged by cholera, there was not a single victim among the numerous persons employed in the perfumery factories of either city.

Cure for Yellow Fever.

A private letter from Her Majesty's Vice-consul at Cape Bolivar to Her Majesty's Acting Consul-General at Caracas states:— "An old woman, named Mariquita Orfila, has discovered a perfect remedy for the black vomit and yellow fever, by means of which several persons have been completely cured after a consultation of doctors had declared that the cases were quite hopeless, and that the patients must die in a few hours. The remedy is the juice of the pounded leaves of the verbena, given in small doses three times a day, and injections of the same every two hours, until the bowels are emptied. The verbena is a wild shrub, to be found growing almost everywhere, and particularly in low, moist ground. All our doctors have adopted its use, and now few or none die of those late fearful diseases. There are two kinds of it, male and female; the latter is most used."

Nature's Ventilation.

Upon the proper adjustments of the dynamical forces which keep up the ceaseless movements of the atmosphere, the life of organic nature depends. If the air that is breathed were not taken away and renewed, warm-blooded life would cease: if carbon, and oxygen, and hydrogen, and water were not in due quantities dispensed by the restless air to the flora of the earth, all vegetation would perish for lack of food. That our planet may be liable to no such calamity, power has been given to the wayward wind, as it "bloweth where it listeth," to bring down from the pure blue sky fresh supplies of life-giving air wherever it is wanted; and to catch up from the earth, wherever it may be found, that which has become stale; to force it up, there to be deflagrated among the clouds, purified and renovated by processes known only to Him whose ministers they are. The slightest change in the purity of the atmosphere, though it may be too slight for recognition by chemical analysis in the laboratory, is sure to be detected by its effects upon the nicer chemistry of the human system; for it is known to be productive of disease and death. No chemical tests are sensitive enough to tell us what those changes are; but experience has taught us the necessity of ventilation in our buildings, of circulation through our groves. The cry, in cities, for fresh air from the mountains or the sea, reminds us continually of the life-giving virtues of circulation. Experience teaches that all air, when pent up and deprived of circulation, becomes impure and poisonous. In referring to ventilation, we are never to forget that, in order to secure Nature's pure air, it is essential to guard against the many sources of its pollution. The air which descends to us is pure; but it is left to man to maintain it so; hence we have to drain our marshes, empty foul ditches, remove cesspools, and see that our streets are sewered and paved. The Deity has given laws for the moral government of society; but He leaves to man, on whom He has bestowed intelligence, the discovery and the application of those scientific means which are necessary to health and physical happiness.—*Captain Maury.*

Artificial Ventilation.

In Wyman's *Practical Treatise on Ventilation* we find these curious results. In a weaving-mill near Manchester, where the ventilation was bad, the proprietor caused a fan to be mounted. The consequences soon became apparent in a curious manner. The operatives, little remarkable for olfactory refinement, instead of thanking their employer for his attention to their comfort and health, made a formal complaint to him that the ventilator had increased their appetites, and therefore entitled them to a corresponding increase of wages! By stopping the fan a part of the day, the ventilation and voracity of the establishment were brought to a medium standard, and complaints ceased. The operatives' wages would but just support them; any additional demands by their stomachs could only be answered by draughts upon their backs, which were by no means in a condition to answer them. In Edinburgh a club was provided with a dinner in a well ventilated apartment, the air being perfumed as it entered, imitating in succession the fragrance of lavender and the orange-flower. During dinner the members enjoyed themselves as usual, but were not a little surprised at the announcement of the provider, that they had drunk three times as much wine as he had usually provided. Gentlemen of sober, quiet habits, who usually confined themselves to a couple of glasses, were not satisfied with less than half a bottle; others, who took half a bottle, now extended their potations to a bottle and a half. In fact, the hotel-keeper was drunk dry. That gentlemen who had indulged so freely were not aware of it at the time is not wonderful; but that they felt no unpleasant sensations the following morning, which they did not, is certainly quite so.

Worth of Fresh Air.

Among the sanitary enactments of the last few years is the Local Government Act, for the better enforcement of appliances for Public Health. An Office has been established specially for the business of this Act, with a well-paid Secretary and Medical Inspector: it arose upon the cessation of the labours of the Board of Health; and the gain by the change may be estimated by the following Hints from an engineering Sanitary Inspector of the Local Government Office:

Sanitary work is not necessarily doing some great thing, but consists more in prompt and efficient attention to small matters. Fresh air is the best disinfectant, but most people, even in England, treat fresh air as if it were an evil. We shut it out of our houses by day, and confine foul air in our rooms by night, especially during the time we use them for sleep. An invalid takes a carriage airing with closed windows; such a ride is, however, in truth, a carriage poisoning. If an open carriage cannot be used on any day in the year with safety, the individual had better not use a carriage; and no room should be occupied which has not an unceasing flow of fresh air through it—not necessarily a draught, but motion. Open flues, open doors, or open windows admit of change of air; not, however, always with comfort to the inmates. But as a room cannot be hermetically sealed up, provision ought to be made for an admission of fresh air, rather than for the stealing in of sewer, drain, cesspool, or sink gases. List up doers, carpet floors, paper window-joints, and block up fireplaces, if contagious diseases are to have their most malignant effects; ventilate houses, by open windows on staircases or in corridors if possible, but by all means ventilate. Cold does not kill so many as foul air, although a low temperature generally increases the weekly bills of mortality. But it is the very poor who suffer most. The Chinese say, "Fools and beggars only suffer from cold; the one have not wit to clothe properly, the others are too poor to clothe sufficiently." Clothing ought to be the protection against cold, not warm and foul air. In every house in which typhus fever or small-pox prevails it will be safer for the inhabitants of such houses to remove the windows rather than to keep them closed. An open shed in a field with warm clothing will be better than a closed room in a town. I have seen fever patients and small-pox patients treated beneath open sheds in the country safely, and I have heard experienced surgeons remark that fresh air and diet were of more avail than medicine. I have seen a British army in hospital and in the field surrounded by foul air, wasting away by fever. I have seen that army restored to health by cleanliness and an admission of fresh air. The air was not cooked nor manipulated by any patented apparatus, but was admitted direct from the vast ocean of fresh air about and above, by slits in the ridge of huts in the Crimea, by the removal of top squares from fixed windows at the great hospitals on the Bosphorus, and by the opening up of flues wherever these could with advantage be formed in those hospitals. The ordinary atmosphere of any country freely admitted and unceasingly changed is the only safe medium in which to breathe. In all countries and under all climates excessive disease to man comes from foul air generated within his dwelling rather than from any external influences. The remedy against disease is, therefore, fresh air. Infection is scarcely possible amid abundance of fresh air. Soap and water can kill contagion if used in time.

The intercepting main sewers of the metropolis, if brought into use, will actually add to existing evils rather than remove them, if these sewers only pass away large volumes of surplus water which now dilute the deposit in many scores of miles of secondary and branch sewers and drains. There are hundreds of open sewer ventilators within the metropolis sending out unceasingly thousands of cubic feet of sewage gases to the streets above. All this vast volume of gas might be cheaply disinfected by being made to pass slowly through charcoal, and all foul sewers may either be cleansed or be disinfected in time.

Town and Country.

Sir E. B. Lytton, in *Blackwood's Magazine*, observes: We who are lovers of the country are not unnaturally disposed to consider that our preference argues some finer poetry of sentiment — some steadier devotion to those ennobling studies which sages commend as the fitting occupations of retirement. But the facts do not justify that self-conceit upon our part. It was said by a philosopher who was charged with all the cares of a world's empire, that " there is no such great matter in retirement. A man may be wise and sedate in a crowd as well as in a desert, and keep the noise of the world from getting within him. In this case, as Plato observes, the walls of a town and the enclosure of a sheepfold may be made the same thing." Certainly, poets, and true poets, have lived by choice in the dingy streets of great towns. Men of science, engaged in reasonings the most abstruse, on subjects the most elevating, have usually fixed their dwelling-place in bustling capitals, as if the din of the streets without deepened, by the force of a contrast, the quiet of those solitary closets wherein they sat analysing the secret heart of that nature whose every-day outward charms they abandoned to commonplace adorers. On the other hand, men perforce engaged in urban occupations, neither bards nor sages but City clerks and traders, feel a yearning of the heart towards a home in the country; loving rural nature with so pure a fervour that, if closer intercourse is forbidden, they are contented to go miles every evening to kiss the skirt of her robe. Their first object is to live out of London, if but in a suburb; to refresh their eyes with the green of a field; to greet the first harbinger of spring in the primrose venturing forth in their own tiny realm of garden. It is for them, as a class, that cities extend beyond their ancient bounds; while our nobles yet clung to their gloomy halls in the Fleet, traders sought homesteads remote from their stalls and wares in the pleasing village of Charing.

Recreations of the People.

The preservation of open places for the recreation of the people is watched with much jealousy by those who take an interest in the assertion of popular rights. Mr. J. S. Mill, the historian, has put in this eloquent plea for their maintenance:

There is room in the world no doubt, and even in old countries, for an immense increase of population, supposing the arts of life to go on improving, and capital to increase. But although it may be innocuous, I confess I see very little reason for desiring it. The density of population necessary to enable mankind to obtain in the greatest degree all the advantages, both of co-operation and of social intercourse, has in all the more populous countries been attained. A population may be too crowded, though all be amply supplied with food and raiment. It is not good for man to be kept perforce at all times in the presence of his species. A world from which solitude is extirpated is a very poor ideal. Solitude, in the sense of being often alone, is essential to any depth of meditation or of character, and solitude in the presence of natural beauty and grandeur, is the cradle of thoughts and aspirations which are not only good for the individual, but which society could ill do without. Nor is there much satisfaction in contemplating the world with nothing left to the spontaneous activity of nature, with every rood of land brought into cultivation which is capable of growing food for human beings, every flowery waste or natural pasture ploughed up, all quadrupeds or birds which are not domesticated for man's use exterminated as his rivals for food; every hedgerow or superfluous tree rooted out, and scarcely a place left where a wild shrub or flower could grow without being eradicated as a weed. in the name of improved agriculture. If the earth must lose that great portion of its pleasantness which it owes to things that the unlimited increase of wealth and population would extirpate from it for the mere purpose of enabling it to support a larger, but not a better or happier population, I sincerely hope, for the sake of posterity, that they will be content to be stationary long before necessity compels them to do so.

This is picturesquely eloquent; but it may be argued that a public " green" or common, in the neighbourhood of a large town, is often a rendezvous for the idle and abandoned, in their brutalizing sports: the great city, like a cauldron, with more evils than that in *Macbeth*, seems to boil over, and deposit its scum upon the circumjacent ground.

The Druids and their Healing Art.

We might expect to find, from the universality of their application, remedies for

the thousand natural shocks
That flesh is heir to

preserved *in perpetuo.* In ancient Britain, the Druids were the depositaries of these secrets.

Amongst the early Britons, the ranks of the priests were recruited from the noblest families: their education, which often extended over a period of twenty years, comprehended the whole of the sciences of the age; and besides their sacred calling, they were invested with power to decide their civil disputes. Their dwellings and temples were situated in the thickest oak-groves, which were sacred to the Supreme Deity. The acorn, and above all, the parasitical mistleto, were held in high veneration: the latter was sought on the sixth day of the moon, and when found was only cut by a priest of the highest rank, for it was accounted a sovereign remedy for all diseases. The practice of the healing art has ever commanded the esteem of the rudest nations: hence it was the obvious policy of the priests, or Druids, to study the properties of plants. Of their progress we have no record; but who knows from what a far antiquity come the traditionary virtues of many of our native plants?

Their famous Mistleto, or *all-heal,* was considered a certain cure in many diseases, an antidote to poison, and a preventive of infection. And, we have, in the present day, a very old *nostrum,* named *Heal-all,* the universal virtues of which are described as equalling the mistleto of our ancestors.

Remedies for Cancer.

A multitude of strange remedies are prescribed for Cancer. When Lord Metcalfe, the Governor of Canada, was beset with this cruel disease, Mr. Kaye, his biographer, tells us: "One correspondent recommended Mesmerism, which had cured Miss Martineau; another Hydropathy, at the pure springs of Malvern; a third, an application of the common dock-leaf; a fourth, an infusion of couch-grass; a fifth, the baths of Docherte, near Vienna; a sixth, the volcanic hot-springs of Karlsbad; a seventh, a wonderful plaster made of rose-leaves, olive-oil, and turnip-juice; an eighth, a plaster and powder, in which some part of a young frog was a principal ingredient; a ninth, a mixture of copperas and vinegar; a tenth, an application of pure ox-gall; an eleventh, a mixture of Florence oil and red precipitate; whilst a twelfth was certain of the good effects of Homœopathy, which cured Charlotte Elizabeth. Besides these varied remedies, many men and women with infallible recipes, or certain modes of treatment, were recommended by themselves and others. Learned Italian professors, mysterious American women, erudite Germans, and obscure Irish quacks—all had cured cancers of twenty years' standing, and all were pressing, or pressed forward, to operate on Lord Metcalfe."

Improved Surgery.

· The basis, and no small portion of the superstructure, of scientific surgery, was laid by the famous Ambroise Paré, who possessed the rare gift of seeing things as they were, and not as his preconceived notions would have them to be. Sharing the common belief that gunshot wounds were, by their nature, poisonous, he used to treat them with boiling oil; but having failed once to apply the usual remedy, he was surprised to find that his patients were much the better for the omission. Thereupon, he renounced the ordinary practice, and from that time gunshot wounds have received a more rational treatment. Paré was the first to revive the practice known to the Arabians of stopping the flow of blood from arteries by tying them. The French Faculty of Medicine ridiculed the innovation as the system of hanging life upon a thread, and declared its preference for the use of boiling pitch which had stood the test of so many centuries; but wounded persons could not be brought to see the force of such reasoning. Anatomy was prosecuted with great assiduity and precision of detail throughout the whole of the sixteenth century, and the way was cleared for Harvey's grand discovery, which he first publicly taught in 1619.

John Hunter introduced what is probably the most capital Improvement in Surgery ever effected by a single man;—namely, the practice in aneurism of tying the artery at a distance from the seat of disease. This one suggestion has saved thousands of lives; and both the suggestion, and the first successful execution of it, are entirely owing to John Hunter, who, if he had done nothing else, would on this account alone have a right to be classed among the principal benefactors of mankind.

Restoration of a Fractured Leg.

M. Flourens has communicated to the Paris Academy of Sciences a letter from Dr. Mottet, giving an account of the Restoration of a Fractured Leg under circumstances of peculiar difficulty. The fracture had been occasioned by a fall of stones on the limb; it was complex, and such that amputation presented peculiar difficulties; still, notwithstanding gangrene and other untoward circumstances, the fracture, being reduced, was kept in its normal position by a peculiar apparatus for the space of a year, at the end of which time the bone was completely regenerated, and the limb perfectly cured without any diminution in length.

The original " Dr. Sangrado."

Thousands may have enjoyed the humour of *Gil Blas* without
suspecting that the genius of Dr. Sangrado had any living proto-
type. Yet such was Botal, who revolutionized the practice of
medicine by a freedom of bleeding that was quite unprecedented.
He bled largely and repeatedly, both young and old, male and
female, in all diseases, whether low in type or acute. " The young
he bled freely, on account of the rapid reproduction of blood in
youth ; the old, because he saw in the practice a conduciveness to
rejuvenescence. He bled freely in low and wasting diseases, even
of a malignant nature, because a richer and better blood was
formed ; in dysentery, because he recognised in it an affinity to
inflammation of the lungs, in which all physicians bled ; in all
forms of flatulency, because of its power to relieve obstructions ;
in short, he had a reason for bleeding in every special distemper,
and when reproached for the indiscriminate routine of practice,
he argued that the more water you draw from a well the purer
and better is that which filters in. From him originated the
system of bleeding in pregnancy, which is continued to this day."
Botal was a man of happy despatch, like Van Helmont, under
whose hands, as his biographer relates, " the sick never languished
long, being always killed or cured in three days." Botal's patients
were probably more often killed than cured ; but they did not
die in vain, for his practice set medical men observing and thinking,
so that good came of it in the end—a great consolation for his
victims, could they have foreseen it.—*Spectator newspaper.*

False Arts advancing true.

After the death of Galen, Medicine ceased to make progress.
Amidst the Gothic invasions the medical sects " dwindled down to
individuals, who achieved for medicine what the monastics effected
for ancient classic literature : they maintained it in the condition
of a small but continuous stream, in the midst of so much charla-
tanism that no man could talk nonsense so gross, or profess supernatural powers so incredible, but that the ignorance of the community would give credit to his assertions." All through the dark
and the Middle Ages astrology, alchemy, magic, and cabalistic
arts predominated ; all physical phenomena were ascribed to occult
causes ; in short, as Sir John Herschel remarks, " If the logic of
that gloomy period could be justly described as ' the art of talking
unintelligibly on matters of which we are ignorant,' its physics
might, with equal truth, be summed up in a deliberate preference

of ignorance to knowledge in matters of every day's experience and use." Sometimes, however, the false arts served indirectly to advance the true. Alchemy led the way to chemistry, and enriched medicine with new remedies, and at least one crotchet of scholastic divinity may be supposed to have done something for the progress of anatomy ; for " the skeleton received, perhaps, an adventitious attention in consequence of the popular belief that, in man, some one particular bone existed of an imponderable, incombustible, and indestructible nature, around which, as a nucleus, all other tissues and organs would collect and re-assume their vital actions at the resurrection. Accordingly, every bone was tested by fire, for the purpose of discovering the hypothetical one." —Dr. Meryon's *History of Medicine.*

Brief History of Medicine.

Great honour is, unquestionably, due to those medical men who by their learning, counsel, and experience, have contributed so many and great things to the improvement of their profession. The art of healing may be considered as a legacy left to us by former ages and enriched by ancient writers, and no doubt ordained by a benevolent Creator for the benefit of His creatures, who, being endowed with reason, are enabled to prosecute Medicine and the collateral sciences with wonderful sagacity. The impossibility of learning medicine properly by experience alone, implies the necessity of studying both ancient and modern writers; but, in the words of Harvey, " men were not to swear such fealty to their mistress Antiquity, as openly and in sight of all to deny and desert their friend Truth." Medical history unfortunately affords many examples of despisers of the mighty dead and of eminent living authorities. Paracelsus burnt the writings of Galen and Avicenna before his pupils, and proclaimed himself the king of medicine. Hahnemann much resembled Paracelsus, for he despised the inspection of dead bodies, and preferred the homœopathic doctrine to pathology; but both had dared to do " aliquid Gyaris vel carcere dignum." Hahnemann's doctrine, that numerous chronic diseases originated in the itch, was neither new, safe, nor true. Dr. C. G. Zieger had many years before promulgated the same idea in a dissertation published at Leipsic in 1758, without boasting, as the other did, that he was engaged twelve years in the discovery. False theories, however, with scientific pretensions, have flourished through many ages. Hence arose homœopathy, kinesipathy, table-turning, and various despicable " isms" of the present day. But, happily for the poor, at least, such lies could not exist in the schools of Harvey, Baillie, and Hunter. The low condition of medicine at the time of Linacre, and the improvement with the aid of Henry VIII. and Cardinal Wolsey, may next be mentioned. Linacre, the founder of the College, and Dean Colet, the founder of St. Paul's School, of grateful memory to the orator, were among the first to restore ancient learning to this island. The College of Physicians having been established, its members were separated from vulgar empirics; but by a new law homœo-empirics may be registered, which was nothing less than legal homicide, and strongly to be protested against.—*Harveian Oration,* 1863.

What has Science done for Medicine?

The practice of Medicine is full of difficulty. Modern Science has done something to aid in the diagnosis, often the most difficult part of the physician's task. Auscultation and the use of the microscope have substituted certainty for conjecture in many cases. But, for this essential preliminary of ascertaining what is the matter with the patient, a combination of faculties is often needed which cannot be communicated in the schools. The power may be developed and improved by use, and corrected by careful observation; but it is born with certain men, and it is not to be gained by teaching or study. Then, supposing the disease to be ascertained, it constantly happens that there is little or nothing to be done that can with any confidence be expected to shorten or reduce the intensity of the attack. The option lies between a system of slight palliatives, almost or quite inoperative, and the application of stronger remedies whose action is uncertain. Fortunately, the effects of medicine in general are far less considerable than is commonly supposed. The statistics of hospitals in which the most different systems of treatment have been adopted do not, indeed, prove that all the systems have been equally good or bad; but they do show that in many diseases there is no known system of treatment that has any marked advantage over others. It is not too much to say that, for one case in which the medicine administered has been of real use, there are ten where the patients would have thriven as well or better without it.

A further difficulty in medical practice has been less noticed than it deserves to be. All that is known of the effect of remedies is the general or average result of a large number of cases in which they have been applied. But no two men are exactly alike in the manner of action of their various organs. When the chemist who has once tried an experiment brings the same substances together under similar conditions, he is absolutely certain that they will act on each other as they did before. Not so is it with the living organism. The idiosyncracy of each patient is more or less unknown to the physician; and till the experiment has been tried, he can have no certainty as to the result of his treatment. It is quite true that the exceptional cases that sometimes arise present apparent rather than real anomalies. There is no reason to suppose that the laws of physics have been suspended by an independent disturbing power when a drug produces on a particular patient an unusual effect. The conditions of the experiment have doubtless been changed by some peculiarity in his organization, which the present means of science are powerless to detect.

The main cause why medicine is still so little advanced is to be found in the backward condition of the science on which it mainly rests. Physiology, including pathology—the first taking cognizance of all the vital functions of organized beings, the second of the disturbance of those functions by disease—is far from maintaining its place in the general march of physical science.—*Saturday Review.*

The Element of Physic in Medical Practice.

The Element of Physic in Medical Practice becomes constantly more simple. Our drugs are fewer and less complicated.* Of course it is all otherwise in pseudo-medicine. Here "specifics" are as rank as weeds. Here little account is taken of natural provisions for the cure of disease. Here physic is everything, and nature and the physician are unimportant. Given the symptoms of a disease and a book of "testings," every old lady thinks herself as competent a physician as Hahnemann. Every disease and symptom of disease has its corresponding remedy, or rather we should say two remedies, for it will nearly always be found that homœopathic patients take two medicines, in equal doses and with equal frequency. Homœopathy abounds in principles. Its great principle is that of "specifics"—that certain medicines have the most definite and designed relation to certain ailments—are *the* thing and the *only* thing. Then there is what we may call the alternating principle, in virtue of which two medicines—each, we suppose, a specific!—are so much better than one. Upon these two principles the enlightened patron of homœopathy is made the receptacle of a most unprincipled amount of physic. We conclude by impressing upon our brethren who are studying medicine in the light of reason and science, the urgency of the duty

* Many years since, the writer heard Sir Lucas Pepys, (some time President of the College of Physicians,) inquire of a druggist at Dorking what use he could possibly make of the many drugs in his shop; "for," added Sir Lucas, "I have only used five or six articles in all my practice."—J. T.

that devolves upon them of so using the element of physic in medical practice as to make more and more apparent the great gulf that is fixed between their practice and the rival quackeries of the day. Let them use medicine so that the most undiscerning patient will perceive that it is only one of many means to an end, auxiliary only to great provisions in the body itself, and for the most part acting, not mysteriously, like quinine, but sensibly or chemically. Let the form of their drugs be unpretentious and inexpensive, so that whatever the cost to the patient may be, he may understand that he pays, not for physic, but for the attention, the skill, and the judgment, of the physician.—*Lancet.*

Physicians' Fees.

In the Court of Exchequer in January, 1863, in an action brought by a physician to recover 21*l.* for services rendered to a patient, it was contended that as there was no special promise to pay, the plaintiff could not recover. Such was the state of the law formerly, physicians being presumed to attend for an *honorarium ;* but an Act was passed to enable registered physicians and surgeons to recover their reasonable charges, subject to such bye-laws as might be passed by the College of Physicians. The latter body, however, it appears, have thwarted the intention of the Legislature by enacting that physicians shall not recover, even though a contract existed ; the object, it seems, being to make the payment of physicians' fees immediate, and to discourage credit. A verdict was found for the plaintiff, leave being granted to move the Court above on the construction of the Medical Act.

Attention has been called to the careless manner in which consulting physicians write their prescriptions ; more especially as regards the dose, the drachm often resembling the ounce, and the writing so generally blotted and crabbed that the dispensers are often obliged to make guesses, with very little light to guide them to a right conclusion. The blame, whenever a mistake occurs, is always attached to the chemist or assistant, without considering the anxiety and trouble they have in deciphering writing worse than falls to the lot of a post-office master. The public have often ridiculed the style of physicians' prescriptions, but will be unable to joke when a mistake more serious than usual occurs.

Prevention of Pitting in Small-pox.

This desirable end is stated to have been attained in the clinical wards of the Royal Infirmary at Edinburgh. The application consists of a solution of india-rubber in chloroform, which is painted over the face (and neck in women) when the eruption has become fully developed. When the chloroform has evaporated, which it very readily does, there is left a thin elastic film of india-rubber over the face. This the patient feels to be rather comfortable than otherwise, inasmuch as the disagreeable itchiness, so generally complained of, is almost entirely removed, and, what is more important, "pitting" once so common, and even now far from rare, is thoroughly prevented wherever the solution has been applied. It may be as well to state that india-rubber is far from being very soluble in chloroform; so that, in making the solution, the india-rubber must be cut into small pieces, and chloroform added till it is dissolved. The medical gentleman who has introduced this treatment has tried several other substances, but found none so generally useful. For instance, gutta-percha was tried. It has the advantage of being very soluble in chloroform, and would have been a very admirable application but for the tendency it has to tear into ribands whenever the mouth is used, or even when the features play. India-rubber, on the other hand, is pliable and elastic, allowing free use of the mouth without any danger (as a rule) of its tearing off. If, however, from some cause or other, a portion is torn off, a fresh application of the solution by means of a large hair-pencil remedies the defect, and the mask is once more complete. Several patients who have had this india-rubber mask applied concur in stating that they found it agreeable to wear, and their faces were perfectly free from "pitting," although other parts of the body, such as the arms, were covered. The credit of this valuable invention and application belongs to Dr. Smart, house physician to the Infirmary.

Underneath the Skin.

All over the surface of our bodies there are scattered millions of minute orifices, which open into the delicate convoluted tubes lying underneath the Skin, and are called by anatomists sudoriparous glands. Each of these tubes, when straightened, measures about a quarter of an inch; and as, according to Erasmus Wilson, whose figures we follow, there are 3528 of these tubes on every square inch of the palm of the hand, there must be no less than 882 inches of tubing on such a square inch. In some parts of the body the number of tubes is even greater: in most parts it is less. Erasmus Wilson estimates that there are 2800 on every square inch, on the average; and, as the total number of such inches is 2500, we arrive at the astounding result that, spread over the surface of the body, there are not less than twenty-eight miles of tubing, by means of which liquid may be secreted, and given off as vapour in insensible perspiration, or as water in sensible perspiration. In the ordinary circumstances of daily life the amount of fluid which is thus given off from the skin (and lungs) during the twenty-four hours varies from $1\frac{2}{3}$ lb. to 5 lb.; under extraordinary circumstances the amount will, of course, rise enormously. Dr. Southwood Smith found that the workmen in the gasworks employed in making up the fires, and other occupations which subjected them to great heat, lost on an average 3lb. 6 oz. in forty-five minutes; and when working for seventy minutes in an unusually hot place their loss was 5 lb. 2 oz., and 4 lb. 14 oz. —*Blackwood's Magazine.*

Relations of Mind and Organization.

We may safely assume, as an established fact, that it is only through the instrumentality of the central parts of the nervous system that the Mind maintains its communication with the external world. The eye is necessary to sight, and the ear to hearing; and so with the other organs of sense. But the eye does not see, and the ear does not hear; and if the nerve which forms the communication between any one organ of sense and the brain be divided, the corresponding sense is destroyed. In like manner it is from the brain that all those impulses proceed by which the mind influences the phenomena of the external world. The division of the nerves which extend from the brain to the larynx destroys the voice. The division of the nerves of a limb causes the muscles of the limb to be paralysed, or, in other words, withdraws them from the influence of the will; the division of the spinal cord destroys at once the sensibility and the power of voluntary motion in all the parts below that at which the division has been made.

The brain has a central organ, which is a continuation of the spinal cord, and to which anatomists have given the name of *medulla oblongata.* In connexion with this there are other bodies placed in pairs. That each of these bodies has its peculiar functions there cannot be the smallest doubt; and it is, indeed, sufficiently probable that each of them is not a single organ, but a congeries of organs having distinct and separate uses.

Experimental physiology, joined with the observation of the changes produced by disease, has thrown some light on this mysterious subject. There is reason to believe that, whatever it may do besides, one office of the *cerebellum* is to combine the action of the voluntary muscles for the purpose of locomotion. The *corpora quadrigemina* are four tubercles which connect the *cerebrum, cerebellum,* and *medulla oblongata* to each other. If one of the uppermost of these bodies be removed, blindness of the eye of the opposite side is the consequence. If the upper part of the *cerebrum* be removed, the animal becomes blind, and apparently stupified, but not so much so but that he can walk with steadiness and precision. The most important part of the whole brain seems to be one particular part of the central organ, or *medulla oblongata.* While this remains entire, the animal retains its sensibility, breathes, and performs instinctive motions. But if this very minute portion of the nervous system be injured, there is an end of these several functions, and death immediately ensues.

These facts, and some others of the same kind, for a knowledge of which we are indebted to modern physiologists, and more especially to M. Magendie and M. Flourens, are satisfactory as far as they go; and warrant the conclusion that there are various other organs in the brain, designed for other purposes, and that if we cannot point out their locality, it is not because such organs do not exist, but because our means of research into so intricate a matter are very limited.—*Sir B. Brodie's Psychological Inquiries.*

Deville, the Phrenologist.

In 1817 a Mr. Deville, a lamp-manufacturer of London, was a member of the Institution of Civil Engineers. He had been originally a pot-boy, then a journeyman plasterer, and afterwards kept a shop for the sale of plaster figures, which he cast. He had risen to a respectable position simply by the force of his natural powers. Mr. Bryan Donkin, a civil engineer, was an early auditor of Gall at Vienna, and subsequently a friend of Spurzheim. He was also, like Mr. Deville, a member of the Institution of Civil Engineers; and when, in 1817, he with others determined to make a collection of casts as records of phrenological facts, Mr. Deville was applied to for his assistance, which he rendered as a matter of business for three or four years. In 1821 he became interested in phrenology, and began to form a collection of casts on his own account. Already, in 1826, Spurzheim said it was finer than any he had seen elsewhere. At Mr. Deville's death, in 1846, this collection consisted of about 5450 pieces; of these 3000 were crania of animals, and the remainder (2450) illustrations of human phrenology. There were 200 human crania, and 300 casts of crania; amongst the latter, those which Baron Cuvier permitted Mr. Deville to take from all the authenticated human skulls in the Museum of Comparative Anatomy of Paris. Mr. Deville was a practical observer, and possessed the large number of 1500 casts of heads taken by himself from persons while living. Amongst these were 50 casts of persons remarkably devoted to religion: 40 of distinguished painters, sculptors, architects, &c.; 30 of eminent navigators and travellers; 80 of poets, authors, and writers; 70 of musicians, amateurs, and composers of music; 25 of pugilists; 150 of criminals; 120 pathological casts illustrative of insanity, &c. Perhaps the most interesting of all are 170 casts which illustrate the changes caused in the cranial conformation of from 60 to 70 individuals by age, special devotion to one pursuit, and the like. Mr. Deville's account of some of these has been published.

" *Seeing is believing.*"

Supreme disregard of the accuracy of the facts on which its conclusions are based, is one of the marks of an uncultivated intellect. It is a part of the credulousness continued from childhood; and is seen in the acceptance, without misgiving, of any *statement* of facts which is made confidently, and without obvious motive for deceit. Not only in matters of science, but in matters of daily life, is this credulity observed. You cannot step into an omnibus, or chat with an acquaintance at the club, without hearing distinct, positive, and important statements respecting the *intentions* of public men,—statements involving their personal honour, perhaps the national safety, and uttered with an air of conviction which would be ludicrous were it not so sad; yet if you happen to ask on what *evidence* the speaker relies, you find perhaps that there is nothing better than surmise or gossip.

The object of the foregoing remarks is to show how easily an inference may be mistaken for a fact, and how habitually men declare they have seen what they have only inferred. Seeing is, in all cases, believing; but in all cases we must assure ourselves of *what* we have seen, carefully discriminating it from what we have not seen but only imagined, and carefully ascertaining whether the facts seen by us are all the facts then present. It is by no means easy to see accurately any series of events; nor, when under any strong emotion, is it easy to prevent the imagination from usurping the place of vision. " Many individuals," says Liebig, " overlook half the event through carelessness; another adds to what he observes the creation of his own imagination; whilst a third, who sees sufficiently distinctly the different parts of the whole, confounds together things which ought to be kept separate. In the Gorlitz trial, in Darmstadt, the female attendants who washed and clothed the body, observed on it neither arms nor head; another witness saw one arm, and a head the size of a man's fist; a third, a physician, saw both arms and head of the usual size."[*]

---

[*] Liebig: *Letters on Chemistry*, p. 28.

There is no popular adage less understood than that " Seeing is believing." With an ill-suppressed irritation at any expression of scepticism respecting things said to have been seen, a narrator asks whether or not he may believe the evidence of his own senses ? That argument seems to him final; and it often happens that his opponent, evading instead of meeting it, retorts :—" No ; the evidence of the senses is not to be trusted, when they report anything so absurd as that. I would not believe such a thing if I were to see it—the absurdity is too glaring."

Both are wrong. Seeing *is* believing; and he that distrusts the evidence of his own sight, will find a difficulty in bringing forward evidence more convincing. The fallacy lies in confounding vision with inference—in supposing that facts are seen which are only inferred. There can be no mistake in trusting to the evidence of sense, as far as that goes. The mistake is supposing it to go much further than it does. It is one thing to believe *what* you have seen, and another to believe that you have seen *all* there was to be seen.—*Blackwood's Magazine.*

Causes of Insanity.

From an interesting Report on Lunatic Asylums in Ireland, issued in 1862, we find that the moral Causes of Insanity predominate in females, the physical causes to a larger extent in males, particularly intemperance and irregularity of life. The cause of disease was ascertained in 2186 cases : in 323 it was intemperance and irregularity; in 183, religious excitement ; in 115, love, jealousy, and seduction. Thirty-seven per cent. of the cases were ascribable to hereditary transmission and intemperance combined. With regard to the hereditary character of insanity, it is observed that mental, like bodily affections, gradually wear out from the intermixture of blood. There was no case found in Ireland in unbroken descent to the fourth generation. On the important question whether insanity is on the increase, there is no certain proof furnished. We know that, with fresh accommodation for the insane, fresh, though long-existing cases, are presented for admission into asylums, creating an apparent increase of lunacy ; and we know that improved treatment and care have tended materially to the prolongation of life among lunatics, and to their consequent accumulation. We know also that science, and even public opinion, now accept as indicative of lunacy affections formerly classed under a different category. Lunacy, also, is now less concealed as a discreditable visitation. Emigration has not taken its proportion of lunatics. But, insanity being in great measure a disease of intellect—one connected with the development of the human mind—it is highly presumable that, in this age of excitement and rapid advancement in arts and sciences, mental affections may be more prevalent than before. In a northern district of Ireland, during the two months of religious revivalism, there were more cases of insanity than in the whole preceding year.

Brain-Disease.

Dr. Forbes Winslow, whose professional life has been devoted to the study of Insanity, in his work *On Obscure Diseases of the Brain, and Disorders of the Mind,* attaches much importance to premonitory ailments, as indicative not only of the fatal mischief which will inevitably succeed them if neglected, but of the only period when remedies can be applied with a fair chance of cure. This period it is difficult even to the medical expert to detect, for the aversion to own any affection of the mind or weakness of the head is so strong, that both patient and friends will often repudiate and ignore it altogether; yet there are unmistakeable signs, such as " headache attributed to derangement of the stomach, vacillation of temper, feebleness of purpose, flightiness of manner, irritability, inaptitude for business, depression and exaltation of spirits; and even weakness of sight, when the optician has been consulted rather than the physician." None of these signs, if caused by Brain Disease, can exist, says Dr. Winslow, for any length of time without seriously perilling the reason and endangering life: yet " it is a well-established fact that seventy, if not eighty, per cent. of cases of insanity admit of easy and speedy cure if treated in the early stage, provided there be no strong constitutional predisposition to cerebral and mental affections, or existing cranial malformation. And, even when an hereditary taint exists, derangement of mind generally yields to the steady and persevering administration of remedies, combined with judicious moral measures, provided the first inclinations of the malady are fully recognised, and without loss of time grappled with. A vast and frightful amount of chronic and incurable insanity exists at this moment in our county and private asylums, which can be clearly traced to the criminal neglect of the disease in the first or incipient stage."

Dr. Winslow insists upon the great importance of self-control as a preventive. He says: " This power is in many instances weakened or altogether lost by a voluntary and criminal indulgence in a train of thought which it was the duty of the individual in the *first* instance resolutely to battle with, control, and subdue. Nervous disorders, as well as insane, delusive thoughts, are thus often self-created. The morbid soon becomes a deranged mind-

s

the insanity manifesting itself in an exaggerated, extravagant, and perverted conception of a notion which had originally some semblance of truth for its foundation.   The self-created, delusive idea may thus obtain a fearful influence over the mind, and eventually lead to the commission of criminal acts."   The forced education of youth frequently leads to mental alienation.   " It is," says Dr. Winslow, " undoubtedly an important element in education to carefully, steadily invigorate and discipline the memory in early life ; but, in effecting this most desirable object, it is our duty to avoid mistaking *natural* mental dulness for culpable idleness, and *organic* cerebral incapacity for criminal indifference to intellectual culture and educational advancement."   Again, the tremendous strain that now taxes the brain-power of society in every direction, is an additional reason why the voice of this minister to the mind diseased should be listened to in time: in the statistics of insanity the terrible fact is admitted, that there is an absolute increase of madness throughout Europe and America.

Dr. Winslow has assembled some very interesting instances of retention of the vigour of the mind in old age, and arrived at, *inter alia*, these conclusions : " 1. That an active and vigorous condition of the mental faculties is compatible with old age. 2. That a continuous and often laborious exercise of the mind is not only consistent with a state of mental health, but is apparently productive of longevity."   It is indeed particularly satisfactory to be told that even in the worst types of mental disease there are some salient and bright spots upon which the physician may act ; and that formidable and apparently hopeless and incurable cases of derangement admit, if not of cure, at least of considerable alleviation and mitigation.

The Half-mad.

The Commissioners in Lunacy have reason to know that there are many, not insane, but who, being conscious of a want of power of self-control, or of addiction to intemperate habits, or fearing an attack or a recurrence of mental malady, but being in all respects free agents, may be desirous of residing as voluntary boarders in an institution for the care and treatment of persons of unsound mind, submitting to a modified control, and conforming to the general regulations of the hospital.   There is not in the statutes for the regulation of registered hospitals any prohibition on such persons being admitted as inmates on the terms above suggested ; provided they contract alone, or jointly with others, to conform to certain regulations expressed or referred to.

Motives for Suicide.

In the *Westminster Review,* New Series, No. 23, we find this suggestive return:

In the year 1851, there were 3598 suicides recorded in France, to each of which the presumed motive was affixed. Out of these no less than 800 are set down to mental alienation; and to that number we should add 70 cases of monomania, 39 of cerebral fever, and 54 of idiocy—all ranking under the general head of uncontrollableness—which will make a total of 963, or more than a fourth of the whole cases. If we now examine the remaining cases, we find "domestic quarrels" next in amount, being no less than 385; while grief for the loss of children amounts to only 46, grief at their ingratitude or bad conduct, 16; sudden anger, only 1. Next in importance to domestic quarrels is the desire to escape from physical suffering: these amount to 313. Debt and embarrassment rank next—203. Want, and the fear of want, 179. Disgust at life—which may properly be called low spirits—stands high—166; shame and remorse, very low, only 7. Thwarted love shows only 91, and jealousy, 25. Losses at play, 6; loss of employment, 25.

Fallacious as all such figures must necessarily be, from the impossibility of always assigning the real motive to the act, they point with sufficient distinctness to certain general conclusions:—First, that insanity is the origin of by far the largest proportion of cases; secondly, that, except the dread of physical suffering, the other large proportions are all of cases which belong to the deliberative kind. In literature it is always passion, and passion of vehement sudden afflux, which determines suicide: the agonies of despair or jealousy, the arrowy pangs of remorse, or the dread apprehension of shame, are the only motives which the dramatist or novelist ever conceives.

Remedy for Poisoning.

Pouring cold water on the face and head appears to be a good remedy in case of poisoning by narcotics. A young woman accidentally swallowed six drachms of a mixture of laudanum and chloroform with some hydrocyanic acid in it. She immediately vomited a portion of the liquid, and then fell down in a state of coma. Professor Harley being called in, he administered hot coffee and nitric ether, and proceeded to effect artificial respiration. No great improvement was perceptible, but on the application of cold water to the forehead the effect was magical. The patient began to breathe more freely, and she lost some blood from the nose. As soon as the affusion of cold water ceased, the coma returned, and was again removed by renewing the affusion; the patient soon moved her arms and legs, and seemed anxious to avoid the stream of water, as if it caused her pain. This treatment was renewed at intervals until the following day, and after the lapse of sixty hours all distressing symptoms disappeared completely.

New Remedy for Wounds.

The *Antwerp Journal* states that perchloride of iron combined with collodion is a good hæmostatic in the case of wounds, the bites of leeches, &c. To prepare it, one part of crystallized perchloride of iron is mixed with six parts of collodion. The perchloride of iron should be added gradually and with care, otherwise such a quantity of heat will be generated as to cause the collodion to boil. The composition, when well made, is of a yellowish red, perfectly limpid, and produces on the skin a yellow pellicle, which retains great elasticity.

Compensation for Wounds.

The Regulations under which pensions and allowances are granted to officers of the Army were revised by a Royal Warrant issued towards the close of 1860. The loss of an eye or limb from injury received in action will be compensated by a gratuity in money of one year's full pay of his then rank or staff appointment. He may be recommended for a pension also, at a rate varying from 400*l.* for a lieutenant-general, to 50*l.* for a cornet ; and if more than one eye or limb be lost, he may be recommended for a pension for each. For minor injuries, " not nearly equal to the loss of a limb," he may receive a gratuity varying from three to twelve months of his then pay. If the injury shall be so diminished as to be " not nearly equal to the loss of a limb," at the end of five years, during which the claimant must be twice examined by a medical board, the pension will then be permanent, otherwise it will cease. No pension or gratuity for these causes will be granted unless the actual loss shall have occurred within five years after the wound or injury was received. This scale of compensation is more liberal than by the previously existing custom.—*Lancet,* 1860.

The Best Physician.

What chiefly characterizes the most eminent physicians, and gives them their real superiority, is not so much the extent of their theoretical knowledge—though that, too, is often considerable—but it is that fine and delicate perception which they owe, partly to experience, and partly to a natural quickness in detecting analogies and differences which escape ordinary observers. The pro-

cess which they follow, is one of rapid, and, in some degree, unconscious, induction. And this is the reason why the greatest
physiologists and chemists, which the medical profession possesses, are not, as a matter of course, the best curers of disease.
If medicine were a science, they would always be the best. But
medicine being still essentially an art, depends mainly upon qualities which each practitioner has to acquire for himself, and which
no scientific theory can teach. The time for a general theory has
not yet come, and probably many generations will have to elapse
before it does come. To suppose, therefore, that a theory of
disease should, as a matter of education, precede the treatment
of disease, is not only practically dangerous but logically false.—
Buckle's *History of Civilization*, vol. ii.

In 1857, Sir John Forbes, M.D., after fifty years of professional experience, left, as a legacy to his successors, the emphatic
avowal, that Nature is, after all, the real physician—since, however human ingenuity may devise means of alleviation and accele-
ration, it is Nature and not Art which cures all curable diseases.
Sir John is, however, far from implying that the art of medicine is
without its use and importance, especially in preventing disease;
but he wishes attention to be more sedulously fixed upon the
degree to which nature can be left entirely to herself, in order that
we might know how, and to what extent, art may with advantage
interfere. There are many cases in which nature, left to herself,
will infallibly kill her patient—say, for instance, in a case of poisoning—whereas the application of a stomach-pump, or a chemical reagent, arrests the evil at once.

Sir John Forbes invites his brethren to collect and classify the
evidence which shows how nature cures disease; and the prejudices which hamper the physician, he indicates in the following
enumeration of current delusions:

1. Ignorance of the natural course and progress of diseases which are
essentially slow and not to be altered by any artificial means, often leads the
friends of the patient to be urgent with the medical attendant to employ
more powerful measures, or at least to change the means used, to give more
frequent or more powerful doses, &c.

2. Ignorance of the power of Nature to cure diseases, and an undue estimate of the power of medicines to do so, sometimes almost compel practitioners to prescribe remedies when they are either useless or injurious.

3. The same ignorance not seldom occasions dissatisfaction with, and
loss of confidence in, those practitioners who, from conscientious motives,
and on the justest grounds of Art, refrain from having recourse to measures
of undue activity, or from prescribing medicines unnecessarily; and leads to
the countenance and employment of men who have obtained the reputation
of greater activity and boldness, through their very ignorance of the true
character and requirements of their art.

4. It is the same state of mind that leads the public generally to give ear to the most ridiculous promises of charlatans: also to run after the professors and practisers of doctrines utterly absurd and useless, as in the instance of Homœopathy and Mesmerism, or dangerous, except in the proper cases, as in the instance of Hydropathy.

5. Finally, it is the same ignorance of Nature and her proceedings that often forces medical men to multiply their visits and their prescriptions to an extent not simply unnecessary, but really injurious to the patient, as could be easily shown.

The sick man is impatient to be well. Ignorant of nature's slow processes, "the strongest and most effective powers of art," says Sir John, "are usually employed for the very purpose of setting aside or counteracting, or modifying in some way or other, the powers of nature. Generally speaking, we may even say that all the heroic arms of physic are invoked purposely to disturb, and obstruct, and overwhelm the normal order of the natural processes."

The Uncertainty of Human Life.

Some men there are who cannot bear the thought of the Uncertainty of Life; since, were they to entertain it, their worldly views would be cut short, and the prospect of fruition, or living to enjoy their gains, be considered so insecure, as to lessen, if not destroy, the inducement to extraordinary exertion. One of fortune's favourites, on being reminded of *the uncertainty of life*, replied, in a confident tone, that had he suffered such a thought to possess him, he should never have got on in the world—the doubt being to him an unwelcome intruder. Every record of human character—every volume of reminiscences that we can take up—almost every day's newspaper,—abounds with evidence of the uncertain tenure of our existence.

In Lord Cockburn's *Memorials*, we read of these three remarkable deaths. At the close of 1809, Dr. Adam, of the High School, Edinburgh, died, after a few days' illness. His ruling passion was for teaching. He was in his bedchamber: finding that he could not see, he uttered a few words, which have been variously given, but all the accounts of which mean—"It is getting dark, boys; we must put off the rest till to-morrow." It was the darkness of death. On May 20, 1811, President Blair had been in court that day, apparently in good health, and had gone to take his usual walk from his house in George-square round by Bruntfield Links and the Grange, when he was struck with sudden illness, staggered home, and died. The day before his funeral, another unlooked-for occurrence deepened the solemnity. The first Lord Melville had retired to rest in his usual health, but was found dead in bed next morning. These two early, attached, and illustrious friends were thus lying suddenly dead, with but a wall between them; their houses, on the north-east side of George-square, Edinburgh, being next each other.

It has always been said, and never, so far as the writer knows, contradicted, and he is inclined to believe it, that a letter written by Lord Melville was found on his table or in a writing-case, giving a feeling account of his emotions at President Blair's funeral. It was a fancy-piece, addressed to a member of the Government, with a view to obtain some public provision for Blair's family; the writer had not reckoned on the possibility of his own demise before his friend's funeral took place.

Dr. Granville, in his work on *Sudden Death*, has related a number of instances of the uncertainty of life, which came to his knowledge between the years 1849 and 1854, from which we select the following:

Mr. Horace Twiss, whose stout frame and laborious habits seemed to promise long life, while sitting in the board-room of one of the Companies of which he was a Director, and in the act of addressing the members, ceased to live, early in May, 1849.

Not long after, at Florence, Harriett Lady Pellew suddenly expired in her carriage, on the drive at the Cascine; and at Paris, the Countess of Blessington, returning home from dinner at the Duchess de Grammont's, was seized with apoplexy, and died next morning, June 4.

In the same year, on September 9, the Grand Duke Michael, brother of Nicholas, Emperor of Russia, a prince of gigantic frame, while reviewing his troops at Warsaw, fell from his horse, and expired a few hours after.

At Rome, Richard Wyatt, the sculptor, was suddenly carried off by apoplexy, May 27, 1851; and on June 7, at Fontaine-bleau, Reynolds, the author of *Miserrimus*, died suddenly.

"I must rise instantly, or I shall be suffocated," said the wife of a banker, on July 8, at Trent Park: she rose, rushed to a window, which she threw open to inhale fresh air: it was the last breath she took in, for she fell a corpse!

In the same year, Audin, the well-known publisher, died suddenly in his carriage, while travelling from Marseilles to Avignon; and Herr Carl Sander, the celebrated German surgeon, expired while seated at his desk, writing a treatise on anatomy.

On New Year's Day, 1852, Sir Charles Wager Watson, of Westwratting Park, while riding briskly to meet the Suffolk fox-hounds, fell from his horse, and on his friends coming up, they found him dead. On April 5, Prince Schwartzenberg was holding a Cabinet council, when he suddenly appeared to gasp for breath, and withdrew: he rallied, and retired to dress for dinner, during which he fell senseless on the floor, and died within an hour from his first seizure.

Mr. Frank Forster, the engineer, on April 13, while writing a letter, was struck with apoplexy, and almost immediately expired. A. N. Welby Pugin, the architect, scarcely of mature age, died suddenly at Ramsgate, September 14; and on the same day, the Duke of Wellington, who had retired to rest apparently quite well on the previous night, died, it is stated of apoplexy, within the brief space of six or seven hours. Dr. Granville states, from the testimony of medical and other near attendants, that, from the very first seizure, when the duke ordered distinctly the apothecary to be fetched *immediately*, down to the last moment of his existence, paralysis of the brain had been complete, for no other comprehensible word could he utter after that direction. On the day before, Dr. Stokoe, the appointed medical attendant to Napoleon I., during the last years of his exile, died suddenly in a public room at York, as he was preparing to continue his journey to London.

On March 12, 1853, Marshal Haynau, having supped with the prime minister, Buol, retired to rest, when, just after midnight, he rang for a glass of water; when the servant returned, his master was gasping for breath, and soon after died. On the same night, the gallant Lieutenant-General Sir Edward Kerrison was found dead in his bed. And, not many days after, Vice-Admiral Zarthmann, while walking in the streets of Copenhagen, complained of vertigo, sank to the ground, and expired in an hour. On April 30, Dr. Butler, Dean of Peterborough, while seated at table with his family, suddenly became insensible, and in ten minutes passed away, almost without a struggle. Maurice O'Connell, the eldest son of "the Liberator," appeared in his usual health in the House of Commons; on the morrow, at midnight, he breathed his last. On December 12, 1853, Dr. Harrington, Principal of Brazenose College, Oxford, having retired to rest in his usual health and spirits, was shortly after seized with spasms, and died before eight o'clock next morning, in his fifty-third year. On the 5th of the same month, Captain Warner, of the "long range," expired suddenly. On a Sunday evening in the same month, a stout middle-aged yeoman was crossing Ovington Park, near Southampton, on his way to the church, which he never reached: the park-keeper found him seated with his back to a tree, his hat on, his umbrella under his arm—dead—with no appearance of convulsion or previous struggle. Visconti, the architect, on December 29, had attended the first meeting of the Imperial Commission for the Exposition building at Paris, and was returning home in his carriage: on the door being opened, he was found dead.

One of the most awfully sudden visitations recorded in our time was the death of Mr. Justice Talfourd, in his fifty-eighth year, March 13, 1845, at Stafford, while delivering his charge to the grand jury. He was speaking of the increase of crime—of the neglects of the rich, the ignorance of the poor—of the want of a closer knowledge and more vital sympathy between class and class—and of the thousand social evils which arise from that unhappy and unnatural estrangement of human interests—when his face flushed and he bent forward on his desk, almost as if the Judge were bowed in prayer by some sharp and overpowering emotion. A moment more, and the bystanders saw him swerve, as if he were already senseless. He was dying, calmly and happily. In a few seconds he was gone—and all that was mortal of the poet was carried to the Judges' Chambers and there laid down in breathless awe. "The people were trembling at the thought of coming before him; but in a minute his function was over, and he was gone to his own account."

Respecting the frequency of these fatal occurrences, Dr. Granville remarks: "Where is the friend, where the acquaintance, or the passing associate at a club, who has not some sad story of the sort, or many of them, to tell you, if you once enter on the dismal subject? From every quarter of the country, from families whom you knew to be in the full bloom of youth, of individuals who were deemed vigorous and in the flower of manhood, we hear as we meet in our daily intercourse, of some one of them having suddenly disappeared from among the living!" Our newspapers abound with such records as the following.

In 1837, a communication to a Bristol journal recorded

"The fearfully sudden decease of Thomas Kington, Esq., of Manilla-hall, Clifton. Apparently without the slightest indisposition he died in his counting-house, Queen-square, Bristol, surrounded by all the accumulations of wealth, and the advantages accruing from the interests of that wide range of commerce, the Melbourne and Australian trade."

And, in the *Times*, June, 1862:

"On the 19th inst., at Nine Elms, very suddenly, Mr. John Miller, on the anniversary of his birth and wedding days, which events he had intended to celebrate at the Star and Garter, Richmond, where he had gone with a few friends, but was suddenly attacked with illness on his arrival there, and was re-conveyed to his own residence, where he expired shortly afterwards, aged fifty."

In 1862, Mr. F. W. Gingell, of Wood House, East Ham, while sitting at dinner with the family, observed to his father, " I have a presentiment that I shall die suddenly :" at the same time his head dropped, and he expired.

Religious Thought.

Moveable Feasts.

The following short explanation of the Moveable Feasts of the Church, and their dependence on Easter, cannot be improved:

" In the English nomenclature Easter Sunday has always the *six* Sundays in Lent immediately preceding, and the *five* Sundays *after* Easter, immediately following. Of these the nearest to Easter before and after are *Palm* Sunday and *Low* Sunday; the farthest before and after are *Quadragesima* (first in Lent), and *Rogation* Sunday (fifth after Easter). Preceding all these are, in reverse order, *Quinquagesima, Sexagesima, Septuagesima*: and following them, in direct order, are the Sunday after *Ascension* (Holy Thursday, Thursday five weeks after Easter); *Whit* Sunday and *Trinity* Sunday. So that Easter Sunday, as it takes its course through the almanacks, draws after it, as it were, *nine* Sundays, and pushes *eight* before it, all at fixed denominations. Looking farther back, every Sunday preceding Septuagesima, but not preceding the fixed day of Epiphany (June 6), is named as of *Epiphany* or after *Epiphany*: the least number of Sundays after Epiphany is one, the greatest number six. Looking farther forwards, all the Sundays following Trinity are named as *after* Trinity in succession, until we arrive at the nearest Sunday (be it before or after) to the St. Andrew's Day (November 30th), which is the first Sunday in Advent. The least number of Sundays after Trinity is twenty-two; the greatest, twenty-seven. From thence, up to Christmas Day, exclusive, the Sundays are named as in *Advent*, and from Christmas Day to Epiphany, exclusive, they are named as Christmas Day, or as the first or second Sunday after Christmas."—*Prof. de Morgan's Book of Almanacks.*

Christmas.

The celebration of Christmas is still rife among us. Its stream of joy is not narrowed, but more equally diffused through society; and although much of the custom of profuse hospitality has passed away, Christmas is yet universally recognised as a season when every Christian should show his gratitude to the Almighty for the inestimable benefits procured to us by the Nativity, by an ample display of goodwill towards our fellow-men:

"What comfort by Him doe we winne,
Who made Himself the price of sinne
To make us heirs of glory?
To see this Babe all innocence,
A Martyr borne in our defence—
Can man forget this storie?"

Ben Jonson.

It is, however, an error of the day to deplore a falling-off in Christmas commemorations; whereas the enjoyment has but assumed a healthier tone. The Past is ever more picturesque than the Present. We stroll into the Great Hall at Westminster, where our Plantagenet kings feasted at Christmas and Epiphany: it is, however, forsaken and dreary; and, looking up roofward, we can scarcely see the louvre through which the smoke of many huge Christmas fires has gone up; or the noble hammer-beams, or the carved angels, and other glories of this majestic roof. But, step into Inigo Jones' banqueting-house, at Whitehall; and there you will see the Lord High Almoner distributing the Royal alms, as he was wont to do centuries since. At Windsor the Sovereign herself is superintending the distribution of her seasonable bounty; the Lord Steward fills the hungry prisoner with good things; the good cheer shines upon Ragged Schools and other havens of charity. The moderation observable in our times is conformable to the precept in the *Whole Duty of Man,* enjoining us not to make the day "an occasion of intemperance and disorder, as do too many, who consider nothing in Christmas and other good times but the good cheer and jollity of them." It is, however, one of the signs of the more gracious and hallowed tone that the singing of Carols has increased of late years; together with the decoration of churches, and the revival of several minor observances, which tend to show the universality of this improved feeling.

Doubt about Religion.

The Bishop of Oxford, in one of his eloquent Sermons upon *the Temptation to Doubt about Religion,* thus describes one class of doubts, and, by implication, of doubters:

"There are the doubts which are the fruits of an evil life, which come forth as the obscene creatures of the night come forth—because it is the night; because the darkness is abroad, and they are the creatures of the darkness. These are, for the most part, self-chosen doubts, bred of corruption and of fear; of a clinging to sin and yet of a fear of its punishment; of a conscious resistance to the ways and the works of a God of purity and truth; of an evil interest which men have in finding revelation to be false, because it is a system which, if true, is fatally opposed to them. Men pursued by these doubts are a fearful spectacle. The terrors which at times shake them are often appalling to witness; and yet even these are less awful than the forced grimace with which they try to laugh them off; vaunting their doubts, like the lonely wanderer who sings noisily to conceal or overcome his fear of the darkness, that they may, if possible, scatter by the loudness of their laugh the besetting crowd of their alarms."

Another class of doubts the Bishop describes are those which address themselves to specific and clearly-revealed points in the revelation, which yet, as a whole, the doubting man does not disbelieve. Against these doubts he would utter his warning, because he believes that their presence, and even their indulgence, is at this moment by no means rare; because their true character is often disguised under the most specious forms; because the young, and among the young the generous, the ardent, the thoughtful, and the inquiring, are often their special victims; and because their cause is one of weakness, both intellectual and spiritual, while their end, when they triumph, is misery here, and, too often, everlasting loss hereafter. Having observed that there must be room for doubts and questions such as these,* the Bishop proceeds:

"It may often seem that these doubts are the pauses of modesty, and these questions the interrogations of an inquiring faith. Thus the doubts are cherished and encouraged under the garb of piety, until a habit is formed in the mind of subjecting the written word and the authoritative declarations of faith to the scrutiny of each man's intellectual faculties; and, according to their decision, of his accepting, modifying, or rejecting them. Now, such a mode of dealing with revelation is exceeding attractive. It promises to make the faith so rational—to give every man a reason for the hope that is in him—to be so free from all forcing of doctrines on him, that it naturally wins to itself young and ardent minds. Yet it is against this that I would so earnestly warn you, and that for the weightiest reasons —for no less a reason than this, that in its very first principle it is subversive of all true faith, and that it is therefore in its consequences full of ruin to the soul."

The relation of the Christian revelation to nature, the Bishop thus intelligibly points out:

"The Christian revelation teaches nothing merely to gratify our curiosity. In this respect it is the very opposite of nature. The handwriting of the Creator in the works of nature seems to be imprinted on them for the very purpose of stimulating our curiosity and training and rewarding our powers of investigation and discovery. In the Christian revelation, on the contrary, nothing is revealed for the sake merely of its being known, but

---

* The Bishop has elsewhere observed, with respect to what he terms "the prescriptive rights of the Church," that, "there always must be subjects upon which good men, from the mere natural law of the mind contemplating one side of a subject with greater interest than another, will arrive at different conclusions."

that the degree of knowledge given us may in some way or other affect our moral and spiritual training."

An Undergraduate of Oxford, in bearing testimony to the influence of these Sermons upon him at the time they were preached, describes the Free Inquiry of the present day as working in three classes of men. With some it was hailed as a relief from the annoyance of a conscience which told them that if the " old paths" were the true ones, there was certainly an ill look-out for them ; and it was a pleasure, therefore, to hear those who ought to know say that the hard things (such as eternal punishment, &c.) which had been told them from their cradles were matters, to say the least, of considerable doubt. With others it was adopted with the gratifying feeling that thus they showed themselves " wiser than their sires," and as intellectual champions " in the foremost files of time," superior to all old wives' fables. With others it was entertained, in a spirit eager for truth, with a painful sense of perplexity—the distress of men who feel that, while they. have conscientiously left the old way as a way averse to all true progress, they neither know nor like to contemplate the issue of the new.

Of these three classes of " free inquirers," the first two were of course contemptible, but the third could not be passed by unheeded ; and after a vehement effort to stand up for truths hitherto on his part unquestioned, the writer felt that he was more or less with them. He then acknowledges to reading the *Essays and Reviews* through three times, which gave him a new freedom, with which he felt self-satisfied: still, he was miserable with uncertainty, for he had nothing beneath his feet but his own private judgment ; and he asks, what was that as regards the truth, when he saw that no two men arrived at the same conclusion? In the midst of all this he went, with others, to hear these sermons: instead of hearing the Bishop steer between conflicting opinions in this matter, our Undergraduate was influenced by these sermons to feel that reverence must go hand-in-hand with knowledge, in order that the true harmony may exist between mind and soul ; that a man's reason and judgment alone are a poor support and comfort, and the kingdom of God *must* be received in the spirit of a little child.*

The Bishop concludes an earnest deprecation of the habit of doubting, with the following awful picture of the death-bed of a victim to this pernicious practice :

" It is not from imagination that I have drawn this warning. I can tell , you of an overshadowed grave which closed in on such a struggle and such

* See *Times*, May 2nd and 5th, 1863.

an end as that at which I have glanced.   In it was laid a form which had
hardly reached the fulness of earliest manhood.   That young man had
gone, young, ardent, and simply faithful, to the tutelage of one, himself I
doubt not a believer, but one who sought to reconcile the teaching of our
Church, in which he ministered, with the dreams of Rationalism.   His
favourite pupil learnt his lore, and it sufficed for his needs while health
beat high in his youthful veins : but on him sickness and decay closed
early in, and as the glow of health faded, the intellectual lights for which
he had exchanged the simplicity of faith began to pale ; whilst the viper
brood of doubts which almost unawares he had let slip into his soul, crept
forth from their hiding-places and raised against him their fearfully envenomed heads.   And they were too strong for him.   The teacher who had
suggested could not remove them : and in darkness and despair his victim
died before his eyes the doubter's death."

Our Age of Doubt.

The intellect of the present generation is usually acknowledged
to have gone off on quite a different tack from that of its predecessor. *Not belief, but doubt, is the present fashion.* Now,
belief and doubt, both of them, have their uses.   Each of them
has its good and its bad side.   Doubt is the more daring and im-
pressive ; but belief, even if sometimes rather illogical, is decidedly
the more amiable.   Let a negative system be true, and a positive
system be false ; still the positive system will call out some of the
best qualities of our nature in a way that the negative system
cannot.   It is certain that the present generation is growing up in
a spirit of greater independence and self-reliance, of less deference
to age, to tradition, to authority of all kinds, than was in vogue
twenty years since.   The change may be for the better or for the
worse, but the fact of the change is undeniable.   Probably, if
minutely examined, it has both its good and its bad side.   The
young men of the present day have gained something in wideness
of view, and at least apparent worldly knowledge ; but they have
certainly lost much that was very attractive in their predecessors.
On the other hand, acts of petty persecution are doing all that can
be done to enlist their best feelings on the side on which it is
wished that they should not be enlisted.   If any man, especially
one of the most conscientious and hard-working officers of the
University, is proscribed and insulted on account of his opinions,
those opinions are at once put in an attractive light to every
generous mind.   Men in authority are slow to believe it, but
there is no policy so foolish as that of making martyrs.—*From the
Saturday Review.*

Mr. Ruskin, in his *Modern Painters*, has this striking passage
upon what he terms " the Faithlessness of our Age :"

"A Red Indian, or Otaheitan savage, has more sense of a Divine existence round him, or government over him, than the plurality of refined
Londoners and Parisians; and those among us who may in some sense be
said to believe are divided almost without exception into two broad classes,
Romanist and Puritan; who, but for the interference of the unbelieving
portions of society, would, either of them, reduce the other sect as speedily
as possible to ashes; the Romanist having always done so whenever he
could, from the beginning of their separation, and the Puritan at this time
holding himself in complacent expectation of the destruction of Rome by
volcanic fire. . . . . Hence nearly all our powerful men in this age of
the world are unbelievers : the best of them in doubt and misery; the
worst in reckless defiance; the plurality, in plodding hesitation, doing as
well as they can what practical work lies ready in their hands. Most of
our scientific men are in this last class; our popular authors either set
themselves definitely against all religious form, pleading for simple truth
and benevolence, or give themselves up to bitter and fruitless statement of
facts, or surface-painting, or careless blasphemy, sad or smiling. Our
earnest poets and deepest thinkers are doubtful and indignant."

A Hint to Sceptics.

Reason is always striving, always at a loss; and of necessity, it
must so come to pass, while it is exercised about that which is not
its proper object. Let us be content at last to know God by his
own methods, at least so much of Him as He is pleased to reveal
to us in the Sacred Scriptures. To apprehend them to be the
Word of God is all our reason has to do, for all beyond it is the
work of faith, which is the seal of Heaven impressed upon our
human understanding.—*Dryden.*

Bishop Mant, writing in a more scientific age than that in
which Dryden flourished, says :

"Persons have, perhaps, been sometimes found who, from their attachment to pursuits of science, and to the acquisition of general knowledge,
have appeared sceptical upon the subject of Divine revelation. But others,
at least equally endowed with intellectual powers, and equally rich in intellectual acquirements, have been serious, rational, and conscientious believers.
Amongst these may be ranked the great apostle, St. Paul, who has been
rarely surpassed in strength of understanding, or in the treasures of a cultivated mind; and in connexion with him it may be added, that 'Luke,
the beloved physician, whose praise is in the Gospel,' was professionally
acquainted with the operations of nature, and the effects of secondary
causes, and thus qualified to appreciate the miraculous and supernatural
character of the works which he has recorded as foundations of our belief."

What is Egyptology ?

The object of Egyptology is to render it a sort of elevated
standing-point, from which all the realms of ethnography and

philology might be surveyed, and the most distant and isolated points brought within range of view. This undertaking has been attempted chiefly by Bunsen, who has completed in five volumes his work entitled *Ægypten's Stelle in der Weltgeschichte* (" Egypt's Place in Universal History," Hamburg, 1845–1857), and has discussed some of the same subjects in a more general and miscellaneous book, or collection of treatises, called *Christianity and Mankind, their Beginnings and Prospects* (London, 1854). It is Bunsen's theory that " the Egyptian language is the point in universal history at which the creative energy of language still shows its original form, just before it raises its pinions aloft, and assumes in the world-ruling nations an entirely different and more spiritual form; while in the other races, according to laws not yet explored, it sinks into the atomic and mechanical, or at best deflects into subordinate ramifications.' — (*Ægypten*, i. 338). Looking back over a period of more than twenty thousand years, this philological speculator recognises a time when the as yet undivided families of Japhet and Shem lived together in a civilized state in Northern Asia. From this undivided Asiatic stock Egypt, according to Bunsen, must be a colony, gradually degenerated into the African type; for the old Egyptian language claims affinity at once with the Aramaic idioms in immediate contact with it, and with the Indo-Germanic tongues, with which it has no direct commerce—(*Report of the Brit. Assoc.*, 1847, p. 280; *Ægypten*, iv., Pref., p. 10). It must be owned that these sweeping conclusions do not rest upon philological inductions of the most accurate kind, and are supported by arguments which are sometimes as arbitrary as they are precarious.—*Encyclopædia Britannica*, 8th edition.

Jerusalem and Nimroud.

The greatest light which has yet been thrown upon the architectural character of the Palace of Solomon, Mr. Lewin (in his *Sketch of Jerusalem*, published in 1861) is of opinion is derived from the recent discoveries in and near Nineveh; Solomon having studiously copied the Assyrian style.

" Take, for instance, the north-west palace of Nimroud, which would almost seem to have been the pattern after which the royal palace at Jerusalem was built. Thus the Nimroud Palace is nearly a square, of about 330 feet each way; and the area of Solomon's Palace is 325 feet by 290 feet. In front at Nimroud was a great hall, 152 feet long by 32 feet wide; and in front, at Jerusalem, was a hall, the house of Lebanon, 150 feet by 75 feet. The halls at Nimroud were supported by rows of pillars, not of stone, but of wood; and the Hall of Lebanon was supported by three rows of cedar pillars, fifteen in a row, making forty-five in the whole. In the centre, at Nimroud, was a spacious open court; and in the centre at Jerusalem was also a court. On the sides, at Nimroud, were suites of apartments three deep, decreasing in width as they receded from the light supplied from the great court; and at Jerusalem were windows in three rows, and light against light in three ranks. At Nimroud, in the rear was a double suite of apartments; and in the rear at Jerusalem were the separate suites of the king and the queen. At Nimroud, the interior walls were lined with sculptured slabs; and at Jerusalem the apartments were also lined with stones carved in imitation of trees and plants."

What is Rationalism?

Rationalism, in its widest acceptation, is applicable to all who follow the dictates of reason, whether in their speculative or practical life. In its more restricted signification it is applied specially to that system of religious opinion whose final test of truth is placed in the direct assent of the human consciousness, whether in the form of logical deduction, moral judgment, or religious intuition, by whatever previous process these faculties may have been raised to their assumed dignity as arbitrators.

The Bishop of Oxford, in one of his Charges, has thus eloquently denounced the present dangerous spirit of Rationalism in the Church:

" Are there not, my reverend brethren, signs enough abroad now of special danger to make us drop our lesser differences and combine together as one man, striving earnestly for the faith once delivered to the Saints? When from within our own encampment we hear voices declaring that our whole belief in the Atonement wrought out for us by the sacrifice on the Cross is an ignorant misconception—that the miracles and the prophecies of Scripture are part of an irrational supernaturalism, which it is the duty of a remorseless criticism to expose and to account for, by such discoveries as that the imagination has allied itself with the affections to produce them, and that they may safely be brought down to a natural Rationalism ;—by such suggestions as that the description of the passage of the Red Sea is the latitude of poetry—that the Avenger who slew the firstborn is the Bedouin host, akin nearly to Jethro, and more remotely to Israel—when the history of the Bible is explained away by being treated as a legend, and its prophecy deprived of all supernatural character by being turned into a history of past or present events—when we are told that had our Lord come to us now, instead of in the youth of the world, the truth of His Divine nature would not have been recognised; that is to say, that it was the peculiar stage in which flesh and blood then were, and not the revelation of His Father who was in heaven which enabled the Apostles to believe in Him—when in

words, as far as opinion is privately entertained is concerned, the liberty of
the English clergyman appears to be complete—when we are told that men
may sign any Article of the National Church, if it is only their own
opinions which are at variance with them—when we are told that they may
sign, solemnly before God, that they allow certain articles of belief, meaning thereby only that they allow their existence as the lesser of two great
evils, and that under the Sixth Article one may literally or allegorically, or
as a parable, or as poetry or a legend, receive the story of the Serpent
tempting Eve and speaking in a man's voice; and in like manner the
arresting of the earth's motion, the water standing still, the universality of
the Deluge, the confusion of tongues, the taking up of Elijah corporeally
into Heaven, the nature of Angels, and the miraculous particulars of many
other events:—when Abraham's great act of obedient faith in not with-
holding his son, even his only son, but offering him up at the express
command of God is commuted by the gross ritual of Syrian notes into a
traditional revelation; while the awe of the Divine voice bidding him slay
his son, and his being stayed by the angel from doing so, is watered down
into an allegory meaning that the Father in whom he trusted was better
pleased with mercy than with sacrifice; when it is maintained that St.
Stephen, full of the Holy Ghost, in the utterances of his martyrdom, and
St. Paul proving from the history of his people that Jesus was the Christ,
would naturally speak not only words of truth, but after the received
accounts—when, I say, such words as these are deliberately uttered by our
ordained Clergy, while the slowness even of English theologians to accept
such a treatment of God's revelation is scoffed at in such words as the following, even by those in our Universities who no longer repeat fully the
Shibboleth of the Reformers, the explicitness of truth and error:—'He
who assents most committing himself least to baseness being reckoned the
wisest;' whilst those who maintained the old truth, I trust with most of
us, my brethren, are branded as Baal's prophets and the four hundred
prophets of the grove who cry out for falsehood—whilst, I say, such words
as these are heard from ordained men amongst us, and who still keep their
places in the National Church, is it not a time for us, if we do hold openly
by the Holy Scriptures as the one inspired voice of God's written revelation
—if we do hold to the ancient Creeds as the summary of the good deposit
—if we believe in the Lord Jesus Christ as very God and very Man—if we
believe in His offering Himself on the Cross as the one only true and sufficient
sacrifice, satisfaction, and atonement for the sins of the whole world—is it
not time for us, laying aside our suspicions and our divisions about small
matters, to combine together in prayer, and. trust, and labour, and love,
and watching, lest whilst we dispute needlessly about the lesser matters of
the law, we be robbed unawares of the very foundations of the faith?'"

What is Theology?

In the widest sense of the word Theology, including both natural
and revealed theology, we have, among theologians who reject revelation, the systems of—(1) *Atheism*, or that doctrine concerning

God which rejects his existence altogether.* (2) *Deism*, or the system which teaches that God is the Creator of all things, but that, having once created them and impressed upon them certain laws for the regulation of their future existence, commonly called the *laws of nature*, He has left them to the government of those laws, and concerns Himself no more with his creation; or, in other words, this system acknowledges the existence of God, but denies his providence. (3) *Theism*, the system which differs from Deism by acknowledging the providence of God. The systems of *Deism* and *Theism* suppose the existence of an Almighty Creator, whose existence is independent of the universe; but there is another system, according to which the laws of Nature are in themselves the external self-existent causes of all the phenomena of the universe, and there is no causative principle external to Nature. This system takes two different forms: *Materialism*, which makes all the phenomena of Nature to result from the physical constitution of matter itself; and the various shades of *Pantheism*, which suppose an intelligent principle (*anima mundi*) to be inseparably connected with everything that exists, and to pervade the whole creation.

Deism properly means belief in the existence of a God, but is generally applied to all such belief as goes no further, that is to say, to disbelief of revelation. It is always applied dyslogistically, and frequently merely as a term of reproach. But the identi word, in its Greek form, *theist*, is not a word of disapproba and, consistently with established usage, may be approp applied as opposed to atheist, when the latter term is correctly used. For it must be observed that the term atheist has been not unfrequently employed in the sense of an unbeliever in Christianity, though at the same time professing theism.—*Penny Cyclopædia.*

Religious Forebodings.

Nearly sixty years since, Southey wrote his famous anticipation of Mormonism, and of some other matters as important as Mormonism, in a letter to Rickman (1805), as follows:

"Here I do not like the prospects: sooner or later a hungry government will snap at the tithes; the clergy will then become State pensioners or parish pensioners; in the latter case more odious to the farmers than they are now, in the former the first pensioners to be amerced of their stipends.

* "Atheist, use thine eyes;
And having view'd the order of the skies,
Think (if thou canst) that matter blindly hurl'd
Without a guide, should frame this wondrous world."
Creech.

Meantime, the damned system of Calvinism spreads like a pestilence among the lower classes. I have not the slightest doubt that the Calvinists will be the majority in less than half a century; we see how catching the distemper is, and do not see any means of stopping it. There is a good opening for a new religion, but the founder must start up in some of the darker parts of the world. It is America's turn to send out apostles. A new one there must be when the old one is worn out. I am a believer in the truth of Christianity, but truth will never do for the multitude; there is an appetite for faith in us, which if it be not duly indulged, it turns to green sickness, and feeds upon chalk and cinders. The truth is, man was not made for the world alone; and speculations concerning the next will be found, at last, the most interesting to all of us."

Folly of Atheism.

Morphology, in natural science, teaches us that the whole animal and vegetable creation is formed upon certain fundamental types and patterns, which can be traced under various modifications and transformations through all the rich variety of things apparently of most dissimilar build. But here and there a scientific person takes it into his foolish head that there may be a set of moulds without a moulder, a calculated gradation of forms without a calculator, an ordered world without an ordering God. Now, this atheistical science conveys about as much meaning as suicidal life; for science is possible only where there are ideas, and ideas only possible where there is mind, and minds are the offspring of God; and atheism itself is not merely ignorance and stupidity—it is the purely nonsensical and the unintelligible.—*Professor Blackie: Edinburgh Essays, 1856.*

The first Congregational Church in England.

In the State-Paper Office has been discovered a manuscript, showing that in the Bridewell of London* were imprisoned the members of the Congregational Church first formed after the accession of Queen Elizabeth. They were committed by the Privy Council to the custody of the gaoler, May 20, 1567. It is, no doubt, to this company that Bishop Grindal refers, in his letter to Bullinger, July 11, 1568:—" Some London citizens," he says, " with four or five ministers, have openly separated from us; and sometimes in private houses, sometimes in fields, and occasionally even in ships, they have held meetings, and administered the

---

* In Blackfriars: originally the Palace of Bridewell, and subsequently a House of Correction.

sacraments. Besides this, they have ordained ministers, elders, and deacons, after their own way." The Rev. Dr. Waddington has discovered some original papers, written by the members of this Church in the Bridewell, signed chiefly by Christian women, together with a statement of the principles of the sect. It appears from these interesting records, which have been kept, though in a loose form, for nearly three hundred years, that Richard Fitz, their first pastor, died in the prison. Dr. Waddington shows, by indisputable evidence, from original papers in the public archives, that the succession of Congregational Churches from the above period is continuous; so that the Bridewell may be regarded as the starting-point of Congregationalism after the Reformation; or, in other words, the origin of the first voluntary church in England, after the Marian persecution, was contemporaneous with the Anglican movement. And it is as remarkable as it is satisfactory, that these touching and simple memorials should have been preserved by the Metropolitan Bishop, and finally transmitted to the Royal Archives.

Innate Ideas, and Pre-existence of Souls.

In the Second Series of *Things not Generally Known*, pp. 147-152, we have illustrated this doctrine at some length; but return to it here for the purpose of quoting an argument directly opposed to the above illustrations, by the writer of the eloquent exposition of Plato, in the *Edinburgh Essays*, 1856:

" Plato was distinguished from all previous philosophers by the prominence which he gave to the doctrine of *innate ideas*. Now, the current opinion in this country certainly is, that these innate ideas were a sort of sublime phantasm blown to the winds by John Locke and the inductive philosophy of external facts which has been achieving such conquests in the modern world from the time of Bacon downwards. But the fact is, that the doctrine of innate ideas, as taught by Plato, never was touched either by Locke or Bacon; and never can be touched in substantials by any thinker who believes that he has thoughts, and that these thoughts have their roots in a simple sovereign and plastic principle which he calls his soul. No doubt there are some pleasant imaginations floating with irridescent colours round the borderland of this Platonic philosophy, which may be blown to the wind by the puff of any cheek, without special inflation from Locke or Bacon. When the great thinker, for instance, pushes his argument for the independence of mind so far as to seem to assert, in positive terms, the existence of ideas in the human soul in ready-made panoply transferred from a previous state of existence into

the present, this must be regarded as a trick of the poet imma-
nent in the philosopher, ever ready to mistake a beautiful analogy
for a substantial argument. Wordsworth, as a philosophic poet,
was certainly more at liberty to illustrate this pleasant fancy than
Plato as a practical philosopher.* *Reminiscence*, as explained by
Socrates in the *Menon* and elsewhere, is not a fact, if the word be
taken in its natural and obvious sense; it is not true that a person
studying mathematics, for instance, when the truth of any profound relation of quantity or number flashes upon his mind, is
recollecting anything that he ever knew before in a previous state
of existence; the simple fact is, that he recognises the evolution
of this truth from other truths of which he finds himself in possession, as a consequence that cannot be avoided when once his
mind is set to work in a certain direction. As certainly as a
sportsman's dog will raise game when it comes near the spot where
the bird is lying, and the scent begins to tell on his eager organ, so
certainly will an idea lurking in a man's mind be hunted out into
startled consciousness by a Socratic questioner. But the simile
limps, like all similes, in one point : the hidden idea is not lying
in the soul, like the bird in the heather, ready-made; it must be
shaped, moulded, and evolved, by a long and sometimes a very
painful process. All that we can legitimately say, therefore, is,
that there lies in every normal human soul the dormant capacity
of acknowledging every necessary truth; and that this capacity is
not borrowed from without. In this sense, and this sense only,
are innate ideas true; and in this sense, unquestionably, they are
very far removed from what may be called a reminiscence."

The Sabbath for Professional Men.

Sir Joshua Reynolds used to say, " he will never make a
painter who looks for the Sunday with pleasure for an idle day;"
and Sir Joshua's journals afford indisputable proofs that it was his
habit to receive sitters on Sundays as well as on other days. This
was naturally displeasing to Dr. Johnson; and we are told by
Boswell, that he (Johnson) made three requests of Sir Joshua, a
short time before his death: one was to forgive him thirty pounds
which he had borrowed of him; another was, that Sir Joshua
would carefully read the Scriptures; and lastly, that he would
abstain from using his pencil on the Sabbath-day : to all of these
requests Reynolds gave a willing assent, and kept his word.

The lax practice of working on the Sabbath is, we fear, too
common. That it is a short-sighted practice there can be no

---

* See the beautiful poem entitled, " Intimations of Immortality.'"

doubt. With respect to it, the Hon. B. F. Butler, of New York, recently made the following statement:

"If I may be permitted to refer to my own experience, I can truly say that, although often severely pressed, and sometimes for years together, by professional occupations and official duties, I cannot call to mind more than half a dozen cases during the twenty-seven years which have elapsed since my admission to the Bar, in which I have found it necessary to devote any portion of the Sabbath to professional or official studies or labours. Of these instances only two, I believe, occurred during my connexion with the Government at Washington, one of which was a case of mercy as well as of necessity, and neither of which prevented my regular attendance at the house of God. The course I have pursued has sometimes compelled me to rise on the ensuing day somewhat earlier than my wont; but an occasional inconvenience of this kind is of small account when compared with the preservation of a useful habit. I am therefore able to testify that it is not necessary to the ordinary duties of professional life, that men should encroach upon the Sabbath; and that the cases of necessity or of mercy, in which professional labour can be required on that day, are few and far between."

"In the Beginning."

That the vast and unknown Antiquity of the Earth, compared with the 6000 years of its supposed existence is but as yesterday, is the first great startling fact which the researches of Geology have brought to light within the last thirty years. "With rare exceptions," says Archdeacon Pratt, "this is become, like the motion of the earth, the universal creed. The prejudice of long-standing interpretation and ignorance of the records which the earth carries in its own bosom regarding its past history, had shut up us and our forefathers for ages, in the notion that the heavens and the earth were but six days older than the human race. But science reveals new phenomena, opens up new ideas, and creates new demands. The torch of nature and reason sheds its light upon the letter of Scripture."

The Rev. Dr. Chalmers was the first to supply this new reading in his *Natural Theology*, vol. i. p. 251, as follows:—"Between the initial act and the details of Genesis, the world, for aught we know, might have been the theatre of many revolutions, the traces of which geology may still investigate, and to which she, in fact, has confidently appealed as the vestiges of so many continents that have now passed away."

"*In the beginning God created the heaven and earth; the earth was without form and void, and darkness was upon the face of the deep,*" is seen to refer to the first calling of matter into existence, and to a state of emptiness and waste into which the earth long after fell, ere God prepared it as the residence of the most perfect of His creatures.

This commentary and explanation was adopted by the late Rev. Dr. Buckland, in his *Bridgewater Treatise:*

"The word *beginning*," he says, " as applied by Moses, in the first verse of the Book of Genesis, expresses an undefined period of time, which was antecedent to the last great change that affected the surface of the earth, and to the creation of its present animal and vegetable inhabitants, during which period a long series of operations may have been going on; which, as they are only connected with the history of the human race, are passed over in silence by the sacred historian, whose only concern was barely to state that the matter of the universe is not eternal and self-existent, but was originally created by the power of the Almighty.   The Mosaic narrative commences with a declaration that, ' *in the beginning God created the heaven and the earth.*'   These few words of Genesis may be fairly appealed to by the geologist as containing a brief statement of the creation of the material elements, at a time distinctly preceding the operations of the first day; it is nowhere affirmed that God created the heaven and the earth in the *first day*, but in the *beginning ;* this beginning may have been an epoch at an immeasured distance, followed by periods of undefined duration, during which all the physical operations disclosed by geology were going on.

"The first verse of Genesis, therefore, seems explicitly to assert the creation of the universe; the heaven, including the sidereal systems and the earth, more especially specifying our planet, as the subsequent scene of the operations of the six days about to be described; no information is given as to events which may have occurred upon this earth, unconnected with the history of man, between the creation of its component matter recorded in the first verse, and the era at which its history is resumed in the second verse; nor is any limit fixed to the time during which these intermediate events may have been going on; millions of millions of years may have occupied the indefinite interval between the beginning in which God created the heaven and the earth, and the evening or commencement of the first day of the Mosaic narrative.

"The second verse may describe the condition of the earth on the evening of this first day; for in the Jewish mode of computation used by Moses, each day is reckoned from the beginning of one evening to the beginning of another evening.   This first evening may be considered as the termination of the indefinite period which followed the primeval creation announced in the first verse, and as the commencement of the first of the six succeeding days in which the earth was to be filled up and peopled in a manner fit for the reception of mankind.   We have in this second verse a distinct mention of the earth and waters, as already existing and involved in darkness; their condition also is described as a state of confusion and emptiness (*tohu bohu*), words which are usually interpreted by the vague and indefinite Greek term chaos, and which may be geologically considered as designating the wreck and ruins of a former world.   At this intermediate period of time, the preceding undefined geological periods had terminated, a new series of events commenced, and the work of the first morning of this new creation was the calling forth of light from a temporary darkness, which had overspread the ruins of the ancient earth."

Such was the modified diluvial theory in which Dr. Buckland brought the weight of his authority to support the views now generally received.

The last Religious Martyrs in England.

In the seventeenth century, as theology became more reasonable it became less confident, and therefore more merciful. Seventeen years after the publication of Hooker's *Ecclesiastical Polity*, two men were publicly burned by the English bishops for holding heretical opinions. These were Legat, burned by King, Bishop of London; and Wightman, by Neyle, of Lichfield. They suffered in 1611. "But this," says Buckle, "was the last gasp of expiring bigotry; and since that memorable day, the soil of England has never been stained by the blood of a man who has suffered for his religious creed."

"It should be mentioned, to the honour of the Court of Chancery, that late in the sixteenth and early in the seventeenth century, its powers were exerted against the exaction of those cruel laws by which the Church of England was allowed to persecute men who differed from its own views." —See *Lord Campbell's Chancellors*, vol. ii.

Liberty of Conscience.

The principle of perfect respect for Liberty of Conscience is the last, the hardest, the most precious conquest of humanity over itself. On its maintenance depends the only real assurance which the world can have even of revealed truth; for where would be the assurance even of revealed truth in a world of mental slaves? England seems chosen as the guardian of liberty of conscience in Europe at the present time. To guard it faithfully is her best tribute to Heaven—her best title to the respect of all that is good and noble in the world. That she has guarded it well will be her glorious epitaph, when, in the revolutions of empire, her power and wealth shall have become a legend of the past. Distance and climate do not change principle. The conscience of the Hindoo is conscience, however clouded, though declaimers may pretend that good is evil and evil good, by the law of the prophet and the institutes of Menu. If it were not so, it would be vain to offer him a purer religion, for he would be incapable of seeing that our religion is purer than his own. Double, treble the number of your missionaries and your bishops. Speed in every way the apostolic work of Christian love. But the sword is forbidden; and not only the sword, but every influence that can compel or induce the heathen to offer to the God of Truth the unholy tribute of a hypocritical profession—the unclean sacrifice of a lie. —*Saturday Review.*

Awful Judgments.

There cannot be a more impious abuse of the authority of the name of God than its employment in solemn asseveration of the truth of that which the utterer knows to be a lie. Such wickedness has been marked with divine vengeance; and Dr. Watts has sought to impress this fact upon the minds of children, in one of his "Divine Songs," telling us how

> Ananias was struck dead,
> Caught with a lie upon his tongue.

An instance of this heinous sin is recorded upon the Market-cross at Devizes, in Wiltshire, in these words:—

"The Mayor and Corporation of Devizes avail themselves of the stability of this building, to transmit to future time, the record of an awful event, which occurred in this market-place in the year 1753; hoping that such record may serve as a salutary warning against the danger of impiously invoking Divine vengeance, or of calling on the holy name of God to conceal the devices of falsehood and fraud.

"On Thursday, the 25th of January, 1753, Ruth Pierce, of Potterne, in this county, agreed with three other women to buy a sack of wheat in the market, each paying her due proportion towards the same; one of these women, in collecting the several quotas of money, discovered a deficiency, and demanded of Ruth Pierce the sum which was wanting to make good the amount; Ruth Pierce protested that she had paid her share, and said, *She wished she might drop down dead, if she had not.* She rashly repeated this awful wish, when, to the consternation and terror of the surrounding multitude, she instantly fell down, and expired, having the money concealed in her hand."

It is not long since, in one of the parish churches of Canterbury, the officiating minister alluded to an awful instance of the interposition of the Almighty, which was presented a few miles from the above city. A woman who was accused of theft positively denied it, and in her protestations solemnly appealed to God in testification of her innocence, and wished she might be struck dead if guilty. She had no sooner used the expression than she fell a lifeless corpse. The articles imputed to her as having been stolen were afterwards found in her house.

Christian Education.

If we look to the nature of the human mind itself, if we consider its longings, how comprehensive is its range, how great its capabilities, how little its best and highest faculties are satisfied with the objects that are placed before us upon earth, how many marks this dispensation bears of being a temporary, and, as it were, an initiatory dispensation, is it not monstrous to pretend that we are giving to the human being such a cultivation as befits his nature and his destiny, when we put out of sight all the higher and more permanent purposes for which he lives, and confine our provision to matters which, however valuable (and valuable they are in their own place), yet of themselves bear only upon earthly ends? Is it not a fraud upon ourselves and our fellow-creatures? is it not playing and paltering with words? is it not giving stones to those who ask for bread, if, when man, so endowed as he is, and with such high necessities, demands of his fellow-men that he may be rightly trained, we impart to him, under the name of an adequate education, that which has no reference to his most essential capacities and wants, and which limits the immortal creature to objects that perish in the use?—*W. E. Gladstone.*

On the whole subject of National Education, how enlarged and liberal are the views taken by the Bishop of Oxford, in one of his recent Sermons. "Our National Education is at this moment surrounded by many difficulties. Among the chief of these are those which spring from the relations of our Church and State. There is no use in disguising from ourselves the fact that these questions exist, and some of them press for settlement. I believe it to be the more manly and the more Christian way freely to admit their existence, and to lend our aid with all honesty in working out their true solution. We cannot, of course, concede one of our principles. We must teach the truth as we have received it — whole, unmixed, uncompromised. But this point secured, whatever we can do we ought to do, by a kindly regard to the feelings of others, by an allowable co-operation and all lawful concession, to loose the hard knot which discord has tied, and unite the hearts of this people in the mighty work of educating its youth to do good service to our God, and to maintain truth and righteousness throughout his world."

The Book of Psalms.

On the Psalms, that inexhaustible treasury of divine wisdom and prophetic inspiration, Hooker asks:

"What is there necessary for man to know which the Psalms are not able to teach? They are to beginners an easy and familiar introduction—a mighty augmentation of all virtue and knowledge; in such as are entered before, a strong confirmation to the most perfect amongst others. Heroical magnanimity, exquisite justice, grave moderation, exact wisdom, repentance unfeigned, unwearied patience, the mysteries of God, the sufferings of Christ, the terrors of wrath, the comforts of grace, the works of Providence over this world, and the promised joy of the world which is to come, all good necessarily to be either known, or done, or had—this one celestial fountain yieldeth. Let there be any grief or disease incident to the soul of man—any wound or sickness named, for which there is not in this treasure-house a present comfortable remedy at all times ready to be found."

With what satisfaction the pious Bishop Horne composed his Commentary on these sacred lyrics of the Sweet Singer of Israel, may be judged from the following passage from the Commentator's Preface:

"Could the author flatter himself that any one would have the pleasure in reading the following exposition which he hath had in writing it, he would not fear the loss of his labour. The employment detached him from the bustle and hurry of life, the din of politics, and the noise of folly. Vanity and vexation flew away for a season; care and disquietude came not near his dwelling. He arose fresh as the morning to his task; the silence of the night invited him to pursue it; and he can truly say that food and rest were not preferred before it. Every Psalm improved infinitely on his acquaintance with it, and no one gave him uneasiness but the last; for then he grieved that his work was done. Happier hours than those which have been spent in these meditations on the Songs of Sion, he never expects to see in this world. Very pleasantly did they pass, and move smoothly and swiftly along; for when thus engaged, he counted no time. They are gone, but have left a relish and a fragrance on the mind, and the remembrance of them is sweet."

Elsewhere the Bishop thus characterizes the Psalms:

"Calculated alike to profit and to please, they inform the understanding, elevate the affections, and entertain the imagination. Indited under the influence of Him to whom all hearts are known, and all events foreknown, they suit mankind in all situations; grateful as the manna which descended from above, and conformed itself to every palate. The fairest productions of human wit, after a few perusals, like gathered flowers, wither in our hands and lose their fragrancy; but these unfading plants of Paradise become, as we are accustomed to them, still more and more beautiful. Their bloom appears to be daily heightened; fresh odours are emitted and new sweets extracted from them. He who hath once tasted their excellences will desire to taste them yet again; and he who tastes them oftenest will relish them best."

The pure and sweet feeling with which this excellent prelate dwells on his past labours, if labours they can be called, could scarcely have been greater, had he foreseen the immense circulation which his work enjoys, and the universal esteem in which it is held.

A more recent Commentator concludes his remarks on the last Psalm with these touching words: " I shall never again so dwell upon them on earth. My God! prepare me for heaven, and for joining there in the songs of the redeemed in the high services of eternity."

The Book of Job.

Diversified are the opinions of the most learned critics concerning the author of the Book of Job, the period at which it was written, in what part of the world the events there recorded occurred; and, though last not the least difficult and perplexing, whether the whole composition may not be regarded rather as allegorical than natural and true. Dr. Mason Good observes of this poem, in his Introductory Dissertation on the Book of Job:—

" It is the most extraordinary composition of any age or country, and has an equal claim to the attention of the theologian, the scholar, the antiquary, and the zoologist—to the man of taste, of genius, and of religion. Amidst the books of the Bible it stands alone, and though its sacred character is sufficiently attested both by the Jewish and Christian Scriptures, it is isolated in its language, in its manner, and in its matter. Nothing can be purer than its morality, nothing sublimer than its philosophy, nothing simpler than its ritual, nothing more majestic than its creed."

Perhaps all our readers may not be aware that, with the exception of the first two chapters and the last ten verses, the book is poetic—it is everywhere reducible to the hemistich form; but whether it is to be considered as dramatic or epic has not been determined. That Moses was the author of this sublime composition seems now almost universally agreed upon by learned commentators. The work itself, moreover, possesses internal evidence to the truth of this statement, many parts of it harmonizing with his acknowledged writings. Dr. Mason Good contends that—

" In his style the author appears to have been equally master of the simple and the sublime—to have been minutely and elaborately acquainted with the astronomy, natural history, and general science of his age—to have been a Hebrew by birth and native language, and an Arabian by long residence and local-study; and finally, that he must have flourished and composed the work before the Egyptian Exody. Now it is obvious that every one of these features is consummated in Moses, and in Moses alone; and that the whole of them gives us his complete lineaments and character; whence there can be no longer any difficulty in determining as to the real author of the poem. Instructed in all the learning of Egypt, it appears little doubtful that he composed it during some part of his forty years' residence with the hospitable Jethro, in that district of Idumæa which was named Midian."

Against the supposition that Moses was the author of the Book of Job, it has been alleged that the word " Jehovah" frequently occurs in it—a word which was first revealed to Moses by the Almighty, preparatory to his undertaking the deliverance of the Hebrew nation. But, although we are told that this term was communicated to Moses for the first time in Exodus vi. 3, we yet find it used nearly thirty times in the Book of Genesis; we may, therefore, with Dr. Mason Good, suppose that he was in possession of this name long before the promulgation of this poem; and the novelty of the communication might have induced him at once to exchange whatever term he had antecedently employed for this new and consecrated term.

It seems now to be universally agreed upon that the land of Arabia Petræa, on the south-western coast of the lake Asphaltites, in a line between Egypt and Philistia, surrounded by Kedar, Teman, and Midian, all of which are districts of Arabia Petræa, situated in Idumæa, is the land of Edom or Esau. With regard to the supposition of some learned authors, that the book is wholly allegorical, Dr. Chalmers does not concur in such a conjecture. He appears to have thoroughly studied the arguments both for and against such a theory, and to have decided against it. He is conclusively of opinion that Job was a real character, and that the history recorded of him is a statement of facts. "There is," says our author, "a very distinct scriptural testimony for the inspiration of his book in 1 Cor. iii. 19."

Uz, where Job lived, was Edom. "We disclaim," says Dr. Chalmers, "all consent to this being an allegorical and not a literal history; and we found our disclaimer on the subsequent references in the Bible to Job as to a real personage; as in James, v. 11, and still more in Ezekiel xiv. 14—20, where he is ranked with Noah and Daniel, whose reality no one doubts. Would the prophet have thus mixed a fictitious with real and historical characters?"

It is also worthy of remark, that the history of Job, although much altered from the original, is still well known among the Asiatics. Though our author does not consider Job's history, as a whole, as being allegorical, yet he thinks the transcendental or supernatural parts of it may be so; and he compares these passages with those in 1 Kings xxii. 19; Zech. iii. 1; and Rev. xii., all of them representations more or less resembling similar ones in Job.—*Times journal.*

APPENDIX.

Great Precedence Question.

The great question relative to precedence which agitated the cities of Dublin and Edinburgh in 1863, arose at the presentation of addresses to the Queen at Windsor by the respective corporations of those two cities, on the occasion of the marriage of the Prince of Wales, when the corporation of Dublin was given precedence, under protest on the part of the corporation of Edinburgh.

The question was subsequently referred to the chief Irish heraldic authority, the Ulster King of Arms, Sir Bernard Burke, LL.D.; and the report which Ulster thereupon wrote was ordered by the House of Commons to be printed. Ulster begins by stating that

"The claim of Edinburgh to the higher precedence is made to rest on the following reasons:—" 1. The Scottish Act of Union being earlier in date than the Irish Act of Union. 2. The arms of Scotland being quartered in the royal shield before the arms of Ireland. 3. By the Acts of Union of Scotland and Ireland, the Peers of Scotland taking rank before the Peers of Ireland."

However, " Dublin founds its claim to precedence on broader and more intelligible grounds; viz.—1. Prescriptive right of Dublin as second city in the dominion of England from the reign of King Henry II., a right unaffected in any way by the Acts of Union. 2. Greater antiquity of the city of Dublin. 3. Greater antiquity of the charters of incorporation of the city of Dublin. 4. Seat of Government and the Viceroyalty being still retained in Dublin. 5. Greater and more dignified privileges of the corporation of Dublin."

Ulster then shows that the quartering of the royal arms, which were capriciously varied at different periods, proves nothing in favour of Edinburgh; and that, by her Act of Union, Scotland was amalgamated with England as Great Britain; while Ireland, though united, preserved in her union a quasi separate position, being still a viceroyalty, with a vice-king and court, having their capital in Dublin.

He concludes by urging that, from the Lord Mayor and Corporation of Dublin being privileged to present their addresses to the Sovereign on the throne at St. James's, Edinburgh not having that privilege,—and from the immense antiquity of the city of Dublin, Dublin is clearly entitled to precedence.

Sir George Grey transmitted this report of Ulster to Garter-King-of-Arms, Sir Charles Young, D.C.L., F.S.A.; Garter gave an opinion, which was also ordered by the House of Commons to be printed. Garter, in his opinion, inclines in favour of Edinburgh, on the grounds—1st, That Scotland occupies the second quarter in the royal shield; 2nd, that England itself became on the accession of James I. an "appanage of the Scottish crown;" 3rd, that as the peers of Scotland were given special precedence by the Irish Act of Union, all other precedence followed "by analogy;" and 4th, that the Mayor of Dublin was not "Lord" Mayor till 1665, while Maitland avers that the style of "Lord" Provost was enjoyed by the chief magistrate of Edinburgh in 1609.

A remark of Sir George Grey's in the House of Commons, wrongly reported, led to the belief that this opinion of Garter was to decide the question. But, on the contrary, the discussion was continued.

Ulster gave, in reply to Garter, a second opinion, which was ordered by the House of Commons to be printed. In his further observations Ulster commences by saying: "The point at issue is not a question of nationalities, or of the relative superiority of Ireland over Scotland, or Scotland over Ireland. That question, a very invidious one, is not now raised, and will, I trust, never be: the only result which could arise from such a discussion would be to wound the feelings and love of country of one or other of two very sensitive peoples. . . . . . The only question to be determined is simply which of the two corporations has the higher precedence?—a right to be determined by municipal charters, royal grants, and other legal evidence." Ulster then still insists on the far longer existence of Dublin. He repudiates the idea altogether that England was an "appanage" of Scotland, any more than France was an appanage of Navarre, when Henry IV., King of the latter country, inherited the crown of France. Appanage has not that meaning. Garter is wrong as to the date of the Mayor of Dublin being "Lord" Mayor in 1665: he was made so by Charles I. 29th July, 1642, while the Provost was not "Lord" Provost till 1667. Ulster concludes for Dublin, on the greater antiquity of Dublin's charters over those of Edinburgh, on it being contrary to all law to construe acts of Parliament "by analogy," and on the undoubted fact, that George IV. conferred in 1821 on Dublin, which Sir Robert Peel emphatically styled "the second city of the Empire," the exclusive (except as to the city of London) honour of presenting addresses to the Sovereign on the throne at Windsor or St. James's.

With these observations of Ulster the question rests in abeyance

INDEX.

U

THE END.

Savill and Edwards, Printers, 4, Chandos-street, Covent-garden.

www.ingramcontent.com/pod-product-compliance
Lightning Source LLC
Chambersburg PA
CBHW031405270326
41929CB00010BA/1337